Forgotten Places

Studies in Criticality

Shirley R. Steinberg
General Editor

Vol. 494

The Counterpoints series is part of the Peter Lang Education list.
Every volume is peer reviewed and meets
the highest quality standards for content and production.

PETER LANG
New York • Bern • Frankfurt • Berlin
Brussels • Vienna • Oxford • Warsaw

Forgotten Places

Critical Studies in Rural Education

Edited by William M. Reynolds

PETER LANG

New York • Bern • Frankfurt • Berlin
Brussels • Vienna • Oxford • Warsaw

Library of Congress Cataloging-in-Publication Data

Names: Reynolds, William M., editor.
Title: Forgotten places: critical studies in rural education / edited by William M. Reynolds.
Description: New York, NY: Peter Lang, 2017.
Series: Counterpoints: studies in criticality; v. 494 | ISSN 1058-1634
Includes bibliographical references.
Identifiers: LCCN 2017009292 | ISBN 978-1-4331-3071-7 (hardcover: alk. paper)
ISBN 978-1-4331-3070-0 (paperback: alk. paper) | ISBN 978-1-4331-4318-2 (ebook pdf)
ISBN 978-1-4331-4319-9 (epub) | ISBN 978-1-4331-4320-5 (mobi)
Subjects: LCSH: Education, Rural.
Classification: LCC LC5146 .F67 2017 | DDC 370.9173/4—dc23
LC record available at https://lccn.loc.gov/2017009292
DOI 10.3726/b11118

Bibliographic information published by **Die Deutsche Nationalbibliothek**.
Die Deutsche Nationalbibliothek lists this publication in the "Deutsche
Nationalbibliografie"; detailed bibliographic data are available
on the Internet at http://dnb.d-nb.de/.

For our friend and fellow scholar
Eelco Buitenhuis
You left us much too soon.

Table OF Contents

List OF Illustrations

LIST OF PHOTOGRAPHS

LIST OF TABLES

Acknowledgements

This book was developed during a period in my life when I encountered a serious health crisis. It has been delayed because of that and I wish to thank all the contributors for their marvelous contributions and patience. I managed to survive that crisis but not without the help, hope and dedication of the most important person in my life, my wife, Susan. Her daily drives, for weeks from Statesboro to the hospitals in Savannah and the hours of her steadfast care and commitment pulled me through. She is always there and I will be forever committed to her as well. I also am grateful for the support of friends and colleagues that visited me during that period and the doctors, nurses and therapists for their expertise. This book on critical studies in rural education was inspired by the forty-two years I have spent working with students in rural public schools and universities. I hope that they learned from me as much as I learned from them. My son, Matthew has served as my computer guru as I worked to submit the text. He managed to tolerate my frequent phone calls. I want to thank Chris Myers for his support of my work over the years and Shirley Steinberg who continues to support my intellectual work.

CREDITS

All photographs used with permission from the Highlander Research and Education Center Archives.

Foreword

Rural Tourist

SHIRLEY STEINBERG

Joe Kincheloe often referred to me as a "callous, urbane sophisticate," ironically acknowledging that, despite my claim to urban roots, a decade and a half of my life was rural … incredibly rural. Born in Baltimore, raised in Los Angeles, at 22, my geographic center was ruptured when I married a Canadian from Southern Alberta, and moved to the epicenter of a prairie to begin my life in a town of never more than 1500 citizens.

Perhaps one of the best ways to observe an area is to be *in it*, but not *of it*. Certainly, I was not in any way "of" a rural area. But being "in" it, and as a participatory human being, I grabbed the opportunity and planned to make rural living my own. I've never been sure who was more culture shocked, me or those who met me; most had never seen a Jew with 99% of the population belonging to one of the town's three Christian denominations. I'm quite positive that no one was prepared for a fast-talking, irreverent LA girl.

The town had no dry cleaners, restaurants, and few paved roads. But it had churches, it most definitely had churches. Not more than ten miles from our borders were three Hutterite colonies, small mini-towns with less than 125 German Christian inhabitants attempting to retain their beyond-rural agrarian lives. We would see them "come to town" on Mondays and Thursdays. Women with polka-dotted scarves hiding their hair, rumored to have silk lingerie tucked beneath the billowing skirts; men with straw hats and black cotton working clothes. Less than 45 minutes down the road was a Blackfoot Reserve (reservation) where Indian [sic] children were bused in at 6am to attend our elementary school.

My first months of rural life consisted of learning to get up before 7 AM, eating porridge for breakfast, getting to know Cal at the local Post Office, and exhibiting joy and wonder when the dusty dirt roads would be oiled once a year; going to the local grocery store where Lewis would fill boxes with my food order, charge them to my account, and then bring the bounty to my house that day, putting them in the kitchen if no one was home. As part of the town doctor's family, I was treated as new royalty, everyone knew me, the American transplant who had never been to a small town and couldn't tell a grain elevator from a missile silo.

I learned to quilt, sitting with 3 and 4 generations of women, tying or stitching enormous quilts by hand, spending weeks binging on wedding quilts, baby buntings, our own new bed dressings. Canning every fall became a passion. Jams and vegetables, all from our garden would shine in new Mason jars after intense weeks of boiling and sealing. Not only did I bake bread, but I learned to grind my own wheat, and bought 50 Hutterite chickens each spring to bottle. I became the town's drama/arts person, judging the annual parade, putting on plays, and creating an arts and crafts guild for women. Several years later I started the Continuing Education program, and hired women to teach aerobics, while I taught off-loom weaving and interior decorating.

A new mother, I became a *La Leche League* leader, and drove 2 hours to the Reserve to teach Native mothers how to nurse. I organized a group of nursing mothers to donate our milk to premature babies, someone would come by the house every day, and we would drop plastic bags into the hands of a medical worker. My breast milk donations extended to babysitting my own nieces and nephew. As four of the sisters-in-law had given birth within two months of one another, we all were filled with milk, lots of it. Within days we discovered the benefit of our bounty by rotating babysitting between us and allowing three of the four mothers to be able to go out sans new baby, sort of an auntie *cum* wet nurse. Nursing my all four babies created a bond, which, over thirty years later, is still strong, and often remembered between the cousins with wonder, and, a bit of shock.

With the birth of each new baby, I would be visited by scores of women at the hospital, Magi bringing clothes and diapers to me as I held court with my latest progeny. The Hutterite ladies would bring me knitted slippers, and let me smell the latest sample of the Avon cologne they kept hidden in their pockets. The Lutherans would bring frozen pierogies and cabbage rolls for my family, and the Mormons would parade in with hand tied or stitched baby quilts and receiving blankets. The doctor (my father-in-law) who delivered each of my babies would march in my private room multiple times each day, grabbing the child and bringing him/her into each patient's room, exhibiting the latest of his growing brood.

If I needed snow shoveled or a fire built, a neighbor would send over her willing husband, and anyone who came by would stand and talk, and talk, discussing the weather, the neighbors, the latest baby, the most recent funeral. There were always topics to discuss, always babies being born and neighbors dying. Within five years, we built a new house bordered on all sides by my in-laws, and 3 sisters-in-law, and our combined yards were populated by plundering cousins, eventually numbering 16, all of whom ran in and out of each home with abandon.

Our children were raised by members of every home in the town. I remember our Meghann disappearing and causing me to hysterically race all over town looking for her. After two traumatic hours, the phone rang, and I was asked if I was missing a naked 3 year old who had appeared on a porch 3 blocks away. The Samaritan noted her family resemblance to cousins and grandparents and by process of elimination had a fairly easy time identifying her and returning her home safely.

Upon reaching 6, my son, Chaim, learned to ride his bike and with it gained an independence and agency that can exist only in a world where two cars on the same road at the same time was a rarity. An idyllic childhood of freedom bounded only by the railroad on one end of town and the cemetery/rodeo grounds on the other. Days were spent roaming between Pigeon Point and the Fish Pond, at a friend's house, or climbing every tree that dared to grow within his youthful demesne. He could disappear for ten hours at time, not a worry, because inevitably someone, somewhere, would see him and report back his last known location via the mysterious, lightning speed communication network that is part backyard fence and part telephone, every small town has one.

As much as I became *in* the town, I continued to realize I was not *of* the town. I had been accepted, engaged, and respected, but was not *one of them*. While elbow-deep in preserves or kneading dough, I was a voyeur, a tourist. One can put the girl in the prairie, but not the prairie in the girl. Conversations were readily found, but I had to watch what I said. Keeping to the harvest, library story hours, and the occasional newcomer, I knew what not to say. The political was silent and my traditionally colorful language was buried, although the *swear jar* at home collected a continual stream of ice cream money. I was a dweller, but not a citizen. Homespun philosophy was pronounced by the men, town council consisted of men, church leaders were men, and women stayed home. We kept busy, but our labors were of the heart, of the hand, and we received what was given to us. I prided myself in my ability to morph into the flat, dry landscape, as a willing participant, I luxuriated in my new talents and abilities to organize and create communities. And I was always watching, figuring out my next move, and I think, wondering if anyone would call me out on my local tourism.

Within ten years, I was bored. I decided to return to university to finish my teaching degree. Two years later I became a high school drama teacher in a city about 30 minutes from town. The day I stood up and began my first class was the day I knew my tour of duty in the hinterlands of Alberta was up. And a year later, I left it all, my home, my partner, my community, and moved to the city. Within months I found that husbands in the town had forbade their wives to go back to university, lest they become like Shirley Steinberg, leave home and ruin their lives.

As simple as a rural life appears, the complexities within rurality are many. Isolation, inability to receive services, intimacy with many in a small area, all these themes pervade a rural existence. Education is a challenge, as it collides with the informal curriculum of one's geographical and ideological place. This place, the rural world, is distinctly not urban, and is not like any other rural place. As un-incredible a rural existence may seem, it is steeped in the incredible. This book begins to unravel the nuanced way of life and philosophical underpinnings of rural living, it brings a critical read to an often poorly articulated state of being, of place. Bill Reynolds has gathered an eclectic collection telling rural tales, creating rural philosophy, and reminding us that often what appears most simple, is indeed, the most complicated.

Shirley R. Steinberg is Research Chair of Critical Youth Studies at the University of Calgary. She is urban.

Introduction

Forgotten Places in the New Gilded Age of Greed and Insensitivity

WILLIAM M. REYNOLDS

One in five poor children in this country lives in a rural area. Yet this group of vulnerable young Americans is seldom on the minds of the public or policy makers when they talk about child poverty in the United States. The image, rather, is overwhelmingly an urban one despite higher poverty rates in rural areas for decades.

—O'Hare (2009, p. 3)

This juxtaposition of robber-baron power and greed is rarely mentioned in the mainstream media in conjunction with the deep suffering and misery now experienced by millions of families, workers, children, jobless public servants and young people. This is especially true of a generation of youth who have become the new precariat (Standing, 2011)—a zero generation relegated to zones of social and economic abandonment and marked by zero jobs, zero future, zero hope and what Zygmunt Bauman has defined as a societal condition which is more "liquid," (Bauman, 2007a) less defined, punitive, and, in the end, more death dealing.

—Giroux (2013, p. 1)

INTRODUCTION

The zero generation as Giroux and Bauman refer to our present society applies to those who live not only in urban and suburban areas but in rural areas as well. Add to this notion of the zero generation what some climate change activists are calling "Decade Zero" of the climate crisis: "we either change now or we lose our chance" (Herron in Klein, 2014, p. 24). There is a heighten sense of urgency to the discussions of youth and the places and environments in which they live. It is easy to forget the rural areas in countries around the world. Urban areas receive more media attention, and are covered more in scholarly publications. But, bifurcating urban and rural is a mistake that can and should be addressed. Education scholars should not set up a mistaken bifurcation between urban and rural education. Certainly there are differences as well as similarities and those should be explored. But the neoliberal agenda is not only out to privatize, corporatize and hence destroy urban and suburban schools but rural schools as well. Not only to destroy rural schools but rural places/communities too. Every aspect of education and living in general is a target for privatization, corporatization and global capitalism. These are issues that create the precariat which includes global populations. This is the multitude that Hardt and Negri discussed in both, *The Multitude: War and Democracy in the Age of Empire* (2004) and *Commonwealth* (2009).[1]

> Those in it [precariat] have lives dominated by insecurity, uncertainty, debt and humiliation. They are becoming denizens rather than citizens, losing cultural, civil, social, political and economic rights built up over generations. The precariat is also the first class in history expected to endure labor and work at a lower level than the schooling it typically acquires. In an ever more unequal society, its relative deprivation is severe. (Standing, 2011, p. 1)

Rural schools, in the United States, served many important roles in the past as centers of social activity and social meaning. They helped to maintain local traditions in particular the identity of rural communities. In many rural areas they became community centers not only for sporting events, but for health issues and general education. Ironically in the 21st century rural schools and even to some extent rural places embody urban and suburban values and serve a globalized neoliberal economic ideology and its agenda.

> The central perception of Globalization is that civilization should be seen through economics, and economics alone. If you add disease prevention or urbanization of preservation of identity (the characteristic of belonging somewhere) to a commercially driven view of human existence, you merely compound the confusion about how the world works. (Saul, 2006, p. 35)

> The ruthless hunt for profit creates a world where everything and everyone is expendable. Nothing is sacred. It has blighted inner cities, turned the majestic Appalachian Mountains into a blasted moonscape of poisoned water, soil and air. (Hedges & Sacco, 2012, p. XII)

The change in rural schools can be attributed to the internet, No Child Left Behind, Race to the Top, standardized exams, Pearson publishing, curriculum, testing, centralization and ultimately as a consequence of neo-liberalism. In terms of rural communities those tasks, once the responsibility and priority of schools, churches and community groups, have been taken over in the 21st century by mega stores like Walmart, Lowes and Home Depot (Schafft & Youngblood-Jackson, 2010). Walmart has become the "community" meeting place. The stores, especially in small communities, have taken on that role while at the same time being an agent for a wealthy family. So the role of Walmart is a meeting place and an anathema.

> I mean, the average worker at Wal-Mart works 28 hours a week, but their wages put them below the poverty line. Which is why when you work at Wal-Mart, they'll give you applications for food stamps, so we can help as a government subsidize the family fortune of the Walton family. (Moyers & Hedges, 2012, p. 2)

So the consequences of this neoliberal money obsessed ideology are horrific. As a result the goal for many rural students and rural dwellers is escape. The urge to escape has been exacerbated by the current mindset. To paraphrase a well-known 1965 song by the Animals written about urban spaces, we have to get out of this place. Rural students frequently give voice to aspirations of making it to the big city, a place to become wealthy. But, not all students in rural American schools have the dream of getting out of rural areas. There are some that are devoted to staying and spending their lives in rural places. Most individuals thinking about those that want to stay in rural communities (Bubbaland) are placing the majority of these students into a particular image, map or cartography (see Chapter 3). These students are portrayed as predominately white. These students are perceived in a stereotypical manner or with a particular identity. The men and women are stereotyped as those who dream of buying that four wheel drive, lift kit enhanced, tool box added and super-sized tired pick-up truck. Mudding that pick-up and having friends over for beer and brats on the weekends. The vision is that most of the more intelligent rural kids leave to get jobs in more affluent suburban/urban areas. That duality is not correct. Bright rural students also stay in their communities and try to make those areas better. Some even stay to work for social and racial justice in those areas. A number of students I taught in the mid-1970s still write to me and tell me of their efforts to improve their rural communities. They serve on school boards and hold other political offices in their communities. These are specific rural communities in upstate New York. As the chapters in this book demonstrate rural education in the United States is not solely a Southern circumstance. And, I would suggest, that not only are rural areas and schools an example of insensitivity in this gilded age, but that insensitivity manifests itself as ignoring the plight of students and families living in those areas world-wide. The suffering and plight of poverty in rural areas is frequently not discussed, mostly forgotten and invisible. One of the worst things you can be in this consumer age is forgotten or erased. "In the information age invisibility is tantamount to death" (Greer, 2004, p. 13). "Constant, unstoppable recommoditization is for the commodity, and so for the consumer, what metabolism is for living organisms" (Bauman, 2007b, p. 13).

> Evil is not confined to war or totalitarian ideologies. Today it more frequently reveals itself in failing to react to someone else's suffering, in refusing to understand others, in insensitivity and in eyes turned away from a silent ethical gaze. (Bauman & Donkis, 2013, p. 9)

It is crucial that we take a critical look at rural education not only in the United States but internationally to understand the necessity of analyzing the class, race, gender, LGBTQ, issues involved in rural schooling and its environment as the authors do in this book. To assist as part of a movement that has as its goal alleviating that suffering and deconstructing neoliberal ideology. Not only rural schooling should be analyzed specifically but its relationship to rural culture and the ways in which media contributes to and forms people's understandings and views of the rural. The internet/cell phone culture has changed the reality of rural life. The stereotypical "backward," out of touch "country bumpkin" is in the 21st century even more ridiculous. Dwellers in remote areas have the ability (maybe more limited) to buy stuff on Amazon just like the rest of us. In the United States the stereotypical picture of the rural citizen, however, is still that portrayed by reality television such as *Here Comes Honey Boo Boo, Swamp People, Lizard Lick Towing and Recovery*, and *Trick My Trucker.*

After having written about the South for a number of years, the South research lead to my thinking about how much of our population inhabits rural areas and my teaching experiences in rural areas. There is, as becomes evident from some of the chapters in this book, a connection between the South and the rural. It is a genuine connection. But our views of rural schooling must be much broader than only discussing the American South. In fact the state with the highest proportion of rural residents is Vermont with 62% of the population living in rural areas. (Merchant, Coussens, & Gilbert, 2006). Demographics illustrate the percentages of rural populations. Rural inhabitants include 19.3% of the population in the US. According to the United Nations the world population of those living in rural areas is approximately 46%. A definition of rural is relevant to the discussion as well. The United States government has 15 different official definitions of rural most of those are from the Department of Agriculture.[2] But, my favorite is from the Department of Education which states: "The term rural means an area that is defined or otherwise recognized as rural by a governmental agency of the State in which the area is located."[3] Again, it is relatively easy to think about United States rural and not the important significance of international rural education and the multiple issues involved. Obtaining definitions of international rural areas is complex because as the United Nations indicates: "there is no internationally agreed upon definition of urban and rural that would be applicable to all countries or even to all countries within a region."[4]

The demographics of children in rural schools in America are revealing. The populations are as follows: 71% White, 10% Black, 13% Hispanic, 2% Asian, 2% American Indian, and 2% two or more races. 24% of public school students attend rural schools. In approximately half of the states' students in rural schools make up the majority of public elementary and secondary school populations. Of the approximately 2.56 million public school teachers, approximately 40% were in rural and small town schools. Compared to teachers in central city schools and urban fringe schools, rural teachers tended to be less well educated, slightly less experienced, younger, and less likely to belong to a minority group. Rural school principals were more likely to be male and less likely to belong to a minority group compared to principals in central city schools and urban fringe schools. These demographics maybe misleading. There have been and continue to be critical pedagogues in these schools. Some of them and their work is included in this reader.

Despite the fact that we think of rural places and rural schools in stereotypical ways. That people who dwell in these areas are not critical thinkers and certainly do not engage in any form of critical activism. That is a mistake. Just in the area of environmental issues alone there are activists who are contesting the neoliberal agenda.

> The anti-fracking movement especially in rural communities in Colorado, Pennsylvania and upstate New York, is one of the most potent grassroots insurgencies in North America. The movement has been able to block the natural gas industry's plans to exploit shale gas in New York State. And it is a huge stumbling block for the industry in many other parts of the United States and Canada. (Hedges, 2015, p. 201)

There are also issues receiving critical attention in rural areas such as health care,[5] education, food,[6] anti-mining activism, and so on. So, to believe that rural areas and the people living in them are just driving around in beat-up old vehicles is a sad misunderstanding and representation which the chapters in this book address and confront.

SECTIONS IN THE READER

I began to think of this book and the idea of rural places when I was writing about the South and I realized that the majority, if not all of my teaching experiences have been in what would be classified as rural environments. And how those experiences have shaped my thinking about the necessity of critical education and critical pedagogy. It is absolutely necessary at this historical moment of oligarchs and neoliberal ideology to place the lens of criticality on questions of rural experience and its manifestations in culture, politics and education. That is what the authors, included in *Forgotten Places: Critical Studies in Rural Education*, attempt. The authors in this text are all important scholars who dwell or have dwelt in rural places both in the United States and internationally. They bring a multiplicity of disciplines and diverse critical perspectives to the study and analysis of rural places. For many reasons, which are elaborated in the chapters that follow, rural places, their impact on lived-experience, and their absence in educational literature, particularly critical educational literature, are addressed. Many critical issues in rural education and rural places are addressed by brilliant writers in this reader. The book is divided into four sections. Many of the chapters could easily move to other sections and putting them into the various sections was done to help the reader organize the various themes or areas highlighted in each chapter. Certainly these are not the last or final comments on rural places. The hope is that this will start discussions about the various topics.

Section I: *Geographies, Cartographies and Rural Culture* presents five chapters the authors; Kelsey Dayle John, Derek Ford, Paul L. Thomas, William M. Reynolds, Jennifer A. Beech, Matthew Guy and Mike Boyer present arguments that discuss issues concerning the conceptualization of rural, politics and critical media literacy. The purpose of this section is to open a critical discussion of the ways the duality between urban/rural, the ways in which media representations of rural inhabitants, rural schools in the United States, Jesus, historical agency and surveillance. These issues open the way for the chapters that follow.

Section II: *Critical Projects and the Rural*, presents projects and issues that are examples of critical work being done in rural areas and with rural inhabitants from Foxfire to Highlander, from migrant education to white women's gender roles to protest, agency and activism in rural areas. These are presented in an historical and critical autobiographical contexts by the authors; Frank Bird III, Robert Lake, Andy Blunden, Carolyn Taylor, Faith Agostinone—Wilson and Todd Price.

Section III: Experiences of the Rural, the largest section of the book, presents compelling critical autobiographies of the lived-experiences of scholars in rural settings. These are not simply chapters that tell the authors stories although they do tell their stories. But, these critical autobiographies place a critical analysis on those narratives. It is one notion to simply tell your story about living the rural experience, it is quite another to place that those stories within a critical context as these authors do. Issues and intersections of ethnicity, race, intergenerationality, schooling, teaching critically and place itself are all brilliantly engaged. The authors; Priya Parmar, Ugena Whitlock, Randall Hewitt, Derrick M. Tennial, Daniel R. Paulson, Bevin Ethridge, Jennifer Job, Kristi Dickey, Susan Kirk, Justin McCrackin, Gina Morris, Rebekah Cordova, E. Bowers and Mark Helmsing offer the reader a provocative look at rural places.

Section IV: International Rural Contexts opens the discussion of the rural to international contexts. This is an area that needs much more critical investigation. In this section scholars present issues related to critical work being done in rural areas of Australia with aboriginal and Torres Strait Islander students, in Jamaica with rural teachers and rural communities and in rural Thailand with critical community pedagogy. The authors, Jon Austin, Amelia Jenkins, Eleanor Blair and Mark Vicars, in this section discuss their critical autobiographical experiences in these various regions.

Again, all of these sections and chapters are provided to foster thought and discussion about places and education that have not received a great amount of attention from critical scholars. I hope the book and its chapters will open discussions and further work in the area of rural cultural studies and critical rural education and also open a dialogue concerning criticality and autobiography. The whole discussion about the duality and cartography of the concept of rural could also open new ideas and new perspectives in this area. The discussions are absolutely significant in this time of "inverted totalitarianism"[7] (Wolin, 2010) which fosters greed, insensitivity and the corporatization of education and our everyday lives. This books attempts to open awareness, through specific places, about the times in which we live and the ways in which students are schooled and the hopes for critical education.

NOTES

1. Hardt and Negri define the multitude as

    The multitude is composed of innumerable internal differences that can never be reduced to a unity or a single identity—different cultures, races, ethnicities, genders, and sexual orientations; different forms of labor; different ways of living; different views of the world; different desires. The multitude is a multiplicity of all these singular differences. (Hardt & Negri, 2004, p. xiv)

2. See: The federal definition of "rural"—times 15, The Washington Post, June 8, 2013. http://www.washingtonpost.com/politics/the-federal-definition-of-rural--times-15/2013/06/08/a39e46a8-cd4a-11e2-ac03-178510c9cc0a_story.html

3. Ibid.

4. See: United Nations Statistics Division *Population density and urbanization* 2013. http://unstats.un.org/unsd/demographic/sconcerns/densurb/densurbmethods.htm

5. See: Rural Health History: Rural health activism over two decades: the Wonca Working Party on Rural Practice 1992–2012. http://rrh.org.au/articles/printviewnew.asp?ArticleID=3245

6. See: Dunford, R. "Peasant Activism and the Rise of Food Sovereignty: Decolonizing and Democratizing Norm Diffusion?" http://ejt.sagepub.com/content/early/2015/11/04/135406611 15614382.abstract

7. Sheldon S. Wolin suggests that inverted totalitarianism

    in contrast, while exposing the authority and resources of the state, gains its dynamic by combining with other forms of power, such as evangelical religions, and most notably by encouraging a symbiotic relationship between traditional government and the system of "private" governance represented by the modern business corporation. The result is not a system of codetermination by equal partners who retain distinctive identities but rather a system that represents the political coming-of-age of corporate power. (Wolin, 2010, p. xxi)

REFERENCES

Bauman, Z. (2007a). *Liquid times: Living in an age of uncertainty.* Cambridge: Polity Press.
Bauman, Z. (2007b). *Consuming life.* Cambridge: Polity Press.

Bauman, Z., & Donkis, L. (2013). *Moral blindness: The loss of sensitivity in liquid modernity.* Cambridge: Polity Press.

Giroux, H. A. (2013, February 27). *The politics of disimagination and the pathologies of power.* Retrieved from http://www.truth-out.org/news/item/14814-the-politics-of-disimagination-and-the pathologies-of power#xiv

Greer, G. (2004). *The future of feminism* (p. 13). Generale Universiteit Maastricht: Dr. J. Tans Lecture.

Hardt, M., & Negri, A. (2004). *Multitude: War and democracy in the age of Empire.* New York, NY: The Penguin Press.

Hardt, M., & Negri, A. (2009). *Commonwealth.* Cambridge, MA: Belknap Press of Harvard University Press.

Harmon, H. L., & Weeks, S. G. (2001). *Rural education—overview, international context.* Retrieved from http://education.stateuniversity.com/pages/2383/Rural-Education.html

Hedges, C. (2015). *Wages of rebellion.* New York, NY: Nation Books.

Hedges, C., & Sacco, J. (2012). *Days of destruction days of revolt.* New York, NY: Nation Books.

Howley, C. B., Howley, A., & Johnson, J. D. (Eds.). (2014). *Dynamics of social class, race, and place in rural education.* Charlotte, NC: Information Age Publishing.

Klein, N. (2014). *This changes everything: Capitalism vs the climate.* New York: Simon and Schuster Paperbacks.

Mann, B., & Weil, C. (1965). We gotta get out of this place. On *Animal Tracks* [vinyl]. Bloomfield, NJ: MGM Records.

Merchant, J., Coussens, C., & Gilbert, D. (Eds.) (2006). *Rebuilding the unity of health and the environment in rural America: Workshop summary.* Washington, DC: National Academies Press.

Moyers, B., & Hedges, C. (2012). *Sacrifice zones: How whole regions of America have been destroyed in the name of quarterly profits.* Retrieved from http://www.informationclearinghouse.info/article 31978.htm

O'Hare, W. P. (2009). *The forgotten fifth: Child poverty in rural America.* Retrieved from http://scholars. unh.edu/cgi/viewcontent.cgi?article=1075&context=carsey

Saul, J. R. (2006). *The collapse of globalism and the reinvention of the world.* London: Grove Atlantic.

Schafft, K. A. & Youngblood-Jackson, A. (Eds.). (2010). *Rural education for the twenty-first century: Identity, place, and community in a globalizing world.* University Park, PA: Penn State University Press.

Standing, G. (2011). *The new precariat: The new dangerous class.* New York, NY: Bloomsbury.

Wolin, S. S. (2010). *Democracy incorporated: Managed democracy and the specter of inverted totalitarianism.* Princeton, NJ: Princeton University Press.

PART ONE

Geographies, Cartographies AND Rural Culture

CHAPTER ONE

The Rural IS Nowhere

Bringing Indigeneity and Urbanism into Educational Research

KELSEY DAYLE JOHN AND DEREK R. FORD

Although the term "urban" seems to be everywhere in educational policy and research, there is little interrogation into precisely what the term "urban" means. One thing that is apparently clear, according to common sense in education, is that the urban is *not* the rural. Rural education is thus defined in the negative sense that it is not urban education, and yet the positive referent here—urban education—is itself ill defined, is itself a victim of undertheorized in educational literature. In this chapter, we want to begin addressing this double-lack in educational research. We do this by weaving together two narratives about the historical production of space. One narrative is that constructed by Marx and critical geographers, which begins with the town/country dialectic inherited by capitalism and ends with a conception of urbanism that is not bound to any particular place or spatial arrangement. The other narrative is one lived by Indigenous peoples in the U.S., and this is a history that has always worked against the division between the town and country. These narratives come into agreement concluding: that there is no such ontological thing as the rural or the urban.

We begin the chapter with a brief orientation to urban educational research in the U.S., which prompts us to question what the urban in this research signifies. To answer this question, we call on Marx's and Engels' writing on the town/country dialectic, which gives a history of how and in what ways the urban and the rural have come to be thought of and lived as distinct entities with their own feel, their own speed, their own aura. For Marx and Engels, whom the dialectic was the operative force of history, nothing is ever fixed or permanent, including the separation of town and country. Marx, for example, wrote about the "urbanization of the countryside, through the industrialization of agriculture" (Smith, 1984/2008, p. 148). Henri Lefebvre's book on the urban, to which we turn next, picks up where Marx left off. Lefebvre argues that the entirety of the globe has been urbanized, and that urbanism, which arose from the city, has escaped the city's confines. In order to understand this thesis, we recall Lefebvre's schematic history of the development of the city, from its first, political iteration, to its latest, urban iteration. At the end, this narrative gives us the insight that the urban isn't about a place today, it's rather about a set of social relations and a patterning of society, about form and not content. The urban is more of a distributed network of production and consumption, of play and work.

While the critical geographic narrative ends up with the overcoming of the urban/rural binary, there is another narrative that troubles and resists this binary from an even earlier historical point, through the lived reality of a different worldview. Indigenous peoples and societies in the U.S. both trouble and add to the urbanization story told by critical geography, and this is what we focus on next. For Indigenous peoples, the very notion of dividing land and space is foreign and destructive (Deloria, 1997; Goeman, 2013). Through Indigenous studies we learn that the urban/rural binary was a colonial construct imposed on Native peoples during the conquest of the Americas. Mapping was a central tool used for the violent expropriation of the land, which Native peoples did not view as a means of production to be owned. Through the creation of reservations and forced relocation programs, the process of settler colonialism works to impose an urban/rural binary on Native peoples and spaces.

WHAT IS RURAL AND WHAT IS NOT

The urban first became an object of educational inquiry with the 1965 Elementary and Secondary Education Act and the Equality of Educational Opportunity Study in 1966, which is commonly referred to as the Coleman Study (Buendía, 2011, p. 2). It seems, however, that the urban is rarely defined. Edward Buendía writes that the earliest urban education policy documents "constructed a population deemed as the urban that has been reduced to racial, economic, cultural and spatial attributes that are seen as corresponding to the totality of their aspirations, experiences and intellectual proclivities" (ibid.). This trend has continued, and Buendía's argument is that even today the urban refers more to populations than to actual places. While critical educational scholars have been doing important work to counter this trend, there is still quite a bit of confusion surrounding the "urban" as an educational and political signifier that arises from a particular worldview originating from a particular place.

For example, in Pauline Lipman's (2011) book, *The new political economy of urban education*, she uses the terms "urban" and "city" synonymously. Indeed, in common parlance one can slip easily between the two. Even in geography, the urban question has historically centered exclusively on the city (Brenner, 2014). But for over four decades now a hypothesis has been making appearances in academic research and social and political movements, a hypothesis that the city and the urban—while absolutely related—are distinct entities. In order to grasp the nuances of this discussion and to ask what it might mean for critical studies in rural education, we want to sketch the development of research on cities and urbanization.

An antagonism has historically existed between the town and the country, or the city and the rural. In a famous section of *The German Ideology*, Marx and Engels (1945/1970) write that this antagonism is fundamental to capitalism for a host of reasons. In the town "individuals must be brought together" to interact with instruments of production "created by civilisation," while in the country individuals "find themselves alongside the given instruments of production as instruments of production themselves," instruments which are "natural" (p. 68). Thus, the difference between the town and the country, for Marx and Engels, related directly to the general division of labor between industry (town) and agriculture (country). This spatial division of labor has important consequences. In the country "property (landed property) appears as direct natural domination," while in the town property appears as the "domination of labour, particularly of accumulated labour, capital." People in the country are "united by some bond" while those in the town "are only held together by exchange." In the country "the domination of the proprietor over the propertyless may be based on a personal relation, on a kind of community," while in the town this domination is maintained through money and exchange. In the country there may still be a unity of physical and mental activity, while in the town there is a division between the two. In other words, the spatial differentiation between town and country signals a differentiation of nature and production, social relations, forms of community and belonging, and subjectivity—or the division of the self into mind and body. This division is previously articulated in science and religion by Descartes—a notion we will see heavily critiqued by Indigenous scholars.

WHITHER THE RURAL?

The relationship between capitalism and the town and country antagonism, argues Neil Smith (1984/2008), is often cited yet seldom deeply understood. He clarifies that capitalism didn't produce the separation between town and country, but rather inherited it from previous modes of production. Further, Smith insists that it is incorrect to read the town and country antagonism as fixed. Rather than being fixed, the separation between town and country actually *erodes* under capitalism, and this is exactly where the distinction between the city and the urban comes into play. Some have even gone so far as to claim that there is no longer any contradiction between the two socio-spatial formations and that urbanization has ushered in a new reality.

Henri Lefebvre begins his 1970 book, *The urban revolution* with this hypothesis. "Society," he writes, "has been completely urbanized" (Lefebvre, 1970/2003, p. 1). Lefebvre quickly follows up with the fact that this urbanization is not yet actual; it is only virtual at the present moment (1970), but it will soon be actual, an accomplished fact. There is a stultifying confusion resulting from not only the conflation of the urban with *the* city, but also from the homogenizing term "*the* city" itself. To correct this, Lefebvre takes us through the history of the production of the contemporary city and, along the way, teases out the distinctions between different phases of urbanization as well as the differing relations between the country and the town, or the rural and the city.

The first iteration of the city is the political city, which could also be referred to as the administrative city. The political city organized political, military, and economic matters, and it was a place of administration, consumption, and exchange. Religious, military, and "noble" leaders are at the helm of this built-form. The political city builds infrastructure—like dams—but production is not a central component of the political city. As a result, the city itself and its populations are produced and reproduced through surpluses extracted from the countryside, and this was accomplished most often through force and ideological persuasion (i.e., religious doctrine). The next form of the city is the mercantile city, and in this iteration the marketplace enters and exchange comes to dominate the city and its functions. This, of course, does not happen at once or without a struggle between the Church and the nascent bourgeoisie. The town-country relationship changes with this transition, as surplus-product from the countryside enters the town voluntarily via the marketplace, and not through coercion. The city gained prominence in economic life as it became a crucial site for the realization of value. Thus, the mercantile city accompanied the rise of ever-increasing networks of places connected through trade. No longer was the city "an urban island in a rural ocean;" instead, it was the country that was "now no more than—nothing more than—the town's 'environment,' its horizon, its limit" (p. 11).

Yet it is with the entrance of production into the city through the emergence of the industrial city that urbanization as it is commonly understood really takes off. The bourgeoisie asserts its domination more completely in this phase of urbanization and the city-form itself becomes subjected to the logic of capital accumulation. Lefebvre referred to this process as an "implosion-explosion." All aspects of social reproduction—communication, transportation, housing, play, and so on—are subjected to the needs and logic of capital accumulation. This is the aspect of implosion: the transformation of the city itself. Yet the search for exchange-value that transforms the city space also transforms spaces outside the city, and this is the explosion. This explosion includes both a transformation in the countryside and the town-country relation as well as a transformation in colonialism. Regarding the former, the city began to totally dominate the countryside which, had hiterhto been "predominately isolated and self-sufficient," but which "now began to depend on urban-industrial production for basic foodstuffs and consumer goods" (Monte-Mór, 2014, p. 263). At the same time, the process of colonialism undergoes a rapid acceleration, as the bourgeoisie seeks ever-cheaper sources of labor-power and raw materials, and new markets for its products.

The industrial city thus propels the city beyond its own limits, casting a net, or an "urban fabric" outward (Lefebvre, 1996). Different territories and socio-spatial formations are woven together, and the boundaries between them are eroded. To take just one "concrete" example, David Harvey (2012) provides a helpful example of the ways in which the industrial city weaves workers from disparate regions together, writing that

> there is a seamless connection between those who mine the iron ore that goes into the steel that goes into the construction of the bridges across which the trucks carrying commodities travel to their final destinations of factories and homes for consumption. (p. 130)

At the same time as the rural is urbanized—through the industrialization of agriculture, the application of advanced science and technology to crop production, the installation of communication networks, the construction of schools, and so on—the urban is ruralized, becomes subject to the dictates of agricultural production writ large.

The urban, then, isn't about a form; it's about a set of social relations, subjectivities, and possibilities. And it is this way of being that has transcended the city as a built-form. Indeed, while it is quite difficult to empirically delineate precisely where the city ends and something else begins (see Brenner & Schmid, 2014), it is impossible to state where the urban ends and begins. This is because, as Andy Merrifield aptly puts it, "the urban is nothing in itself, nothing outside dynamic social relations, nothing outside of a coming together of people" (2013, p. 37). The city is anywhere that differences encounter one another, anywhere that work, play, and desire flower.

INDIGENEITY, BINARIES, AND MAPPING

The story that Marx and Engels and their kin in critical geography tell us about urbanization is important, we believe, for understanding contemporary socio-spatial relations. In particular, the breaking down of the binary between the urban and the rural helps us to grasp the ways in which social patterning occurs today.

Yet there are also crucial historical and theoretical limitations to the critical geographic story as told by Lefebvre and his later companions, for this story, in the end, represents but one worldview, one that arose predominantly from the study of European society. We have to be careful, then, not to transpose that story onto other spaces, histories, and peoples. What we want to do now is turn to another worldview that both challenges and articulates a similar conclusion as critical geography's theory of urbanism. To adequately interrogate urban/rural binary and to uncover the spatial dynamics of the present moment, we believe that we need to turn to Indigenous knowledges. Such a move is necessary because Indigenous peoples have been troubling, interrogating, and resisting divisions of space since European contact. The United States is a settler colonial society, and any discussion of space must first look to settler colonial studies as a way to understand the organization, naming, and claiming of space.

Settler colonial studies addresses issues and ideologies in settler colonial nations, specifically issues of land accumulation and the harmful effects on peoples and society that continue to systematically operate from a colonial ideology. Settler conceptions of space require the "need to turn land into property" (Goeman, 2013 p. 104). Goeman (2013) writes about colonial cartographic ideology saying, "Maps, in their most traditional sense as a representation of authority, have incredible power and have been essential to colonial and imperial projects" (p. 16) where land was turned to property.

For Native communities, maps have always been a tool of colonization for both the physical and metaphorical mapping of lands and bodies (Goeman, 2013). From the first major mapping expedition conducted by Lewis and Clark to the Dawes Act (which marked and divided communal Native lands into propertied containers belonging to individual families) Natives have had maps forced upon them and their communities. In the age of exploration, expeditions for map making provided the tools and knowledge necessary for economic expansion through domination. As a result of these practices and the capitalist need to accumulate land, ways of knowing became institutionalized and normative through the systematic reproduction of settler colonial expansion and its accompanying ideology (Harley, 1989; Pickles, 1992). Designations of "town" and "country" were not native to the territory known today as the United States prior to European contact; they were only made by other nations who violently seized spaces from Indigenous peoples, settled on these spaces, and instituted the authority to name and develop them. John Mohawk (2000) writes that excess wealth concentrated in urban centers lead to colonization as a necessity in order to maintain wealth as populations grew. He says, "excess population provided both motive and opportunity for unleashing colonizers on distant lands" (p. 32).

The driving force of settler colonialism is the material and ideological. There is, in other words, an ideology about the inferiority of some peoples and the superiority of other peoples that is irretrievably tied up with the question of land acquisition, which was central to the formation of the U.S. As Marx (1867/1967) writes toward the end of the first volume of *Capital*, "the expropriation of the mass of the people from the soil forms the basis of the capitalist mode of production" (p. 719), what Marx referred to as "so-called primitive/primary accumulation." Marx here is critiquing the story the narrative that bourgeois political economy tells about the origins of capitalism, which is roughly as follows: Once upon a time there existed two kinds of people. One type was "diligent, intelligent, and, above all, frugal" and the other type were "lazy rascals, spending their substance, and more, in riotous living" (p. 667). At a certain moment in time, the political economist says, it came to be that the latter type had nothing left to sell except their own labor. In radical contrast to this origin story, Marx demonstrates that it was actually "conquest, enslavement, robbery, murder, briefly force" (p. 668) that were the primary mechanisms through which the initial capital—and the conditions necessary for capitalist production—were produced and accumulated. In the U.S., settler-colonialism was part and parcel of this strategy. And mapping—the drawing of boundaries—was absolutely central to this iteration of primitive accumulation, for it went hand in hand with the forced and murderous expropriation of Native peoples from their land. Inferiority was solidified with the designation of cities as areas of "civilization" for Europeans and "rural" areas inhabited by Indigenous peoples as "uncivilized." Only after land was labeled and borders were drawn could it be stolen and then codified, so that the one with the map was the one who was able to lay claim to the land.

Thus, the very notion of the urban/rural divide is a colonial concept, one that originated with colonial and capitalist thinking about and relation to land, the land seen purely as a means of production to be exploited for profit. This divide was imposed on Indigenous communities through colonization. Prior to this, Indigenous communities had complex systems of trade, governance, and production that did not map onto any rural/urban or country/town binary (Forbes, 2001). Though Indigenous peoples may have had separate spaces for growing and trading crops, separating the spaces was not the primary framework for understanding the relationship to the land or the production. The relationship instead centers stewardship, the sacred, and connection. Dunbar-Ortiz (2014) gives several examples of Indigenous peoples' systems of corn production pre-contact to show that North America was a thriving network organized through a radically different world view. She writes that the main source of trade was corn—which was believed to be a sacred gift from God which was meant to be stewarded by people on Earth. She gives one example of the Haudenosaunee Confederacy, which "avoided centralized power by means of a clan-village system of democracy based on collective stewardship of the land" (p. 24). From this system, corn was dispersed evenly throughout clans, eliminating a system of commerce in which production and distribution took place in distinct and separate, opposed spaces.

THE RESERVATION

Newcomb (2008) writes that the relationship between Indigenous peoples and the U.S. (including the establishment of reservations) has always been puzzling and unclear. Scholars who work on issues of Indian law and policy write extensively on structures of *power* that underlie policies of subjugation for Indigenous peoples. The processes of colonization are not logically straightforward but, as indicated earlier, are intertwined with religion, ideology, science, and industrialization. Central to the discussion of power is the taking, settling, and naming of Indian reservations—areas of land that the United States marked off and reserved for Native communities through the practice of mapping. Reservations were established to ease conflicts between settlers and Indigenous peoples in "rural" areas and were upheld through treaties with the U.S. government's Bureau of Indian Affairs (Dunbar-Ortiz, 2014). The process of marking and maintaining reservation spaces is inseparably linked to modes of control and separation in settler colonial societies. Two major Acts in particular—the 1830 Indian Removal Act and the 1887 General Allotment Act—officially remove, rename, and designate spaces for Indigenous peoples by way of domination of the U.S. government. However negatively purposed reservation spaces are, Indigenous peoples have resisted by making these areas of empowerment, survival, and resistance. The reservation has, by necessity, always betrayed any town/country dialectic, for although reservations are never in or too close to city centers, they themselves are centers of culture, language, spirituality, commerce, and all of those things that hold Indigenous social formations together.

After the creation of reservation spaces, relocation programs started in 1950s, further creating and complicating separations for Native peoples by splitting up peoples in already separate spaces, adding another fold to the history of urbanism. Relocation programs were introduced to purposefully separate Native families and clans (Goeman, 2013, p. 94). Goeman points to this division as significant because not only was it a spatial separation but a cultural separation aimed at dismantling traditions, languages, and spiritual practices. Instead of practicing their traditional ways, Native peoples who were forcibly relocated to cities to become "productive" members of the working class and were then forcibly assimilated as urban Indians (Twiss, 2015, p. 66). This would follow Native peoples and create a binary within Indian identity, which Goeman calls the "urban/reservation Native" (p. 7). This dichotomy has fractured solidarity among Indigenous communities by designating reservation Indians as more Native than urban Indians. This rez/urban dichotomy is a primary example of how fracturing the notion of Indian identity can fracture unified resistance from Indigenous peoples by eroding solidarity.

RESISTING SPATIAL BINARIES THROUGH INDIGENOUS KNOWLEDGE

Indigenous knowledges teach us that the use of the terms urban/rural, insofar as they denote a binary, are inherently colonial terms for colonial ideas and practices of separation Along with sectioning off land, settler colonial societies employ divisions in epistemology, methodology, and knowledge making. Most Indigenous scholars trace the institution of binaries in academic work to Descartes' famous lines that separate body and mind in his *Discourse on Method*. Linda Tuhiwai Smith (2012), for example, writes a map she names *decolonizing methodologies* for Indigenous scholars and communities who intersect the research university. She addresses the separation of self and knowledge that permeates academic research. Another prominent Indigenous scholar, Vine Deloria (1997), writes extensively on resisting colonial divisions which separate space/land from its existence as a living entity in scientific research. This separation has historically dis-credited any knowledges or worldviews that do not fit in the dominant colonial paradigm— where space is non-living and external to human existence. Indigenous scholars contest these divisions in all areas of academic research by resisting this type of binary thinking.

Mishuana Goeman, an Indigenous geographer, troubles the binary of on/ off reservation (Goeman, 2013) in a text committed to re-mapping space using Indigenous cartography. The urban/reservation binary is a primary representation of how space connects to a colonial understanding of what it means to have legitimate Indian identity and connection to land. She writes about her experience with the dichotomy of reservation/urban Native identity both literally and figuratively as a way to reconcile her movements from place to place as a child. Her family members were neither fully urban nor fully reservation Natives, yet she embraces this contradiction as a way to challenge colonial binaries in full. She says,

> who is actually a "real" Indian, is often motivated by the spatial politics. I confront in this project. Critical scholars, until the last decade had divided up American Indians into two categories: traditionalists and progressives. In many ways this split is also spatial, as supposedly progressives leave the rez and traditionalists stay at home. (Goeman 2013, 103)

She goes on to argue that a "Native" identity is one that creates culture and community even outside the boundaries of the reservation. Finally, she also argues that the on/off reservation distinction is a colonial notion because the boundaries of the reservation were created by the U.S. as a tool of control over Natives. Therefore, adapting one's identity as either authentic or inauthentic based on their spatial relationship to the settler state's establishment of reservation lands is a colonial practice. This distinction becomes especially important for the large number of urban Indians who were relocated from reservations into cities where they formed their own Native communities in urban spaces far away from their perspective reservations. Just as it is impossible to name a space as "urban," it is equally impossible to designate a legitimate Native identity using settler colonial spatial relations. Today Native peoples hold on to their identity, languages, and world views even if they are forcibly separated from their land. This dis-connection with land is not condoned, but enforced by a permeating settler colonial relationship to land. Today Natives leave reservation spaces for a number of reasons while at the same time utilize the borders of the reservation to protection lands and members.[1]

WHAT, AND WHERE, IS RURAL EDUCATION?

The urban/reservation dichotomy is a distinction that is important to understand because community identity is wrapped up with the space in which the people constituting that community live. Most reservation communities are thought of as "rural" spaces in the American imaginary, but these spaces serve as epicenters for Indigenous resistance and collective being, while at the same time being separate to the space of the "urban Indian." Indigenous peoples have used their anti-colonial worldviews to resist these divisions in space and identity by arguing that the reservation/urban Native is a dualism brought about by settler colonialism. The process of dichotomizing spaces breaks down with the institution of reservations in "rural" areas. Furthermore, Indigenous communities resist by making "rural" reservations their epicenters, further troubling this binary. The dichotomy breaks down a second time with the institution of relocation programs, which further troubles the urban/reservation dichotomy by creating a division within a division. The American Indian experience is not necessarily diasporic but draws a unique parallel between what it means to occupy a specific space, when that space has been demarcated as a tool for social, cultural, and spatial control. Indigenous peoples, using their anti-colonial worldviews, have resisted these divisions.

There is no doubt that the place in which one engages in the educational relationship and process impacts the educational experience. Thus, we believe that it is absolutely imperative that we think not only about the relations between place, space, and education, but also that we think deeply about how to conceptualize each of those terms. Our intention in this paper has not been to argue that, because the urban/rural binary doesn't hold, that all space is smooth and undifferentiated. On the contrary. There are problems, issues, possibilities, and constraints that are specific to particular places and to particular types of places and the power relationships represented by naming and claiming these spaces. At the end, then, the call in this paper is to reject the urban/rural divide as something that has been complicit in the settler colonial project and as a binary that itself has been challenged by both critical geographers and Indigenous peoples. Instead of thinking about places as fixed and static entities, defined in opposition to other fixed and static entities, we should turn our attention to *social processes*, to the ways in which we live, work, play, desire, and, hopefully, cooperate.

NOTE

1. It is important to note that reservations, borders, and binaries are not totally permeable in Indigenous worldviews. Many Indigenous nations have utilized frameworks of sovereignty, nations, and borders for greater survival and self-determination. See Barker (2005) for more discussion on the complexity of sovereignty and borders.

REFERENCES

Barker, J. (2005). For whom sovereignty matters. In J. Barker (Ed.), *Sovereignty matters: Locations and contestations and possibility in Indigenous struggles for self-determination* (pp. 1–31). Lincoln: University of Nebraska Press.

Brenner, N. (2014). Introduction: Urban theory without an outside. In N. Brenner (Ed.), *Implosions/explosions: Towards a study of planetary urbanization* (pp. 14–35). Berlin: Jovis.

Brenner, N., & Schmid, C. (2014). The "urban age" in question. In N. Brenner (Ed.), *Implosions/explosions: Towards a study of planetary urbanization* (pp. 310–337). Berlin: Jovis.

Buendía, E. (2011). Reconsidering the urban in urban education: Interdisciplinary conversations. *Urban Review*, 43(1), 1–21.

Deloria, V. (1997). *Red earth white lies.* Golden, CO: Fulcrum Publishing.

Dunbar-Ortiz, R. (2014). *An Indigenous peoples' history of the United States.* Boston, MA: Beacon Press.

Forbes, J. D. (2001). The urban tradition among Native Americans. In S. Lobo and K. Peters (Eds.), *American Indians and the urban experience* (pp. 5–28). New York, NY: Altamira Press.

Goeman, M. (2013). *Mark my words: Native women mapping our nations.* Minneapolis, MN: University of Minnesota Press.

Harley, J. B. (1989). Deconstructing the map. *Cartographica, 26*(2), 1–26.

Harvey, D. (2012). *Rebel cities: From the right to the city to the urban revolution.* London and New York, NY: Verso.

Lefebvre, H. (1970/2003). *The urban revolution* (R. Bononno, Trans.). Minneapolis, MN and London: University of Minnesota Press.

Lefebvre, H. (1996). Right to the city. In E. Kofman and E. Lebas (Eds.), *Writings on cities* (pp. 63–181). Malden, MA: Blackwell Publishing.

Lipman, P. (2011). *The new political economy of urban education: Race, neoliberalism, and the right to the city.* New York, NY and London: Routledge.

Marx, K. (1867/1967). *Capital: A critical analysis of capitalist production (vol. 1).* New York, NY: International Publishers.

Marx, K., & Engels, F. (1945/1970). *The German ideology: Part one.* New York, NY: International Publishers.

Merrifield, A. (2013). *The politics of the encounter: Urban theory and protest under planetary urbanization.* Athens, GA and London: The University of Georgia Press.

Mohawk, J. (2000). *Utopian legacies: A history of conquest and oppression in the western world.* Sante Fe, NM: Clear Light Publishers.

Monte-Mór, R. L. (2014). What is the urban in the contemporary world? In N. Brenner (Ed.), *Implosions/explosions: Towards a study of planetary urbanization* (pp. 260–267). Berlin: Jovis.

Newcomb, S. (2008). *Pagans in the promised land: Decoding the doctrine of Christian discovery.* Golden, CO: Fulcrum.

Pickles, J. (1992). Texts, hermeneutics, and propaganda maps. In T. J. Barnes & J. S. Duncan (Eds.), *Writing worlds: Discourse, texts, and metaphors in the representation of landscape* (p. 211). London: Routledge.

Smith, L. T. (2012). *Decolonizing methodologies: Research and Indigenous peoples.* London: Zed Books.

Smith, N. (1984/2008). *Uneven development: Nature, capital, and the production of space.* Athens, GA and London: The University of Georgia Press.

Twiss, R. (2015). *Rescuing the gospel from the cowboys: A Native expression of the Jesus way.* R. Martell & S. Martell (Eds.). Downers Grove, IL: InterVarsity Press.

*Kelsey Johns research is funded by the NSF Grant No. (DGE-1247399).

CHAPTER TWO

Teaching Against Provincialism IN THE Conservative, Anti-Intellectual Rural South[1]

PAUL L. THOMAS

Confederate flag, Tillman Hall = provincialism

Often ignored behind the whitewashed myth of the Founding Fathers and the so-called birth of a nation taught in public schools is that the Declaration of Independence was strategically limited to white males only due to, in part, delegates from South Carolina who balked on including language rejecting slavery (The Deleted Passage of the Declaration of Independence, 2015). Where I was born and raised, and then taught public school for 18 years, my home state of South Carolina was also first to secede from the Union, hand-in-hand with Georgia, Mississippi, Texas, and Virginia in, explicitly, defense of slavery. South Carolina rebuked the Union for its "deference to the opinions and wishes of the other slaveholding States," such as Mississippi who declared bluntly: "Our position is thoroughly identified with the institution of slavery—the greatest material interest of the world" (The Declaration of Causes of Seceding States, 2014).

Even as slavery began to collapse under the weight of its inhumanity and immorality, free whites in South Carolina *increased* the number of slaves—with nearly half of families owning slaves by 1850—at the beginning of the Civil War (Remove confederate flag this week, 2015). South Carolina also offered the political world John C. Calhoun, Ben Tillman, and Strom Thurmond—embodiments of racism as political capital. Even as we move into the second decade of the 21st century, the South continues to cling to false narratives, refusing to face the facts above while waving a flag and pledging allegiance to a tradition many simply do not understand. This is the bigoted provincialism in which teachers much teach and students must learn all across the rural South.

Throughout the 1980s and 1990s, I taught in the rural upstate South Carolina high school I attended as a student. One of my non-fiction units for American literature included a consideration of persuasive writing, beginning with Ralph Waldo Emerson and Henry David Thoreau and then examining Thoreau's influence on Gandhi and Martin Luther King Jr. The last works of that unit focused on Booker T. Washington, W. E. B. Du Bois, King, and Malcolm X—a dedicated and extended honoring of black history and debate that was much more than a token nod such as black history month.

One class session when I was handing out King's "Letter from Birmingham City Jail" remains with me to this day. A white male student brushed the photocopy of King's letter off his desk top and into the floor with a hissed, "I ain't reading that nigger." My class included black students, but my being white and this student's own life experience had taught him his perverse righteous indignation was entirely justified; he might as well have snarled "heritage, not hate," the recurring defense of keeping the Confederate battle flag on top of South Carolina's capitol building and then on the statehouse grounds—before its contentious removal in 2015.

More calmly than I should have, I returned the handout to his desk with my hand on the papers, and looking him in the eye, I explained he would never say that word again in my room, and he would in fact read what I had assigned. For many if not all of my students, this was probably the first time they had witnessed a white male—from their home town, in fact—take such a stand. In all-white situations throughout my life in the South, racist slurs and veiled racist comments and jokes have been *and remain* a cruel norm.

The debate about removing the Confederate battle flag from South Carolina state grounds was resurrected after violence erupted twice in the state—the police officer shooting of Walter Scott and the massacre at Emanuel African Methodist Episcopal Church, both in Charleston. The rhetoric around the flag debate, despite the horrific nature of the two killings, were often lies about the flag somehow not being a racist banner of slavery from the beginning, and the narratives have mostly omitted the racist intent of resurrecting that flag in the early 1960s as an ugly middle finger to desegregation and civil rights for blacks. The state representatives and senators who were democratically elected but chose to clutch still that flag exposed ugly truths about denial and racial inequity surviving and even thriving today.

Bringing down that flag was a symbolic act itself, but it was also a *movement* that continued to include real admissions about race inequity and new policies that could this world a better place. To bring down a flag, to change the names of buildings, to remove statues—these are necessary acts of facing, not erasing, history. Memorials that honor the dishonorable are indignities to the true value of history, or even heritage. There is no dishonor in admitting failures; in fact, facing the past and acknowledging human's inhumanity to humans is the most honorable thing we can do. However, what is morally right continues to be muted against the power of anti-intellectualism in the South, a norm that is nearly as powerful as the entrenched racism and classism that plagued the region—and continues to blunt the effectiveness of the public school system.

Below, then, this chapter investigates the many aspects of racism and classism that constitute the provincialism of the South and how that remains a barrier to liberatory education (Sargis, 2008). As LaBrant (1946) confronted:

> Do the very words we use and our attitudes toward them affect our tendency to accept or reject other human beings? … A basic understanding which needs to be taught in school and home is that the existence of a word does not at all prove the existence of any thing. Children do not understand this; nor do all adults. … We have much of this word magic indirectly taught in our classrooms. (pp. 323, 324, 326)

Education in the South is a battle waged against word magic.

THE SELF-DEFEATING SOUTH, WORDS NOT SPOKEN: RACISM AS A SCAR AND CANCER

Born and raised in a very small rural town in upstate South Carolina, I have lived my entire 56 years in the South. Most of that life has been spent teaching, and a large span of that career was in the high school I attended, among redneck children mostly just like me, where we explored literature. A key text for me each year while I was a high school English teacher was William Faulkner's "A Rose for Emily," and if you are not from the South, and you want to come close to understanding the South, read that story carefully. The shocking revelation at the end of the story—behind the locked door, the pillow and the bed, the "iron-gray hair"—is as close as you can come to understanding the South if you are not *from* here. (Equally powerful windows into the South are Alice Walker's "Everyday Use" and Flannery O'Connor's "A Good Man Is Hard to Find.")

What these works of literature expose is that we are a self-defeating people, we Southerners, a sort of ignorant pride, a blind faith in tradition and a steely determination to do as we damn well please. We'd rather cling to our ignorance (a long-standing tradition) than do the right thing—especially if someone else is telling us to do the right thing. The South, you see, is stuck in a perpetual arrested development, a fixed childhood/adolescence: We're going to smoke, drink, and make out in *our own car* and there is nothing you can say or do to stop us.

That "we," however, is the *white* South (both literally and its controlling psyche), and that is the problem. (One element of "A Rose for Emily" that is important here is the "we" narration of the town. ("When Miss Emily Grierson died, our whole town went to her funeral," it begins.) So if you think articles such as "8 disturbing trends that reveal the South's battered psyche"—which asks, "So what is it that perpetuates decades of poverty in the Deep South?"—helps you understand the South, you need to consider carefully what is absent in the 8 trends:

1. Southern states have the most poor people. …
2. Deep South states have no minimum wage. …
3. Deep South has lowest economic mobility. …
4. South has lowest per capita spending [b]y state government. …
5. Forget about decent preventative healthcare. …
6. One result: people self-medicate in response. …
7. Forget the lottery, just pray to Jesus. …
8. And hold onto that gun! (Rosenfeld, 2014)

What is essentially absent in this piece, an examination of trends that confuses markers for root causes? Race, and more directly, racism.

Notably, the piece mentions race in only one place, and then only "white," with blacks reduced to a negation, not white: As you would expect, the vast majority of people falling under the poverty line in the poorest states do not have white faces—although there are poor whites. The Henry J. Kaiser Family Foundation compiles state poverty rates by race. In the poorest states, whites account for smaller percentages of the poor than blacks (Poverty rate by race/ethnicity, 2016). When anyone in the U.S., especially the South, examines poverty, "poverty" becomes the convenient term that can be uttered as a device for ignoring poverty and denying racism (Perry, 2014). Mention the disturbing racial imbalance of drug arrests (whites and blacks use marijuana at the same rates, but blacks suffer the brunt of arrests) or mass incarceration (white males outnumber black males 6 to 1 in society, but black males outnumber white males 6 to 1 in prisons), and the response will invariably turn to the suggestion that poverty is the cause, not racism. This is the sort of provincialism, bigoted logic, that pervades the South, and corrodes formal education committed to critical inquiry.

Of course, if mass incarceration were a function of poverty and not racism, since twice as many whites as blacks are in poverty, the prison populations would be two white males to every black male. So in order to answer why the 8 trends noted above *exist*, why they are *tolerated*, we must name and then confront the reason: racism. Racism as a historical scar. Racism as a contemporary and undiagnosed, untreated cancer—and undeniably traceable to slavery, especially in the rural South. Yet, formal schooling often bends to whitewashed myths about the Civil War in Southern schools, reinforcing, not confronting the bigoted logic behind "heritage, not hate."

The self-defeating South is the function of right-wing political leadership that campaigns with coded language and images (Desmond-Harris, 2014)—the infamous Jesse Helms "hands" commercial in his run against Harvey Gantt, for example—and then implements policy along racial lines, *even when the consequences of that policy also negatively impacts the large white poverty populations in the South*: right-to-work laws, limited social program funding, shrinking funding for public institutions, resisting universal healthcare, lingering calls for breaking the wall between church and state, supporting school choice, ignoring the re-segregation of schools (public, charter, and private), and doubling down on gun access and ownership.

If we are seeking root causes to answer "So what is it that perpetuates decades of poverty in the Deep South?," we must acknowledge the lingering power of racism, and then we must also confront how rurality in the South allows that racism to remain powerful, even though it now is mostly coded (although blatant expressions of racism remain common in the South). And that dynamic is both entrenched in Southern culture and then reflected in many public schools, if not most. In 2017, we must not discuss inequity and poverty, especially in the context of the South, without also naming the historical and contemporary racism driving many of the consequences of social dynamics and public policy. "The violence of breaking down the door seemed to fill this room with pervading dust"—Faulkner's collective narration of "A Rose for Emily" describes the climax of an entire community finally facing the truth.

For the U.S., I would argue, the South is our Emily, and we remain unwilling, possibly unable, to break down the door, look at the hair on the pillow and admit that we have skeletons in our closet—racism, both a scar and a cancer we refuse to treat. However, the way to making that bold move remains the potential of liberatory education, which is often absent in the mostly provincial schools remaining in the South.

ON SOUTHERN HERITAGE AND PRIDE

When writing about my redneck past—born, raised, and now having lived my entire life in the upstate of South Carolina—I reached back to my grandparents and parents as a way to give context to who I am and how I "got to be this way." In the waning days of June 2015, in the sort of near-100-degree heat we tend to suffer in July and August, South Carolina was exposed to the rest of the U.S. and world in a way that is hard for me as a Southerner to face: nine innocent souls slaughtered in a racist rage, the Emanuel church shooting in Charleston mentioned earlier. While the domestic terrorist responsible for this logical consequence of a people hopelessly clutching a culture of violence in the form of the right to bear arms and willfully blind to the lingering racism that stains our refrain of "life, liberty, and the pursuits of happiness" sought to start a race war. Instead, however, a state and national conversation began about the embarrassment that is Southern Heritage, raised like a petulant bully's middle-finger on the grounds of South Carolina's Capitol until the Confederate battle flag was finally removed (again).

I have never felt pride about being a South Carolinian, a Southerner, or an American—these are all mere coincidences of my birth. It makes no real sense to me, this personalizing geography and then mangling history and ideology in order to create barriers among people. As a high school teacher in South Carolina for nearly two decades, I was guaranteed that my students would bristle at my confronting them about the flag fetish among many white students, mostly males. As a life-long witness to Southern Heritage, I have come to recognize that we are not unique but representative in the South of the worst aspects of patriotism, nationalism, and jingoism—making a commitment to a false narrative to preserve an ideology that ultimately is self-defeating and dehumanizing.

Those most fervent about Southern Heritage and fundamentalist faith in the South have something important in common: an incomplete at best and missing at worst understanding of either the history of the South (and the Confederacy) or the Bible. These gaps in historical accuracy can be traced to the reality that public schools continue to avoid those facts since they work against the provincialism, the bigoted provincialism, of the South. There is a selectivity to calling on history and scripture that exposes the real commitments of the fervent: holding onto a world that insures other people remain inferior.

"Heritage Not Hate" is propaganda (Comer, 2015), and as Aldous Huxley (1937) notes: "The propagandist's purpose is to make one set of people forget that certain other sets of people are human." It is the cruelest sort of irony that Southern Heritage advocates misrepresent history as many fundamentalists misrepresent Christianity because those false narratives seek to dehumanize and divide (Lozada, 2015). Yes, my family and community shaped who I am and how I became who I am today—both in part through my formal schooling and then significantly as I have taught in the South over thirty years. And I am certain the South and South Carolina have played roles in that story of me as well.

But I have no specific idea if any of my ancestors participated in any way in the Civil War or slavery; I must imagine that those ancestors in the South during those eras were like most people—in most ways directly or indirectly complicit in horrible human acts. I must imagine that because we are directly and indirectly complicit now in horrible human acts—some so large and pervasive that most cannot see them (our consumer culture that includes the wealth of the few on the labor of the discardable many). I have no desire to contort reality around my ancestors or the history of the region I happen to be born in as an act of somehow justifying my own value as a person. And certainly, as a critical educator committed to liberatory education, I reject using formal education and the disciplines themselves to create history in the image of bigoted reconstructions.

Southern heritage and *pride* are abstractions that allow a callous disregard for the very real world around us—a world that is unnecessarily violent *of our own making*, a world that is horribly inequitable *of our own making*, and a world trapped in the labels of "heritage" and "Christian" but unwilling to learn from history or act on "Love your neighbor as yourself" (Matthew 22:39, New International Version). As a person and as a critical educator, I simply cannot endorse or defend a past that reveals all the ways we have failed each other. It seems instead that today and every "today" we are called to imagine how the world can be better and then do something to make that happen.

I am grateful in many ways for the life my grandparents and parents afforded me, all of which is tied to the place of my life and education, but my life has also included making choices to set aside many things that redneck past inculcated in me, things that do not fill me with pride, but shame. The enduring possibilities of human dignity have been my guideposts that I found in literature (not garbled and romanticized history or cherry-picked bible verses): William Faulkner and Flannery O'Connor, Ralph Ellison and Alice Walker, Langston Hughes and e.e. cummings, Margaret Atwood and Haruki Murakami, Milan Kundera and Adrienne Rich. These came to me not from cultural norms, but from the best and bravest educators throughout my high school and undergraduate years.

The moral barometers who ultimately saved me remain the voices I hear daily: Kurt Vonnegut and James Baldwin. Vonnegut (1998) writes through Eliot Rosewater from *God Bless You, Mr. Rosewater*:

> "Go over to her shack, I guess. Sprinkles some water on the babies, say, 'Hello, babies. Welcome to Earth. It's hot in the summer and cold in the winter. It's round and wet and crowded. At the outside, babies, you've got about a hundred years here. There's only one rule that I know of, babies—:
>
> "'God damn it, you've got to be kind.'"

And Baldwin (1960) confesses in "They Can't Turn Back": "It took many years of vomiting up all the filth I'd been taught about myself, and half-believed, before I was able to walk on the earth as though I had a right to be here."

I feel no pride in being a South Carolinian, a Southern or an American; I did not choose any of that geography. But when I read Vonnegut and Baldwin, I am proud to be a fellow human and I feel a sudden rush of hope found in the pages of literature—as author Neil Gaiman (2013) recognizes: "You're also finding out something as you read vitally important for making your way in the world. And it's this: The world doesn't have to be like this. Things can be different."

And this is my confession: While white parents gave me life, black authors saved my life—and that gift came from teachers and learning opportunities that were liberatory, and thus confrontational to the provincialism of my region, of my upbringing. As an educator especially, then, I have debts to pay, and I must pay them forward—things I cannot do clutching a past that has failed us all.

JAMES BALDWIN: "ON SUCH SMALL SIGNS AND SYMBOLS DOES THE SOUTHERN CABALA DEPEND"

James Baldwin published "They Can't Turn Back" in 1960 just as I was about to enter this world. Baldwin—black, gay and from the North—was witnessing a world from which I—white, straight and from the South—would in many ways be exempt, although it was the same world. In this essay, Baldwin was charged by *Mademoiselle* to report on student activism in Florida after the Greensboro (North Carolina) sit-in, which the editors framed, in part, as follows:

> More than any other event, the Greensboro sit-in launched the 1960s, a decade of political activism and students were on the cutting edge of social change. In 1960, the writer James Baldwin visited Tallahassee, Florida. to report on student activism there. Baldwin ruminated on the underlying causes of black protests and marveled at the militancy and idealism of the younger generation. To Baldwin, the movement challenged all Americans to rethink whether "We really want to be free" and whether freedom applied to all Americans or only to part of the population. (Italics in original)

"I am the only Negro passenger at Tallahassee's shambles of an airport," Baldwin (1960) begins, as he paints an immediate picture of the tensions between blacks and whites that defined his world:

> If she were smiling at me that way I would expect to shake her hand. But if I should put out my hand, panic, bafflement, and horror would then overtake that face, the atmosphere would darken, and danger, even the threat of death, would immediately fill the air.

In Charleston, South Carolina—about 300 miles away from Greensboro and 50-plus years later—racial tensions escalated from "threat" to execution. In the wake of the mass shooting of the #Charleston9 (an eerie and disturbing echo of the Little Rock Nine), the political and public response focused on the Confederate battle flag on the Capitol grounds in South Carolina as well as in both government and private contexts across the South and U.S. Time and place, then, do not erase the power of Baldwin's second paragraph:

> On such small signs and symbols does the southern cabala depend, and that is why I find the South so eerie and exhausting. This system of signs and nuances covers the mined terrain of the unspoken—the forever unspeakable—and everyone in the region knows his way across this field. This knowledge that a gesture can blow up a town is what the South refers to when it speaks of its "folkways." The fact that the gesture is not made is what the

South calls "excellent race relations." It is impossible for any northern Negro to become an adept of this mystery, not because the South's racial attitudes are not found in the North but because it has never been the North's necessity to construct an entire way of life on the legend of the Negro's inferiority. That is why the battle of Negro students for freedom here is really an attempt to free the entire region from the irrational terror that has ruled it for so long.

The South Baldwin describes—and the inherent tensions of both public and educational lives—was cracking under the weight of "separate but equal" as that myth crashed into a rising refrain of civil rights. As Baldwin notes, "the viewpoint of the white majority" dictated the narratives about and for blacks—and whites.

After the racist massacre in Charleston, as the South and the nation wrestled with symbolism—a flag—we also confronted a tarnished but enduring myth-turned-slogan, "Heritage Not Hate," as Tony Horwitz (2015) explains:

> Some of those who invoke the "heritage, not hate" mantra are disingenuous. On the day of the [Charleston] shooting, I was in rural east Texas, touring a small town with a businessman who displayed the rebel flag on his truck. After telling me "it's heritage, not hate," he proceeded to refer to a black neighborhood as "Niggertown" and rant against the Martin Luther King, Jr. holiday.
>
> Most flag defenders, however, are sincere when they say they cherish the banner as a symbol of their ancestors' valor. About 20 percent of white Southern males of military age died in the Civil War. In South Carolina the toll was even higher, and thousands more were left maimed, their farms and homes in ruins. For many descendants of Southern soldiers, the rebel flag recalls that sacrifice, and taking it down dishonors those who fought under the banner. No one wants to be asked to spit on their ancestors' graves. ...

This deep-seated and genuine conflict in the white Southern psyche is both real, and troubling. However, such conflicts between belief/custom and informed understanding reinforce the necessity for formal education to rise above replicating cultural norms and seeking ways to interrogate that provincialism through critical inquiry. Horwitz continues:

> But a deeper problem remains, and not just among those who cherish the Confederacy. Nationwide, Americans still cling to a deeply sanitized and Southern-fried understanding of the Civil War. More often than not, when I talk to people about the conflict, I hear that it was about abstract principles like "state sovereignty" and "the Southern way of life." Surveys confirm this. In 2011, at the start of the war's sesquicentennial, the Pew Research Center asked more than 1500 Americans their view as to "the main cause of the Civil War." Only 38 percent said the main cause was slavery, compared to 48 percent who answered states' rights.

These realities of the contemporary South and entire nation confirm that Baldwin (1960) in the turbulent cusp of the 1950s/1960s at Florida Agricultural and Mechanical University continue to ring true—especially in the context of the failures of both society and formal education:

> The South is very beautiful but its beauty makes one sad because the lives that people live, and have lived here, are so ugly that now they cannot even speak to one another. It does not demand much reflection to be appalled at the inevitable state of mind achieved by people who dare not speak freely about those things which most disturb them. ...
>
> It is very nearly impossible, after all, to become an educated person in a country so distrustful of the independent mind. The fact that F.A.M.U. is a Negro university merely serves to demonstrate this American principle more clearly: and the pressure now being placed on the Negro administration and faculty by the white Florida State Board of Control further hampers the university's effectiveness as a training ground for future citizens. In fact, if the Florida State Board of Control has its way, Florida will no longer produce citizens, only black and white sheep. I do not think or, more accurately, I refuse to think that it will have its way but, at the moment, all that prevents this are the sorely menaced students and a handful of even more sorely menaced teachers and preachers.

Our contemporary world remains too often silent, just as our schools continue to be in the service of the status quo—failing more often than not the very students most in need of public and higher education. Just as Baldwin's (1960) recognition of the power of symbolism in the South speaks to today, his words strike also at the heart of the return of segregated and inequitable schooling across the entire U.S. (Thomas, 2014):

> For the segregated school system in the South has always been used by the southern states as a means of controlling Negroes. When one considers the lengths to which the South has gone to prevent the Negro from ever becoming, or even feeling like, an equal, it is clear that the southern states could not have used schools in any other way.

In his role as witness, Baldwin details his own journey among black leaders and students in Florida, and one student leads him to note:

> But this [the historical perspective] does not, and cannot exist, either privately or publicly, in a country that has told itself so many lies about its history, that, in sober fact, has yet to excavate its history from the rubble of romance. Nowhere is this clearer than in the South today, for if the tissue of myths that has for so long been propagated as southern history had any actual validity, the white people of the South would be far less tormented people and the present generation of Negro students could never have been produced.

For South Carolina and the U.S., pulling down a flag was not an act of erasing history, but a moment, a momentum for facing a history long masked behind the veneer of whitewashing. Baldwin's time spent with student protestors in Florida spurred in him angst—an angst not unlike those who fear *now* that the flag removal will be but a passing symbolic act with little real change to follow: "And all this, I think to myself, will only be a page in history. I cannot help wondering what kind of page it will be, whether we are hourly, in this country now, recording our salvation or our doom," Baldwin (1960) muses. However, Baldwin's closing words suggest hope, a hope embodied in young blacks then who were in a different world than the one into which Baldwin was born. And Baldwin believed in the promise of young black activism grounded in a bold recognition of the real history of race in the U.S.:

> They [black student activists] cannot be diverted. It seems to me that they are the only people in this country now who really believe in freedom. Insofar as they can make it real for themselves, they will make it real for all of us. The question with which they present the nation is whether or not we really want to be free. It is because these students remain so closely related to their past that they are able to face with such authority a population ignorant of its history and enslaved by a myth. And by this population I do not mean merely the unhappy people who make up the southern mobs. I have in mind nearly all Americans.
>
> These students prove unmistakably what most people in this country have yet to discover: that time is real.

Hope and angst again cling to the U.S. in the wake of the mass shooting in Charleston, in the wake of political leaders who defended the Confederate flag on one Friday (and for years) only to reverse course after a weekend (and likely some motivation from the very CEOs politicians had invoked as evidence the flag was not a real issue), in the vacuum of the national refusal to confront the violent gun culture that arms the racism we are begrudgingly admitting.

In Baldwin's (1992) refuting of William Faulkner—whose white man's calls for patience from blacks—we have more evidence of the relevance of Baldwin in a time of racial unrest:

> But the time Faulkner asks for does not exist—and he is not the only Southerner who knows is. There is never time in the future in which we will work out our salvation. The challenge is in the moment, the time is always now. (p. 126)

As we consider formal schooling, then, we must admit that Falkner represents the sort of normative schooling typical of education, while Baldwin's critical confrontations continue to be mostly absent from those same lessons. Faulkner speaks to the bigoted provincialism that Baldwin would not tolerate.

BALDWIN: "IT IS APPARENTLY VERY DIFFICULT TO BE AT ONCE A SOUTHERNER AND AN AMERICAN"

The South is littered, however, with more than Confederate battle flags, even once it was removed from the state house grounds. As Baldwin (1992) explains in his refuting of Faulkner:

> Any real change implies the breakup of the world as one has always known it, the loss of all that gave one an identity, the end of safety. And at such a moment, unable to see and not daring to imagine what the future will now bring forth, one clings to what one knew, or thought one knew; to what one possessed or dreamed that one possessed. Yet, it is only when a man is able, without bitterness or self-pity, to surrender a dream he has long cherished or a privilege he has long possessed that he is set free—he has set himself free—for higher dreams, for greater privileges. (p. 115)

Whether you are from the South—as I am, during my 56th year in the area where I was born—to understand the South and its bigoted provincialism we must return to Faulkner's (1995) "A Rose for Emily" and place that story in the context of Baldwin's "Faulkner and Desegregation," and M. E. Bradford's (1966) "Faulkner, James Baldwin, and the South."

In the shocking ending to "A Rose for Emily," the town (that community and place so sacred to Faulkner [1995], as Bradford [1966] emphasizes) and the reader discover that Emily has spent much of her life sleeping with the corpse of her mysteriously vanished lover. Not to be overly simplistic, but in that scene, Emily *is* the South and her act *is* the cancerous core of what best captures that region's ideological commitment—cling to the *corpse of tradition* no matter what. It is the steadfast clinging that matters, not the thing itself.

Baldwin's (1992) response to Faulkner's call for Southern blacks to be patient about integration at mid-twentieth century deftly dismantles the inherent contradictions, the incessant paternalism, and the disturbing lack of awareness embodied by Faulkner himself. While Faulkner seems oblivious to the message in his own work, Baldwin, a black man from Harlem, the North, echoes the warning of "A Rose for Emily":

> [S]o far from trying to correct it, Southerners, who seem to be characterized by a species of defiance most perverse when it is most despairing, *have clung to it* [emphasis added], at incalculable cost to themselves, as the only conceivable and as an absolutely sacrosanct way of life. They have never seriously conceded that their social structure was mad. They have insisted, on the contrary, that everyone who criticized it was mad. (p. 118)

Further, Baldwin's understanding of the South remains as perceptive now as when he originally confronted Faulkner:

> It is apparently very difficult to be at once a Southerner and an American. ... It is only the American Southerner who seems to be fighting, in his own entrails, a peculiar, ghastly, and perpetual war with all the rest of the country. ...
>
> The difficulty, perhaps, is that the Southerner clings to two entirely antithetical doctrines, two legends, two histories. ...
>
> The Southern tradition, which is, after all, all that Faulkner is talking about, is not a tradition at all: when Faulkner evokes it, he is simply evoking a legend which contains an accusation. And that accusation, stated far more simply than it should be, is that the North, in winning the war, left the South only one means of asserting its identity and that means was the Negro. (p. 120)

And finally to grasp fully the South, Bradford's (1966) apologist reading of Faulkner (punctuated with "We in the South") as well as a distinct *misreading* of Baldwin offers the full shape that characterizes the South: Faulkner as embodiment, Emily as metaphor, Baldwin as moral witness, and Bradford as contorted intellectual justification. However, in the South, this is never merely academic or something *past*—despite how often these facts are ignored or whitewashed in schools, and even reinforced by the very buildings in which students are supposed to learn.

CLEMSON'S TILLMAN HALL AND THE TRAGEDY OF SOUTHERN TRADITION: "YES, BUT ..."

The Faulkner/Baldwin/Bradford clash has been resurrected in the Tillman Hall debate at Clemson University—not as a unique case, but a representative one, Clemson University in its founding, its physical plant, and the myriad names with which it is associated. Tillman Hall at Clemson University bears the name of a former South Carolina governor, Benjamin Tillman, who "established an agricultural school that would become Clemson College, as well as Winthrop College" (Benjamin Ryan Tillman, 2016). Those not from the South likely find these recurring tensions unfathomable, notably the battles about the Confederate flag, first on the capitol and then on the capitol grounds. The Faulkner/Baldwin/Bradford dynamic detailed above is now being played out by students calling for renaming Tillman Hall, Clemson faculty voting to support renaming, administration appearing to call for patience, and then a counter-protest supporting the tradition of the hall's name.

The Tillman Hall controversy is significant for how it represents the provincialism of the South, but its place in a public university intensifies how that provincialism remains entrenched in the educational system and how that system of formal education is also resistant to rising above corrosive narrative and clinging to a corrupted past.

Apologists for tradition in the South, like Bradford (1966) for Faulkner, expose the contradictory mindset confronted by Baldwin. Those who rush to add "yes, but ..." in defense of Tillman, for example, are likely to interject the "yes, but ..." strategy to refute Martin Luther King Jr. (Bouie, 2015). "Yes, but" Tillman was governor and if not for him, no Clemson! "Yes, but" King was a socialist and adulterer.

As a life-long Southerner, I have witnessed these patterns regularly throughout my life. It is the logic of the South. I am a child of the South, the Bible Belt where "sparc the rod, spoil the child" dominates "turn the other cheek." Again, as Baldwin (1992) recognized, the South clings like Emily not to tradition but to the fabricated legend. And it is there that the hypocrisy of "yes, but …" is fully exposed. Apologists for Tillman cling to Tillman's *ill-gotten status* during his life, a status reflecting the most dehumanizing qualities of the South during Reconstruction and the early 20th century. Critics of Tillman, however, recognize that his racism outweighs any so-called accomplishments. Will Moredock (2014) notes as one example:

> Tillman went to the U.S. Senate in 1895, where he remained until his death in 1918. He used the Senate floor and the Chatauqua circuit to become the nation's loudest and most famous proponent of white supremacy, or in his own words, "preaching to those people the gospel of white supremacy according to Tillman."

"It's true, South Carolinians would do well to remember Tillman's legacy," argues Paul Bowers (2015), addressing directly the naming of Tillman Hall:

> But we shouldn't honor it, which is exactly what we're doing by keeping his name on a building at a public university. …
>
> It's another thing entirely for it to be named after Tillman, a progenitor and perpetuator of American apartheid who led lynch mobs during Reconstruction and boasted about it until his dying day.

To honor Tillman as well as many others like him is to make Emily's mistake—clinging to a corpse that should be buried beneath a marker, not to honor but to remind us of all that we must not embrace again. Apologists for tradition are emboldened by those calling for patience, like Faulkner, who prompted Baldwin (1992) to punctuate his essay with urgency:

> But the time Faulkner asks for does not exist—and he is not the only Southerner who knows it. There is never time in the future in which we will work out our salvation. The challenge is in the moment, the time is always now.

•

Learning and teaching in the South remains trapped in the provincialism of the region that is mostly reflected in and perpetuated by how schools work and how the disciplines are taught. Critical literacy and liberatory pedagogy would require formal education to interrogate the false narrative of the Confederate flag or Southern heroes such as Lee or Tillman, men honored with buildings and statues all across the Bible Belt.

The South, as I have detailed, has a distinct history that continues, but the South is not unique in that the problems of formal education failing its liberatory possibilities characterizes schools across the U.S., a country just as apt to cling to the decayed carcass of false narratives as we have in the South.

NOTE

1. Sections adapted from https://radicalscholarship.wordpress.com/2015/07/09/removing-confederate-battle-flag-from-state-grounds-facing-not-erasing-history/; http://loulabrant.wordpress.com/2014/02/04/the-words-of-my-mouth-1946/; https://radicalscholarship.wordpress.com/2014/03/16/the-self-defeating-south-words-not-spoken-racism-as-a-scar-and-cancer/; https://radicalscholarship.wordpress.com/2015/06/24/on-southern-heritage-and-pride/; https://radicalscholarship.wordpress.com/2015/06/25/james-baldwins-they-cant-turn-back-1960-on-such-small-signs-and-symbols-does-the-southern-cabala-depend/; https://radicalscholarship.wordpress.com/2015/01/19/clemsons-tillman-hall-and-the-tragedy-of-southern-tradition/

REFERENCES

Baldwin, J. (1960). They can't turn back. *History Is a Weapon*. Retrieved from http://www.historyisaweapon.com/defcon1/baldwincantturnback.html

Baldwin, J. (1992). *Nobody knows my name*. New York, NY: Vintage.

Benjamin Ryan Tillman. (2016). *Biography*. Retrieved from http://www.biography.com/people/benjamin-ryan-tillman-9507546#governor-of-south-carolina

Bouie, J. (2015, January 19). Happy Robert E. Lee Day! *Slate*. Retrieved from http://www.slate.com/articles/news_and_politics/politics/2015/01/robert_e_lee_day_some_southern_states_still_celebrate_the_confederate_general.html

Bowers, P. (2015, January 17). Of course they should rename Tillman Hall. *Paul Bowers, Professional Writer*. Retrieved from http://paulmbowers.tumblr.com/post/108256495085/of-course-they-should-rename-tillman-hall

Bradford, M. E. (1966). Faulkner, James Baldwin, and the South. *The Georgia Review, 20*(4), 431–443.

Comer, M. (2015, June 23). Hey white southerners, let's talk about our Confederate heritage. *Matt Comer*. Retrieved from http://www.mattcomer.net/1070/hey-white-southerners-lets-talk-about-our-confederate-heritage/

The Declaration of Causes of Seceding States. (2014). *Civil War Trust*. Retrieved from http://www.civilwar.org/education/history/primarysources/declarationofcauses.html

The Deleted Passage of the Declaration of Independence (1776/2015). *BlackPast.org*. Retrieved from http://www.blackpast.org/primary/declaration-independence-and-debate-over-slavery

Desmond-Harris, J. (2014, March 15). 8 sneaky racial code words and why politicians love them. The Root. Retrieved from http://www.theroot.com/8-sneaky-racial-code-words-and-why-politicians-love-the-1790874941

Faulkner, W. (1995). *Collected stories of William Faulkner*. New York, NY: Vintage.

Gaiman, N. (2013). Neil Gaiman lecture in full: Reading and obligation. *The Reading Agency*. Retrieved from http://readingagency.org.uk/news/blog/neil-gaiman-lecture-in-full.html

Horwitz, T. (2015, June 24). How the South lost the war but won the narrative. *TPM*. Retrieved from http://talkingpointsmemo.com/cafe/how-south-lost-the-civil-war-won-narrative-confederate-flag

Huxley, A. (1937). *The olive tree, and other essays*. London: Chatto and Windus.

LaBrant, L. (1946, June). The words of my mouth. *English Journal, 35*(6), 323–327.

Lozada, C. (2015, June 19). How people convince themselves that the Confederate flag represents freedom, not slavery. *The Washington Post*. Retrieved from https://www.washingtonpost.com/news/book-party/wp/2015/06/19/how-people-convince-themselves-that-the-confederate-flag-represents-freedom-not-slavery/

Moredock, W. (2014, February 5). Ben Tillman was a racist, terrorist, and murderer: It's time to take down his statue. *Charleston City Paper*. Retrieved from http://www.charlestoncitypaper.com/charleston/ben-tillman-was-a-racist-terrorist-and-murderer-its-time-to-take-down-his-statue/Content?oid=4857402

Perry, I. (2014, March 12). The risk of playing down racism. Room for Debate. *The New York Times*. Retrieved from http://www.nytimes.com/roomfordebate/2014/03/12/the-assumptions-behind-obamas-initiative/the-risk-of-playing-down-racism

Poverty Rate by Race/Ethnicity. (2016). *The Henry J. Kaiser Family Foundation*. Retrieved from http://kff.org/other/state-indicator/poverty-rate-by-raceethnicity/

Remove Confederate Flag This Week. (2015, July 14). *Greenville News*. Retrieved from http://www.greenvilleonline.com/story/opinion/editorials/2015/07/04/editorial-remove-confederate-flag-week/29641931/

Rosenfeld, S. (2014, March 12). 8 disturbing trends that reveal the South's battered psyche. *Salon*. Retrieved from http://www.salon.com/2014/03/12/8_disturbing_trends_that_reveal_the_souths_battered_psyche_partner/

Sargis, J. (2008, July). Liberatory education for autonomy. *The International Journal of Inclusive Democracy*, *4*(3), 1–4. Retrieved from http://www.inclusivedemocracy.org/journal/pdf%20files/pdf%20vol4/Liberatory%20Education%20for%20Autonomy.pdf

Thomas, P. L. (2014, May 16). Racial segregation returns to US schools, 60 years after the Supreme Court banned it. *AlterNet*. Retrieved from http://www.alternet.org/education/racial-segregation-returns-us-schools-60-years-after-supreme-court-banned-it

Vonnegut, K. (1998). *God bless you, Mr. Rosewater*. New York, NY: Dial Press Trade Paperback.

CHAPTER THREE

Rural Place

Media, Violent Cartographies, and Chaotic Disruptions

WILLIAM M. REYNOLDS

I was raised in rural south Jersey, and there was no culture there. There was a small library, and that was it. There was nothing else.

—PATTI SMITH

Much of the value of critical analyses of cartography lies in the ways in which they disrupt institutionalized geopolitical mappings by displacing what are regarded as stable worlds, substituting them with historically contingent ones.

—OPONDO & SHAPIRO (2012, P. 1)

THE RURAL AND VIOLENT CARTOGRAPHIES

What distinguishes the map from the tracing is that it is entirely oriented toward experimentation in contact with the real ... The map is open and connectable in all of its dimensions; it is detachable, reversible, susceptible to constant modification. It can be torn, reversed, adapted to any kind of mounting, reworked by individual, group, or social formation. It can be drawn on a wall, conceived as a work of art, constructed as a political action or as a mediation.

—DELEUZE & GUATTARI (1987, P. 12)

In a more general way, one has to admit that every individual and social group conveys its own system of modelising subjectivity; that is, a certain cartography—composed of cognitive references as well as mythical, ritual and symptomatological references—with which it positions itself in relation to its affects and anguishes, and attempts to manage its inhibitions and drives.

—GUATTARI (1995, P. 11)

> Too much of public education is devoted to unfitting children for community life. With regard to rural life, this has been accomplished by disseminating the message that physical labor is demeaning and that rural people are largely unworthy of respect.
>
> —OEHLSCHLAEGER (2011, P. 52)

In their text *A Thousand Plateaus*, Deleuze and Guattari enumerate the characteristics of the rhizome. One of the principles of the rhizome is that of cartography or mapping. Referring to earlier work, Michael J. Shapiro elucidates his use of "violent cartographies" as ways of "imagining" warring spaces that become, in Foucauldian fashion, "frames" around which policy debates from any number of areas can be rendered intelligible to citizens.[1] "Maps of enmity" have driven domestic U.S. elections and subsequent policy decisions by their victors, the strongest one has been the "red/blue" state divide or perhaps in this context, the rural/urban divide. The red/blue divide is interconnected to rural/urban mapping. Here is Shapiro's explanation of the concept:

> [The] bases of violent cartographies are the "historically developed, socially embedded interpretations of identity and space" that constitute the frames within which enmities give rise to war-as-policy (Shapiro, 1997, p. ix). Violent cartographies are thus constituted as inter-articulations of geographic imaginaries and antagonisms, based on models of identity-difference. (Shapiro, 2007, pp. 293–294)

The notion of violent cartographies, elucidated by Shapiro, forms an interesting way to analyze conceptualizations of the rural. For years the rural as a mythical or ritualistic place has been an object or frame of humor, other, or curiosity. The 21st century concept of the rural is centuries away from the manner in which Romantic poets like, Blake, Wordsworth, and Shelly conceived the pastoral (read rural) as places to "escape" the evil of the cities, where as Wordsworth indicated, the "world was too much with us; late and soon" (Perkins, 1967, p. 289). Images of hillbillies, trailer park dwellers, backwoods ignorance, and a like are frequently reinforced by various forms of media from political news shows to situation comedies to reality shows. There is a violent cartography at work in the mapping of the rural. This is the result of reducing the rural to a fixed concept, a stereotype. Shapiro discusses cartography and the connections among Deleuze and Foucault. Deleuze, when speaking about Foucault's notion of the diagram in *Foucault* (1986) discusses this reduction or restraining of a cartography:

> A diagram is a map, or rather several superimposed maps. And from one diagram to the next. New maps are drawn. Thus there is no diagram that does not include, besides the points which it connects up, certain relatively free or unbound points, points of creativity, change, and resistance, and it is perhaps with these that we ought to begin in order to understand the whole picture. (Deleuze, 1988, p. 44)

The concept of violent cartographies for the purposes of this analysis is that violent mappings, cartographies diagrams work to contain or destroy those free, creative resistant unbound points. That is how power operates politically in the formation of the rigid diagramming or dismissal of notions of rural, rural existence and in particular in this case of certain types of media to reinforce those segmented, defined and contrived places. When speaking of the rural the geography has narrowed considerably. When the rural is represented or even casually thought about, visions of Appalachia, or the Ozarks emerge and certainly the common-sense view is of southern places. But, these are rural places, mostly forgotten or demeaned. Rural places are North, East, West and South in North America and around the world. This narrow view works to destroy ideas that the rural(s) are also places or points, as Deleuze indicates, of creativity, change and resistance. It can be related to Deleuze and Guattari's notions of territorialization, deterritorialization, and reterritorialization and the ways in which they relate to the diagram, the map, and for the purpose of this work, place. First, notions of rural place/space need to be discussed so as not to solidify an overarching definition of them. Discussions of rural place should not attempt to paradoxically territorialize the rural. Territorializing would attempt to define "stable, coded patterns that make up the internal and external organization of the environment of living things, which may be transcoded as part of other larger milieus" (Young, 2013). Attempting to give a particular place a given stability, can also give us a diagram that involves both order and chaos this will be seen in later parts of this work. Places do not always fit their frames and can slip in and out of them. What might be created is a type of deterritorializing of territories which have become over the years coded such as the rural. A type of chaotic disruption, of the given or at the very least a discussion of the manner in which the code has evolved and become commonsense and taken-for-granted.

Perhaps a chaotic disruption of the frame(s) of rural place can develop a notion that not only do rural places manifest some of the attributes that are reinforced by media, but critical media literacy can facilitate a deconstruction of some of those notions and develop for such places creativity, change and resistance. One example of a disruption of place comes in the phenomenon of the presidential campaign of Bernie Sanders. "Bernie Sanders is an improbable politician. Independent, occasionally irascible, he came from the far left and an urban background to win elections in one of the most rural states in the country" (Taibbi, 2015). Framed places can be disrupted. At the very least a discussion of these diagrams can move rural places from within the shadows of the forgotten and stereotypical. All of these issues demonstrate power and politics operating within notions of the violent cartographies. The politics of place will also be addressed.

MEDIA AND THE RURAL

We think lines are the basic components of things and events. So everything has its geography,[2] its cartography, its diagram. What's interesting, even in a person, are the lines that make them up, or they make up, or take or create.

—DELEUZE (1995, P. 33)

What seldom gets talked about—and when it is, often with irreverent humor and contempt—is the poverty of rural America, particularly rural white America: Appalachia, the Ozarks, the Mississippi Delta, the Dakotas, the Rio Grande Valley, the Cotton Belt.

—GURLEY (2015, P. 1)

In the past the television shows portraying rural life/country living were for the most part situation comedies with an occasional musical variety show—*The Real McCoys* (1957–1963), *Petticoat Junction* (1963–1970), *Green Acres* (1965–1971), *The Beverly Hillbillies* (1962–1971), *The Andy Griffith Show* (1960–1968), *Gomer Pyle* (1964–1969), *Hee Haw* (1969–1997), *Mr. Ed* (1961–1966), and *The Dukes of Hazzard* (1979–1985).

From West Virginie they came to stay in sunny Cali-forn-i-a. Grand Pappy Amos and the girls and the boys of the family known as the Real McCoys.

I make a livin catching big ole catfish. But, I don't use a rod and reel, that's right. I use my hands and feet. We call it noodlin Oklahoma style.

Now we have countless country (rural) reality television. *Duck Dynasty* (2012), *Moonshiners* (2011), *Swamp People* (2010), *Here Comes Honey Boo Boo* (2012–2014), *Hillbilly Hand Fishin* (2011), *Rocket City Rednecks* (2011–2013), *Ax Men* (2008–present), *Sons of Guns* (2011–2014), *The Call of the Wildman* (2011–present), *American Loggers* (2009–present), *American Pickers* (2010–present), *Born Country* (2007–present), *Welcome to Myrtle Manor* (2013–2015), *Lizard Lick Towing and Recovery* (2011–2014), *Redneck Rehab* (2012), *Appalachian Outlaws* (2014–present), *Party Down South* (2014–2016), and on and on. Interestingly enough the number of so-called reality television shows has increased from 4 in 2000 to 320 in 2010 (Screen Rant, 2016). One change from the days of the *Real McCoys* to the days of *Hillbilly Hand Fishin* is that in the initial shows rural living was either to be escaped (Beverly Hillbillies) or glorified (Andy Griffith Show) and in the present day of reality television rural living/county life is an object of curiosity and ridicule. Pozner (2010) explains it in this way:

It's true that millions of people have become reality TV junkies, initially drawn in by a sort of cinematic schadenfreude. That "What's wrong with you/" reaction is the viewer's equivalent of rubbernecking at an accident. Sometimes it makes us laugh, sometimes it shocks us, but we're unable to turn away from the cathartic display of other people's humiliation.

> Often it makes us feel superior: No matter how bad our problems may be at least we aren't
> as fill-in-the-blank (pathetic, desperate, ugly, stupid) as those misguided enough to sign up
> for such indignities on national TV. (Pozner, 2010, p. 16)

Additionally the media of television/video has changed tremendously in the last ten years. Many "cable television shows" are accessible on a number of medium from Netflix to You Tube. All of the television programs I discuss are easily accessible via a variety of sources from television to computers. These media representations of rural life, however, they are obtained/viewed territorialize a violent cartography, a diagram and an identity. They construct those representations of the rural in a number of ways. The power of situation comedies and rural reality television operate in different ways to accomplish this territorialization. First, we can discuss the outwardly "innocent" and humorous ways in which television from the 1960s through the 1980s operated. Second, we can analyze the influence of reality television in continuing and altering those notions constructed decades ago and moving them into the 21st century. One common construction of the early shows, but replicated in the reality shows of the 21st century is that the "rural" is framed as an exclusively white experience. Approximately 15% of the population of the United States lives in rural areas defined as an area/town with a population fewer than 50,000. Despite the fact, that rural population racial demographics break down (2010) as 78% white, 8.2% Black, 9.3% Hispanic, 1.9% Native American (53.8% of Native Americans live in rural areas) (HAC, 2010). There are relatively few if any media representations of Black, Hispanic or Native American rural experiences. When there are representations, there is what Pozner (2010) explains as "Erasing Ethnicity and Encoding Bigotry" (pp. 161–195). Of course these rural experiences exist and the reasons for their erasure is something that will be explored.

> Representation in the media is often key to our ability to feel valued and to believe that
> world holds positive possibilities for people who look like us and share similar backgrounds
> and identities. Yet when a community's main media presence consists of mockery, misrep-
> resentation, or demonization, invisibility may be preferable. (Pozner, 2010, p. 195)

Third, chaotic disruptions of these violent cartographies are discussed.

THE RURAL DIAGRAM

What are the common characteristics that develop as a violent cartography or diagram of rural places in pre-reality television? Many programs exhibit the characteristics that emerge as territorializing our thoughts about rural places. Two major programs are *The Real McCoys* (1957–1963), and *Green Acres* (1965–1971). There are several characteristics of these and other shows of the same historical period that contribute to a type of violent cartography. I would highlight three.

First, there is a sharp contrast drawn between city and country life. Second, there is a humorous glorification of the white, "simple life", family values, and "country living." Third, low income struggles and agricultural life is portrayed as "normal."

The contrast between city and rural life is most accentuated in the show *Green Acres*. In the program Manhattan lawyer Oliver Wendell Douglas buys a farm in poor condition in Hooterville from a con man Eustice Haney. He drags his high status, Hungarian wife to the farm where they try to make it a place to be. The point being that they are leaving the good life to live in Hooterville. The contrast between urban and rural is even emphasized even in the show's theme song.

> New York is where I'd rather stay.
> I get allergic smelling hay.
> I just adore a penthouse view
> Dah-ling I love you but give me Park Avenue. (Lennie72, 2013)

The show intertwines rural living and farming which in many cases is true, but is not the only form of life in rural communities but if a viewer watched many shows of that historical period it was framed in that manner. The portrait is painted that life in the country is somehow not as good nor as sophisticated as life in urban areas. Hay and pitchforks versus Penthouse apartments and expensive stores. The cartography is made by not so subtle images of clothes, houses and vehicles. Oliver driving a tractor in a suit is surely a statement. An imitation of the painting, *American Gothic* by Grant Wood is also presented in the introduction to the show as Oliver stands with a pitchfork next to his wife, Lisa, dressed not in her sophisticated New York dress but in a denim shirt and jeans. The wealthy wife has donned the clothes of the country. All of the images and lyrics of this situation comedy count for more than just a cute, funny and quaint television program. As much as we or viewers of the past enjoyed the show a cartography was being constructed, continued and reinforced in the popular media and in the minds of the American public.

In the *Real McCoys*, what viewers saw was not so much a contrast between urban and rural as a glorification and reinforcement of the rural family with the all-knowing patriarch as head of the household and the pleasures and complications of life on the farm. The patriarch was usually able to solve the complications.

> From the hills of West Virginia, Amos McCoy moves his family to an inherited farm in California. Grandpa Amos is quick to give advice to his three grandchildren and wonders how his neighbors ever managed without him around. (IMDB, 2015)

Even though this situation comedy was on television form the late 50s to the early 60s and seen in various forms on the internet, the image of the rural white family that it portrays has a lasting effect on various representations of the rural family that have followed and continues the reinforcement of a type of violent cartography.

Both of these television programs demonstrate the image and frame that working in agriculture (life on the farm) is both something to be held in esteem and something that is to be separated from work or leisure in the urban environment. As stated previously working with your hands is somehow not as desirable as working in the city even though that might be with your hands as well. The cartography gets a distinct etching from these early rural television shows. That frame reinforces the attitude and image that rural areas are simple, somewhat backward and certainly not places of creativity or political resistance.

Reality television shows move the framing of the rural to a new concentrated "glad I don't live there" frame. This schadenfreude experience gets us to tune into shows such as: *Hillbilly Handfishin,* and *Swamp People.* But why do viewers continue to watch:

> because these shows frame their narratives in ways that both play and reinforce deeply ingrained societal bias about women and men, love and beauty, race and class, consumption and happiness in America. (Pozner, 2010, p. 17)

What are the characteristics of these country/rural reality shows that continue the territorializing of the rural. First, they accentuate, reinforce and replicate the stereotypical jargon and lifestyle that we have come to recognize as rural. Second these media representations pull us away from the "innocent" country life to a much grittier, malicious and in your face existence. Third, there is an emphasis on an anti-intellectual existence, which reinforces common narratives of people living in rural environments as ignorant. It makes this anti-intellectualism a laughing manner.

> This is key. It's true that millions of people have become reality TV junkies, initially drawn in by a sort of cinematic schadenfreude.[3] That "What's wrong with you?" reaction is the viewer's equivalent of rubbernecking at an accident. Sometimes it makes us laugh, sometimes it shocks us, but we're unable to turn away from the cathartic display of other people's humiliation. Often it makes us feel superior: No matter how bad our problems may be, at least *we* aren't as fill-in-the-blank (pathetic, desperate, ugly, stupid) as those misguided enough to sign up for such indignities on national TV. (Pozner, 2010, p. 16)

Hillbilly Handfishin takes place in Oklahoma. A place that has been increasingly associated with conservative politics, cowboys and country folk (see Chapter 11). It was where people were traveling away from to California a place to escape in the days of the dust bowl and the major setting for John Steinbeck's *Grapes of Wrath.* Oklahoma has that diagram. In this show, the main character, Skipper Bivins, and his co-noddler, Trent Jackson take urban dwellers on noodlin' expeditions. That is catching large catfish with your hands and feet.

Again, the distinction is made between urban and rural when in the trailer for season one Skipper says "This ain't Boston." In this series the two noodlin boys take urban dwellers to the creeks to face snakes, beavers, catfish and murky waters to catch with hands and feet the bona fide country fish –the catfish. The boys are usually dressed in jeans and are bare chested as they take the urban dwellers into the country wild. As the host says "This is nothin like Boston, no matter what your brother says it's no camping trip but there is no bigger rush" (Helman, Greensfeld, & Gallagher, 2015). So, the stereotypical lifestyle and jargon (a particular way of speaking mostly associated with Southern dialect) are typical of these 21st century reality programs. This show demonstrates that the pleasant stereotypical country life of Green Acres—driving a tractor with your suit on, is replaced by the gritty down and dirty rural life of muddy water, snakes and a "case of culture shock for Jersey girls, and LA boys" (Helman, Greensfeld, &Gallagher, 2015). There is a sense that an intellectual background is not helpful or necessary in these Oklahoma Handfishin expeditions. There is a distinction made between "book smarts" and urban sophistication and they are pointless compared to fishing expertise and survival skills for rural living. Although the anti-intellectual aspects are not specifically stated there is an implicit orientation toward the anti-intellectual. This reality show demonstrates the reinforcement of the rural diagram. It elaborates the perceived differences between urban and rural. Pozner (2010) discusses the ways in which reality television shows reinforces stereotypes. "Because this genre that calls itself 'unscripted' is carefully crafted to push all our culturally ingrained buttons" (p. 46). The author is discussing gender issues (which exist in these rural reality shows as well) but our cultural stereotypes also are about our sense of place.

Swamp People another gritty rural reality show about alligator hunting as a way to make a living in the Southern Louisiana Bayou (a marshy lake or wet land). The original cast of characters included Troy Landry (The best alligator hunter in American, the King of the Bayou) and his son Jacob. Gator hunting is not an exclusively male occupation as demonstrated by Liz Cavalier (Queen of the Bayou) and her daughter Jessica. The show is extremely popular with over 125 episodes about gator hunting. "Out here the law of the land is No guts. No gators" (Boag, Watts, & Diaz, 2016). This reality show reinforces the images of rural life. The occupation of alligator hunting is certainly not one familiar most people in the United States of internationally. It accentuates the diagram of rural living. In this particular reality program the main characters speak a dialect of Louisiana Creole. It is certainly different from the everyday language of most Americans. In fact, some of the episodes of *Swamp People* are captioned so viewers can understand the language. The unique language is viewed as another separation of rural living from "mainstream" existence. This language is characterized is characterized by viewers as humorous and no quite normal. A second characteristic of the rural reality shows is that they work to change our perceptions of the innocent country life to a malicious, "in your face" existence. Certainly hunting alligators for a living and the hazards and risks involved in that labor are not the quant home life represented in the early television shows dedicated to representing rural existence.

These alligator hunter are rugged, tough people. As with Hillbilly Handfishin', the sense of anti-intellectualism is present. Again, the stereotypical intellectualism is replaced with survival knowledge. Apparently rural folks don't read books they learn how to survive with rugged jobs in places with threatening creatures.

These reality shows do reinforce and perpetuate the violent cartography of the rural diagram. The millions of views watching these shows are bombarded with stereotypical representations of rural life that persist in the 21st century. These is little discussion or representation of alternative notions of rural living and alternative ways of presenting it. That is where we turn next.

CHAOTIC DISRUPTION

I am an invisible man … I am a man of substance, of flesh and bone, fiber and liquids—and I might even be said to possess a mind. I am invisible, understand, simply because people refuse to see me.

—ELLISON (1995, P. 3)

No one is seeking timeless paradise; and no one, however nostalgic, is really seeking to turn back the clock to return to Burdy's Bend of segregation and starvation. What people are seeking is not so much the home they left behind as a place that they feel they can change, a place in which their lives and strivings will make a difference—a place in which to create a home.

—STACK (1996, PP. 198–199)

The rural, as the media represents it, swirls in frames that are somewhat othered. Certainly as this type of violent cartography continues there will be a continuing reduction in the percentage of the population of the United States living in rural areas. People are leaving rural areas in the pursuit of "better" jobs, and a more affluent lifestyle. This phenomenon is given the name rural flight or rural exodus.

Rural America, which encompasses nearly 75% of the land area of the United States, currently accounts for about 16% of the country's population, the lowest in the nation's history. In fact, it has been almost a century since people living in rural America outnumbered those who resided in metro areas. (Doering, 2013, p. 1)

The world-wide rural population is much larger. Demographics illustrate the percentages of rural populations. Rural inhabitants include 19.3% of the population in the United States. According to the United Nations the world population of those living in rural areas is approximately 46%.

A chaotic disruption of this violent cartography of the rural is to begin or continue to make evident that rural areas in the United States are more than simply Bubba land, hand fishin' or gator catching which, as I have tried to demonstrate, both the early situation comedies and more recent reality television have success-fully constructed and that the struggles and resistances of the world's population living in rural areas are significant and require research that accentuates those issues. In many ways one of the tools of violent cartography is to simply ignore or erase as they are solidifying their frame(s) concerning the rural. Certainly ignoring, in a malicious way, the struggles and political movements which have been and are in rural areas. The concept/cartography that only poor "redneck" conservatives live in red state rural areas is clearly a way to perpetuate and solidify that notion which, of course, has political implications particularly in the 2016 presidential cycle as well as other arenas such as education and community building. But this violent cartography erases all of the progressive work, accomplishments and possibilities that have taken place and are taking place in rural areas.

> And from diagram to the next, new maps are drawn. Thus there is no diagram that does not also include, besides the points which it connects up, certainly relatively free or unbound points, points of creativity, change and resistance, and it is perhaps with these that we ought to begin on order to understand the whole picture. (Deleuze, 1988, p. 44)

It is this violent cartography that desires to keep our perceptions of rural "folks" as poor, dumb, beer drinking, pick-up driving, and country music loving. When we look at kids who have been brought up and go to school in rural areas the same frame exists. Rural students frequently give voice to aspirations of making it to the big city. But, not all students in rural American schools have the dream of getting out of the rural area. There are some that are devoted to staying and spending their lives in the rural area. Most people thinking about those that want to stay in rural communities (Bubba land) are placing the majority of these students into a particular image. These students are predominately white. They are thinking of these students in a stereotypical manner. The men and women who dream of buy-ing that four wheel drive, lift kit enhanced, tool box added and super-sized tired pick-up truck. Mudding that pick-up and having friends over for beer and brats. The vision is that most of the more intelligent rural kids leave to get jobs in more affluent suburban/urban areas. That duality is not correct. Bright rural students also stay in their communities and try to make those areas better. Some even stay to work for social justice in those areas. That chaotic disruption. So, again, the television shows whether from the 1950s–1980s or the reality television shows continue the violent cartography and reinforce our images and do not express the possibilities of resistance and progressive history within rural areas. The history of Caesar Chavez and The United Farm Workers Union and the struggles and accomplishments of farm workers and the connected work on migrant workers, The United Mine Workers Union and the struggles over coal mines in areas such as West Virginia, and around the world; The American Indian Movement and the struggles of Native Americans are all ignored when it comes to cartographies of the rural. Raising issues and discussing these movements begins that disruption. In education rural schools certainly are ignored. I remember beginning told that since all of my teaching experience was in rural schools and those schools were in economically depressed areas, I would never get a job at the prestigious suburban schools. Apparently working with rural communities had somehow tainted me. But, when you think about education and the rural and people living in rural environments, Paulo Freire's concepts, although not directly linked to this cartography notion and certainly coming from a different philosophical tradition ring with its echoes. The violent cartography of the rural divides people, even people living within the rural environment itself. It makes people more easily controlled, divided and therefore oppressed.

> The more alienated people are, the easier it is to divide them and keep them divided ... These focalized forms of action, by intensifying the focalized way of life of the oppressed (especially in rural areas), hamper the oppressed from perceiving reality critically and keep them isolated from the problems of oppressed women and men in rural areas. (Freire, 2006, p. 142)

Additionally, Freire states:

> It is indispensable for the oppressors to keep the peasants isolated from the urban workers, just as it is indispensable to keep both groups isolated from the students. (Freire, 2006, p. 145)

A chaotic disruption of the cartography, frame, or diagram of the rural is necessary. The disruptions can occur in a number of ways. The struggle will be to contradict, create and disrupt deeply embedded cartographies about the rural raising issues of race, class, gender, LGBTQ, social justice, progressive movements, union history, and connections between rural and urban situations using free and unbounded lines. Those issues are tackled throughout this book. Additionally music can be used to disrupt cartographies of situations such as life on Native American Reservations. The discussion of Reservation Rap Music or Rez Rap both in the United States and Canada can be shown and discussed as disruptions to erased history of native peoples. Individual artists and groups such as: Drezus, Red Eagle, Tru Rez Crew, and Wahwahtay Benis. These artists disrupt the diagram constructed about Native Americans and their dwelling places as well as a bold assertion of the genocide that was inflicted on Native Americans in North America. There also needs to be much additional work done on African-American existence in rural environments. Books such as; *The Promised Land: The Great Black Migration and How It Changed America* (Lemann, 1996) which discusses the South to North Migration of Blacks. *The Warmth of Other Suns: The Epic Story of America's Great Migration* (Wilkerson, 2011), *Why African-Americans are moving back to the South* (Sisson, 2014), and *Call To Home: African-Americans Reclaim The Rural South* (Stack, 1996), The last book involves research that is being conducted concerning the return of Blacks to rural areas or what has been called reverse exodus. Of course, discussions of farm workers, and the farm workers union is a chaotic disrupter. *From the Jaws of Victory: The Triumph and Tragedy of Cesar Chavez* (Garcia, 2012), other ethnicities must be added to any discussion of rural education. Not only ethnicities their narratives and diagrams of the rural but an analysis of social class and poverty should be deconstructed as well. These chaotic disruptions, indeed may be a type of violent cartography to violent cartographies, which always already portray the rural as other.

NOTES

1. For a full explanation of cartography see Reynolds and Webber (2009).
2. See Deleuze (2005, pp. 92–99).
3. Schadenfreude is a German word that means "taking pleasure in the misfortune of others" (Pozner, 2010, p. 16).

REFERENCES

Boag, P. (Writer) & Watts, M. (Writer) & Diaz, A. (Director). (2016). Swamp people [Television series]. Retrieved from https://www.youtube.com/watch?v=std9MIhXTB0

Deleuze, G. (1988). *Foucault*. Minneapolis, MN: University of Minnesota Press.

Deleuze, G. (1995). *Negotiations 1972–1990*. New York: Columbia University Press.

Deleuze, G. (2005). *Francis Bacon: The logic of sensation*. Minneapolis, MN: University of Minnesota Press.

Deleuze, G., & Guattari, F. (1987). *A thousand plateaus: Capitalism and Schizophrenia*. Minneapolis, MN: University of Minnesota Press.

Doering, C. (2013, January 13). As more move to the city, does rural America still matter? *USA Today*. Retrieved from http://www.usatoday.com/story/news/nation/2013/01/12/rural-decline congress/1827407/

Ellison, R. (1995). *Invisible man* (2nd ed). New York, NY: Vintage Books.

Freire, P. (2006). *Pedagogy of the oppressed* (30th anniversary edition). New York, NY: Continuum Press.

Garcia, M. (2012). *From the jaws of victory: The triumph and tragedy of Cesar Chavez*. Oakland, CA: University of California Press

Guattari, F. (1995). *Chaosmosis: An ethico-aesthetic paradigm* (P. Bains & J. Pefanis, Trans.). Bloomington, IN: Indiana University Press.

Gurley, L. (2015, October 22). *Why the left isn't talking about rural American poverty*. Retrieved from http://inthesetimes.com/rural-america/entry/18526/why-the-left-isnt-talking-about-rural american-poverty.

Helman, S. (Developer). & Greensfeld, A., & Gallagher, S [Producers]. (2015). *Hillbilly Handfishin: Noodlin Time Trailer*. Retrieved from: https://www.youtube.com/watch?v=fHVi43U9JLg.

Housing Assistant Council. (2010). *Race & ethnicity in rural America*. Retrieved from http://www.ruralhome.org/storage/research_notes/rrn-race-and-ethnicity-web.pdf

IMDB. (2015). *The real McCoys.* Retrieved from http://www.imdb.com/title/tt0050053/

Lemann, N (1996). *The promised land: The great black migration and how it changed America.* New York, NY: Vintage Books.

Lennie72. (2013). *Green acres intro~HD with lyrics.* Retrieved from https://www.youtube.com/watch?v=wzT1kO_-xbQ

Oehlschlaeger, F. (2011). *The achievement of Wendell Berry: The hard history of love.* Lexington, KY: The University Press of Kentucky.

Opondo, S. O., & Shapiro, M. J. (2012). *The new violent cartography: Geo-analysis after the aesthetic turn.* New York, NY: Routledge.

Pozner, J. L. (2010). *Reality bites back: The Troubling truth about guilty pleasure TV.* Berkeley, CA: Seal Press.

Reynolds, W., & Webber, J. A. (2009). *The civic gospel: A political cartography of Christianity.* Rotterdam: Sense Publishers.

Screen Rant. (2016). Retrieved from http://screenrant.com/reality-tv-statistics-infographic-aco-149257/

Shapiro, M. J. (1997). *Violent cartographies: Mapping cultures of war.* Minneapolis, MN: University of Minnesota Press.

Shapiro, M. J. (2007). The new violent cartography. *Security Dialogue, 38*(3), 291–313.

Sisson, C. M. (2014, March 16). Why African-Americans are moving back to the South. *The Christian Science Monitor.* Retrieved from: http://www.csmonitor.com/USA/Society/2014/0316/Why-African-Americans are-moving-back-to-the-South

Stack, C. (1996). *Call to home: African Americans reclaim the rural south.* New York, NY: Basic Books.

Taibbi, M. (2015, November 30. The Case for Bernie Sanders: His critics say he's not realistic – but they have it backwards. *Rolling Stone.* Retrieved from http://www.rollingstone.com/politics/news/the-case-for-bernie-sanders-20151103?page=3

Wilkerson, I. (2011). *The warmth of other suns: The epic story of America's great migration.* New York, NY: Vintage.

Wordsworth, W. (1967). The world is too much with us late and soon. In D. Perkins (Ed.), *English romantic writers.* New York, NY: Harcourt Brace Jovanovich, Inc.

Young, E. B. (2013). *The deleuze and guattari dictionary.* New York: Bloomsbury Academic.

CHAPTER FOUR

Fat Guys IN THE Woods Naked AND Afraid

Rural Reality Television as Prep-School for a Post-Apocalyptic World

JENNIFER A. BEECH AND MATTHEW GUY

As cultural theorist and critical pedagogue bell hooks argues in *Cultural Criticism and Transformation*, pop culture is "the primary pedagogical medium for the masses of people globally who want to, in some way, understand the politics of difference" (1997). Following from hooks, we argue that no examination of rural education would be as efficacious, then, without an examination of how the rural is figured in the popular medium of t.v. in general and reality survival shows in particular. We examine how the current cultural obsession with the post apocalypse—whether Biblical or germ warfare (think *Walking Dead*)—is driving middle-class, urban folks to desire what they consider to be rural, working-class knowledge. Two reality shows—*Naked and Afraid* and *Fat Guys in the Woods*—are of particular interest for the ways in which they operate on several pedagogical levels to "teach" or create a desire for rural, working-class survival skills. Further, using Julia Kristeva's notion of "the abject," or those repressed elements of our nature that must stay hidden so that our subjectivity/civilization does not fail, we assert that the prepper mindset and the consumer industry fostered by this obsession with the apocalypse, appeal to an "abject" fear of the apocalypse, evoking a crisis in identity by turning the following false binaries on their heads: urban/rural; city sophistication/country crudeness; and book smarts/common sense. Our work is inspired by hooks' call for critical citizens and educators to watch such media as what she terms "enlightened witnesses— critically vigilant about what is being told to us and how we respond to what is being told."

RURAL REALITY SURVIVAL SHOWS AS TESTING
AND TRAINING GROUND

For those less familiar with these shows, a little background is in order. *Naked and Afraid*, which first aired on Discovery in 2013, follows two survivalists (one male, the other female) in their attempt to survive naked and with one survival tool each in a remote wilderness for twenty-one days. In this scenario, the survivalists—who are initially assigned a Primitive Survival Rating (PSR) based upon their projected skills, experience, and mental strength—supposedly already possess rural survival knowledge. Hence, on a pedagogical level, the show works to field test their actual skills; each participant's PSR is re-evaluated upon completion of the challenge or at the point that one or both taps out. For viewers, the show offers us not only the opportunity for voyeuristic entertainment, but also a chance to engage in visual learning. This notion of learning by watching is reinforced on the show's website, as viewers can take the PSR quiz. Based strictly upon knowledge learned from watching the show, we each scored a 9 out of 10—not that we can actually perform the tasks we identified. (As it turns out, neither can some of the so-called survivalists.) The website also offers an interactive forum called the Social Survivalist, in which viewers can compete to answer survival-related trivia. In our observation, these types of interactive outlets do seem to foster some surface-level knowledge about survival, as well as a desire to gain such knowledge. In fact, shows like *Walking Dead*, *Preppers*, *Naked and Afraid*, and *Fat Guys in the Woods* have spawned a whole survivalist industry, which targets average Joe's and Jane's with survival manuals, kits, and even bootcamps. Indeed, many of the participants on the show list "survival expert" as their main or secondary profession. Although the Bureau of Labor Statistics does not yet recognize "outdoor survival expert," Simplyhired.com (2016) lists the average salary of a survival expert at $64K—suggesting that folks are willing to pay someone in this growing field quite a bit for his or her expertise.

Watching the show from a critical perspective reveals the limits of holding the title of survival expert when faced with actual rural survival situations. For instance, many of the experts who claim fire starting capabilities struggle—and often fail—to light fires under less-than-ideal circumstances (such as freezing rain, when dealing with wet wood, or after their fire starter has gotten wet). Hence, the show can prove a useful pedagogical tool for discussing the differences between textbook and applied knowledge. As enlightened witnesses, we imagine these "experts" sitting in some urban facility demonstrating their bow or flint fire starting technique with dry materials and feeling quite proud of themselves. After watching several episodes, it's not hard to imagine some of the former clients of these so-called experts wanting their money back. We also question the efficacy of learning based solely upon watching—an ironic commentary offered in the parody episode of *Naked and Afraid* featuring the comedic actors Seth Rogen and James

Franco, which aired in December 2014. Rogen brought as his survival tool a roll of toilet paper, Franco a pair of sunglasses, and when asked how they prepared for the show, Franco answered: "just by watching it." Likewise, in Season 1, Episode 8 of *Fat Guys in the Woods*, 33 year old social worker Parker, says prior to coming on the show, "I feel like if you watch enough about the outdoors, you can kind of be an outdoorsman and not go out" (2014).

This leads us to a preliminary discussion of the second television show we focus on, *Fat Guys in the Woods*, a series which makes no pretense towards an enlightened view of gender roles. For instance, to quote Creek Stewart, the show's survival expert, his primary objective is "to teach [the 3 urban guys] the survival skills that make a man, a man." This message is reinforced on the show's website, which informs us: "With the help of The Weather Channel's resident Survival Expert Creek Stewart three guys will face nature's reckoning and find out what they are truly made of." (Spoiler: it's manliness). Pay attention to how the following quote from the website, which explains the premise of the show (which first aired in 2014), sets up binaries between rural and urban knowledge, skills, and values:

> *Fat Guys in the Woods* takes man's oldest and most primal struggle to the sweatpants-wearing couch potatoes of today. Man made fire, built shelter, and hunted food with his own two hands ... but as he got smarter, his waist got bigger.

In this figuration, urbanity is equated with sloth and gluttony and—by implication—femininity. The word "smarter" is telling, for it signals a hierarchy of knowledge that places industrial and technological knowledge above what might be deemed more traditional, old-school, rural knowledge. Bill C. Malone's discussion of ruralism as reflected in country music applies, as well, to these reality t.v. shows: "In short, ruralism linked country singers to the nation's most cherished myth, the deeply held belief that our country began its existence as a republic of rural virtue" (Malone, 2002, p. 23). Malone goes on to note that ruralism appeals to Americans "through its fantasies of rough-and-ready independence, its evocations of nostalgia, and its suggestion that old-time ways carried with them a brand of morality superior to that of modern times" (Malone, 2002, p. 28). Stewart's job is to help these fat guys "conquer mother nature" in the course of their 3-day wilderness survival experience, and his own website—Creekstewart.com—which advertises his training camps and other events, warns viewers, "Remember, its not IF but WHEN," and provides a reference to Ezekiel 38:7 ("Get ready; be prepared, you and all your hordes gathered about you and take command of them"). Clearly, Stewart—and by implication, the show's producers—seeks to claim Biblical authority as exigency for helping participants (the fat guys, as well as the male viewing audience) reclaim the masculinity, knowledge, and morality that have supposedly been forsaken with urbanity. The show, then, operates at the level of forensic rhetoric—indicting men for losing their way—and deliberative rhetoric—serving as a means of redemption through a pedagogy of rural masculinity.

TURNING FROM THE ABJECT TO THE RURAL

Let's turn our attention to these shows' either explicit or implicit goal for participants (and viewers vicariously), to discover their "rural" selves by conquering mother nature, at least as she is constructed within the shows. We find Kristeva's work provocative for teasing out the impetus behind and ramifications of the current obsession with preparing for the apocalypse. In her work *The Powers of Horror*, she writes:

> On close inspection, all literature is probably a version of the apocalypse that seems to me rooted, nor matter what its socio-historical conditions might be, on the fragile border (borderline cases) where identities (subject/object, etc.) do not exist or only barely so—double, fuzzy, heterogeneous animal, metamorphosed, altered, abject. (Kristeva, 1982, p. 207)

Kristeva says this after the section on the genre of apocalyptic literature, seen of course in works like the *Book of Revelations*, but a genre she works to connect to modern authors along the lines of Celine and Dostoevsky. Her words here point to an ongoing concern in her writing, the subject's confrontation with the at times unstable foundations of its own identity, yet they also point to a concern with the survivalist shows being discussed, that of the "fuzzy, heterogeneous" borders of identity. Kristeva takes up the question of the abject, an idea she takes great pains to define, not necessarily as an object, as we will see, but more precisely as an effect on the subject.

Rooted firmly in Freudian-Lacanian psychology, Kristeva's notion of the abject is the signifying of something that "disturbs identity, system, order" (Kristeva, 1982, p. 4). Relying also on structuralism, Kristeva puts forth the abject as more signified than signifier, indicating that what the abject is does not weigh as much as what the abject means. Examples of the abject given by Kristeva are "filth, waste, or dung," in addition to "defilement, sewage, and muck," as Leon S. Roudiez translates it (Kristeva, 1982, p. 2)—in short, the traces our own repressed, "natural" selves that one must confront and overcome to earn the title "civilized," or for our purposes here, "survivor," which we argue relates indirectly to the current notions surrounding the identity "rural." Kristeva's more famous, and perhaps by design more personal, example is,

> When the eyes see or the lips touch that skin on the surface of milk—harmless, thin as a sheet of cigarette paper, pitiful as a nail paring—I experience a gagging sensation and, still farther down, spasms in the stomach, the belly. (Kristeva, 1982, pp. 2–3)

Gross, yes, but academically, one has to argue, not universal, and that is the point: Kristeva locates the abject in the unfamiliar, the unfocused, and thus solely in the subjective. Human subjectivity arises, according to Lacanian psychology, once it splits from the Mother, symbolically, not physically. The important word here, "symbolically," emphasizes that the split, the distance between self and Mother, must be overcome only through the realm of the symbolic, through the realm of language, the realm of the Father, the realm of the Law. To paraphrase Kristeva, the signifier of the Father replaces the breast of the Mother. Whatever was nourished before the split must now be enunciated or signified, a move that is at once repression and uncovering as the subject struggles to don the identity it needs to engage its new state of existence. Ultimately there is a constant vigil by the subject for what is to be normalized or internalized, arising in a constant anxiety the subject creates about his identity, an anxiety shows like *Preppers*, *Naked and Afraid*, and others exploit to make their binaries seem more organic, more intrinsic. Such anxiety creates a desire for enculturation as "mimesis," the "means" by which the subject "becomes homologous to another in order to become himself." As Kristeva states, "laws, connections, and even structures of meaning govern and condition me" (Kristeva, 1982, p. 13). Identity comes from the enfranchisement of the subject by the Other, "an Other who precedes and possesses me, and through such possession causes me to be" (Kristeva, 1982, p. 10). Again, it must be emphasized, that what could in a sense be considered fundamental, organic, or even just intrinsic to the subject must be repressed, and what is actually outside, foreign, or just Other, must be integrated into my identity, and deemed natural, normal, even instinctual.

Relating this further to rural reality survival shows, the abject, therefore, is the sudden eruption into my world of paradoxically unfamiliar yet instinctual meanings that show my own self to in fact operate as foreign to my subjectivity—precisely what ensues when our city slickers are misplaced into these rural survival situations! Kristeva's best definition perhaps is that the abject shows to me "what I permanently [must] thrust aside in order to live" (Kristeva, 1982, p. 3). The *Fat Guys*' website asserts of its participants,

> Free of life's usual comforts (a bed, showers, a takeout menu) and forced into nature's most challenging situations, these men will put down those potato chips and fight to prove themselves. At the end of the day survival is simple … just don't die.

The contestants from both shows, though, are in a sense forced to set aside their own civilized subjectivity, and, in the midst of the abject of nature which comes in the form of bugs, animals, mud, or whatever else, turn to their more "rural" selves, as if such an identity must be there to just survive. In Kristeva's—and by extension, these shows'—framework, the abject is not some object imbued with its own meaning, or assigned its own meaning by my culture: the abject operates as a signified, not as a signifier signaling a repeatable meaning: "the abject is not an object facing me which I name or imagine," for the abject cannot have "a definable abject" (Kristeva, 1982, p. 1). This indefinability gives the abject its power over the subject, a power that destabilizes meaning itself, or, as with these survivalist shows, a power that destabilizes binaries and borders. The abject, which

Kristeva says "draws" the subject "toward the place where meaning collapses," i.e., the apocalyptic is "a 'something' that I do not recognize […] A weight of meaninglessness, about which there is nothing insignificant, and which crushes me" (Kristeva, 1982, p. 2). In shows like *Naked and Afraid*, we can see loneliness, hunger, desperation, anxiety, fear, or the most potent, incompatibility, fulfilling this role of a "crushing" something for most participants. Going back to the concrete examples Kristeva gives of the abject, such as waste, bodily fluids, or the skin on milk, the abject is not merely discomforting or gross:

> It is thus not lack of cleanliness or health that causes abjection but what disturbs identity, system, order. What does not respect borders, positions, rules. The in-between, the ambiguous, the composite. The traitor, the liar, the criminal with a good conscience, the shameless rapist, the killer who claims he is a savior … Abjection […] is immoral, sinister, scheming and shady: a terror that dissembles, a hatred that smiles. (Kristeva, 1982, p. 4)

Here, we wonder: can the abject be the ineptitude of the contestant who claims he's a survivalist? Can it also be that which erodes survival, like hunger, insect bites, dehydration, or even incompatability, however it may erupt into the show? The response to the abject logically arises from the superego, and thus from a more shared concept of civilization, signaling the abject as what is "perverse because it neither gives up nor assumes a prohibition, a rule, or a law [but instead] turns them aside, misleads, corrupts" (Kristeva, 1982, p. 15). More directly, Kristeva says that the abject "confronts" the subject "with those fragile states where man strays on the territories of animal" (Kristeva, 1982, p. 12). This edge of civilized man is where one finds the apocalyptic, the abject, and ultimately, where one finds the binaries of urban/rural, male/female, combative/supportive, or even survivor/failure, strengthened and affirmed.

CONSUMERISM AND THE COMMODIFICATION OF RURAL SURVIVAL

What kind of an apocalypse are we dealing with in these shows, though? What exactly is the disaster we are preparing for? In short, the answer is nothing, but everything. In some shows like *Preppers*, the apocalypse is merely what happens after everything collapses, either economically, politically, or environmentally. The apocalypse knows no political biases, which ironically binds the progressive fearing environmental disaster to the conservative preparing himself for the apparently inevitable collapse of social and political foundations. As Gwendolyn Audrey Foster points out, "our apocalyptic obsessed culture" has "grown to the point that it both permeates and informs our daily lives" (Foster, 2014, p. 2), such that it soaks into the mindset of nearly every political, religious and cultural persuasion.

Obviously, then, such a widely shared sense of impending doom must remain in general terms if it is to be tapped into by popular culture, and that, frankly, is where it is at its most compelling and yet its most functional. Briefly defined, the word "apocalypse" comes from the Greek *apokalupsis*, derived from *apokaluptein*, which means to "uncover" or "reveal." Catherine Keller points out that "prebiblically, the term connotes the marital stripping of the the veiled virgin" (Keller, 2005, p. 1). Kristeva points to the word's etymological derivation from the idea of vision, but points out that "it must be understood as the contrary revelation of philosophical truth" (Kristeva, 1982, p. 154). That is, the religious connotations of revelation in the apocalypse are unavoidable, in that the utmost foundations of our world are upended, overturned, and the nebulous truths we hold to be solid are cast aside. Such a wide net of "apocalypse" shows that "no ideological interpretation can be based on" it, for "what principle, what party, what side, what class comes out unscathed, that is, identical to itself, from such a thorough critical conflagration?" (Kristeva, 1982, p. 154).

To define the apocalypse in such general and, well, rather apocalyptic terms makes sense of the nonspecific abject upon which it relies, as Kristeva defines the abject. It also, it seems, allows the more political interpretations of the apocalypse and the abject to circulate within culture, for it is culture that demands that we leave the abject, that we jettison the more defiled elements of our selves, to gain the identity that culture gives to us. As Kristeva points out, the abject, the subject and sublimation of which "is eminently productive of culture," (Kristeva, 1982, p. 45) is that which can be aligned with the maternal body from which we extract ourselves, or our "selves," so that we can create our identity in the realm of the Symbolic, the realm of language and culture. Kristeva writes

> A representative of the paternal function takes the place of the good maternal object that is wanting. There is language instead of the good breast. Discourse is being substituted for maternal care. (Kristeva, 1982, p. 45)

Kelly Oliver says it more directly when she points out that for Kristeva, "the authority of our religion, morality, politics and language comes through the repression of horror [i.e., the abject], adding that "our culture is founded on this horror" (Oliver, 1993, p. 101). Ultimately, this means that the abject erupts into our world as the overturning of our intimate understandings of authority, which make up our identities, those socialized "selves" that we construct, or feel compelled by society to construct, in order to obtain or even enunciate our desires. Kristeva locates this relation between authority and repression in religious rituals of defilement, such as in the codes of the sacred in Leviticus. "Defilement is what is jettisoned from the *symbolic system*" (Kristeva, 1982, p. 65) Kristeva writes, adding that such defilement serves as the "translinguistic spoor of the most archaic boundaries of the self's clean and proper body" (Kristeva, 1982, p. 73). Leviticus articulates the proper handling of the abject, from proper foods to its preparation, to the codes surrounding menstruation, disease, and even burial.

This becomes a long way of saying that the bugs, the blood, the swelling of the flesh, the vomit, the maggots, in fact, every instance of abjection witnessed voyeuristically by watching *Naked and Afraid* serves as more than just entertainment. The abject in the scenarios put forth by the show serve to the participants and to the audience as reminders of the tenuous nature of our own cultural selves, scenes which, ironically, we find both repellent and compelling. Of course, Kristeva goes into detail about the ambivalent attraction and repulsion felt by subjects witnessing the abject, which we need not delve into, but voyeurism has been an element of the formation of fetishes and phobias for psychoanalysts from Kristeva going back to Freud, and furthermore, for Kristeva, phobias (and we could argue, fetishes) are condensations of the unnamable abject into the nameable object. Thus the camera work in *Naked and Afraid* allows spectators to be omniscient voyeurs, encountering solid instances of their own fears as they are encountered vicariously by participants, but it also allows spectators to operate as confessors whenever hand-helds are used by contestants as a diary, whereby they quite often confess their fears and resentments about the very abilities of their partners to stick it out all the way to extraction from the scenarios. In Season 3, Episode 3 "Hearts of Darkness," contestant Carrie is shown early and often complaining about her survival partner Tom, as well as the jungle, the insects, the weather, and the utter boredom of their predicament. She asserts that she could most likely survive the scenario by herself, and wonders aloud just where Tom's so-called survivalist skills are. Likewise, in Season 2, Episode 2, "Damned in Africa," Eva says of her partner Jeff, "I'm wondering if he's starting to lose it a little bit."

These fears concerning others, sometimes themselves, resonate in two distinct ways. First, they accompany the onslaught of the abject captured and enhanced by the show, which help link the experience of the abject to the crises of identities that are the real meat of the shows. Numerous scenes of the snakes, spiders, predators, plants, and insects in each scenario are repeated often throughout the episodes, as are images of the insect-bitten skins, the mud, the swellings, the grimaces, the pains, etc. that mark the participants. Mosquito sounds are often added throughout the episodes, as in Season 2, Episode 1 "Man Vs. Amazon," as are images of bugs crowding the night vision cameras. Other enhancements of the abject include the added layers of flies buzzing when Luke and Lyndsey discover a dead kudu in Season 3, Episode 1 "Primal Fear," an image which in itself links nature to the abject, but gets added dimension with the almost unnoticed foley work. In that same episode, Luke handles some "predator poop" to assure Lyndsey that the cave they are considering is far too dangerous to stay in. He also eats grubs from the ground, saying that he can detect a faint "poop taste" in them. In fact, the repeated scenes of eating, whether its palm hearts hacked out by machetes and kukris to lizards, turtles, snakes, bugs, and all other sorts of exotic fauna, serve to confront us with the abject. Kristeva, in her discussion of defilement codes in Leviticus, says that "orality signifies the boundary of the self's clean and proper body" (Kristeva, 1982, p. 75), so that the eating that must be undertaken in *Naked and Afraid* must often be seen as compromise, a relenting of the boundaries of the civilized self if one must survive. In that same episode where Luke discovers that a cave may actually be the home of a predator, and where he eats the grubs for some much needed protein, he confesses to the camera that feels "a lot of guilt and shame" about not having a fire started soon enough. Thus the encounter with the abject, be it living beside it or in it, or having to take it into one's body in order to survive, is always an assessment of one's identity, of the ability of oneself to be the person who must engage whatever aspect of the abject being encountered, rather than fall victim to the abject. Fear of the actual worth and stamina of identity accompanies the bravery of engaging the abject and surviving.

That assessment of identity resonates in a second way, in that almost any identity held over from our so-called civilization, be it Army-vet, survivalist, athlete, or just outdoor enthusiast, can only serve as an indication of just how much one can draw from the more authentic and necessary "rural" identity one needs when survival is actually, at least within the parameters of the show, required. The whole notion of a PSR rating reinforces the idea that some unspoken yet implicitly understood ultra-survivalist identity stands forth as the actual measure of whatever survivalist identity one creates within the limits of civilization, creating an anxiety even amongst contestants that they may not have that actual "rural" identity needed, and have been duped into believing the survivalist identity they have heretofore created is, like the society it is built from, set to disintegrate when the apocalypse, the true revelation of the abject, appears. A self-described "mountain man" like Luke survives to extraction, as does the New York construction worker Charlie in Season 4, Episode 7 "Columbian Conflict," yet both AK and Tyler tap out of Season 2 Episode 1 "Man vs Amazon" to have EJ, another Army vet, and Laura, step in. At one point Tyler, a military vet like Charlie, says "thirteen months in Afghanistan didn't do to me mentally and physically what being out here in the jungle has done." Furthermore, identities not associated with being a survivalist, such as homemaker, vegetarian or rock climber, may in fact endanger the ability to survive by suddenly making the contestant collapse in the face of the abject.

Like all reality television shows, *Naked and Afraid* gathers up contestants for the drama accompanying tension, anxiety and conflict, and at times even enunciates such reservations about contestants in the show. When there are vegetarians, like Dani in Season 4, Episode 7 "Columbian Conflict," and Angela in Season 4, Episode 6 "Lord of the Rats," the narrator often voices the concern that the viewer must latch on to, that as vegetarians, the aversion to "much needed protein" may compromise their ability to survive, reflected at times in their early PSR ratings.

Despite this, and quite comically, many of these vegetarians survive and, in fact, both Dani and Angela come to the aid of their male partners. Dani goes out to get a toad for Charlie who is suffering from lack of nourishment, and Angela jumps off the boat when she is being extracted to help her partner, Darrin, swim to the boat because his hip gets injured. The point, though, is not that the vegetarian identity coincides with the rural identity needed for survival. The point is that the vegetarian identity, like the impatient woman identity or the bossy male identity or the too luxuriate female identity or the too stubborn male identity, does not compromise or undermine the rural identity required to actually survive to extraction. One good element of the show is that while certain stereotypes of men and women are engaged by the show, as given above, the show also presents either the upsetting of expectations of those stereotypes, or it will go against any such stereotyping. Women are often complaining, and men are often bossy, but so too are women also good leaders and men quite sensitive to the emotional states of their female partners. All of which, again, goes to reinforce the idea that once the apocalypse arrives and society crumbles, the identities we have heretofore built will crumble, but the true, authentic "rural" identity that one may or may not have, will be the only way to survive the abject that the apocalypse reveals.

In her book *Hoarders, Doomsday Preppers, and the Culture of the Apocalypse* (2014), Foster forwards the rather grim thesis that "our culture of narcissistic doom wants more than anything to create a climate of fear and isolation, in which we are forced to endlessly consume and die emotionally, as willing participants in late-stage capitalism." She goes so far as to assert that as we live in a society that is "increasingly stratified into the very rich and the very poor, human misfortune and visions of apocalyptic doom have become our principle source of entertainment" (Foster, 2014, p. 2). Although Foster does not discuss *Naked and Afraid* or *Fat Guys in the Woods*, we can clearly identify these shows within the genre of what she calls "apocotainment"—since Stewart habitually begins almost every episode by scaring the week's 3 participants (along with the viewing audience) as motivation to learn primitive survival skills. Employing what we will call a "pedagogy of fear," Stewart sets himself up as the pedagogue exemplar—as his voiceover introduces the first episode: "If you can survive a week with me, you can take on anything." (Recall Stewart's prediction of the post-apocalypse on his personal web site.)

Because of the very different set up of the show, for *Fat Guys,* we turn to the premier episode as important for establishing the premise of and exigency for a show. Season 1, episode 1: "Sub Zero Teepee Build" introduces us to 3 friends from Los Angeles who have all come to spend a week with Stewart: 28 year old Matt, whom we are told has been so career-focused that he has let his health go; Jesse, a 27 year old writer; and Ben, 34, who is a substitute school teacher. Upon their arrival at a remote location in the Smokey Mountains of Tennessee, Stewart greets these "friends from the big city" with a story that he claims is from recent headlines in the area: he tells of 3 hikers on the Appalachian Trail who just 5 hours into their hike use a cell phone to call for help; by the time the rangers arrive, they suffer from severe hypothermia and frost bite. Cue ominous music and a turn of Jesse to the camera: "We were having fun, and Creek got serious real quick. Scared all of us." Before they can even start, their own ability to reveal their "rural" or "survivalist" identity is indirectly questioned, heightening the anxiety they have about such identity. Similarly, in Season 1, Episode 8, after Creek has warned his apprentices of the brutal few days ahead of then, Atlanta coffee shop worker and aspiring lawyer Chris discloses to the viewing audience, "Creek told me there were four things to surviving out here, and, honestly, all I heard was death, death, death, death." In a different episode, Big Fellow, an African-American chef from Detroit, admits, "I'm not gonna lie; I'm scared," and after his final night alone, he kids Stewart, "Creek, do you realize that in every scary movie, the black dude dies first?" (Season 1, Episode 6, 2014) As Kristeva writes, anxiety in reaction to the abject creates a desire for enculturation as "mimesis," the "means" by which the subject "becomes homologous to another in order to become himself" (Kristeva, 1982, p. 13).

After a trek into the woods and fashioning a primitive wickiup from logs and leaves in that premier episode, Stewart lectures Matt, Jesse, and Ben on how to make use of a "mountain man fire starter kit." Superimposed on the screen is a text box directed towards viewers that explains, "High-carbon steel found in many tools and knives is the best type of metal to create a spark with flint." These text boxes appear periodically, clearly positioning viewers as pupils, as well. Happy to listen and, hopefully, watch as Stewart build them a fire, the three become rather disgruntled when after this brief dissertation about mountain man fire starting techniques, Stewart tosses the steel and flint out into the woods, forcing his pupils to search the creek bed for flint rock and highlighting the importance (at least for those not on their couches) of learning by doing. Likewise, Stewart models how to build snares, and then has the guys make their own snare, by which they secure a rabbit. Stewart is adamant about the importance of all three men participating in the quite abject experience of skinning, preparing, and cooking the rabbit. While cooking their catch, the guys reminisce over their last meal, which they admit to just shoving food into their mouths. Jesse says,

> Two days in, and I feel like I'm already taking habits home. Just the idea of being conscious of everything you're doing is something that everyone should do, but I do not do. Heart disease is in my family, and I am not doing enough avoid a fatal heart attack.

Here, these fat guys stand in as the abject which viewers potentially fear for themselves, and as viewer comments on the episode replayed on YouTube indicate, many viewers are unable to take seriously this narrative of salvation through brief survival experiment, recognizing the show for its place in a commodified survival industry: user "fullstrutn" writes, "one weekend will change these guys,,,,sorry. this just another 'photo op' for an 'adventure.'" At one point as an aside to the viewers, in a bit that feels very much like an advertisement, Stewart lectures about the usefulness of a compact survival blanket that can fit in one's pocket. As he models securing the blanket between two trees, he lies on the ground under it, telling viewers how because the blanket can reflect up to 80% of a user's body heat, as well as the heat of a fire, it can mean the difference between life and death. Subtext to potential advertisers: advertise your reflective blanket here now! Subtext to viewers: buy one. Special links on the Weather.com, like "Advertise with Us," and "Ad Specs" tell potential advertisers: "Weather offers a full suite of Standard, Rich, and Custom Ad formats across our screens: Weather.com, Mobile, Tablet, and Cable"—harkening back to Foster's recognition that "Apocalyptic gloom sells" (2) and making it impossible for us as enlightened witnesses to miss the capitalistic subtext of the show.

Day five into every episode, Stewart separates each man to survive one night alone and then rewards the "fat guy" whom he judges to demonstrate the best survival skills with the same knife kit he uses: the Blackbird SK-5 in a Hedge Hog Leatherworks case. Underlying the narrative of redemption through a manly return to nature, every show can be read as a series of product placements for items that are for sale on Stewart's online store: notifbutwhensurvivalstore.com. Take, for instance, Season 2, Episode 4: Knife Skills in the Swamp, in which Stewart takes three overweight disc jockeys into the Dead Lake Swamp area of the Florida panhandle. DJ Lopez says of himself, "The only time I go out is for lunch," while Mike relates that as a recovering alcoholic, he has replaced the bottle with food; meanwhile, Jim admits to being at a crossroads in wanting to lose weight so that he can watch his newly born granddaughter grow up. Minutes into the show, Stewart lectures: "As a survivalist, I definitely understand the importance of tools to survive in an environment like this. And I consider your survival knife the most important tool, and this week, that choice is yours." Suddenly, Stewart flashes open his coat to reveal a vest sporting at least 8 different knives. Stewart praises Mike for choosing a Kukri as a chopping tool, noting that a good tactical hatchet can mean the difference between "knife and death." At one point as the 4 men sit around whittling sticks in order to construct a turtle trap, Stewart fondly remembers the first Rambo knife he received at age nine. Not surprisingly, these knives each are available on *Not If But When Survival Store* (which he never mentions directly on the show). At the beginning of every episode, Stewart issues each guy a backpack containing a few survival tools, one of which is usually a stainless steel water bottle containing enough water for their first day. However, for Season 1, Episode 4, Stewart deviates and gives the guys, instead, a personal straw water filter. A quick search reveals several options for purchasing such filters on two sites with which the show's survival expert is affiliated: the Frontier Emergency Water Filter (willowhavenoutdoor.com) and the Aquamira Frontier Bug Out Straw, as well as the Life Straw (notifbutwhensurvivalstore.com). While this product placement is not necessarily sinister, when considered in conjunction with what is not emphasized on the show, we must question the value of the pedagogical imperative of the show. Whereas the goal of critical pedagogy is to foster what Freire calls conscientization and engaged citizenship, the end game of Stewart's pedagogy of fear is to promote consumerism, which, as Marxist criticism points out, is the selling of ideology and identity inasmuch as it is selling products. Again, Foster's analysis with doomsday narratives is instructive:

> One of the interesting things about our fascination with our own demise is our lack of interest in the demise of the Earth. it is not that we are not interested in the end of the Earth and the destruction of other species. No. our interest in Earth, the environment, and other species is primarily in their usefulness to humanity. (Foster, 2014, p. 46)

Repeatedly, the participants in *Fat Guys* focus on a superficial momentary transformation in their own thinking about themselves—not about their responsibility to the woods or to their environment. Mike's words are telling: "You spend the first half of life trying to kill yourself and the second half trying to stay alive" (Season 2, Episode 4). His week-long survival experience does not foster obligation to the rural or to the earth. Again, the dominant narrative is: buy the right tools so you "just don't die."

CONCLUSION

In conjunction with our discussion of rural reality survival shows, we would emphasize that even official definitions of the term rural operate around oppositions. As Donehower, Hogg, and Schell note, "As a quantitative measure, the Department of Commerce's Bureau of Census defines rural as essentially not urban" (2007, p. 2). Donehower, Hogg, and Schell take a very different approach to rural literacy from that forwarded by either of the shows we have discussed: "Rural literacies, then, refers to the particular kinds of literate skills needed to achieve the goals of sustaining life in rural areas [...] and create the public policies and economic opportunities needed to sustains rural communities" (Donehower et al., 2007, p. 4). Participants in both *Naked and Afraid* and *Fat Guys in the Woods* are concerned only with their own immediate survival. Neither show overtly forwards any sense of responsibility to the rural environment or communities surrounding the landscape on which the survivalists must test or learn their skills. For the extraction of the surviving participants of *Naked and Afraid XL*, set in Columbia, viewers paying close attention to every detail will observe the boats of the extraction crew guarded by 50 caliber machine guns. As enlightened witnesses, we know these weapons are not there to ward off dangerous caiman. Rather, the unremarked upon subtext is that our survivalists have been in dangerous territory not simply due to natural environmental hazards; more likely, they have been in drug running zones. Viewers are not meant to focus on that; viewers are supposed to celebrate—along with the survivalists—the conquering of mother nature. Likewise, survivalists and the viewing audience are in no way directed towards a concern for local peoples. The rural is, instead, a playground for those with enough resources to take anywhere from a week to 21 days or more off to face their own worst fears. This pedagogy of fear works on oppositions. It's not so much about testing who the survivalist are as it is about testing who they are not: not man enough, not fit enough, not tough enough, or, ultimately, not the best shopper. Viewers of *Naked and Afraid*, for instance, can question—and judge—the survivalist who brings fishing line or a snorkeling mask as their supposed survival tool. Viewers of *Fat Guys in the Woods* can rush to online survivalist stores to purchase their own reflective survival blanket or knife and in doing so, feel superior to the poor sap who was has not purchased wisely or—worse yet—not shopped at all.

Kristeva's ideas concerning the abject resonate with texts of all kinds that speak to anxieties and crises of identity, power, or even existence, and this is especially true for the whole "survivalist" genre of fictional and reality shows. Shows like *Doomsday Preppers, Life After People, The Colony* or even *The Walking Dead*, along with movies like *The Hunger Games* and the recent *Mad Max* reboot, are upfront about the apocalyptic core of their presentations, but it could be argued nevertheless preserve a distance between their subject matter and the viewers. Zombies, total global economic collapse, or even catastrophic climate change, seem to be unlikely, if not impossible. Shows like *Naked and Afraid* and *Fat Guys in the Woods* collapse this distance, essentially by dropping their onscreen participants, and thus their viewers, into that abject which stands ambiguously at the edge of their own civilized selves. The apocalypse these survivalist shows present thereby becomes more personal, more present, more internalized, and more powerful.

REFERENCES

Creek Stewart. Retrieved May 15, 2015 from creekstewart.com

Donehower, K., Hogg, C., & Schell, E. (2007). *Rural literacies*. Carbondale, IL. Southern Illinois Press.

Fat Guys in the Woods. Retrieved February 14, 2016 from Stories.weather.com/fat-guys-in-the-woods.

Fat Guys in the Woods (2014, August 10). Sub zero teepee build [Season 1, Episode 1]. Weather Channel.

Fat Guys in the Woods (2014, August 31). Eat bees to survive [Season 1, Episode 4]. Weather Channel.

Fat Guys in the Woods (2014, September 14). Trial by fire [Season 1, Episode 6]. Weather Channel.

Fat Guys in the Woods (2014, September 28). The pit. [Season 1, Episode 8]. Weather Channel.

Fat Guys in the Woods (2015, June 28). Knife skills in the woods [Season 2, Episode 4]. Weather Channel.

Foster, G. (2014). *Hoarders, doomsday preppers, and the culture of the apocalypse.* New York, NY: Palgrave Macmillan.

hooks, b. (1997). *Cultural criticism and transformation* (Sut Jhally, Prod.). Media Education Foundation.

Keller, C. (2005). *Apocalypse now and then: A feminist guide to the end of the world.* Minneapolis, MN: Fortress Press.

Kristeva, J. (1982). *The powers of horror.* New York, NY: Columbia UP.

Malone, B. C. (2002). *Don't get above your raisin': Country music and the Southern working class.* Champaign, IL: University of Illinois Press.

Naked and Afraid. Retrieved February 14, 2016 from nakedandafraid.discovery.com

Naked and Afraid (2013, July 28). Beware the bayou. [Season 1, Episode 6]. Discovery Channel.

Naked and Afraid (2014, March 23). Damned in Africa [Season 2, Episode 2]. Discovery Channel.

Naked and Afraid (2015, June 7). Columbian conflict [Season 4, Episode 7]. Discovery Channel.

Naked and Afraid (2014, March 16). Man vs. Amazon [Season 2, Episode 1]. Discovery Channel.

Naked and Afraid (2014, December 7). Franco and rogen [Season 3 Special]. Discovery Channel.

Not If But When Survival Store. Retrieved February 1, 2016 from notifbutwhensurvival.com

Oliver, K. (1993). *Reading Kristeva: Unraveling the double-bind.* Bloomington and Indianapolis, IN: Indiana UP.

SimplyHired. Retrieved February 14, 2016 from www.simplyhired.com

Willow Have Outdoor. Retrieved February 14, 2016 from willowhavenoutdoor.com

CHAPTER FIVE

Finding Jesus

Schooling in the Age
of Mass Surveillance

MICHAEL BOYER

I ask the pardon of those teachers who, in dreadful conditions, attempt to turn the few weapons they can find in the history and learning they "teach" against the ideology, the system and the practices in which they are trapped. They are a kind of hero. But they are rare, and how many (the majority) do not even begin to suspect the "work" the system (which is bigger than they are and crushes them) forces them to do, or worse, put all their heart and ingenuity into performing it with the most advanced awareness (the famous new methods!)
—LOUIS ALTHUSSER (1970)

My high school guidance counselor knew my family worked in factories and were not college educated. "Don't worry about taking Spanish; you only need a foreign language if you are planning to attend college," he said. Mr. Z knew where we lived, government housing, *the white peoples' projects* the kids at school called them. He was a nice enough guy, and really I'll never know his true intentions. His advice could have been to motivate me or to provide the factory with another worker; regardless, it angered me enough I decided that very day to hatch a plot to escape the postindustrial shell of a town where I grew up just east of St. Louis.

I remember my grandfather's advice, as the adage says, *Go west young man; go west*. So the day after my eighteenth birthday, I did just that, stopping off along the way to attend community college, university, and eventually graduate school to obtain a teaching credential before landing my first teaching job. I went as far west as possible, running into the Pacific Ocean where I was hired to teach English to *Newcomers*, migrant Mexican students, at a high school tucked away in a rural community in the Pacific Northwest. In no time I fashioned an affinity with the students living in this little town. Like most new teachers, I imagine, when I started teaching I was enthusiastic, ready to save the world; but really I didn't know much.

So I tried to remember the things I learned in my teacher preparation program, mostly methods and writing lesson plans. In hindsight it was most absurd; even more so were the lectures on making sure to never be too nice to your students too soon, to never share information of a personal nature, and for god's sake—never touch a student! But there was one professor, a Freirian scholar, who prepared me quite differently; he taught me to teach from the heart, and to share my humanity. Also, he cautioned me to be skeptical of pre-packaged literacy materials and to develop curriculum naturally, drawing from the life experiences of learners. So, I began that first year scared but determined; I shared stories about growing up poor and going to school in a small town in Southern Illinois, about moving a lot, and about growing up with many cousins extending from a matriarchal clan, and eventually my students began to trust me enough to share their personal stories.

Students told stories of walking for days to cross the desert and about the need to come north to send money to their family members struggling to survive in Mexico. Their stories were like nothing I had ever heard, powerful. Soon we began to negotiate the content for the course day by day deciding to write bilingual autobiographical narratives as the content they would focus on to learn English, but also for me to learn Spanish, blurring the lines between teacher and student, we both had something to offer, it was a trade. Over the months we published a series of narratives, student artwork, and photographs of each author, and in retrospect, this was an exciting time as a young teacher; however, the following year I was involuntarily transferred, ending up at a school located fifty miles from my home. A year turned into several and in time I decided to leave this community to complete doctoral studies with the hope of someday sharing my experience with the next generation of educators in a teacher preparation program. We loaded up the truck and ventured forward to start a new chapter, returning to the good life, the university.

Accordingly, I had just returned to Boise, while cursing under my breath in the scorching summer heat, unloading boxes from the moving truck, a box buckled under the strain of the load spewing its contents all over the parking lot. As I started cleaning up the mess of papers, I recognized the black and white photocopied books of stories and artwork we had made together over a decade ago in that ESOL class. I studied the face of each young author, analyzing each narrative, trying to relive a simpler time that I thought had vanished forever. Hours passed before I found myself sitting alone in my storage unit, without chemicals I swear, I had experienced a form of time travel, reliving a special moment shared with a group of teen aged kids who had taught me so much more than my teacher preparation program ever could.

I felt horrible, how had I allowed myself to lose them? At once it dawned on me; I would find the kids who had made such a lasting impact on my life. I wanted to talk to them, to know where these authors are today, and admittedly, it was strange to imagine them, ten years later, as adults. So I got on Facebook and found several former students who were willing to meet and reconnect; in time this quest to reunite with former students would turn into a qualitative research project. I collected several student narratives, but in this chapter I am going to share just one.

My research was driven by two primary questions. First, what are the personal and educational narratives of *one and a half generation* migrant students from Mexico living in the rural Pacific Northwest? And, how are these "micro-narratives" tied to larger "macro-narratives", and why is an understanding of the intertwining of the two essential for bilingual teachers to act in solidarity with students?

Thus, the following retrospective narrative account, told by one of my former students, a young man I call Jesus, describes his experience attending high school as a member of *the one and a half generation*. Members of the one and a half generation are undocumented as they were born in Mexico and brought to the United States as young children. As is the case with Jesus, members of the 1.5 generation are *Americanized* through attending public schools. Yet after high school, due to the lack of a social security number, they are unable to obtain financial aid to attend college, unable to work most jobs, and in Oregon, even unable to obtain a driver's license. However, before sharing Jesus' story, permit me to briefly explain how I will analyze his story and draw upon it to continue to tell my own.

MICRO-NARRATIVE THEMES AND ARCHETYPAL GENRE

My approach to the analysis of Jesus' story focuses on two general aspects of stories, *discourse and narration* (Genette, 1980) or *what* is told in the story and *how* the story is told (Labov, 1972, White, 1973). To better understand *what* is told in the story, I elaborate *themes* to locate the micro-narrative in a larger socio-historical context by placing myself within the hermeneutic tradition in which past and present are constantly fused (Gadamer, 1988). From within this tradition, I am positioned to interrogate Grand Narratives (Clandinin & Connelly, 2000), or metanarratives (Lyotard, 1984) about immigrants from Mexico. Stated simply, we can only understand Jesus' story (i.e., make sense of it) with reference to other texts, and in turn our understanding of these other texts is modified by our understanding of this text. The study of teacher and student agency in the face of adversity is of particular importance in the connections to broader political, social, and cultural developments made in this work; for this reason allow me to give a brief background of immigration and educational policy.

IMMIGRATION NARRATIVES AND ECONOMY

What stands out most in the history of migration from Mexico to the US is the reoccurring theme of the US gaining access to an abundance of cheap Mexican labor (Bustamonte, 1997). For example, in the 1920s and into the Great Depression, anti-immigrant sentiment blamed Mexican workers for high unemployment; the government's response was *repatriation* or forced deportation. However, during World War II, the United States war economy depended on Mexican labor to meet production needs and created the Bracero Program, a system of "colonial labor exploitation" (Gonzalez & Fernandez, 2003, p. 26). For the decades following the Bracero era, circular migration was practiced, meaning workers would travel between the two countries to do seasonal work. However, the 1986 Immigration Reform and Control Act (IRCA) and the 1996 Illegal Immigration Reform and Immigration Responsibility Act (IIRIRA) ended circular migration patterns and resulted in further militarization of the border (Gonzales-Berry & Mendoza, 2010).

In more recent times, the North American Free Trade Agreement (NAFTA) of 1994, an agreement designed by transnational corporations to reduce tariffs to trade and investment, caused an increase in migration. As a result of NAFTA, an influx of subsidized cheap imported corn from the US devastated local Mexican farmers, putting them out of business; and, as soon as the policy took effect between Canada, the US, and Mexico, the minimum wage in Mexico dropped, manufacturing wages went down, and the number of Mexicans fleeing poverty increased drastically (Bigelow, 2006, p. 19). Being compelled to move in search of work can be understood as economic forces or technologies of economy utilized by the state since the Enclosure Movement in 16th century England, and perhaps dates back to the Roman Empire; these technologies have been described as free market globalization, or neoliberal ideology (Gabbard, 2008).

While NAFTA increased the number of people coming north, at the same time, several laws were passed that focused on mandatory detention for non-citizens: the Illegal Immigration Reform and Responsibility Act of 1996 (IIRIRA), the Antiterrorism and Effective Death Penalty Act of 1996 (AEDPA), and the USA Patriot Act of 2001 (Bosworth & Flavin, 2007). Prior to the enactment of these laws, those caught entering the country without proper documents were sent back; today they are routinely taken into custody. Hence, the number of prisoners doing time for immigration offenses, distinct from criminal offenses, grew 859% from 1985 to 2000 (Bosworth & Flavin, 2007, p. 138).

Moreover, the Obama administration has deported more than two million people, dwarfing any previous administration (Goodman & Gonzáles, 2014). To carry this out, there are two divisions within DHS tasked with immigration enforcement: Customs and Border Protection (CBP) is responsible for enforcement *at* the border, and Immigration and Customs Enforcement (ICE) is responsible for immigration enforcement *within* the United States. Part of the militarization of the border has resulted in the expansion of the jurisdiction of ICE further inland by partnering with Sheriff's departments (Goodman & González, 2014). How does this aggressive immigration apparatus affect the lives of emergent bilingual students, their families, and their teachers in schools?

Many of my colleagues over the years are unaware or apathetic to the reality of migrant students and their families and symptomatic of the manner in which teachers have swallowed Master Narratives about schools and the larger society: That they are democratic in nature. Yet, a critical reading of history reveals how democracy in western nations serves an illusory purpose to hide dominant ideologies, which have always been more capitalistic than democratic. Foucault, Burchell, Gordon, and Miller (1978) explains,

> To govern a state will therefore mean to apply economy, to set up an economy at the level of the entire state, which means exercising towards its inhabitants, and the wealth and behavior of each and all, a form of surveillance and control as attentive as that of the head of a family over his household and his goods. (p. 92)

Consider the following example of how official policy narratives that criminalize workers function to apply economy.

In the decade following 9/11 (September 11, 2001), the detention budget for ICE increased from 864 million dollars to 2 billion dollars annually. Contributing to this growth are the US Government's "criminal alien" enforcement programs, which began in the 1990s and are now part of the Secure Communities program that links ICE, the Department of Justice, and local law enforcement (Miller, 2014). Secure Communities produce most detainees for detention facilities by widening the enforcement and deportation capabilities even more by creating the category of "crimes of moral turpitude" which include charges of fraud, forgery, and possessing a controlled substance (p. 222). The logic of neoliberalism drives private detention facilities to contract with ICE in what has been called *the immigration gold rush*. Miller (2014) provides the example of the Corrections Corporation of America (CCA) that made 95 million dollars in 2005 by contracting with the Department of Homeland Security; in 2011 it was making 208 million dollars per year from these contracts. The for profit incarceration industry depends on an increased criminalization of migrants. What role does the history of migrant schooling play within the larger socio-political context?

ENGLISH PROGRAMS AS FORMS OF SURVEILLANCE AND CONTROL

Mexican children attended legally segregated schools in the United States until the mid-20th century; Mexican children were targeted for deculturalization by programs "designed to strip away Mexican values and culture and replace the use of Spanish with English" (Spring, 2011, p. 223). For example, in 1918, Texas made it a criminal offense to teach in any language other than English; Anglos believed Mexican culture discouraged "the exercise of economic entrepreneurship and cooperation required in an advanced corporate society" (p. 224).

Contemporary notions of bilingual and multicultural education resulted as a historical response to institutionalized deculturalization programs that lasted for nearly two centuries (Spring, 2011). Multicultural education and bilingual education were born from the struggles waged by African Americans, Mexican/Latinos, Asians, and American Indians during the height of the Civil Rights Movement of the 1960s and 70s. However, bilingual programs are less common today than English only program models.

For roughly a dozen years, I have worked in English as Second Language (ESL) classrooms. Other acronyms for the same type of language program model are ESOL (English for Speakers of Other Languages) and common today, ENL (English as a New Language). In *ESOL*, instruction is provided in English often with little to no support in the student's primary language. Generally, English instruction is provided in a *pullout program*, which consists of English lessons for thirty minutes to an hour per day. There are a number of different language instructional program models being used by school districts across the nation with a wide range of the amount of primary language literacy that is provided alongside English Instruction. In the model called *submersion*, students are in English only with no additional language support. In the US, this approach is illegal as a result of *Lau v. Nichols* (1974) however; many students often find themselves in submersion settings (Banks & Banks, 2013) as policy defines knowledge assessed in English as legitimate.

The No Child Left Behind Act 2001 (NCLB) continues an agenda set forth in the policy report of *A Nation At Risk* in 1983, to build a national culture based on a market driven rationale cloaked in the language of school reform (Gabbard, 2008) and should be viewed as part of the broader crisis of democracy of which militarization is a central aspect (Saltman and Gabbard, 2008, p. 225). Changes to language policy under NCLB effectively erased ideological gains made over the preceding thirty years, and moved from the *language as resource* orientation backwards to a position of *language as problem*, discouraging maintenance bilingual programs and promoting English-only approaches (Hornberger, 2006, p. 230).

NCLB certainly has amplified the high stakes testing and so called accountability environment, however Foucault et al. (1978) explains the origins of current school reform techniques as being as old as the state itself, explaining "The success of disciplinary power derives no doubt from the use of simple instruments; hierarchical observation, normalizing judgment, and their combination in a procedure that is specific to it, the examination" (p. 170). In time test preparation has just become part of the school day, part of the "normalization" process. This discourse of high stakes testing, as progress monitoring for the benefit of students, works to conceal how statistical data gathering is used as part of the art of government and how the examination has been used as a form of surveillance for centuries. More on these techniques of surveillance will follow the narrative of a former student I call Jesus.

RURAL SCHOOL LIFE: JESUS' MICRO NARRATIVE

I was in third grade when I came to the US; I think I was nine. I didn't know English, but I had a bilingual tutor that sat with me in class and helped me follow what was happening. It took me no longer than half a year and I already knew what everybody was saying. In elementary school I felt welcomed by the other kids and the teachers. My teachers cared about me.

Throughout my years in elementary and secondary, ESL class is the place I felt like I could go and where I didn't have to be afraid. This was the only place where I could talk to somebody that I knew was going to understand me.

Jesus orients the reader to the setting of his story, but then moves to a building *complication* or a *crisis* in his narrative, stating that the place where he initially felt safe and understood "changed once I got to middle school." Jesus explains a change in school culture when he moved from elementary to middle school, stating that he began to "feel bullied by other students and by school staff". Where he once felt "cared for" by his teachers, at the middle school he felt like school staff viewed him as suspect, stating:

The ESL teacher was always after me; he wouldn't leave me alone. They were always investigating me. They were focused more on busting people than trying to teach people. This is how they acted towards Mexicans. Through the years, I was pulled from class, and a few fellow students, to have field [drug] tests done on us. In one year, I got maybe 5 to 6 field tests done to me.

He adds, "This is just how they acted toward Mexicans." After the second time being pulled from class, Jesus told his parents what had happened at school. But, he felt like his parents who did not attend school in the US, were unable to understand the serious nature of his problems. (The school did not notify Jesus' parents about the drug tests.)

Jesus' parents told him maybe he was just, "hanging around the wrong group." But Jesus clarifies, "All I was doing was sitting down to eat with Hispanic kids." He states, "When I would sit down to eat, a bunch of my friends would sit with me ... it's just that we feel like all we have is each other because nobody else will understand us." As Jesus continues his narrative, a pattern of suspicious and punitive behavior on the part of school staff emerges, which left Jesus feeling vulnerable. His feelings of alienation became compounded by the advice of his parents, who are undocumented; as they cautioned him to "not bring attention to the family".

Jesus describes repeatedly being subjected to "field tests" performed by Principal Lugosi and Officer White (pseudonyms) which were similar to road-side sobriety tests. "It would start by them stating, 'We have information from various people that you might be under the influence.'" Although he was always "found to be clean," Lugosi and White would keep him out of class for an hour or more at a time, repeatedly asking him to "rat on other people", or to inform on his peers. Jesus' describes being pulled from class for drug testing as becoming a routine occurrence.

However, the final time Jesus was detained from class, he assumed he would be given another "field test" by the principal or resource officer, but this time the principal's office was full of police officers. "They said I was under investigation and arrested me." Jesus gives a detailed explanation of the crisis as it unfolds:

> The officer and Mr. Lugosi said they had me on camera giving something wrapped in a napkin to a girl [allegedly drugs] who got busted. They said, "A few people say you are the main guy." I told them I had no clue what they were talking about. The cops said they had evidence, "now we just need you to admit to it." As I was being arrested, he searched my pockets, "Alright you have the right to remain silent …" I was done you know.

At this point Jesus becomes the object of investigation, cast as a criminal rather than being seen as worthy of being treated with dignity.

Jesus continues, "It's like you have no power. Even when you try to say no, it's a yes, you have to say yes." He describes a lack of agency sharing feelings of being defenseless, insisting he was at school to learn and "They [staff] were there to do whatever they wanted to do to me." He also describes his fear of the police dog and the swarm of armed officers who searched through his cell phone, laptop computer, and even forced him to remove his clothing,

> They made me take everything off, my shoes, coat, everything. They made me take it off. And they kept trying to still have me confess. So by the time my mom got there I was in the principal's office handcuffed with my pockets turned out and my pants undone hanging down under my waist.

As police strip Jesus of his clothing, he feels completely disempowered, he states, "I was done," meaning he had given up any hope of resisting. He becomes visibly emotional during our conversation while describing the humiliation of his mother seeing him in the principal's office disrobed, handcuffed, and vulnerable.

To summarize the events, Jesus was called into the principal's office, searched, handcuffed, read his Miranda Rights, and was about to be taken away to jail. In narrative terms, the *problem* appears to be moving toward a *resolution*. However, at the last moment, Jesus' mom appeared on the scene and the police made Jesus and his mom a deal. He explains:

> My mom was crying. The cops said, "If you sign this confession you can go with your mom, we'll take these handcuffs off of you, you can go home."

Jesus' mom said, "If you did wrong you need to admit to it." Jesus pleaded his innocence. After discussing the situation with his mother, the problem comes to a head as Jesus explains: "My mom wanted me to be free, she said, 'Yea, sign for it.' My mom made the decision." With his description of his mother's decision, Jesus' story moves toward its *conclusion*. In the case of Jesus' story, the conclusion can be deemed a tragic failure, indicated not only by his description of his feelings of powerlessness, but also appear in Jesus' reflections on the ultimate results of signing a confession to selling drugs at school.

> I ended up with probation, kicked out of school. I never graduated; I am still one-half credit short from receiving my high school diploma. This kept me from being able to apply for my papers [temporary work visa and reprieve from deportation] under Obama's deal. (Department of Homeland Security, 2012)

Jesus' reflection below can be understood as corresponding to a narrative's *evaluation* in which commentary is provided on "the meaning or consequences of the crisis or complicating action." He explains:

> My mom doesn't speak English. She had no clue what was going on, she was just going along with what was happening. My probation officer told me, "These people are after you. They think they have you good." I wouldn't rat on anybody so they made an example out of me.

Jesus' story indicates a change in the way he viewed school as a young child and his perception of the way school staff viewed him as a teenaged Mexican student. His identity changes from the beginning of his narrative of being a "fast learner" with teachers that "cared about him" to being suspected of being involved with criminal activity and eventually "being on probation and kicked out of school." Ultimately, this is the action that contributes to his inability to improve his legal status under Obama's executive order known as DACA that could have potentially protected him, at least temporarily, from deportation as well as providing him an avenue to attend college.

Jesus' ends his *evaluation* by describing his mother's lack of legal and cultural capital as an undocumented laborer and the manner in which the school and police took advantage of this fact:

> [She] doesn't speak English and is not [formally] educated. She has no understanding of the whole American concept of "rights" at all. She is from rural Mexico where there are no rights for poor people.

Jesus' description of how he was treated in secondary school has profoundly affected his life options articulated in what can be interpreted as the *coda* of his narrative. In bringing his account into connection with the present and drawing it to its final conclusion, Jesus explains, "Now I'm working odd jobs, just making ends meet, mowing lawns."

NARRATIVES AND HISTORICAL AGENCY

In *Life as Narrative*, Jerome Bruner (1990) explains that how one constructs a personal narrative is really the act of how one constructs reality. He contends that linguistic patterns set during the act of telling one's life story are instrumental in shaping one's actions and have implications for how one chooses to live one's life in the present moment as well as in the future. How does Jesus' micronarrative shape his reality and connect to the larger socio-historical context?

In *Metahistory: The historical imagination in nineteenth century Europe,* White (1973) explains how historians and philosophers of history Hegel, Marx, Nietzsche and Croce use different styles and narrative modes in their representation of past events. One of these tactics is emplotment, or "the way by which a sequence of events fashioned into a story is gradually revealed to be a story of a particular kind" (p. 7). White explains, *the comedy, tragedy, satire, and romance* (or combination of two) "has its implication for the cognitive operations by which the [narrator] seeks to 'explain' what was 'really happening' during the process of which it provides an image of its true form" (White, 1973, p. 11).

According to White (1973), the reconciliations at the end of a tragedy are somber; "they are more in the nature of resignations of men to the conditions under which they must labor in the world." These conditions are seen as unchangeable, eternal, man must work within these inalterable conditions; "They set the limits on what may be aspired to and what may be legitimately aimed at in the quest for security and sanity in the world" (p. 9). Sadly, White's (1973) description of the tragic mode of emplotment describes the way Jesus perceives his lack of choices and options in his life story illuminating the manner by which emergent bilingual students are often *pushed out* of school at the secondary level by school districts mandated to raise test scores, or face sanctions, under the federal No Child Left Behind (NCLB) law (Lukes, 2012). There are several other themes that contribute to Jesus being *pushed out* of school.

Theme: The War on Drugs Narrative

Foucault reminds us (1988), "power produces reality; it produces domains of objects and rituals of truth" (p. 194) We can view the way Jesus was pushed out of school and into the criminal justice system as part of the Master Narratives used to promote incarceration ideology targeting poor brown and black people, who make up the majority of a growing population that is currently either incarcerated, on parole, or on probation (Alexander, 2011). And, young men who do not graduate from high school, of all races, are 47 times more likely to be incarcerated than their peers of a similar age who had graduated from a four-year college or university (Sum, Khatiwada, & McLaughlin, 2009).Viewed as a continuation of incarceration as a preferred means to deal with *surplus population*, this approach dates back at least four hundred years to the advent of the modern nation state itself (Foucault & Khalfa, 2006). Jesus' narrative illustrates the danger of the convergence of racialized ideologies in contemporary times, as youth of color are targeted as *illegals*, and by the *War on drugs rationale* within the dominant Ideological State Apparatus, the school (Althusser, 1970). The War on Drugs narrative has led to militarized policing in schools, paralleling the manner in which it functions in general society.

Just as increased border security is tied to fears of domestic terrorism, the political rationality for increased security measures, which have effectively militarized our schools, is often presented in language about preventing a Columbine type shooting incident. Apart from the fact that these measures have proven ineffective at preventing similar tragedies from happening, this type of rationality distracts the public from questioning the correlation between violent shooting incidents and pharmaceutical medications used by shooters during these incidents (Corsi, 2012). The frequency with which antidepressants and stimulants, legitimized drugs, are prescribed would suggest that they have been quite effective at creating docility in most users, but not without risk of side effects including violent outbursts and increased suicidal tendencies in children. Ideological narratives of *fighting a War on Drugs* permits doctors to prescribe drugs to control the behavior of "difficult" children and has become normalized as a secondary measure when children fail to internalize institutional rules and norms.

Theme: Criminalization of Youth of Color

Sociologists who study racial formation theory describe the colonial origins of race: "The state from its very inception has been concerned with the politics of race" (Omi & Winant, 1994, p. 81). Today, in what some refer to as America's "post-racial" era, Alexander (2011) author of *The New Jim Crow: Mass Incarceration in the Era of Colorblindness*, documents how fundamental structures of society have not radically changed in the United States since the Jim Crow era; rather the language has changed to justify it. In the era of colorblindness, it is no longer socially acceptable to use race, explicitly, as a justification for contempt, and social marginalization. Rather than rely on race, the state uses the criminal justice system to label people of color "criminals" and then engage in the inhumane practices supposedly left behind (Alexander, 2011).

Similarly to the way the "War on Drugs" has framed the issue of addiction as a crime, criminalizing migration only makes sense if people are convinced that migrants are criminals or pose a risk to the safety of U.S. citizens. Criminalizing undocumented workers becomes the rationale used to reinforce cultural notions of "the other" (Said, 1993) which convince otherwise good people to go along with, or fail to question, narratives that inflict harm. As educators we are not immune to repeated xenophobic media narratives that normalize the concept of being illegal and most are unaware of the origins of this social construction.

Theme: Illegality

Europeans have used religion, race, and nationality—one's citizenship—to divide people into categories for more than one thousand years. Historically, social caste has been used as justification for forcing the *other* to work for those defined as superior; doing society's most undesirable and dangerous jobs (Chomsky, 2014).

In the US, race determined who qualified to become a US citizen until the Fourteenth Amendment was passed in 1868. Followed by, the 1882 Chinese Exclusion Act that, "codified in immigration law the elision of racist and nationalist discourse," barring Chinese from becoming citizens based on race, but also excludeding the Chinese from entering the US based on nationality (Miller, 2014, p. 284). Language used in the quota system that restricted immigration of southern and eastern Europeans in 1921 also viewed people such as Italians as a race and a nationality. During the 20th century the legal category of *national origins* was linked to race as a legal identification to determine status, originally to exclude undesirable Europeans. "For the first time white Europeans were treated as legally *other* and subordinate, the way conquered and racially differentiated peoples–African and Indian–had been since the first days of British settlement" (Chomsky, 2014, p. 34). Foucault (1988) explains the effects of this kind of rationality,

> Political rationality has grown and imposed itself all throughout the history of western societies. It first took its stand on the idea of pastoral power, then on that of reason of state. Its inevitable effects are both individualization and totalization. Liberation can only come from attacking, not just one of these two effects, but political rationality's very roots. (p. 85)

Controlling freedom of movement of the *other* dates back to the origins of the modern nation state itself; today *nationality* or *country of origin*, which emerged alongside ideologies of race, continues to be the dominant political justification used to exclude and marginalize poor people of color. (Chomsky, 2014)

The Role of Compulsory Schooling

When the economy is bad and anti-immigrant rhetoric is commonplace, language policies tend to reflect hostilities toward immigrants who prefer to maintain their

Spanish while learning English. Historically, the United States has favored educational programs that transition students to English as soon as possible, rather than supporting bilingualism and language rights for students (Banks & Banks, 2013). Once again, let us utilize a wider historical lens for perspective.

Foucault provides a useful historical perspective to understand how we have come to normalize the video surveillance monitoring every space inside and out of the middle school where I work today. And, as radical truth teller Edward Snowden's *Guardian* interview with Glenn Greenwald (2013) revealed the states' mass collection of email, phone calls, and online activities using *War on Terror* rationality, Foucault's (1988) genealogies map the moral, scientific, and political rationale used to govern populations from medieval times through the Enlightenment and into the contemporary era, expanding the historical context to view the origins of compulsory schools beyond the post-revolutionary common school movement.

Foucault (1988) locates the origins of schools within monasteries dating back to the Middle Ages, having common roots with the military, asylum, hospital, and prison, all of which developed in accordance with the needs of the modern nation state as technologies to control growing urban populations in western European societies. To be sure, the goal of schooling in the United States, from the beginning, was to turn a multilingual and multicultural society into a single culture society "Common school reformers believed that education could be used to ensure the dominance of Protestant Anglo American culture, reduce tensions between social classes, eliminate crime and poverty, stabilize the political system, and form patriotic citizens" (Spring, 2011, p. 79).

This history informs the present, illuminating the reality that schooling was never meant to benefit all students; its main function has been social control. And not only do schools control people, they control knowledge by preserving and distributing "legitimate knowledge" (Apple, 2004; Foucault, 1988). Curricular discussions in the US about how to reproduce the social classes for the types of future work and places students are meant to occupy within the capitalist structures once were out in the open, less of a secret. Curriculum was overtly modeled around the factory and used as a means to teach students the hierarchical corporate structure as natural and the normal social arrangement. As Jesus' narrative indicates, these systems are still very much commonplace in schools today in the form of a postmodern hidden curriculum (Apple, 2004).

For too long, the commonly held view of compulsory school as a benevolent institution has provided an efficient form of social control. Yet, when we employ a critical historical lens to examine the practices of English only, or the normalization of military tactics like police searches conducted with dogs, code red lockdown drills, SWAT team drug raids, we realize these activities train students to conform, be fearful docile bodies; they learn to internalize the school as their protector, thus promoting complete reliance on, and conformity to the state.

DISMANTLING MASTER NARRATIVES: MY OTHER ME

Geographer James Anderson and sociologist Liam O'Dowd refer to "a paradox of origins" in the creation of borders around the world where there is *a legacy of violent origins*, "whether in national conflict, political revolution, or the slaughter of native populations". They call it the "politics of forgetting" whereas the violent origins of boundaries "needs to be played down or concealed for territorial democracy to perform its legitimizing functions" (as cited in Miller, 2014, p. 185). Acritical approaches to teaching based on ideas of cultural neutrality and/or color blindness perpetuate this *politics of forgetting* in Oregon's schools. In the field of education, Chomsky and Macedo (2000) refer to this as *the social construction of not seeing*, which conceals the reality that *Oregon was founded as a racist utopia* from land taken from the Paiute, Umpqua, Siletz, Klamath, Nez Perce, and other native peoples by force. Founded in 1859, with exclusion laws that prohibited blacks from even moving to Oregon until 1926, it has a history of elected officials openly associating with the Ku Klux Klan in Portland, which was one of the most segregated cities north of the Mason-Dixon Line until the mid-twentieth century (Novak, 2015).

My experience working in schools affirms that power relations function to fragment knowledge, deskilling both students and teachers who are forced to collect absurd forms of data, and focus on generalizable methods scripted by textbook companies to improve standardized test scores at the expense of actively constructing knowledge and sharing wisdom. My personal experience aligns with Tim Wise's statement about white people (2008), and likewise, teachers who *are not mean spirited, or hard-hearted people*, yet, in my years of working alongside them I have observed that many hold unexamined xenophobic perspectives about *the other* in general and about migrants from Mexico specifically. These worldviews are constructed through mainstream media discourses that converge with official policy narratives to demonize migrants and cloak economic structures that rely on an influx of cheap labor from countries south of the Rio Grande. And, to revisit my question, why do teachers need to understand students' micronarratives as connected to these larger macro-narratives? At least part of the answer can be found in Althusser's (1970) description of the majority of teachers:

> So little do they suspect it that their own devotion contributes to the maintenance and nourishment of this ideological representation of the School, which makes the School today as "natural", indispensable-useful and even beneficial for our contemporaries as the Church was "natural", indispensable and generous for our ancestors a few centuries ago.

To "begin to suspect the work the system forces them to do" (Althusser, 1970) requires a critical understanding of our students, and of equal importance, an understanding of history to reveal the manner in which the *ideological state apparatuses* and *repressive state apparatuses* work in tandem to reproduce the relations of production. Thus, educators who take up the weapon of history can challenge society's Master narratives and refuse to be complicit in sustaining a status quo that creates a permanent underclass of migrant youth by currently failing to graduate *one of two emergent bilingual students* (Scott, 2012); in sum, developing historical literacy broadens our perspective of the many currents shaping an otherwise unquestioned reality by uncloaking dominant ideologies in schools while forcing teachers to also re-examine their own identities. As Foucault (1988) warns us, "The relationship between rationalization and the excesses of political power is evident. And we should not need to wait for bureaucracy or concentration camps to recognize the existence of such relations" (p. 59). For teachers to challenge Master Narratives requires exercising historical agency to organize and to take action inside and outside the classroom. Teachers and parents can demand more dual immersion language programs from their local school boards, and occupy offices of elected officials to demand an immediate expansion of DACA and passage of the Dream Act. Additionally, teacher education must meet the challenge of preparing teachers to dismantle Master Narratives by expanding current notions of diversity through integrating critical theory throughout teacher preparation programs to equip teachers to challenge simplistic explanations of "high drop-out rates" that tend to blame the student and/or his/her home culture.

Exercising agency as teachers requires directly connecting our own well-being to the well-being of our students. Once again, Foucault reminds us of two very important facts: One, "Power is only a certain type of relation between individuals" and two, "There is no power without potential refusal or revolt" (1988, p. 84). Thus, micro-narrative histories raise important questions like, what if Jesus's story happened to my teen aged son; and, how can we prevent similar tragedies? We can begin to disconnect self, as teachers and students, from the state to write a new chapter by acknowledging western cultural tendencies to otherize, described by Edward Said (1993), which "involves establishing opposites and 'others' whose actuality is always subject to the continuous interpretation and re-interpretation of their differences from 'us'" (p. 332). Rather than identifying with the state, teachers must connect their identity to that of their students to coauthor a new chapter informed by personal knowledge of one another, which in turn requires a commitment to self-knowledge. Detaching our identities from the institution of school requires living an examined life, to know ourselves as part of history and as part of the natural world, further requiring us to interrogate the symbolic order and to privilege the fluid and evolving aspects of identity to begin to see all things as connected (Jacobs, 2013). To be sure, this process is never final; rather it requires a continuous responsibility to author our life stories in integrity. The key to finding Jesus can be found in ancient Mayan philosophy and requires us to peer into the mirror, to become one another, to act as the collective "we" gracefully expressed in the poem, "In Lak' Ech", by Luis Valdez:

Tú eres mi otro yo.
You are my other me.
Si te hago daño a ti,
If I do harm to you,
Me hago daño a mi mismo.
I do harm to myself.
Si te amo y respeto,
If I love and respect you,
Me amo y respeto yo.
I love and respect myself.

REFERENCES

Alexander, M. (2011). *The new Jim Crow: Mass incarceration in the age of colorblindness.* New York, NY: New Press

Althusser, L. (1970). Ideology and ideological state apparatuses, first published in La Pensee. Retrieved February 2, 2015 from https://www.marxists.org/reference/archive/althusser/1970/ideology.htm

Apple, M. (2004). *Ideology and curriculum.* New York, NY: RoutledgeFalmer.

Banks, J. A., & Banks, C. A. M. G. (2013). *Multicultural education: Issues and perspectives.* Hoboken, NJ: John Wiley and Sons.

Bigelow, B. (2006). *The line between us: Teaching about the border and Mexican immigration.* Milwaukee, WI: Rethinking Schools.

Bosworth, M., & Flavin, J. (2007). *Race, gender, and punishment: From colonialism to the war on terror.* New Brunswick, NJ: Rutgers University Press.

Bruner, J. (1990). *Acts of meaning.* Cambridge, MA: Harvard University Press.

Bustamante, J. A. (January 01, 1997). Mexico-United States labor migration flows. *International Migration Review, 31,* 1112–1121.

Chomsky, A. (2014). *Undocumented: How immigration became illegal.* Boston, MA: Beacon Press.

Chomsky, N., & Macedo, D. P. (2000). *Chomsky on miseducation.* Lanham, MD: Rowman & Littlefield Publishers.

Clandinin, D., & Connelly, F. (2000). *Narrative inquiry: Experience and story in qualitative research.* San Francisco, CA: Jossey-Bass Publishers.

Corsi, J. (2012, December 18). *Psych meds linked to 90% of school shootings.* Retrieved February 10, 2016 from http://www.wnd.com/2012/12/psych-meds-linked-to-90-of-school-shootings/#q93KcY-WPS9jOo2JC.99

Department of Homeland Security. (2012, November 16). Deferred Action for Childhood Arrivals. Retrieved on February, 8, 2015 from http://www.uscis.gov/humanitarian/consideration-de-ferred-action-childhood-arrivals-daca Foucault, M. (1988). *Michel Foucault, politics, philosophy, culture: Interviews and other writings 1977–1984.* New York, NY: Routledge.

Foucault, M., Burchell, G., Gordon, C., & Miller, P. (1978, 1991). *The Foucault effect: Studies in governmentality: with two lectures by and an interview with Michel Foucault.* Chicago: University of Chicago Press.

Foucault, M., & Khalfa, J. (2006). *History of madness.* London: Routledge.

Gabbard, D. (2008). *Knowledge and power in the global economy: The effects of school reform in a neoliberal/neoconservative age.* New York, NY: Lawrence Erlbaum Associates.

Gadamer, H. (1988). *Truth and method*. New York, NY: Crossroad.

Genette, G. (1980). *Narrative discourse: An essay in method*. Ithaca, NY: Cornell University Press.

Greenwald, G. (2013, June 11). *The Guardian*. Edward Snowden: The Whistleblower Behind the NSA Surveillance Revelations. Retrieved February 15, 2016 from www.theguardian.com/world/2013/jun/09/edward-snowden-nsa-whistleblower-surveillance

Gonzalez, G. G., & Fernandez, R. A. (2003). *A century of Chicano history: Empire, nations, and migration*. New York, NY: Routledge.

Gonzales-Berry, E., & Mendoza, M. (2010). *Mexicanos in Oregon: Their stories, their lives*. Corvallis: OSU Press.

Goodman, A., & González, J. (2014, April 10). *Democracy Now!* Retrieved from www.alternet.org/immigration/activists-debate-tactics-combat-over-2-million-undocumented-migrants-deported-obama

Hornberger, N. (2006). *Nichols to NCLB and global perspectives on US language education policy: Imagining multilingual schools: Languages in education and glocalization*. In O. García, T. Skutnabb-Kangas, & M. C. Torres-Guzmán (Eds.), England: Multilingual Matters.

Jacobs, D. T. (2013). *Teaching truly: A curriculum to indigenize mainstream education*. New York: Lang.

Labov, W. (1972). *Language in the inner city*. Philadelphia, PA: University of Pennsylvania Press.

Lukes, M. (Sept. 6, 2012). *Pushouts, shutouts, and holdouts: Adult education pathways of Latino young adults*. Migration Policy Institute. http://www.migrationpolicy.org/article/pushouts-shutouts-and-holdouts-adult-education-pathways-latino-young-adults

Lyotard, J. F. (1984). *The postmodern condition: A report on knowledge*. Minneapolis, MN: University of Minnesota Press.

Miller, T. (2014). *Border patrol nation: Dispatches from the front lines of homeland security*. New York, NY: City Lights Publishers.

Novak, M. (2015). *Oregon was Founded as a Racist Utopia*, retrieved: http://gizmodo.com/oregon-was-founded-as-a-racist-utopia-1539567040

Omi, M., & Winant, H. (1994, 2014). *Racial formation in the United States: From the 1960s to the 1990s*. New York, NY: Routledge.

Said, E. (1993). *Culture and imperialism*. New York, NY: Knopf.

Saltman, K., & Gabbard, D. (2008). Militarization. In D. Gabbard (Ed.), *Knowledge & power in the global economy: The effects of school reform in a neoliberal. New York: Lawrence Erlbaum Associates*.

Scott, D. (2012, December 6). Graduation data shows states struggle with English learners, *Governing*. Retrieved April 1, 2015 from http://www.governing.com/blogs/view/gov-graduation-data-shows-states-struggle-with-English-learners.html

Spring, J. (2011). *The American school: A global context from the Puritans to the Obama Era*. Boston, MA: McGraw-Hill Higher Education.

Sum, A., Khatiwada, I., & McLaughlin, J. (2009). The consequences of dropping out of high school: Joblessness and jailing for high school dropouts and the high cost for taxpayers. *Center for Labor Market Studies Publications*. Paper 23. Retrieved http://hdl.handle.net/2047/d20000596

Valdez, L. (1990). From "Pensamiento Serpentino". Retrieved February 14, 2016 from http://culturalorganizing.org/no-poetry-is-illegal/

White, H. (1973). *Metahistory: The historical imagination in nineteenth-century Europe*. Baltimore, MA: Johns Hopkins University Press.

Wise, T. (2008). *The pathology of privilege: Racism, white denial & the costs of inequality*. Retrieved October 14, 2014 from http://www.mediaed.org/assets/products/137/transcript_137.pdf

PART TWO

Critical Projects
AND THE Rural

CHAPTER SIX

Foxfire

Educational Deliverance in the Land of Deliverance

FRANK BIRD III

In this journey of life I have always been a teacher, learner and a searcher. I first taught swimming lessons when I was twelve years old in our back yard pool. Over the years since then I have either been a teacher or indirectly involved in teaching, training and always learning. I have crossed the streams in my life that I have encountered using bridges, dangling ropes, jumped a few smaller ones, waded across and found the most satisfying method stepping one stone at a time through the water. When I did cross the stream I had accomplished something and along the way I did become a great swimmer. My sojourns to North Georgia often find me sitting alongside a stream, waterfall or river reflecting on my day.

My first thought in applying this idea of a stream to education came as I read through numerous papers, articles, and blogs some condemning and some redeeming of the public education sector. In my undertaking reflecting on my experiences with the Foxfire Approach to teaching in Rabun County Georgia, a river is literally an active part of the story. Public Education is not something that is easily positioned into definitive boxes. There are as many various separate individual aspects as there are children and communities where public education is taking place. There is fluidity to learning with the many differing learning styles and perceptions alone. Teachers tend to forget that each child brings to the table a unique and often alien set of psychological, physiological, cultural, and often moral pieces that can be as varying as the gravel in the stream.

In a historical perspective the industrial revolution at the turn of the 19th century impacted education. Education was quick to be pulled into place as an integral aspect of preparing workers for the assembly line more so than developing a consensus of individuals who could choose their own direction. Individuality was suppressed in order to become efficient. It was nearly a hundred years ago John Dewey would argue that traditional, industrialized education stifled individualism and democracy. Society needed progressive education as he called what the format of education he proposed (Dewey, 1938). John D. Rockefeller was considered the initiator of industrialized, standardized education; he was on The General Education Board in 1906. Rockefeller wanted employees who would do his bidding. He wanted to strip away individualism and in doing so create the basis for many politicians and our leader's view of what education should be (H. A. Ozmon, 2003). This rigid construct is akin to building a dam on a stream or building a bridge providing a once and done approach eliminating creativity and innovation. John Dewey saw education as a means to achieving democracy and individuality as well as community. Dewey thought that modern industrial society had submerged individuality and sociality. Because of the confusion of modern society, he argued, the school should be an institution where the individual and social capabilities of children can be nurtured. The way to achieve this is through democratic living (H. A. Ozmon, 2003).

John Dewey wrote and described the concepts and ideas that would one day be embodied in the Foxfire Approach to teaching. A classroom where teacher and students are in an osmotic relationship learning from each other building on experiences of each other and acquiring new learning as you go. Experience was the basis for John Dewey's idea and it was having those contextual experiences to provide the basis for the content being covered. Dewey's idea of a Democratic classroom is what Foxfire would become.

Education is crossing the stream of life one way is through the Foxfire Core Practices used stepping stones. Foxfire was a deliverance from the tedious industrialized monotony of traditional education. I have learned over the years if you honestly approach education and learning there is no one way or method that always works (Dewey, 1938). In 1966 I was a junior in high school in a steel town outside Philadelphia. My first awareness of rural Georgia was in passing through on family trips to Naples Florida. This was on old Route 1, a lonely two lane that snaked along the east coast through Georgia prior to the interstate system. I have vivid memories of stopping for gas and the white only rest rooms and outhouses behind the gas stations for coloreds. What I saw of Georgia was at that time not in a positive light. In 1972 I was teaching special education in a small private program in Macon Georgia prior to IDEA. One Saturday night I went to see Burt Reynolds starring in the movie Deliverance. The fictional film took place outside Atlanta Georgia in Rabun County which has on its eastern border the now infamous Chattooga River. Thus my introduction to Rabun County was definitely one of fear.

I never thought at that time in my life I would one day be sitting down with several former students of those early Foxfire classes who wrote a blistering essay about the impact of the movie Deliverance on Rabun County. Three former students were hired for a year as staff writers through a grant in 1973 to interview residents as to the impact the movie made on the area (Puckett, 1989). In recent years I have interviewed and discussed Foxfire with two of the writers and former students Barbara Taylor Woodall and Laurie Brunson Alteri on many occasions. It was around this time I was intrigued with some books that had just recently been published entitled Foxfire. The Foxfire books were composed of a series of literally how to articles about rural life in Appalachia written by high school students from Rabun County. It would be nearly forty years till I was actually standing in the Foxfire Class at Rabin High School Tiger Georgia.

The Foxfire Approach to teaching had its start in the fall of 1966 when a recent college graduate Eliot Wigginton was hired to teach literature in a rural Georgia High school. Elliot Wigginton writes he went to Rabun Gap to teach because he wanted to live in Rabun Gap and that's all. No great sense of mission or purpose as far as the school and its students they really were of little concern. He wanted to live in that part of the country after spending his summer at a family lodge on Lake Rabun and teaching was a legitimate way to get there and support him (Wigginton 1986 (Wigginton, 1986). The classes were made up of residents of Rabun Gap-Nacoochee School and the local youth. At that time there was not a public high school in the area in Rabun County. Rabun County had a two lane in and back then most of the roads were dirt. The county student's costs were covered by the state department of education (Foxfire, 2016). Traditionally many local youth by high school age had dropped out and were either farming or working in various small industries in the area (Puckett, 1989). The school residents were youth who were not succeeding at home or in school and their parents were paying for a very nice boarding school. The Rabun-Nacoochee school had been founded as a vocational agricultural program and students worked on the farm within the school. This was an easy mix for a progressive educational idea to have some room to grow. This mixed group of students had one thing in common they did not want to be in school (Wigginton, 1986).

Robert Fried in The Passionate Teacher, considers the main issue in schools is that of students not wanting to be there (Fried, 1995). As it happens on the first day of school the teacher Elliot Wigginton's podium is set on fire with lighter fluid and he found himself seriously contemplating what comes next (Wigginton, 1986). Mountain folks can be serious and perhaps it was an omen he needed a new profession. Undaunted he did return the next day and continued in Rabun County for nearly thirty years after. He mentions several times in his journals and entries in his books of his frustration on that first day. Wigginton stated (1985):

> One of the bleakest fall days in 1966, 1 walked into my first period class, sat on top of my desk … and said, very slowly and very quietly, "Look this isn't working. You know it isn't and I know it isn't. Now what are we going to do together to make it through the rest of the year." (p. 32)

Elliot Wigginton learned lesson one of being a new teacher which is always the hardest. How do you keep the students interested and motivated? Wigginton was looking for a way to get across to the residents and mountain kids who really had no desire to be in school let alone learn anything he was trying to teach (Foxfire, 2015). Bobby Starnes a past President of the Foxfire Fund offers:

> Eliot Wigginton tried several approaches, but just could not get the students' attention. With inspiration from the writings of John Dewey, Wigginton asked the students what would interest them. What could they do as a class to make the English curriculum interesting? Several ideas were discussed, and the students ultimately chose to produce a magazine. The students would develop basic writing skills while creating content for their magazine. Some of the students decided to write articles based on information and stories gathered from their families or neighbors and stories about the pioneer era of southern Appalachia. (p. 1)

Elliot Wigginton was trying to provide an education that delivered the components of a good literature program. He wanted the students to learn to write and read better. He wanted them to take pride in their work and effort and he wanted them to be successful. The idea of talking with and interviewing the elders of the community provided the students with engagement and ownership of the projects. This was their community and it was their story. John Dewey points out:

> Mankind likes to think in terms of extreme opposites. It is given to formulating its beliefs in terms of Either-Ors, between which it recognizes no intermediate possibilities. When forced to recognize that the extremes cannot be acted upon, it is still inclined to hold that they are all right in theory but that when it comes to practical matters circumstances compel us to compromise. Educational philosophy is no exception. The history of educational theory is marked by position between the idea that education is development from within and that it is formation from without; that it is based upon natural endowments and that education is a process of overcoming natural inclination and substituting in its place habits acquired under external pressure. (Dewey, 1938)

It was not until 1970 that a concrete list of what is Foxfire was written down. Wigginton and the Foxfire program developed the first set of Core Practices for use with a project sponsored by the Institutional Development and Economic Affairs Services. That first set established a clear basis and outline for the central practices of Foxfire. The practices have evolved over time with teachers input and suggestions (Puckett, 1989). The current Foxfire Core Practice one is; From the beginning, learner choice, design and revision infuses the work teachers and learners do together (Foxfire Core Practice One, 2016). It was from the students the idea for a magazine evolved.

The success of the Foxfire program was due in large part to the fact the students chose to create a magazine. Since the magazine was their choice, the students were deeply invested in the work of creating it. The magazine product itself was not the solution to classroom woes that so many teachers thought it would be. Kaye Collins a former student and staff member said, "It seemed that people couldn't understand the importance of the difference between the magazine, which was the choice we made, and the fact that we made a decision." (Foxfire Fund, 2016) Bobby Starnes former president of the Foxfire Fund adds (2002):

> Although this first conversation did not produce the outcomes he hoped for, it was the beginning, and his trip down this path ultimately led to the creation of The Foxfire Magazine. (p. 3)

As Wigginton approached the students with the idea two things were clear. Students would make the final decision and whatever the project they did choose it must help them learn the English curriculum. After much soul searching and seeking of direction Eliot Wigginton's students hit upon the idea of a student produced magazine based on the history of the local community. (Stames, 2002) In the book Sustainable schools authors Craig Howley and John Eckman quote Eliot Wigginton (1997):

> The venture clicked. ... Students previously bored, indifferent, and disruptive—started doing research and writing assignments eagerly. They began to understand how the local knowledge and wisdom ... contributed to their lives, helped them make sense of their world, and was valuable in its own right. (1997, p. 56)

The new magazine would need a name and his students would need to pick one. The idea of student choice came back to him from his education graduate courses and readings on John Dewey and the Democratic classroom. (Starnes, 2002, p. 4) Many times people ask why the name Foxfire and the response from Wigginton was always the same "Foxfire" is the name that the English class picked, in 1966, for the student-produced magazine that they chose to create, containing stories and interviews gathered from elders in their rural southern Appalachian community. Other potential names on the list included "ginseng", "yellow root", and "bloodroot", which are also native to the North Georgia area where the students lived. The term "foxfire" is a name commonly applied to several species of bioluminescent fungi that grow on rotting wood in damp forests. These fungi typically produce a dim blue-green glow that can be seen only in dark, starlit areas, away from any artificial lights or moonlight. Other names associated with these glowing fungi include "faerie fire" and "will o' the wisp". (Starnes, 2002)

Over the past five years I have talked with Barbara Taylor Woodall on many occasions and always left ready to return to Rabun County and Foxfire. Barbara was a Foxfire student in 1971 and it was Foxfire that inspired her to stay in school and eventually to write her first book, It's not my Mountain anymore (Woodall, 2015). Barbara pointed to the student ownership of articles and the Foxfire magazine. The students would decide what to write about and do the leg work involved in interviews and photographs. Students would transcribe tapes and develop their articles only to be proofed and edited by fellow students. Barbara used the word engagement numerous times in our talks. The students were engaged and took pride in the work that they were doing conserving their heritage. The students wanted to participate and be part of this endeavor. Many afternoons students would gather at the Karan's Café just outside Mountain City Georgia. The Foxfire students would discuss upcoming ideas and articles over pie and sweet tea (Woodall, 2015).

A publisher friend of Elliot Wigginton suggested a book comprised of the numerous articles gathered and in 1971 the first Foxfire book was published and was soon a best seller. It was followed shortly by Foxfire II and III. The quality of the students work and interest about the elder's tales and wisdom led in 1972 to the publication of the first Foxfire book and the series now has thirteen volumes of mountain lore all researched and written by high school students (Wigginton, 1986). To date nearly nine million books have been sold. National attention came as the success of the Foxfire books and magazine spread nationwide (Puckett, 1989).

Wigginton would travel around the country talking about Foxfire and students from the program would travel along as well and tell of their experiences in the program. In the early 1970s on a trip to California Barbara Woodall had never been away from home let alone flown on an airplane. As they went out to eat Barbara would not order anything to eat. Finally Wigginton asked what was wrong and Barbara told him her mother said not to eat anything she wouldn't have at home. A bucket of Colonel Sanders solved the problem (Alteri, 2013).

It was not long until other schools sought to "Foxfire" and many efforts were not successful. John Puckett came to Georgia to do research on the program and his dissertation was based on nearly eighteen months in Rabun County. He saw firsthand the enthusiasm and involvement of students and questioned aspects of the program (Puckett, 1989). Puckett interviewed previous students and current students, teachers of Foxfire and teachers who had not been successful. He raised questions about the literature curriculum of using writing articles to teach literature. He found students from Foxfire were not always successful in college classes (Puckett, 1989). Talking with former students myself I found all I spoke with stayed in school because of Foxfire and several went on to be writers in their own right (Collins, 2015). It took recognizing that the magazine was only a vehicle for mastering curriculum mandates, and the effort to understand, communicate and replicate the projects educational success led to the development of a set of practices that guided their work. (Starnes, 2002) It was in this effort that Wigginton found how much his ideas mirrored John Dewey's philosophy of education. Wigginton states (1985):

> One paragraph into Experience and Education by John Dewey and things began to crystallize. By the time I finished it, I was shaking my head in amazement. On every one of its less than a hundred pages, insights leaped out into the air and I found myself pounding the arm

of my chair and saying, "That's right, damn it, that's exactly right." All of those discoveries I had made about education Dewey had elucidate into complete clarity fifty years and more before. And he showed me how incomplete my own philosophy still was. (p. 280)

Dewey's philosophy became central to the formation of all the work that followed. Growing out of this work was the Foxfire Course, later named level one, and currently is known as the Foxfire Course for Teachers. This thinking and interest lead to Foxfire networks around the nation and to a solidifying of the ten core practices taught in the Foxfire Approach to teaching today.

Kaye Carver Collins discussed Foxfire and her high school days when the books became best sellers and Foxfire received its first check from the publishers. The students had made another choice to buy acreage on the side of Black Rock Mountain and build a living museum of Appalachia. The idea consisted of finding old cabins and either through donation or purchase move to the land. The first check went towards buying land. Today there are numerous cabins, chapels, barns and other buildings of a by gone era. In one wagon barn is one of the last remaining covered wagons from the trail of tears (Collins, 2015).

The magazine is still published although now in the Rabun County Public High School where it has been since 1976. (Starnes, 2002) At the high school a group of teacher's taught in a Foxfire manner. Literature, Social Studies, Music and Science were taught based on Foxfire principles. Today only the magazine class is left although the former music students The Foxfire Boys are known in bluegrass circles around the south. A progression from the program was a concerted effort to coordinate teacher training in this process. The first attempts to replicate the Foxfire experience in many ways were simply clones. High Schools wanting to publish a magazine and many times did not meet with success. Teachers would refer to their effort as "doing Foxfire". (Starnes, 2002)

There was a high failure rate among teachers claiming to be "doing Foxfire" that led teaching staff and students to believe that teachers had not understood the concept underlying the magazines success—weaving tightly two ingredients: student choice and academic integrity. Kaye Carver Collins, an early magazine student who traveled to many sites to work with teachers and learners as they developed magazines, put it this way: "It seemed that people couldn't understand the importance of the difference between the magazine, which was the decision we made, and the fact we made the decision. (Starnes, 2002)

As the books sales began to slow Elliot Wigginton began looking for additional sources to fund the growing program in Rabun County. National grants and teacher networks offered a possible solution. At one point a national teachers magazine was being published of success stories and ideas. Around the country teachers were taught how to teach others the Foxfire method (Puckett, 1989). Foxfire was a nationally recognized program until the middle 1990's when a scandal involving Eliot Wigginton stopped the flow of grant money (Smith, 2008).

Dr. Smith went on to say, "it was at this time we knew to save Foxfire we had to make some adjustments" (Smith, 2008) Kaye Collins said the support of the community was over whemling when the scandal broke and everyone wanted the program to continue. Lee Carpenter added to Bobby Starnes book in the following (2002):

> Today, Foxfire is an organization that continues to support teachers work in schools across the nation, as well as an organization fully committed to preserving the original classroom model, grounded in the Appalachian culture, in Rabun County, Georgia. The Foxfire magazine celebrates its 50th Anniversary, our commitments to grassroots organization, to innovative systems of broad based volunteerism, to the inclusion of teachers through a wide variety of experiences and programs, and our participatory decision making process make Foxfire a unique and complex educational organization. And we are still exploring new ways to further these commitments—the current partnership with Piedmont college, in nearby Demorest, Georgia, allows education students to integrate the foxfire Approach into teaching practices at an early stage, in the hope that they won't have the same struggles in their first classroom the way Foxfire's founder did in 1966. (p. 7)

I was involved in one of Piedmont's first rekindled teacher courses back in 2005 while working on my Specialist degree. The experience and interactions in our cohort were most interesting. Twenty plus teachers of all ages of students experimented with Foxfire for a semester. Several now still use Foxfire in their classrooms. I tend to use variations and pieces of Foxfire due to the nature of my resource and co-teaching classes.

In the Foxfire Approach, learning environments are characterized by student involvement and action, by thoughtful reflection and rigorous assessment, by imagination and problem solving, by applications beyond the classroom for what is learned, and by meaningful connections to the community. In these classrooms, students build the ability to work collaboratively and assume responsibility for their own learning processes. (Foxfire, 2015) If you visited a classroom where the Foxfire Approach is used, you would see a dynamic learning environment characterized by student involvement and action, rigorous assessment and evaluation, reflection, imagination, and problem solving. You would notice a blurring of the lines between community and classroom, resulting in a community learning laboratory that extends the classroom beyond the school walls (Smith, 2009). You would see teachers and learners working together to make decisions about how they will learn, how they will assess and evaluate what they learn, and how they will use what they learn in meaningful ways. Foxfire is based around eleven Core Practices and these hold the key to the approach. (Foxfire, 2015)

Core practice one is right out of Dewey and progressivism and in line with Dewey about building a democratic classroom, motivation and providing student choice. Core Practice One: From the beginning learner choice, design and revision infuses the work teachers and learners do together (Foxfire, 2015).

The central focus of the work grows out of learners' interests and concerns. Most problems that arise during classroom activity are solved in collaboration with learners, and learners are supported in the development of their ability to solve problems and accept responsibility (Starnes, 2002)." Alfie Kohn (1998) described the research on student choice and interest as "so compelling that it is ... difficult to understand how anyone can talk about school reform without immediately addressing the question of how students can be given more say about what goes on in their classes"(p. 11).

There is in Foxfire, open inquiry-based as indicated within Core practice two: The work teachers and learners do together clearly manifests the attributes of the academic disciplines involved, so these attributes become habits of mind (McDermott, 2016). Through collaborative planning and implementation, students engage and accomplish the mandates. In addition, activities assist learners in discovering the value and potential of the curricula and its connections to other disciplines (Stames, 2002). Borrowing from John Dewey,

> For I am so confident of the potentialities of education when it is treated as intelligently directed development of the possibilities inherent in ordinary experience that I do not feel it necessary to criticize here the other route nor to advance arguments in favor of taking the route of experience. (Dewey, 1938, p. 89)

The concept of Problem centered-design, encouraging and motivating fits well into Core Practice three: "The work teachers and students do together enables learners to make connections between the classroom work and surrounding communities, and the world beyond their communities (Smith, 2009). Because learners engaged in these kinds of activities are risk takers operating on the edge of their competence, the classroom environment provides an atmosphere of trust where the consequence of a mistake is the opportunity for further learning (Starnes, 2002)." Alfie Kohn writes: "John Dewey reminded us that the value of what students do 'resides in its connection with the stimulation of greater thoughtfulness, not in the greater strain it imposes.' (Kohn, 2004, p. 43)"

Dewey was convinced that teachers need to be facilitator's more than traditional teachers which find credence in Core Practice four: "The teacher serves as facilitator and collaborator (Smith, 2009). Teachers are responsible for assessing and attending to learners' developmental needs, providing guidance, identifying academic givens, monitoring each learner's academic and social growth, and leading each into new areas of understanding and competence" (Starnes, 2002, p. 34). Dewey felt the teacher should be a "co-partner and guide in a common enterprise— the child's education as an independent learner and thinker." (Dewey, 1938 p. 10)

Constructivism is what this is all about Core Practice five: Active learning characterizes classroom activities (Smith, 2009). Rather than completion of a study being regarded as the conclusion of a series of activities, it is regarded as the starting point for a new series (Starnes, 2002, p. 88)." Walker states, "At the heart of Dewey's ideal view of education was the idea of learning from experience." (Smith, 2008)

With children imagination is perhaps the most important aspect and is reflected in Core Practice six: The learning process entails imagination and creativity (Smith, 2009). It is the learner's freedom to express and explore, to observe and investigate, and to discover that are the basis for aesthetic experiences. These experiences provide a sense of enjoyment and satisfaction and lead to deeper understanding and an internal thirst for knowledge (Starnes, 2002, p. 98)." Eisner adds,

> Inviting students to use their imagination means inviting them to see things other than the way they are. And, of course, this is what scientists and artists do; they perceive what is, but imagine what might be, and use their knowledge, their technical skills, and their sensibility to pursue what they have imagined. (Eisner, 1998, p. 199)

It is about collaboration and the building of community as shown in Core Practice seven: Classroom work includes peer teaching, small group work and teamwork (Smith, 2009). Every learner is not only included, but needed, and, in the end, each can identify her or his specific stamp upon the effort (Starnes, 2002). When there is ownership learning becomes second nature. "If we want the kids to take ownership in their own learning they have to see us—the faculty and administration—doing just that. When they see us taking risks and exploring new ideas, they'll follow suit (Sergiovanni, 1994, p. 168). Learners' work will "bring home" larger issues by identifying attitudes about and illustrations and implications of those issues in their home communities (Starnes, 2002)." Parker Palmer adds,

> As I make the case that good teaching is always and essentially communal, I am not abandoning my claim that teaching cannot be reduced to technique. Community, or connectedness, is the principle behind good teaching, but different teachers with different gifts create community in surprisingly diverse ways, using widely divergent methods. (Palmer, 1998, p. 115)

A critical aspect of Dewey's thinking of a democratic society is involved in, Core Practice eight: Work intended for audiences the learners want to serve or engage evokes the best efforts by the learners and provides feedback for improving performance (Smith, 2009). The audience, in turn, affirms the work is important, needed, and worth doing (Starnes, 2002, p. 68)." John Dewey states in his Pedagogic Creed (18971938):

> I believe that all education proceeds by the participation of the individual in the social consciousness of the process. This process begins unconsciously almost at birth and is continuing shaping the individuals powers saturating his consciousness forming his habits training his ideas, and arousing his feelings and emotions. Through this unconscious education the individual gradually comes to share in the intellectual and moral resources which humanity

has succeeded in getting together. He becomes an inheritor of the capital of civilization. The most formal and technical education cannot safely depart from this general process. It can only organize it or differentiate it in some particular direction. (p. 17)

In today's world in the end it is always about assessment and this is addressed in Core Practice nine: The work teachers and learners do together include rigorous, ongoing assessment and evaluation (Smith, 2009). Teachers and learners employ a variety of strategies to demonstrate their mastery of teaching and learning objectives (Starnes, 2002)."

There is a significant responsiveness to Core Practice ten: Reflection, an essential activity, takes place at key points throughout the work (Smith, 2009). One of the crucial elements for teachers and students is reflection. It is this reflective activity that evokes insight and gives rise to revisions and refinements (Starnes, 2002)." Elliot Eisner states, "Dewey's emphasis on the importance of creating communities of learners so that children could learn from each other was one of the hallmarks of good progressive education practices." (Eisner, 1998, p. 94)

I was privileged to be able to visit the Foxfire class at Rabun county High School in Tiger Georgia and to interview and talk with students and teachers. I was able to see the Core Practices in action and see the intricacies and interactions of learners and teachers. Mr. Mark Ernest then principal of Rabun High School was proud of the Foxfire history and tradition at the school. By chance a quick PowerPoint I did of photos I took while there is listed on the school website, "What does a Foxfire class look like?" Two teachers at this time, Mr. Justin Shook, English teacher and Mr. Justin Spillers, Business teachers worked together to facilitate the Foxfire classes. Justin Shook explained: "When No Child Left Behind and Georgia State mandates required stricter adherence to Standards it was difficult to teach the Foxfire class as a journalism class and it became part of the business program." (Shook, 2008)

The first Foxfire classes at Rabun High School were in 1976 when the new High School opened up. Since that time the Foxfire magazine has been published twice a year. Fifty years of stories, interviews and photographs and for me being able to sit and talk to students currently involved was very special. I was able sit in on two classes of Foxfire in which I was allowed to spend some time with the students asking questions and watching the next magazine come into being. I asked the two teachers what they thought of Foxfire. Justin Shook commented that, "Foxfire has a tradition at Rabun High School and at first some students think it will be an easy class but find out soon it is a lot of work and the students keep each other going. (Shook, 2008) Justin Spillers spoke to me about the Core Practices.

We have them up around the room and we do follow to the letter the eleven Core Practices and the students know this. Each student is assigned by the editors not teachers jobs to complete from marketing of the magazine, proofing, editing, photography, transcribing tape recorded interviews and photography. (Shook, 2008)

Foxfire is an idea not a package. It is a way of teaching that would be what some teachers are already doing and alien for some. It is difficult to try and draw together twelve years of involvement in a program and cram into a few words. It is a critical part of rural Georgia and for great teachers around the country.

REFERENCES

Alteri, L. B. (2013, July 15). *Foxfire student* (F. Bird, Interviewer).

Collins, K. (2015, July 15). *Foxfire interview* (F. Bird, Interviewer).

Dewey, J. (1938). *Experience and education*. New York, NY.

Eisner, E. (1998). *The kind of schools we need: Personal essays*. Portsmith: Heienmenn.

Fried, R. (1995). *The passionate teacher*. Boston, MA: Beacon Press.

H. A. Ozmon, C. O. (2003). *Philosophical foundations of education*. Upper Saddle River, NJ: Merrill Prentice Hall.

Foxfire. (2015, August 21). Foxfire Core Practices. Mountain City, GA, USA.

Foxfire. (2016, March 13). Foxfire Core Practices. Mountain City, GA, USA.

Kohn, A. (1998). *The schools our children deserve*. Boston, MA: Houghton Mifflin.

Kohn, A. (2004). *What does it mean to be well educated*. Boston, MA: Beacon Press.

McDermott, H. S. (2016). *The Foxfire Approach: Inspiration for Classrooms and Beyond*. Rotterdam: Sense.

Puckett, J. L. (1989). *Foxfire reconsidered: A twenty year expreiment in progressive education*. Chicago, IL: Univerity of Illinois Press.

Sergiovanni, T. (1994). *Building Community in Schools*. San Franciso: Jossey-Boss.

Shook, J. (2008, October 15). *Teacher foxfire* (F. Bird, Interviewer).

Smith, H. (2008, June 23). Foxfire. (F. Bird, Interviewer)

Smith, H. (2009). *The development of the foxfire core practices*. Demorest, GA: Piedmont College.

Starnes, B. A. (2002). *From Thinking to Doing: The Foxfire Core Practices Constructing a Framework to Teach Mandates Through Experience-Based Learnin*. Mountain City: The Foxfire Fund.

Wigginton, E. (1986). *Sometimes a shining moment*. Garden City, NY: Anchor Books.

Woodall, B. (2015, July 15). *Sitting and talking about Foxfire over lunch* (F. Bird, Interviewer).

CHAPTER SEVEN

Myles Horton AND Highlander Folk School

An Enduring Exemplar of Rural Education for Democratic Engagement

ROBERT LAKE AND ANDY BLUNDEN

Figure 7.1. Anti-Highlander billboards were distributed across the South in 1965.
Used with permission from the Highlander Research and Education Center Archives

In a 1981 interview with Bill Moyers, Myles Horton recalled the day in late 1959 when Sheriff Elston Clay came to put a padlock on the door of the Highlander Folk School. Some of the news reporters that were there said "What are you laughing about?" I was standing outside laughing, and they took a picture of me standing there laughing. And the sheriff padlocked the building I said "My friend here, you know, he thinks he's padlocking Highlander ... Highlander is an idea-you can't padlock an idea".

MOYERS & HORTON (1982, P. 250)

By 1959 this "idea" of Highlander that Horton spoke about had proven to be a highly successful exemplar of equipping leaders for grassroots labor union organizing and civil rights activism. Consequently, this work was fiercely contested, met violence and was under continual surveillance from the FBI and local authorities. Horton's formal career in this work spanned more than 50 years yet it was evident even from his early teens, that the "idea" of democracy as an unfinished, lifelong process had possessed his being. Like Dewey he believed that democracy "is a growing concept that has to do with moving in a certain direction" (Horton, 1998, p. 174). In this chapter we examine the past, present and possible future of Highlander through written and oral narratives, songs and recorded interviews. In particular we explore and discuss the ways that Horton and the staff of Highlander have continuously focused on the cultural assets and indigenous knowledges of rural people in empowering citizens for self-governance and transformative social change by remaining faithful their vision that "people's needs make an educational program" (Horton, 2003, p. 217). Horton's view that democracy is a "growing concept" that results from moving in a "certain direction" is wonderfully substantiated by his life history which is where we turn in this inquiry.

HORTON IN HISTORICAL CONTEXT

Myles Horton was the first of four children, born in 1905 into a poor white family at Paulk's Mill outside of Savannah in Western Tennessee. His parents were former school teachers and Presbyterians, both from families which had lived in Tennessee for many generations. Myles's father, Perry, having had a grammar school education, had secured a job as a county official, while his mother, Elsie, was a respected and active member of the community. Myles attended the elementary school at nearby Brazil, and completed eighth grade, which was as far as the school went. Thanks to help from a family friend he was able to enter the nearby Cumberland Presbyterian College in the autumn of 1924, where he would receive biblical training. It was here also that Horton read Shelley. From Shelley, Horton learned that it was right to stand up to authority in support of social justice, and never to be afraid of punishment or to submit to the temptation of rewards.

Because Horton came from a poor family himself, his heart always reached outward to those in that condition. There is a story he tells about a defining moment that took place while riding a train during his college days that helped served as a catalyst in his decision to commit his life to helping people in poverty. As he was looking at the Cumberland Mountains scenery from the train in rural Tennessee he saw a house near the tracks.

> As I got closer I saw a 15 year-old-girl standing on the porch, hanging by one arm around the pillar that held up the porch, hanging there looking at that train with the most forlorn look I think I have ever seen. Such a sad look. I just said to myself, she sees this train going by, and

to her it represents getting away from that poverty that's drying her up. No hope. Nothing. No future. This train could take her away but she doesn't have the money to get on this train, or she wouldn't know where to go if she got on it. I started crying right there because it was such a sad picture of hopelessness. That picture stayed in my mind and is still in my mind, and I still cry when I think about it. That helped me understand the cruelty of the system that blighted what could have been a beautiful life. That helped, in a way, my determination to try to do something about that situation. (Horton & Freire, 1990, pp. 229–230)

During the summer breaks, Horton had been running a Bible class for children for the Presbyterian Church in Ozone, Tennessee. In 1927, he expanded his class to include adults, and attracted an ever widening circle to a program of community education in which he encouraged participants to share their problems and seek solutions to these problems through discussion and talks by invited experts. The residents of Ozone appreciated him so much they urged Horton to forego his last year of college and stay on teaching at Ozone. But Horton was well aware of his own limitations, and after promising the community that he would return he set off on a journey to discover how real social change could be achieved through education by first focusing on his own intellectual development.

UNION THEOLOGICAL SEMINARY

A local Congregationalist minister, Abram Nightingale, helped Horton work his way through a reading program covering the history and culture of the South, the social problems of Appalachia and the moral issues of modern capitalism. In the summer of 1929, Nightingale persuaded Horton to apply to the elite Union Theological Seminary in New York. To his own surprise, Horton was accepted. Here he met the radical socialist theologian, Reinhold Niebuhr who was to become his lifelong friend, mentor and supporter. Horton's honest and straightforward approach to learning was refreshing to Niebuhr. For example, early in their relationship Horton informed Niebuhr that he would have to drop his class because he could not understand his lectures. It turns out that that many students felt that way but were afraid to speak up. Niebuhr's reply to Horton was "Myles, you've got to stay. If you don't understand, something's wrong. You've got to go back in, because these people won't tell me the truth", (Niebuhr in Horton, 1998, p. 35). It was while he was at seminary that Horton first encountered the work of Karl Marx.

It was then that I discovered about Marxism and analysis of society on a class basis. … So I found from Marx that I could get tools, not blueprints, tools that I could use for analyzing society. That helped me to analyze. Then I had to get a synthesis of my religious background and my understanding of economic forces. (Horton, 2003, p. 123)

Even so, Horton stated that when it came right down to becoming a member of the Communist party, that the party officials in America viewed him as someone who had too many of his own ideas to go along with any organization for which he would have to be subservient. Later when Horton was asked if he had ever been a member of the communist party he said "Lord, no, we were more radical than the communists. We wanted real democracy" (Horton quoted in Smith, 2007, p. 4).

UNIVERSITY OF CHICAGO

After completing his course at the seminary in 1930, he attended the University of Chicago where took classes with Robert Park and learned about group problem solving and conflict and he also acquainted himself with the ideas of John Dewey. Horton continued to read and toured the country, studying utopian communities, community education projects and Native American communities. He became convinced that utopian communities which cut themselves off from the wider community were of little value in achieving social change. He also visited Jane Addams at Hull House on several occasions, but nothing he saw satisfied him. He completely rejected the conception of vocational education, which, like school education, was intended only to fit people into the status quo, and he was hostile to programs which served to "educate people out of their class." For Horton, none of these projects had very little potential to effect social change.

DENMARK

During his time in Chicago, he heard about Nikolaj Frederik Severin Grundtvig and the Danish folkehøjskoler movement. In 1931 he travelled to Denmark with Don West to see if these Folk Schools lived up to their reputation. He was disappointed, partly because he felt that the spirit which had animated the early folkehøjskoler had been lost, and partly because he realized that the folkehøjskoler belonged to a certain times and a certain culture and could not be transplanted into 20th century America. Nonetheless he noted with approval the following features of the folkehøjskoler all of which he was later to adopt at the Highlander Folk School:

Students and teachers living together;
Peer learning;
Group singing;
Freedom from state regulation;
Non-vocational education;
Freedom from examinations;
Social interaction in non-formal setting;
A highly motivating purpose;
Clarity in what for and what against. (Horton, 1998, pp. 52–53)

Before returning home he wrote to himself:

> What you must do is go back, get a simple place, move in and you are there. The situation is there. You start with this and let it grow. You know your goal. It will build its own structure and take its own form. You can go to school all your life, you'll never figure it out because you are trying to get an answer that can only come from the people in the life situation. (Horton, 2003, p. 3)

Horton returned to Tennessee and was given a farmhouse in Monteagle, which is in Grundy County—one of the poorest counties in the USA, where he established the Highlander Folk School in 1932, in the depths of the Great Depression.

THE GREAT DEPRESSION AND THE BIRTH OF HIGHLANDER

Horton was clear from the outset about the motivating purpose of his project:

> From the start it was aimed at reaching southern workers who would be willing to build a new social order. We wanted to use education as a tool to bring about social change in the South. … I thought there ought to be a revolution in this country. (2003, pp. 8 and 125)

There were three major elements to Highlander's programs. Firstly, they delivered community education, much like what he had been doing in Ozone years before, for the local community in Monteagle. As a result of this service he earned the loyalty of the community, and when Highlander was firebombed, raided by the police or the Ku Klux Klan, witch-hunted in the press, shot at and subject to all manner of slander and legal attack, the community stuck by them. But this component was never going to bring about social change.

The second element was the residential program. Horton actively engaged with organizations in the region, in the early days, mainly the labor unions, and encouraged them to send to Highlander emerging grass-roots leaders—not people who were on the union payroll and owed allegiance to the bureaucracy, but shop-floor people whose loyalties remained with their peers. Students would come typically for two or three weeks and over time they built up to classes or 20 or 30 students.

The third element was what he called the extension program. This entailed taking the Highlander staff and students out to picket lines or whatever struggles were going on at the time and doing whatever they could to help the workers. This included actively participating in picketing, research, fund-raising and publicity as well as running Highlander-type courses on the picket lines, including singing and the use of activist theatre as well as discussion groups. Workers from these struggles would then be selected on the same kind of criteria as for the residential courses, and brought back to Highlander for a few days or longer if possible.

When students left Highlander, and went back to their organizations, in 90% of cases they took up full-time leadership positions. Highlander maintained contact with them and continued to help them work through the problems that arose while remaining firm in their stance that without local leadership the work in the south simply would not be successful. In a letter written by Niebuhr describing the Highlander project to potential supporters he wrote "we believe that neither A. F. of L, nor Communist leadership is adequate to their needs. Our hope is to train *radical* labor leaders" (Niebuhr quoted in Horton, 1998, p. 61). These potential leaders had grown up in a region where there was a strong distaste for outside, top down influences and Horton was one of their own as well.

Highlander also had at any given time some graduate students, typically from Northern universities, working with Highlander for research or practicum. Everyone at Highlander, without exception, participated in every activity on an absolutely equal footing with everyone else. This included both the manual work needing to be done about the farm (money was so short, growing their own food was obligatory and there were no salaries paid), discussion and participation in struggles during the extension program. By this means, Horton and the Highlander built up a great network of support which could be called upon when required. They knew everyone and everything that was going on in the South, and their reputation in the labor movement grew accordingly. Experts were invited to address classes to provide information about specific problems when the students requested it, but frequently they were sent home again if their input was not specifically requested by the students.

The history of Highlander is marked out by a succession of projects. At specific junctures, Highlander would let go of programs that they had been running, and hand them over to the organizations they had been serving so that they could run them on their own behalf, rather than by sending recruits to Highlander. Then Horton would intensively research a new domain of activity, often leaving Highlander for extended periods to go and live and work and organize in an area, before launching a new program. Horton was able to anticipate with remarkable success the emergence of new social movements. Indeed his programs could only work in close connection with a growing social movement.

The first project, beginning in 1932, growing slowly under terribly difficult conditions, was work amongst the poorest stratum of workers in the labor movement. The CIO (Congress of Industrial Organizations, originally Committee for Industrial Organization—dedicated to industrial or general unionism as opposed to craft unionism) was founded in 1935, and Highlander was subsequently accepted as their official educational arm. That is, Horton started working with the hitherto unorganized sections of the working class just as the move towards industrial unionism was emerging, and three years before the American Federation of Labor set up the Committee for Industrial Organization.

By the mid-1940s, Horton began to hand the union education program back to the CIO unions and turned to the poor farmers in the South in collaboration with the National Farmers' Union, 90% of whose members were in the North. In the late 1940s and early 1950s he turned to the movement against racial segregation, a few years before the *Brown vs. Board of Education* case was heard in the Supreme Court, and their unanimous finding announced on May 17, 1954 triggered the school desegregation struggle.

The Civil Rights Movement grew out of this struggle, and Highlander was deeply involved with all those who became leading activists well before the Birmingham Bus Boycott in 1955. They handed their education program back to the Southern Christian Leadership Conference to run themselves in the mid-1960s and turned back to where they had started from, to address the problems of poverty in Appalachia, and an array of cooperative ventures emerged as a result of their work.

The program Highlander ran for the labor movement in the first years had something approximating to a curriculum. The core curriculum was labor economics, labor history, public speaking, union tactics, dramatics, labor journalism and what they called 'parliamentary law', i.e., formal meeting procedure. From 1937, they used the ACWA (Amalgamated Clothing Workers of America) rule book and a mock AF of L Convention held at the end of each term to teach meeting procedure. Myles Horton ran classes on union problems, including organizing methods, strike tactics and race relations. Participants would write and produce a short play on a labor theme and role-play the negotiation of a union contract.

However, Horton became dissatisfied with this program: "We were giving answers to questions that were not being asked, trying to make their practices fit our theories (Horton, 2003, p. 21). They went on to develop the unique approach which led to Highlander becoming arguably the greatest force for social change in the South.

Horton realized that people were coming to Highlander looking for experts who would give them the answers to their problems. But this was never going to work. They had been habituated to regard their own experience and that of their peers as worthless, and yet it was only by analyzing their own experience and taking their own experience as a starting point that they had a chance of resolving their problems and learning from it. But they were the experts in their own experience. Horton believed that adults learned through experience and every adult had something like the same amount of experience: but they needed to learn how to analyze that experience. The staff at Highlander might indeed have a lot of knowledge and solutions to offer, but unless this knowledge arose out of the workers' own experience, it would mean nothing to them. The first task was to get people to voice their problems and talk about their own experience, together with others, including their peers as well as the staff. Very soon others would chime in with similar experiences and people would begin to search for further information about these problems—where they may have arisen in the past, how others had resolved them, and so on as well as seeking background information, such as the relevant legal codes, underlying economic conditions, and so on. Horton said that once people learn to analyze their own experience and that of their peers, 90% of the time they find that what they thought was their problem was not at all, and begin to dig deeper. Consequently the Highlander staff was then able, as equals, to share their experience, suggest books where answers may be found, invite experts to come and answer questions which have arisen in the discussion the answers for which were not readily available. No material was ever introduced except as it arose from a life situation presented for discussion by the students who have come to Highlander. The students tended to remain convinced that they would have to get the answer from an expert, but even when staff or invited experts believed they had the answer, it would not be provided, nor any suggestion given that they had a solution. The workers had to find the solution to their own problems by analyzing their own experience and pursuing questions that arose out of the analysis of their own experience. Sometimes staff would put questions to the group, so as to focus the discussion and help the discussion move in a productive direction, but never provided answers; sometimes they would help manage domineering personalities or other difficulties that might put up barriers to discussion, that's all. And of course their experience with running such workshops allowed them to prompt participants in profitable directions with well-aimed questions.

This reliance on the experience of poor people as the source of solutions to their own problems and as being as valuable as the experience of any expert was crucial to the egalitarianism which prevailed at Highlander. People learned not only to value their own experience and that of their peers but they also came to feel comfortable interacting with middle-class people, academics and so on, as equals, confident in their own knowledge.

COLLECTIVE DECISION MAKING

Horton found that poor people, especially uneducated or young people, or people in minority groups, not only regarded their own knowledge and experience as worthless, but had become habituated to having every important decision in their life made for them, and being told at every point what they should do, to the extent that they were quite incapable of making a decision for themselves, let alone as part of a group. And yet the ability to make a decision, and even more importantly, to make a *collective* decision together with their peers was the very essence of liberation—it meant taking charge of their own lives. Collective decision making was also central to the very meaning of learning.

> Learning and decision making are inseparable. People learn from making decisions and making decisions helps them learn. The motivation for decision making, like the motivation for learning, comes through genuine involvement in an undertaking considered

worthy of the effort and possible to achieve. ... Significant learning proceeds *in the process of shared decision making*. (Horton, 2003, pp. 246–247)

The day-to-day running o-f the school would be placed in the hands of the students. At the beginning of each residence, the staff would inform the students about what previous students had done and then it would be left to the students to decide everything. The students usually found this situation distressing at first, but staff would absolutely refuse to give directions or make suggestions. The same applied to the problems which workers brought with them to Highlander for resolution. There is a story told in which a group of workers and Horton were on the front lines of a difficult strike involving 2000 workers. At a certain crucial point the workers found that they did not know what they were going to do, and demanded of Horton that he tell them what they should do. Horton refused, and a worker put a gun to Horton's head saying that if he didn't tell them what to so he would shoot him. Still Horton would not give way (Moyles & Horton, 1982, p. 264).

So this is what Highlander was doing: teaching poor people to trust their own experience and that of their peers and helping them learn how to analyze that experience and forcing them to take charge of their own lives by participating in the process of shared decision making and taking responsibility for those decisions.

During the first phase of Highlander's work, with the CIO, shared decision making meant forming committees, having meetings and so on and making decisions the way decisions have always been made in the labor movement, by Majority. Horton said that he never agreed with majority voting, but this is what the workers needed to take charge of their lives in and through the union movement.

Figure 7.2. 1937-Highlander Staff organizing workers at a Tennessee lime plant.
Used with permission from the Highlander Research and Education Center Archives

GROUP SINGING AND DRAMA ON THE FRONT LINES OF CONFRONTATION

"Sing and fight! Right was the tyrant king who said: 'Beware of a movement that sings'"
—WOBBLIES, QUOTED IN FOWKE, GLAZER, & BRAY (1973, P. 9)

From the time he spent in Denmark, Horton learned to "first enliven, then enlighten" (Adams & Horton, 1975, p. 92). Once consistent source of "enlivening" came through the dynamic of group singing. This dynamic was present from their start in 1932 and onward. By 1939, Highlander had its own mimeographed song-book which was used on picket lines as well as in classrooms where "enlightening" on specific union organizing problems took place. An overview of the history of the use of music and drama at Highlander can be summed up by the two main areas of focus of their work in equipping labor leaders and civil rights education. Without question the outstanding leader of song and use of drama during the labor period was Myles Horton's wife, Zilphia, who came to Highlander in 1935. Zilphia studied music at the College of the Ozarks, in Arkansas and is described by those her new her as a warm, personable and inspiring woman of the people. "People who wouldn't usually sing with strangers would sing with her. There was a quality about her that inspired trust" (Adams, 1975, p. 73). This was quality was imperative when leading group singing on the front lines of a picket in the line of fire quite literally. For strikers in this period of violent resistance to unions, group singing was far more than "holding hands and singing kubayah". Singing strikers discovered that the power of harmonic resonance increased their courage and sense of community.

Figure 7.3. Early 1940s Zilphia Horton at a Street Rally.
Used with permission from the Highlander Research and Education Center Archives

One story in particular is a striking example of this dynamic at work. The setting is Chattanooga, Tennessee sometime in the 1930s during a parade held on George Washington's birthday. In a taped interview Zilphia narrates this powerful account.

> There was a minister in the parade, a band, children and strikers. We were marching two by two behind the band and when we marched by the mill, they opened up on us with a machine gun. Several People were hit. The woman on my left [Highlander's librarian, Hilda Hulbert] was hit in the ankle. I looked around and the police had disappeared. There had been quite a few of them around, too. One was lying in a ditch. I said to him "What are you doing there"? He said, "Well lady, I've got a wife and three kids!" In about five minutes after the firing stopped, a few of us stood up at the mill gates and started singing, "We shall not be moved." And in about ten minutes, people began to come out from behind the barns and little stores around there, and we stood and sang "We shall not be moved." That's what won them recognition. That what a song means in many place. That song is almost a labor hymn. (Z. Horton quoted in Adams, 1975, p. 75)

From 1935 to 1952 while Zilphia was director of the Highlander workshops, "nearly one hundred labors plays were written by Highlander staff members or students" (Adams, 1975, p. 72). In fact, drama was used to teach contract negotiations, parliamentary law, public speaking or union problems. In the case of Highlander, drama provided a powerful tool not only for helping adults learn to read, but it also strengthened their identity as agents for radical social change through the process of participation in leading activities.

Drama and music were both central to Highlander's many activities during the Civil Rights era, so much so in fact, that one cannot think of the movement as a whole without picturing people marching and singing across the Southern United States. Two of the central figures in this era were Guy and Candie Carawan. Guy first came to Highlander in 1953 with one of Woody Guthrie's musician friends, Ramlin' Jack Eliot. He moved to Highlander in 1959 at the urging and recommendation of Pete Seeger. Candie came to Highlander in 1960 from Fisk University in Nashville, Tennessee and married Guy a short time later. In a personal interview, one of Martin Luther King's closest colleagues, C. T. Vivian spoke about Guy Carawan's role during the Civil Rights Movement.

> I don't think we had ever thought of spirituals as movement material. When the movement came up, we couldn't apply them. The concept has to be there. It wasn't just to have the music but to take the music out of our past and apply it to the new situation, to change it so it really fit. ... The first time I remember any change in our songs was when Guy came down from Highlander. Here he was with this guitar and tall thin frame, leaning forward and patting that foot. I remember James Bevel and I looked across at each other and smiled. Guy had taken this song, "Follow the Drinking Gourd"—I didn't know the song, but he gave some background on it and boom—that began to make sense. And, little by little, spiritual after spiritual began to appear with new words and changes: "Keep Your Eyes on the Prize, Hold On" or "I'm Going to Sit at the Welcome Table." Once we had seen it done, we could begin to do it. (Vivian, in Carawan & Carawan, 2007, p. xix.)

The one song that Guy Carawan and the entire Highlander community will most be remembered for is *We Shall Overcome* which would go on to become the definitive anthem of Civil Rights movement. Zilphia Horton learned this song which was really an adapted church hymn from the early 20th century, from Lucille Simmons, one of the African-American women that led the 1945–1946 tobacco workers' strike in Charleston, South Carolina. After Zilphia died, Guy Carawan taught this song on the front lines of the battle over desegregation throughout the south. Myles Horton tells a story about how the second verse was born during a weekend session at Highlander in 1959, a youth choir from Montgomery, Alabama visited Highlander and enjoyed the inclusive environment of racial equality there.

> They were looking at a movie called *Face of the South*. It was dark. Suddenly, raiders came in with flashlights. They must have been vigilantes and some police officers, but they weren't in uniform. They demanded the lights be turned on, but they couldn't get anybody at Highlander to do it. They were furious you know, running around with flashlights. In the meantime, the kids started to sing "We Shall Overcome." It made them feel good. The raiders yelled, "Shut up and turn on the lights!" Then some kid said, "We're not afraid." Then they started singing, "We are not afraid. We are not afraid." That's when that verse was born, the night of the raid. (Horton, 1989, p. 31)

Guy was invited to the first meeting of the Student Non-violent Coordinating Committee (SNCC) in April 1960, and taught this song to over 200 participants who became leaders of the Civil Rights Movement and took this song back home with them to many different communities. (We will discuss their role in more detail at the end of this article). Perhaps Wyatt Tee Walker, a close associate of Martin Luther King said it best in describing the role this song played at the heart of the freedom struggle.

> One cannot describe the vitality and emotion this hymn evokes across the Southland. I have heard it sung in great mass meetings with a thousand voices singing as one. I've heard a half dozen sing it softly behind the bars of the Hinds County Prison in Mississippi. I have heard old women singing it on the way to work in Albany, Ga. I've heard the students singing it as they were being dragged away to jail. It generates power that is indescribable. It manifests a rich legacy of musical literature that serves to keep body and soul together for that better day which is not far off. (Walker, in Carawan & Carawan, 2007, p. 8)

In the spring of 1960, Candie was one of the first white students to participate in the non-violent training workshops led by James Lawson. During a phone interview with Candie, she stated that one of the central activities that took place in these workshops, was "role playing about how to protect yourself" during non-violent protests (2/20/15, personal communication). These strategies were used in real life confrontation across the South on the many fronts of the struggle for racial justice in sit in's and freedom rides.

CONFRONTING SEGREGATION

In the South, segregation had the force of law. What further complicated matters was that many union activists in the South were also Klan members. Nonetheless, Horton always made it known to the unions sending members to Highlander that Highlander was an integrated school. Racial segregation increasingly became a barrier to Highlander's objectives, however. Whenever they had tried to build unions, coalitions or virtually anything else, they eventually came up against the barriers of racism. Highlander always stood firm against the pressure to segregate, but for a number of years the unions selected segregated groups to send to Highlander. On one celebrated occasion, Horton invited a black worker to a union class. A member of the KKK whose union was paying for the course objected and demanded that the black worker be excluded. Horton refused and said that if he didn't like it he (the Klan unionist) could leave. Objecting that he had paid for the course, he grumbled, but stayed, and surprisingly he learned from the experience; as a union official he later included black members in the groups he sent to Highlander from his own union. Over time, the people coming to Highlander just accepted it. Horton did not make integration a topic of discussion, but people just learned through the experience of learning together, and eating and working together and sharing bedrooms and bathrooms together, and working towards common goals, that it wasn't so terrible after all.

Between 1932 and 1947, 6,800 students had participated in Highlander residences and over 12,000 workers had participated in extension classes. This work transformed the labor movement in the South, the more so because Highlander graduates invariably moved into leadership positions representing the lowest grades of the proletariat in the South, and they remained in touch with Highlander afterwards. Despite the progress Highlander had made towards integrating the unions, few Highlander graduates believed that integration could be extended to the rest of the South beyond the union movement.

The relationship with the conservative CIO leadership was becoming untenable however. Anyone who openly advocated political action beyond the narrow pursuit of union wages and conditions faced expulsion. The CIO responded to the House Un-American Activities Committee witch-hunt by demanding their affiliates, including Highlander, make declarations of opposition to and dissociation from Communism. Highlander's refusal to comply meant parting ways with the CIO. The responsibility for union education was handed back to the CIO to run for themselves, but the methods developed by Highlander which was encouraging initiative from the ranks of the union movement, were not continued by the CIO. Highlander had gone as far as it could in organizing the lowest ranks of workers in the South into unions; it was time to move on.

The war had created demand for farm produce and the end of the war only increased demand, and Horton determined that it was time to turn to the poor farmers of the South. The next phase of their work was directed at educational work amongst farmers, both black and white, assisting them in developing cooperatives and encouraging the growth of the National Farmers Union.

Highlander was able to use the contacts they had made through their union work to make new contacts with farmers, and after 5 or 6 years working amongst farmers they had built up a broad layer of support amongst both black and white sections of the rural poor in the South and a large number of cooperative ventures were being operated by farming communities, giving them a degree of independence from the agribusinesses which had always exploited them.

Until 1954 only 10–15% of students at the school were black, but during the summer of 1954, in the wake of the Supreme Court finding on school segregation, about 50% of the workshop participants were black. For the next decade, a majority of those coming to Highlander would be black as Horton became convinced that a social movement was building up in the South.

Horton did not attempt to suppress racial conflict within the school, but the experience of living together and working towards a common goal invariably led to participants accepting the egalitarian and integrated regime at Highlander and they were invariably full of praise for these practices by the time they left.

THE CIVIL RIGHTS MOVEMENT FROM THE GRASS ROOTS UPWARD

A one-week workshop for the United Furniture Workers of America held in May 1954 included 35 blacks and whites from 16 locals. The course covered the use of formal meeting procedure and all the usual topics of interest to unionists, but they also discussed the importance of union participation in the drive for school desegregation.

At that time, there was a lot of interest in the UN and the new world situation following the end of the war, and Highlander held workshops where people could learn about the United Nations and the progress being made by the National Liberation Movements around the world. Horton particularly sought out blacks who were relatively free of pressure from white people, either because they ran their own businesses serving the black community, or were preachers in the black churches which were all owned by their black congregations.

In August 1954, the bus owner/driver, Esau Jenkins, and the retired school-teacher, Septima Clark, attended one of these workshops. They came from Johns Island, one of the Sea Islands of South Carolina, one of the most deprived and marginalized areas in the country, where people spoke a dialect incomprehensible to outsiders. Jenkins drove the bus that took people to work on the mainland every day and he had been trying to teach people to read while driving his bus, so they could register to vote. According to the constitution of South Carolina, poor black people had to prove they could read by reading the Constitution of South Carolina, before they were allowed to vote.

A two-week summer workshop on school desegregation in May 1955 attracted 50 teachers, unionists, students and community leaders, among them Rosa Parks, whose fare to Monteagle had been paid for by the Alabama branch of the NAACP. A July 1955 workshop on the UN was attended by a young beautician, Bernice Robinson, who was inspired to help her cousin, Septima Clark, promote community activity on Johns Island.

The visit of Esau Jenkins, Septima Clark and Bernice Robinson to Highlander led to Highlander's most successful program—the Citizenship Schools, and within a few months of attending Highlander, Rosa Parks triggered the famous Montgomery Bus Boycott, conventionally taken as the beginning of the Civil Rights Movement. Rosa Parks had made no plans while at Highlander, but she went home with a different spirit. According to her own testimony Rosa Parks' decision to refuse to give up her seat to a white man and to force the police to arrest her was because at Highlander she had found respect as a Black person and white people that she could trust. This gave her the courage to insist on being treated with respect and confidence in eventual victory.

After Esau Jenkins raised the problem of voter registration in the Highlander workshop, Highlander took on this project, and Horton spent several months, on and off, in Johns Island, learning the dialect and familiarizing himself with

Figure 7.4. Desegregation workshop at Highlander in 1955. Rosa Parks is at the end of the table. Six months later, her actions sparked the Montgomery Bus Boycott.

Used with permission from the Highlander Research and Education Center Archives

—See more at: http://highlandercenter.org/media/timeline/#sthash.X9LmMX9g.dpuf

people's lives there. A room was rented and Bernice Robinson was appointed teacher; Bernice was given no direction as to how to teach and had no teaching experience. Her curriculum consisted of what she had learned about respecting others at home and later at Highlander. This can be summarized as treating people with respect and as equals, beginning from their experience and responding to people's problem as they saw them. On January 7, 1957, she stood nervously before her first class and said "I'm not a teacher. I really don't know why they wanted me to do this, but I'm here and I'll learn with you. I'll learn as I go along." She pinned a copy of the Universal Declaration of Human Rights up on the wall and told her students that by the end of the term she wanted them all to be able to read it. She had brought with her reading material from her local elementary school but immediately realized that these were inappropriate for her adult class. Allowing the problems raised by the class to set their program, they worked on writing their own names and moved on to reading the labels on supermarket cans, filling out work dockets, filling in the blanks in a mail order catalog—all those practical everyday tasks which frustrate the illiterate person. In two months the enrollment increased from 14 to 37. The object was to register to vote and use the majority that blacks had in the state to advantage; so the final examination was to go down to county courthouse and register to vote. Throughout the program, approximately 80% of the class passed the exam at the end of the approximately three-month term.

Septima Clark was appointed director of the program, which became known as the Citizenship School, and rapidly spread across the south. New teachers were apprenticed to Bernice by observing her at work in the classroom, and these new teachers in turn trained others. By 1961, over four hundred teachers had been trained, and there had been over four thousand students. By 1970, approximately 100,000 illiterate African-Americans had learned to read and had registered to vote, and many hundreds of black people, none of them with teaching credentials of any kind, had been trained as teachers by the former beautician Bernice Robinson and her apprentices. Very many of these teachers would go on to become activists in the Civil Rights movement. The program, together with Septima Clark as Director, was subsequently handed over to the Southern Christian Leadership Conference to run it as their program.

The runaway success of the Citizenship School was possible only thanks to the fact that there was a revolutionary situation in the South. Horton was able to detect this in its earliest stages and provided the kind of education which not only gave black people the confidence to stand up to the system and offer leadership to their communities, and the knowledge that there were elements of the white population who could be expected to support them, but also the means to analyze their situation and draw on the experience of the black communities in the South to overcome the barriers erected against them.

Angeline Butler attended Highlander in the Spring of 1959.

In the spring of 1959 the Fusons took a group of Fisk students to Highlander. There we discussed the South, race relations, and the change that needed to come to the South and met long-time activists … In the company of these older activists, we held informal self-exploratory discussions that allowed us to see ourselves in the larger scheme of things in the South and the world. We also discussed more democratic ways of organizing. The central idea of Highlander was that people needed to talk and listen to one another until they could discover some common ground, some agreement on what changes needed to be made. Once a consensus was reached, only then could a method be applied.

Highlander provided an opportunity for black folks and white folks to sit down together, to experience communication as human beings. We had dinner together, washed dishes together, slept in bunk beds in the same room side by side, laughed, and shared humorous stories. We were able to touch one another and to see up close the obvious differences. We had to realize we each had God's light within us, that we were all from the *same* source and deserved to share the same opportunity in life.

In the fall of 1959, I heard about the workshops on nonviolence at Clark Memorial Church. With the help of members of the Nashville Christian Leadership Council— … Rev. C. T. Vivian and others—Rev. James Morris Lawson Jr. organized and conducted the workshops. Lawson was a divinity student at Vanderbilt University and a field worker with the pacifist organization called the Fellowship of Reconciliation. He had traveled to India to study the philosophy of Mahatma Gandhi and had already served time in jail as a Conscientious Objector to the Korean War. I recruited other students from Fisk to attend the workshops: Peggy Alexander and Diane Nash were among the female students who responded. Mary Anne Morgan from Meharry Medical College in Nashville came also.

In these workshops what we were all talking about was our future. A new phase of my life began as we addressed the truth about our place in the society and how the society looked upon us as a people. We studied Mahatma Gandhi, the life of Jesus Christ, and Thoreau. Pretty soon we applied their teachings of nonviolence and civil disobedience to the fundamental inequality of people in Nashville's segregated society. We began to define clear targets that needed changing. We wanted access to all services in establishments where we spent money—lunch counters in five-and-dime stores, department stores, bus stations, and drugstores. (Holsaert, Richardson, & Noonan, 2012)

The first lunch counter sit-in was staged by four black students from North Carolina Agricultural and Technical College at the Woolworth lunch counter in Greensboro, North Carolina, on 1 February 1960. On 1 April 1960, Highlander held its seventh annual college workshop entitled "The New Generation Fights for Equality," the focus of which was demonstrations, college students, and the civil rights movement. Two weeks later, sit-in leaders, many of whom had participated in the Highlander workshop, met in Raleigh, North Carolina, to form the Student Nonviolent Coordinating Committee (SNCC), which would confront segregation head on.

THE QUEST FOR DEMOCRATIC ENGAGEMENT CONTINUES

Toward the end of the 1960s and through the 1970s, Highlander was involved in helping Appalachian coal miners organize for healthier working conditions. In the 1980s they were closely entwined with grassroots environmental reform and still are involved in this work presently.

Figure 7.5. In the early 1980s residents of Bumpas Cove, Tennessee, protested toxic dumping in their community. Highlander supported their efforts.

Used with permission from the Highlander Research and Education Center Archives

–See more at: http://highlandercenter.org/media/timeline/#sthash.X9LmMX9g.dpuf

When Horton died in 1990, his legacy did not since he had spent his whole life working himself out of a job. According to the Highlander website they continue the original mission to serve "as a catalyst for grassroots organizing and movement building in Appalachia and the South. We work with people fighting for justice, equality and sustainability, supporting their efforts to take collective action to shape their own destiny." (2016, n.p) retrieved from: http://highlandercenter.org/

This is more explicitly stated further down the pages of their website.

> [Highlander is] continuing to fight for justice and equality through organizing and leadership development among Latino immigrants, LGBTQ leaders in the south. They also host annual conferences for culturally and ethnically diverse young people with a focus on encouraging the use of culture to enhance social justice efforts, and helping organizations in diverse constituencies develop new strategies and alliances. (ibid.)

CONCLUSION

The more the people become themselves, the better the democracy
—Freire quoted in Horton & Freire (1990, p. 145)

The "idea of Highlander" remains unfettered and will continue to do when and where there are people that are treated as equals without being patronized. It will flourish when indigenous ways, culture and personhood are not monolithically labeled as rural southern white, black, or Hispanic or that the urban or "northern" way of doing things is inherently better. Horton himself and the people that were drawn to his "idea" serve as an enduring testimony, that democratic education for social justice can happen anywhere when there is an emphatic focus and unwavering insistence that everyone can participate and contribute, that each person has cultural assets and unique human experiences from which we can all learn. The ebb and flow of cultural trends is in a constant state of change. Today for example, at Highlander you are more likely to hear the influence of spoken word poetry or hip hop than Celtic and English influenced folk music. But even this evolution in popular musical trends is consistent with the Highlander's position of honoring cultural heritage since even these 21st century sounds can be traced to the oral traditions of West Africa that found their way to America through the slave trade. The cultivation of personal agency is still central to the unfettered "idea of Highlander" whether the issues of social justice emerge in the 20th or 21st century or any century for that matter. We are sure that Horton "the radical hillbilly" with a radical love for people would agree. We close with this quote from very end of Horton's conversation with Paulo Freire.

MYLES: I'm going to read a short little poem here. You can figure out who wrote it. "Go to the people. Learn from them. Love them. Start with what they know. Build with what they have. But the best of leaders when the job is done, when the task is accomplished, the people will all say we have done it ourselves." Who wrote that? Who could have written it?

THIRD PARTY: You could have written it. Paulo could have written it.

MYLES: It has taken a long time for people to come to these ideas hasn't it? This was written in 604 B.C. by Lao Tzu. Isn't it wonderful?

(Horton & Freire, 1990, pp. 247–248)

REFERENCES

Adams, F., & Horton, M. (1975). *Unearthing seeds of fire: The idea of Highlander*. Winston-Salem, NC: J. F. Blair.

Carawan, G., & Carawan, C. (2007). *Sing for freedom: The story of the civil rights movement through its songs*. Montgomery, AL: New South Books

Fowke, E., Glazer, J., & Bray, K. I. (1973). *Songs of work and protest*. New York, NY: Dover Publications.

Holsaert, F. S., Richardson, J., & Noonan, M. P. N. (Eds.). (2012). *Hands on the freedom plow. Personal accounts by women in SNCC*. Champaign, IL: University of Illinois Press.

Horton, M. (1989). Thou shalt not teach. In B. Schultz & R. Schultz (Eds.), *It did happen here: Recollections of political repression in America*. Berkeley, CA: University of California Press.

Horton, M., & Freire, P. (1990). In B. Bell, J. Gaventa, & J. Peters (Eds.), *We make the road by walking. Conversation on education and social change*. Philadelphia, PA: Temple University Press.

Horton, M. (1998). *The Long Haul. An autobiography*. New York, NY: Doubleday.

Horton, M. (2003). In D. Jacobs (Ed.), *The Myles Horton Reader. Education for social change*. Knoxville, TN: University of Tennessee Press.

Moyers, B., & Horton, M. (1982). The adventures of a radical hillbilly: An interview with Myles Horton. *Appalachian Journal, 9*(4), 248–285.

Smith, A. J. (2007). *The early years of Highlander Folk School and its adversaries: 1932–1942*. Unpublished Master's Thesis. Retrieved from http://dighistory.org/portfolio/the-early-years-of-highlander-folk-school-and-its-adversaries-1932–1942

The Liberatory Potential AND Constraint OF Working-Class Rural Women's Gender Roles WITHIN THE United States

FAITH AGOSTINONE-WILSON

Working-class rural women in the United States represent a compelling intersection of economics, race, gender, and social geography. Location alone is a powerful mediating factor, shaping identity and experience. The life of a working-class rural woman in Vermont is going to be vastly different than one in Nevada in terms of landscape, politics, and culture. Economic changes also impact rural women's identities as farms and factories close and Wal-Mart becomes the primary employer of a region. Diversity is also becoming the norm in rural communities, with majority older and white populations passing away, replaced by younger, more diverse families. Therefore, the image of the unchanging rural landscape and the women who occupy it is more nostalgia than fact.

Socialist/Marxian feminist theory provides a useful way to examine issues of identity surrounding working-class rural women. Socialist feminism "holds that women's consciousness, or standpoint, emerges from the social context of their lives, specifically from the sexual division of labor and from women's subordination to men" (Sachs, 1996, p. 14). Vogel (2013) asserts that a useful dialectical materialist feminism has to have five key elements. First, it has to express a clear dedication to women's liberation and genuine equality (not just equality of opportunity) for all people. Second, it has to be capable of providing a coherent analysis of what is happening to women now, as well as seeking to understand how things have become the way they are. Third, it has to provide theory to accompany the history. Fourth, a vision has to be created for future social organizing that remains consistent with history and theoretical framing. Fifth, when "the woman question" is asked, an answer has to be demanded in the form of practical strategies.

Socialist feminism goes further than traditional leftist conceptualizations of women's oppression as a shared experience among all women (Brown, 2013; Vogel, 2013). In particular, the family becomes the site of analysis concerning where oppression plays out, complicating more determinist explanations of why working-class women find themselves in a subordinate role despite having made gains in terms of legal equality and the workplace (Whatmore, 1988). The development of the family from clan-based social structures to patriarchal extended families to the monogamous nuclear family has been the result of historical and political changes from the transition of pre-class societies to capitalist ones (Brown, 2013; Vogel, 2013. The family is further shaped by changes in labor, as in the case of rural communities losing family farms and livable wage factory work.

Additionally, critical rural/southern scholarship (Cloke & Little, 1997; Pruitt & Vanegas, 2015; Reynolds, 2014; Sachs, 1996; Thomas, 2011) and critical rusticity (Boso, 2013; Herring, 2010) provide important frames to use when analyzing issues of identity and rural women, along with concepts such as metronormativity and urbanormativity, which seek to problematize the tendency of urban-centered research to represent the rural as "an empty space removed from racial, ethnic, and socioeconomic stress or inequality" (Herring, 2010, p. 85). Critical rusticity addresses LGBTQI intersectional concerns by highlighting how activism organized around sexuality also needs to include rural spaces and not assume that everything happens in the city (Herring, 2010). Far from being hinterlands to which people are exiled, the rural contains compelling aspects of place that center people's ways of being, albeit in contradictory ways.

Using socialist-feminist and critical rural theories, this chapter will first discuss the complexities in defining "rural" and how this is linked to identity, including demographic definitions of the rural, the historical impact of post-Great-Migration policies, and the various identities of rural, working-class women. Next, the liberatory aspects of rural female identity will be explored, tied to the openness of rural spaces. Finally, the barriers that rural women encounter are presented and examined in turn: economic factors, agrarian ideology, rural patriarchy, and domestic violence/reproductive rights. For clarity, this chapter is primarily addressing rural, working-class women within the United States, with the understanding that there are key differences between the experiences of rural working-class women throughout the globe.

RURAL AS PLACE AND DISTINCTIVE IDENTITY

Pruitt and Vanegas (2015) explore the concept of legal geography in their analysis of the urbanormative characteristics of the law. They find that laws become variably applied on the basis of material space, with those in positions of authority often ignoring the rural in their application of the law:

> In our increasingly metro-centric nation, where rural populations are dwindling and marginalized both literally and symbolically, most federal appellate judges appear to have little experience with, or understanding of, typical socio-spatial features of rurality: transportation challenges, a dearth of services, lack of anonymity, and—frequently—extreme socioeconomic disadvantage. (p. 77)

For Sachs (1996), the rural is an experiential construct that represents social and political conflicts over the meaning of identity and the environment that goes far beyond the specifics of territory. Rural identity is also mediated by particular historical situations through human labor and is not a static or trans-historic concept (Brown, 2013).

Though portrayed in literature and popular media as unchanging and stable, what we think of as "rural" is currently undergoing dramatic shifts demographically, economically, and culturally. Much of this is happening as non-white groups start to view themselves as rural or Southern, for example, and as whites decrease their affiliation with that place-based identity (Greene, 2007). This section presents a sketch of rurality in the areas of definitions, the impact of the Great Migration era policies on the South, and working class women's roles.

Defining "Rural"

Rurality is challenging to define because relying on population thresholds alone is problematic. For example, a small town next to a large city could technically have a population below 2,500, but it wouldn't be considered *culturally* rural (Websdale, 1998). Interestingly, the U.S. Census doesn't have an official definition of *rural*, instead referring to it as "encompassing all population, housing, and territory not included within an urban area" (Defining Rural Population, n.d., para. 3). Essentially, the government has established *rural* as *not-urban*.

The Federal Office of Rural Health Policy uses further means to delineate rurality, such as the Rural-Urban Commuting Area codes with further refinements to define areas with low population density (no more than 35 people per square mile). Using this low population density definition, currently 57 million people (18% of the U.S. population) occupy rural spaces (para. 7). This would include all regions of the U.S., representing a vast land mass of diverse geographies, economies, dialects, cultures, occupations, ethnicities, and sexualities (Boso, 2013; DeKeseredy, Muzzatti & Donnermeyer, 2014; Greene, 2007; Websdale, 1998).

Despite the increasing diversity of those making up rurality, researchers have documented some general cultural characteristics held in common that further define rural. These include a relative homogeneity in terms of conservative political beliefs, religiosity and suspicion of outsiders though these can vary in intensity (Hardesty & Bokemeier, 1989; Pruitt, 2007; Websdale, 1998). Cultural homogeneity is reinforced by closeness within the community and a general lack of privacy, despite living in relative isolation geographically. Reinforcement of norms often occurs through public shaming and gossip and reliance on extra-legal means of control as part of "taking care of business." In fact, D'Antonio-Del Rio, Doucet, and Chauvin (2010) have proposed the use of their Southern Subculture Index as a means of assessing what they view as a Southern propensity toward violence by examining the factors of county of residence, adherence to Evangelical Protestantism, and Scots-Irish ancestry.

Post-Great Migration Policies

Situating rural working-class women's identity in a dialectical-historical way requires an understanding of the significance of government policies aimed at shaping rural populations. In what is referred to as the Great Migration, from 1910 to 1970, black and white southerners moved to the North and Midwest in search of employment, a higher standard of living, and escape from oppression (Eichenlaub, Tolnay, & Alexander, 2010). Bageant (2010) carefully documents his Great Migration experiences growing up in a rural white working-class family in his memoir, *Rainbow Pie*. The memoir also serves as a historical analysis of the Appalachian region, connecting Scotch-Irish settlers to current political views of the white underclass. As a whole, Southern migrants didn't fare dramatically better immediately after their move north or long-term, though the Great Migration is often portrayed as an American Dream social experiment with a successful outcome (Eichenlaub et al., 2010).

During this same period of mass migration, policy researchers began to focus their attention on rural populations, particularly in the South where poor whites were viewed as genetically inferior, degenerate, shiftless and in need of state-based reform (Banes, 1992). Mainstream narratives of the New Deal tend to reflect an unquestioned, urbanormative viewpoint: that government invested massive amounts of money to provide infrastructure for an economy in collapse (Coleman, 2010). By connecting consumption to democracy and citizenship, policy makers found an interest convergence in ramping up relief programs during the Great Depression, where it was harder to explain away economic inequality. There were also growing concerns that the labor unrest happening in the cities would spread into rural populations.

Rural women were the key to cementing the consumption-based national model within the home (Coleman, 2010). The Farm Security Administration's (FSA) community farm program of the 1930s is an example of state intervention that shaped rural working-class women's lives. In order to receive assistance via government funding of tracts of land, farmers had to abide by a set of regulations, including roles of women, as an aspect of lifestyle transformation. For farm women, "this meant greater regulation to the domestic sphere and a subsequent marginalization of the outside tasks that many women undertook in support of their families" (p. 202). These cooperative farms were meant to be a prototype for future interventions into the lives of farmers "so that they could fully participate in the burgeoning consumerism that was redefining American culture and identity" (p. 202).

Contrary to portrayals of rural women as uneducated and backward, history presents countless instances of female-operated agricultural production. As one example, Sachs (1996) examines the chicken and egg trade and found that from the mid-1800s to the 1940s, Pennsylvania women from one county alone oversaw the raising of 80,000 chickens and 6 million eggs on their family farms (p. 107). It was the introduction of mechanization and large-scale farms, along with agricultural associations that brought the enterprise under the control of men.

Often monetary assistance to farmers inadvertently drove rural women indoors, further alienating them from agricultural labor. Sachs (1996) traces similar pathways in the dairy trade where women found themselves displaced with the arrival of factory farming and the introduction of machinery. Tractors have also played a major role in shaping gendered labor on farms, where men primarily design, own and operate large farm equipment. This demonstrates the impact that machinery has on gendered work, and that under capitalism, the benefits of technology do not tend to go directly to the workers, often being used against them (Brown, 2013).

The Great Migration era also included an influx of mineral extraction corporations into the South. Websdale (1998) outlines how coal companies in East Kentucky, under the guise of civilizing the region, created discord and hegemonic rule in many communities. When violence would emerge, it was blamed on the cultural tendencies of hillbillies to resolve their problems by feuding. Indeed, Cobb (1992) finds that country music during this time often expressed skepticism and disdain for technology wrapped in the guise of "progress."

Sohn's (2003) ethnographic work with Appalachian working-class women who were non-traditional college attendees revealed negative experiences with past schooling where teachers openly criticized them and their friends' appearance and mannerisms. At the same time, the teachers' pets were the more socially-acceptable middle-class students, even though the teachers themselves had shared the same rural, working-class backgrounds before they entered the middle class. Often these experiences created a lingering sense of skepticism on the part of the adult students about higher education and fears that they would lose their mountain identity.

Women's Roles

Pruitt (2007) asserts that "geography matters" as a category of identity, because it impacts social, legal, and cultural aspects of life. Therefore, "experiencing a rural upbringing or being a long-time rural resident can be a critical aspect of how a woman sees herself" (p. 425). Economic and structural changes happening in many rural regions, from closure of family farms and factories to the introduction of low-wage, part-time service jobs, has also transformed rural women's family forms, roles within those families, and erased some geographic boundaries between country and city (Lattimer & Oberhauser, 2005; Sachs, 1996).

Female rural identity is also mediated strongly by social class, with the very labels of "country" or "hillbilly" immediately marking one as being poor or working-class (Peterson, 1992). These motifs appear regularly within country music, with variants that come in and out of "style" in popular culture, with "redneck" on the commercial ascendency while "hillbilly" or "cowgirl" rarely heard. Linkon, Peckham, and Lanier-Nabors (2004) found that rural women working-class students "tend to embrace the ethos of a stable identity" and didn't tend to "perform" as middle-class students did, especially for self-promotion, in university or professional settings (p. 152). At the same time, as Hubbs (2011) explains, "Working-class women 'have always been positioned at a distance' from femininity, a historically specific construction that was indicatively bourgeois from its eighteenth-century beginnings" (p. 60). This section examines the more common identity constructs for working-class rural women, organized along a continuum from most to least "acceptable" to mainstream rural patriarchal ideology: farmwife, redneck, farmer, and misfit.

Farmwife. The farmwife role is best defined by Sachs (1996):

> Designation of women as farmwives defines them primarily in relation to their husbands … thus, farmwives share many of the duties of housewives, but in addition, they perform various activities related to the farm enterprise, such as bookkeeping, milking cows, running errands, supervising farm labor, growing and preserving food, various farm chores, and "filling in" or doing what needs to be done. (p. 134)

Keller (2014) found that even though farmwives regularly engaged in work we would traditionally associate with farm labor, they self-identified along the lines of traditional gender roles (i.e. refusing the label of "farmer"), or referred to themselves as "helping out" rather than performing chores essential to the maintenance of the farm. This is along the lines of the strategy of *emphasized femininity*, where women attempt to conform to gender norms as a means of enabling males to "save face" and thereby preserve rural patriarchy (Keller, 2014; Pompper & Crandall, 2014).

Brasier, Sachs, Kiernan, Trauger, & Barbercheck (2014) provide a useful theoretical overview on further situating the farmwife identity. They first discuss three models of marriage on farms which include the *agrarian marital model* (partnership between husbands and wives with distinct roles for each), *industrial marital model* (wives do the housework only) and the *symmetrical model* (roles based on individual preferences). The symmetrical model was represented most by younger farm couples, where women and men would interchange chores. These models of marriage are also influenced by the family farm as an institution, ideologies of masculinity as they relate to who is or isn't a "farmer," and de-traditionalization, which allows for women to take on a wider range of farm jobs depending on needs that arise. Brasier and colleagues found that the size and type of the farm had significant impacts on the marital models being lived out.

Redneck

As an identifier, *redneck* is specifically tied to whiteness and being lower-to-working-class. To a lesser degree, it is also linked to rural settings, though the term is more widely geographically applied today (Hubbs, 2011). Though often portrayed as hell-raising and rebellious, the redneck female identity construct is still quite deferential to rural patriarchy, "attaching to maleness and connoting a rough style of masculinity, often, but not exclusively, southern" (p. 47). Redneck (male and female) is also a stock character type appearing frequently in horror, slasher, and pornographic films, presented as "either the perpetrators and/or victims of extreme forms of violence" or sexuality (DeKeseredy et al., 2014, pp. 180).

The redneck female identity is highly mediated by commercialism, which presents a model of a "hard," "authentic" woman who likes to kick back with the boys. Indeed, as an example of this marketability, Hubbs (2011) describes the efforts of R. J. Reynolds in the late 1980s to expand the target market of the Marlboro brand to include what they dubbed the "virile female." This persona was identified as young, white, possessing a high school diploma or less, liking to party, and "significantly male-identified, into boyfriend and what he is doing," tractor pulls, and hot rod shows (p. 59). Coincidentally, this persona is presented to a T in the form of Gretchen Wilson and her 2004 hit anthem "Redneck Woman," which is meant to represent an authentic portrayal of working-class, rural white females and hard living.

Farmer

Though the identity still maintains ties to rural masculinity and patriarchy, rural women moving away from farmwife to self-identifying as *farmer* is becoming an increasingly common phenomenon, accompanying the growth in the number of women owning and working on farms (Brasier et al., 2014; DeKeseredy et al., 2014; Keller, 2014). The farmer identity represents heterogeneous pathways, from marrying into a family who has farmland to purchasing one's own land as a single woman. Rural women also claim the farmer identity by "explicitly drawing on bodily difference to show that women can get the job done if they have the right knowledge" (p. 92). Jackie, one of the women Keller (2014) interviewed in her study of female farmers, considered herself a mentor and trainer of women, showing them practical skills such as equipment maintenance and strategic use of body strength like removing a fence post with their lower body rather than the upper body as men tend to do.

Misfit

There are rural women who do not tend to fit into the specified gender roles outlined above (though they can claim those labels), usually due to being lesbian, politically liberal/left, feminist, anti-war, vegan/vegetarian, atheist/agnostic, or any range of identities that tend to be seen as oppositional to the patriarchal rural ideology. Yet they maintain deep connections with rurality both as a place and a way of life. Greene's (2007) analysis of the country folk duo the Indigo Girls shows that "that it is possible to deconstruct southern identity and then rebuild it such that it is more inclusive and thus more complex than the old notion of southern identity as essentially conservative, white, male, and Protestant" (p. 171).

Despite the automatic association of sexual minority status with urban settings, LGBTQI people live in every county of the United States, with roughly 64,000 same-sex couples living in rural areas (Boso, 2013, p. 17). Those numbers are likely higher if one includes single people and those who have not disclosed their sexuality. The presence of rural gays and lesbians has prompted Garringer (2013) to begin a nationwide oral history project to gather the experiences of individuals who are re-shaping rural America and who prefer rural spaces to urban ones. Indeed, Boso (2013) points to the many legal and cultural constraints involved when rural LGBTQI individuals relocate to urban locations, leading many to prefer to remain in small towns and communities.

OPENINGS AND POSSIBILITIES

Girls, Guns, and Rods Magazine (2015) is published and written by women, and features advertising by women-owned businesses related to hunting, fishing, and the outdoors. The goals of the magazine include reaching out to an often-neglected demographic of rural women who take the outdoors seriously, and to encourage girls 16 and under to become interested in hunting and fishing, whether for competition or for fun. One meme posted on the magazine's Facebook page shows a young girl holding a fish she has just caught, with the caption "The world needs more pictures of girls holding fish … and fewer pics of them holding cameras in front of bathroom mirrors" as a way to emphasize getting away from the narrow world of vanity and appearance. Many of the authors relate being exposed to the outdoors since the age of three or four and directly socialized into hunting by fathers and other male relatives, and, in some cases, by older female relatives.

Though there are boundary-busting representations of women, including photographs of them dressed in full hunting gear (complete with dirt on their faces for full camouflage) and hunting with their male relatives and other women, such as all-girl alligator or duck hunt retreats, the predominant representations of the women in the magazine are younger, white, able-bodied, slender, and middle class (based on the ability to purchase expensive hunting gear), or come from two-parent, heterosexual households. So though the presence of women in hunting and outdoors sports is refreshing, one gets the sense that if additional boundaries were crossed, such as articles about hunters who are openly lesbian, interviews with members of left/liberal hunting groups, or women opposed to trophy hunting or being too overtly "male" or heavy set in appearance, that their presence wouldn't be as welcomed in this publication. So long as enough males remain in charge of hunting and outdoor sportsman culture and are the primary socializers of women into hunting and fishing, heteronormative, conservative, rural patriarchy remains unharmed.

Self-reliance discourse, present in the magazine's articles, is also intensely ablest, with the unspoken admonition that unless you can take care of yourself, you are somehow a burden on others (Goodley, 2011). This, of course, feeds nicely into an already strong neoliberal, anti-government sentiment which seeks to replace laws and social services with atomized networks of DIY experts. Instead of having laws and policies in place to penalize sexual harassment and domestic violence, the answer is to create more independent-minded, strong rural women who will kick the offending guy in the balls or arm herself for a confrontation. A good ol' gal is supposed to "take care of her own" which means not troubling others when it comes time to take care of business. Anything that goes beyond one's immediate scope of home or family is an intrusion into the community and not acceptable.

The above example illustrates the many contradictions inherent in the identities of rural women. With every instance of working against the norms in rural life, a counter-posed repressive element emerges to restrict the absolute freedom of women; therefore an uncritical celebration of alternative rurality is partial at best. Yet there still remains much potential and possibility in terms of working class female identity when it comes to rural geographies:

> Winding roads slow travel time; driving thirty miles may take an hour, though longer if the traveler gets stuck behind a coal truck. The women would say that the remoteness, which might frustrate a city dweller, is desirable because of the freedom it gives them. They caution against an interpretation that isolation somehow implies a lack of culture or lack of intelligence. (Sohn, 2003, p. 425)

Most of the freedom we associate with the identities of rural women originates in the Old West where the landscape itself and harsh conditions literally ruptured traditional gender roles. Rutter (2005) notes that Western states such as

Utah and Colorado were among the first to grant women the right to vote. Esther Morris became the first justice of the peace in 1870 in Wyoming and Kansas had its first woman mayor in 1887, leading to the election of an all-female council in 1888 (p. 97). As Rutter explains,

> A Western woman's concerns were naturally more practical than theoretical ... Most had killed rattlesnakes off their porches with double-barreled shotguns, patched up gunshot wounds, taken potshots at wolves and coyotes in the chicken coop, battled drought and flood, and read the Bible by candlelight. Shouldering heavy loads and performing important tasks had given Western women a brand of independence other women had not yet enjoy ... these women weren't the sort who sat about passively ... if a situation was getting out of hand—be it rustlers, bandits, drunks, gamblers, or prostitutes—you took care of it. (pp. 95–96)

Thomas' (1989) ethnography of rural women from different regions of the U.S. also found similar accounts of practical know-how and acknowledgement—not romanticization—of hard work. They described the importance of being adaptable and versatile, whether it was women needing to be able to do manual labor or men needing to cook. Thomas found that the women she interviewed would often describe themselves as "tomboys," "mannish" or "daddy's boy" and expressed a definite dislike of "being indoors," i.e. housework.

Since its commercialization and wide distribution in the 1920s, country music has provided another arena for unique ways to be rural and female (Banes, 1992). Loretta Lynn's songs—many of them written by herself—portray a distinct working class, practical woman's point of view. Her music addressed adultery, birth control, women's inequality, and what it was like to be poor (Shipka, 2010). Lynn's career emerged on the scene at the same time as the height of the Great Migration, and she represented many of the disruptions to traditional gender expectations of women during this time. Roba Stanley, an early-era musician, played the banjo and sang about enjoying the single life and having several boyfriends (Banes, 1992). Before extreme commercialization, these early-era female artists directly challenged male control while unapologetically asserting their own authentic life stories. Indeed Lynn's music portrays men as weak and gullible, in need of strong women to fend off competitors, as in her 1968 hit, "Fist City" (Shipka, 2010). Even today, violent retribution at the hands of women shows up in songs like Carrie Underwood's "Before he Cheats" and the Dixie Chicks' "Goodbye Earl."

Despite past practices of researchers to frame rural women's labor through traditional notions of farming as a male-dominated enterprise, in reality women occupy a wide array of roles within agriculture, from operating machinery and caring for animals to accounting and marketing goods (Whatmore, 1988). Sachs (1996) outlines the long, connective history women have had with agriculture and the land (though they own less than 1% of it), which is currently under threat due to climate change, corporate farming, and displacement. In the 1900s South, complex informal networks of regional food distribution were overseen by women, where rural women would bring farm products to markets, selling them to urban housewives (Sharpless, 2012).

The number of principal operators of farms who are women has grown by nearly 50% between 1997 and 2007 (Brasier et al., 2014, p. 284; Keller, 2014, p. 76). In particular, women are an increasing presence in sustainable and organic farming, which is one of the more female-friendly areas of agriculture. Additionally, in the 1970s, groups of women purchased and attempted to run collectives as part of a woman's land movement effort. Eighty of these projects were started by women between 1970 and 1990, most of whom were lesbians, a group not often associated with rural life (Sachs, 1996, p. 51; Valentine, 1997). These examples point to the potentially liberating aspects of rural female identities. As Sachs (1996) puts it, "although patriarchal family structures and cultural traditions tend to confine rural women, their subordination remains incomplete" (p. 6).

BARRIERS AND CONSTRAINTS

Despite the many potentially liberating elements of rurality for women who occupy rural places, there are numerous interacting constraints, pointing to the contradictory nature of female rural identity overall. Economic factors involve rural poverty, lack of access to health care and services, and a changing job market. The rural adherence to agrarianism and attendant lack of class-consciousness, along with the model of self-reliance, constrain women. Rural patriarchy further restricts identities of women, with the enforcement of old boy networks and traditional gender roles. Finally, domestic violence and lack of access to reproductive health services are heighted for rural working-class women because of their geographic isolation and urbanormative legal tendencies.

These constraints are highly interactive. For example, rugged individualism as part of an agrarian ideology more deeply inscribes patriarchal and religious oppression and can make women less likely to seek help if they are being abused. Capitalism can philosophically support agrarianism and individualism with free enterprise rhetoric as wages fall, making women afraid to leave abusive partners. Even though economic factors, agrarianism, rural patriarchy and domestic violence/reproductive restrictions are examined in turn in this section, this by no means suggests that they stand alone. Most of the time these are highly integrated problems that make them more challenging to unpack. As Brown (2013) explains, "both class and gender oppressions must be grasped in their totality and their relation to each other for an adequate understanding of capitalism" (p. 53).

Economic Factors

Despite the media's association of minority groups and urban areas with poverty, rural regions experience higher rates on just about every economic indicator, from income to health, to education. In 2012, the rate of rural poverty stands at 17.1%, higher than the national average of 15% (Housing Assistance Council, 2014, para. 2), though this is likely a conservative representation of actually experienced poverty due to the government's extremely low cutoff levels for household income. Certain regions can also experience poverty more intensely, such as central Appalachia which has a poverty rate of 22.1%, far above the national norm (Lattimer & Oberhauser, 2005, p. 273). Rural poverty tends to be more lasting and harsh in rural regions, due to a combination of geographic isolation, cuts in welfare programs, hostility toward unions, and loss of jobs (Lattimer & Oberhauser, 2005; Norris, 2012). The rural poor also reside in states with smaller budgets and barriers to health care (Lattimer & Oberhauser, 2005).

Mirroring national trends, rural working-class women and children make up the majority of households in poverty (Lattimer & Oberhauser, 2005; Pruitt & Vanegas, 2015; Websdale, 1998). In response to a lack of resources and a cultural climate that is often hostile to seeking outside assistance from government agencies, women have developed intricate informal assistance networks, such as trading childcare with each other, sharing transportation, or material goods (Pruitt, 2007). Shenk and Christiansen (2009) compared the views of older rural women in the United States and Denmark and found that even though they shared a connection to the land and family, Danish women viewed social services as a right that should be available to anyone whereas U.S. rural women saw such assistance as only for the most desperate and vulnerable.

Rural working-class women are also economically impacted by their relationship to property or land. Despite doing most of the labor globally, men "still own the land, control women's labor, and make agricultural decisions in patriarchal social systems" (Sachs, 1996, p. 6). Further, "women's limited access to land is usually defined by their relationships to men, specifically by their husbands' or fathers' ownership or access to land" (p. 45). Exclusion from land ownership has a long history, as when nearly all of the rural black female population and a large portion of rural white women worked as tenant farmers between 1865 and 1940 (p. 50). Currently, as agriculture continues its shift from the family farm model to large, corporate agribusinesses, rural women have not seen their own situations improve. Instead, land ownership falls into the hands of fewer men and is not transferred to women (Lattimer & Oberhauser, 2005).

Gringeri (1993) traces how the erosion of locally owned business networks in rural regions due to the arrival of Wal-Mart and other fast food and retail chains has contributed to the transformation of rural economies from agriculture-based to service and informal sector labor. Rural working-class women are directly impacted by this change as they represent a vulnerable population for low-wage jobs. Gringeri presents the example of industrial homework, a form of local out-sourcing where sets of assembly jobs are portioned out to individual families, like putting sets of bolts together that are then shipped to a larger facility for assembling. Homework jobs have low pay, no security, and no insurance benefits because they don't require the infrastructure of a traditional factory. In some cases, families are required to pre-purchase equipment needed for these jobs. In West Virginia, 20% of households reported participating in informal economic sector jobs, either as a primary source of income or for supplemental income (Lattimer & Oberhauser, 2005, p. 279).

Therefore, working-class rural women face a unique set of economic challenges that are tied to the availability of living-wage jobs, segregation by race and gender (often exacerbated by agribusiness and extractive industries), lower levels of education, geographic isolation, and lack of access to social services. As DeKeseredy, Muzzatti and Donnermeyer (2014) explain, "the withdrawal of meaningful, living wage employment opportunities seriously undermines the life world, moral codes and habitus of ordinary people" (p. 181). When agrarian and patriarchal ideologies are added to the mix, they often reinforce these economic conditions.

Agrarianism

Sachs (1996) outlines the significance of agrarianism as a political ideology that shaped the early United States, with a legacy that continues today. Beginning with Thomas Jefferson's promotion of the family farm and land ownership as a way to "tame" the landless white working class and remove Native Americans from their lands, agrarianism purports a superior way of life through rurality. Women's roles in agrarianism are meant to support the notion that farming and rural living are more moral than city life. Sachs also sees the connection between the emergence of agrarianism and the expectations of middle-class urban women to become experts of the domestic sphere. As a way of tapping into this connection, the dating site Farmersonly.com markets itself on the agrarian notion that rural women have tradi-tional morals and that "city folk just don't get it." Agrarianism works today through the narratives of poverty pride and self-sufficiency, which carries with them mes-sages of anti-solidarity and promotes disdain for the concept of a social safety net.

Poverty Pride

A close cousin to "don't get above your raisin'," poverty pride is an enduring theme in country music, where the working-class is portrayed as more authentic and noble than the wealthy and that poverty is preferable than being rich (Hubbs,

2011; Horn, 2009; Peterson, 1992). Common sentiments of poverty pride include deep minimizing of economic hardship and abusive households: "we were poor but we had each other," "we didn't realize we were poor" "we were beat [spanked] but we still turned out fine" or "folks don't know how to be committed to each other anymore." These are often defensively employed whenever being faced with domestic crises or larger social problems. As with the perpetuation of rural patriarchy described below, poverty pride inadvertently reinforces the ruling class and deflects analysis away from capitalism and onto individuals and the family. It is a complex and insidious form of false consciousness, wrapped in a homey and harmless guise of nostalgia.

Poverty pride functions to erode solidarity among the working class as a solution to ending oppression. As Peterson (1992) explains regarding poverty pride in country music, "a working class identity based on manual labor is celebrated. It is celebrated, however, in a way that invites self-identification with hegemonic forms" (p. 60). As an example, country music is filled with class markers, but they are immediately funneled into individual acts, patriotism, or religion as solutions to social problems. Rather than calling for acts of opposition to the ruling class, poverty pride simply points to one's past poverty and how "they still turned out fine." As a testament to the failure of poverty pride as a social strategy, Peterson presents the example of a meeting between Merle Haggard and Richard Nixon. Commenting on one of Haggard's songs, Nixon praised "just keep on singing songs like that 'Workin' Man Blues,' Merle, and maybe we can get some of these people off their asses" (p. 68).

Self-Sufficiency

As Websdale (1998) maintains, "Notions that people are self-sufficient and survive and thrive because of their own choices and energy are important in rural regions" (p. 99). Self-sufficiency is a powerful narrative that implies weakness on the part of anyone who isn't able to cope using the resources around them. Lest we think that this is unique to rural cultures, Websdale finds similar discourses around domestic violence in general, blaming women for not "choosing" to leave an abusive partner. Applied to women, bootstrapism has devastating effects. Other functions of self-sufficiency include portraying farm life as liberating, as often seen in literature promoting "simple living" or off-gridding. Aside from the ablest discourses that attend these lifestyles, they overlook the inescapable role of women's domestic labor which is made all the more difficult without the assistance of modern technologies.

Self-sufficiency discourse also fits nicely into the neoliberal construct of the privatized family able to bear all costs without relying on the state. In what is framed as an anti-government viewpoint, agrarianism insists on communities "doing it on their own," such as churches providing charity, not the state. For rural working-class women, these attitudes—on top of rural patriarchy and structural economic barriers—can often discourage them from seeking assistance if they are in abusive relationships (Websdale, 1998). The geographic isolation of rural communities can also reinforce the notion that one is on one's own and has to rely on one's own skills to survive. However, in her ethnographic work with farm women, Sachs (1996) found that they were *more* supportive of concepts of state intervention such as child and health care, funding for education, farm relief, and job incentives than the men.

Rural Patriarchy

Rural patriarchy is an active process of socially constructing gender relations through the rural family and the church, linked to capitalist production and influenced by history and class (Sachs, 1996). Within rural communities, traditional family norms in combination with religious networks often work against rural women's abilities to resist in what we might think of as urbanormative feminist ways (large-scale, socially conscious, politically active), leading researchers to conceive of this group as self-sabotaging and choosing victimhood (Sachs, 1996). Yet contesting patriarchy is a far different matter when courts will sentence couples to attend church, for example, "so that they could learn the virtues of the Christian family" as a way to overcome domestic violence (Websdale, 1998, p. 141).

For rural working-class women, the persistent cultural pressure to not "get above your raisin" is taken up a few notches when being female is added to the equation. Not only are rural women not supposed to act like they are better than their family and friends (which can include something as simple as going back to college), they are not supposed to "get above their gender" when it comes to maintaining traditional, heteronormative, binary male/female boundaries. This section addresses specific ways that rural patriarchy establishes barriers to equality for women, often integrating into a woman's own identity and making it appear that she is "choosing" to identify with oppressive ideologies. Women therefore participate in maintaining rural patriarchy through (1) deference (describing their work as "helping" men) and (2) being "one of the boys."

Helping

Bhandari, Bullock, Anderson, Danis, and Sharps (2011) note key differences between urban women and rural women's coping skills. Urban women utilize exercise, meditation, self-talk, and support networks to cope with negative or abusive situations where rural women tend to rely more on self-abnegation like denial or minimizing the situation. As an example of the "helping" dynamic, Sohn (2003) outlines how rural working-class women struggle to maintain a balance between their identities of being a college student while retaining their social connections to their friends and family. Sachs (1996) highlights how viewpoints of women who are in these positions can often be interpellated with rural patriarchal ideology, taking the form of denial, forgetting, repressing memories, or depression, all as a means of disappearing and pushing away their own interests to make room for male identities.

In their ethnographic research with farm women, Thomas (1989) and Sachs (1996) found that they repeatedly referred to their work as "helping," primarily as a means of retaining rural patriarchal roles and enabling spouses to save face. Helping can also take on a class dynamic, with rural working-class women attempting to emulate the persona of the upper-class southern lady with her "decency and good manners," maintaining gender role boundaries, and upholding traditions of family and Christianity (Pompper & Crandall, 2014). Of course, this creates immediate contradictions with the realities of the working-class family under capitalism.

One of the Boys

A second way rural patriarchy is maintained through the actions of women is by direct male identification, a more openly aggressive form of coping than helping. Being "one of the boys" or a female redneck, is another coping strategy that maintains a constant referential discourse to men. As an example, Hubbs (2011) presents the contrast between two country songs, Kitty Wells' "Honky Tonk Angels" and Gretchen Wilson's "Redneck Woman." Wells focuses her critique on men and their role in shaping the wayward woman by their mistreatment of them while Wilson "makes common cause with redneck men and draws on cherished symbols of good ol' boy ideals and prerogatives to articulate its manifesto" (p. 62). Sachs (1996) finds that such identification with patriarchal ideology can often buttress racism, homophobia, and xenophobia rather than ending women's oppression.

For Hubbs (2011), Wilson's "Redneck Woman" "uses self-resourcing techniques and song craft to affirm the distinctiveness and legitimacy of the redneck woman, and does so in solidarity with redneck men," not to assert a separate female identity (p. 46). Horn (2009) finds that while Wilson and the redneck woman persona in general might on the surface appear to be challenging gender norms within country culture, they never fully overturn them. By contrast, country artists such as k.d. lang, an open lesbian with a more androgynous form of presentation, represents a far bigger threat to the rural status quo and patriarchy. As with many rural working-class women, Wilson has to "maintain the paradoxical balance between being a rebel and conforming to the traditional, family-oriented norms of the industry, which shy away from challenging sexual roles" (Horn, 2009, p. 471).

Domestic Violence and Reproductive Restrictions

The context of the patriarchal family looms large for rural working-class women, particularly in the areas of intimate partner violence (IPV) and lack of access to abortion services. Though these remain pressing issues for urban and suburban women, the factor of geographic isolation heightens the risks for rural women. Rates of domestic violence among rural populations can be challenging to measure, because national surveys such as the government's National Intimate Partner and Sexual Violence Survey (NISVS) use zip code to determine location, but doesn't present an urban-rural snapshot of results. Additionally, not all police departments have uniform ways of tracking IPV and it is more likely to go unreported by victims than in urban areas (Intimate Partner Violence in Rural America, 2015). Based on data that is known, nearly 23% of rural women have reported being a victim of IPV, compared to 15.5% for urban areas (p. 3). Bhandari et al. (2011) state that taken together as a group, 40–80% of low-income women experience IPV compared to 25% for the national average (p. 837); an indication that class bears heavily on domestic violence no matter the geographic location. Studies of women in Appalachia have uncovered rates as high as 28% for IPV (physical and sexual abuse) during pregnancy (p. 834).

Notions of women "choosing" to stay or theories of learned helplessness on the part of victims are ineffective enough but are especially urbanormative when applied to rural contexts, where "exiting relationships are significantly more dangerous for rural women than for their urban and suburban counterparts" (DeKeseredy et al., 2014, p. 189). This is even more apparent when children are involved. Rural women who have already separated from a violent relationship are over three times more likely to be raped by their former partner than urban/suburban women (p. 189). Increased levels of gun ownership and ideological notions of masculinity tied to firearm ownership have also placed rural women at greater risk—even though most guns are used for hunting in rural regions, Websdale (1998) found that rural victims of IPV reported firearms being used as a way to intimidate and injure the victim, children, family members and pets, sometimes culminating in murder.

Isolation also perpetuates domestic violence and rural patriarchy, both in terms of geography and psychology. However, at the same time that rural victims of IPV experience isolation geographically, they have a *lack* of privacy when it comes to an abusive partner and his allies. Rural women experience compromised confidentiality because the victim's business is easily known by police, social service agents, her church and family, many of whom know each other or could be related to each other (Bhandari et al., 2011; Websdale, 1998). This often discourages women from reporting abuse.

Access to reproductive health services is another significant barrier facing rural working-class women. Currently, there are only 739 remaining abortion clinics in the U.S., the majority located in urban areas (Johnston, 2015, para. 2). Recent laws against abortion, such as the requirement that clinics have hospital-level infrastructure in order to provide abortion services, end up impacting smaller, rural clinics the most, as in Texas, which only has 7 remaining clinics, all in urban areas (Bassett, 2014, para. 1). For women who *do* decide to have children, even they are faced with an increase in the number of rural hospitals that are closing their maternity wards, leaving the nearly half a million women who give birth annually in these facilities having to drive to urban areas to receive care (Andrews, 2016). Left without options, an increasing number of working-class rural women are resorting to desperate means to end a pregnancy, such as in Texas where between 100,000 to 240,000 women have attempted to self-induce an abortion (Levintova, 2015). All of this takes place within the larger context of consolidation of health care facilities as more hospitals close and merge (Dafney, 2014).

Pruitt and Vanegas (2015) assert that current abortion regulations have the most significant effects on rural working-class and poor women who live longer distances from abortion providers and should therefore be declared unconstitutional. The language of these restrictions on abortion indicate that an undue burden hasn't been sufficiently established, as in claiming that rural women can always commute to a larger, urban hospital that meets the regulations, thereby applying an urbanormative set of standards to the realities of rural working-class women. The inadequacy of undue burden as a standard applied to rural women also emerges with pharmacists who opt out for religious reasons of filling contraceptive prescriptions. In urban areas, women could travel to another facility, but less populated areas may only have one place to obtain medicine.

CONCLUSION

This chapter has presented some of the complexities surrounding rural working-class women and the shaping of their identities. First, it has established that concepts of rurality are challenging to define and sociological concepts are not always standardized, making data about rural working-class hard to find. Second, rural, working-class women are more demographically varied than once thought, though they may have several factors in common.

Third, there is a need to challenge the urbanormative nature of research and law when it comes to inquiry about rural women. While urban and suburban working-class women might have closer access to social services, rural women face geographic and cultural isolation. Finally, concepts of socialist feminism are needed to situate our dialectical understanding of rural working-class women, both historically and currently. Experiencing a combination of economic constraints—exacerbated by geography—and the ideologies of rural patriarchy and agrarianism, rural working-class women are part of the proletariat. Their liberation, like the liberation of the working-class as a whole, will only happen with the abolition of capitalism:

One half of humanity will always be responsible for childbirth, but this does not imply an inevitable inequality between men and women. Women are not an absolute other that exist only in nature and outside of the social sphere. Instead, for humanity to reach its full potential, this biological factor must be superseded. A new unity between humanity and nature must be reached [and] is only possible if the gender-inequalities stemming from social organization are overcome. (Brown, 2013, pp. 30–31)

REFERENCES

Andrews, M. (2016, February 24). More rural hospitals are closing their maternity units. *Shots: Health News from NPR*. Retrieved from http://www.npr.org/sections/health-shots/2016/02/24/467848568/more-rural-hospitals-are-closing-their-maternity-units?utm_medium=RSS&utm_campaign=news

Bageant, J. (2010). *Rainbow pie: A redneck memoir*. Victoria, Australia: Scribe Publications.

Banes, R. (1992). Dixie's daughters: The country music female. In M. McLauren & R. Peterson (Eds.), *You wrote my life: Lyrical themes in country music* (pp. 81–112). Langhorne, PA: Gordon & Breach Publishers.

Bassett, L. (2014, October 3). Situation in Texas is 'urgent' after 13 abortion clinics close overnight. *Huffington Post*. Retrieved from http://www.huffingtonpost.com/2014/10/03/texas-abortion-clinics_n_5927698.html

Bhandari, S., Bullock, L., Anderson, K., Danis, F., & Sharps, P. (2011). Pregnancy and intimate partner violence: How do rural, low-income women cope? *Health Care for Women International, 32*, 833–854.

Boso, L. (2013, February). Urban bias, rural sexual minorities, and courts' role in addressing discrimination. *UCLA Law Review*. Retrieved from: http://williamsinstitute.law.ucla.edu/wp-content/uploads/Boso-Urban-Bias-Rural-Sexual-Minorities-05.09.12.pdf

Brasier, K., Sachs, C., Kiernan, N., Trauger, A., & Barbercheck, M. (2014). Capturing the multiple and shifting identities of farm women in the northeastern United States. *Rural Sociology, 79*(3), 283–309.

Brown, H. (2013). *Marx on gender and the family: A critical study*. Chicago, IL: Haymarket Books.

Cloke, P., & Little, J. (Eds.). (1997). *Contested countryside cultures: Otherness, marginalization, and rurality*. New York, NY: Routledge.

Cobb, J. C. (1992). From Rocky Top to Detroit City: Country music and the economic transformation of the South. In M. McLauren & R. Peterson (Eds.), *You wrote my life: Lyrical themes in country music* (pp. 63–79). Langhorne, PA: Gordon & Breach Publishers.

Coleman, A. (2010). Rehabilitating the region: The New Deal, gender, and the remaking of the rural south. *Southeastern Geographer, 50*(2), 200–217.

Dafney, L. (2014, January 16). Hospital industry consolidation—still more to come? *New England Journal of Medicine*, DOI: 10.1056/NEJMp1313948. Retrieved from: http://www.nejm.org/doi/full/10.1056/NEJMp1313948

D'Antonio-Del Rio, J., Douchet, J., & Chauvin, C. (2010). Violent and vindictive women: A re-analysis of the southern subculture of violence. *Sociological Spectrum, 30*, 484–503.

Defining Rural Population. (n.d.). *Federal office of rural health policy*. Retrieved from http://www.hrsa.gov/ruralhealth/aboutus/definition.html

DeKeseredy, W., Muzzatti, S., & Donnermeyer, J. (2014). Mad men in bib overalls: Media's horrification and pornification of rural culture. *Critical Criminology, 22*, 179–197.

Eichenlaub, S., Tolnay, S., & Alexander, J. T. (2010, February). Moving out but not up: Economic outcomes in the great migration. *American Sociological Review, 75*(1), 101–125.

Garringer, R. (2013, July). *About.* Retrieved from: https://countryqueers.com/about/

Girls, Guns, and Rods Magazine. (2015, January/February). *Introductory Issue.* Retrieved from: http://viewer.epageview.com/Viewer.aspx?docid=a6b31d77-9c4f-4458-8517-a41a00dc3bd8

Goodley, D. (2011). *Disability studies: An interdisciplinary introduction.* Thousand Oaks, CA: Sage Publications.

Greene, K. (2007). Southern misfits: Politics, religion, and identity in the music of the Indigo Girls. *The Southern Quarterly, 44*(4), 155–174.

Gringeri, C. (1993). Inscribing gender in rural development: Industrial homework in two Midwestern communities. *Rural Sociology, 58*(1), 30–52.

Hardesty, C., & Bokemeier, J. (1989, February). Finding time and making do: Distribution of household labor in nonmetropolitan marriages. *Journal of Marriage & the Family, 51*, 253–267.

Herring, S. (2010). *Another country: Queer anti-urbanism.* New York, NY: New York University Press.

Horn, A. (2009, October). "Keepin' it country": What makes the lyrics of Gretchen Wilson hard? *Popular Music & Society, 32*(4), 461–473.

Housing Assistance Council. (2014, September 16). *Rural poverty decreases, yet remains higher than the U.S. poverty rate.* Retrieved from http://www.ruralhome.org/sct-information/mn-hac-research/rrn/990-official-poverty-rate-2014

Hubbs, N. (2011, Winter). "Redneck woman" and the gendered poetics of class rebellion. *Southern Cultures*, 44–70.

Intimate Partner Violence in Rural America. (2015, March). *National Advisory Committee on Rural Health and Human Services.* Retrieved from: http://www.hrsa.gov/advisorycommittees/rural/publications/partnerviolencemarch2015.pdf

Johnston, A. (2015, January 2). The number of abortion clinics in the United States gets lower every single year. *Bustle.* Retrieved from: http://www.bustle.com/articles/56149-the-number-of-abortion-clinics-in-the-united-states-gets-lower-every-single-year

Keller, J. (2014). "I wanna have my own damn dairy farm!": Women farmers, legibility, and femininities in rural Wisconsin, US. *Journal of Rural Social Sciences, 29*(1), 75–102.

Lattimer, M., & Oberhauser, A. (2005). Exploring gender and economic development in Appalachia. *Journal of Appalachian Studies, 10*(3), 269–292.

Levintova, H. (2015, November 17). Up to 240,000 women have tried to give themselves abortions in Texas. *Mother Jones.* Retrieved from: http://www.motherjones.com/politics/2015/11/thousands-texas-women-are-trying-self-induce-abortions

Linkon, S., Peckham, I., & Lanier-Nabors, B. (2004, November). Struggling with class in English studies. *College English, 67*(2), 149–153.

Norris, A. (2012). Rural women, anti-poverty strategies, and black feminist thought. *Sociological Spectrum, 32*, 449–461.

Peterson, R. (1992). Class unconsciousness in country music. In M. McLauren & R. Peterson (Eds.), *You wrote my life: Lyrical themes in country music* (pp. 35–62). Langhorne, PA: Gordon & Breach Publishers.

Pompper, D., & Crandall, K. (2014). The erotic-chaste dialectic and the new southern belle code at the high school prom: Feminine gender role stress across ethnic and socio-economic factors. *The Journal of Popular Culture, 47*(5), 937–951.

Pruitt, L. (2007). Toward a feminist theory of the rural. *Utah Law Review, 2*, 421–488.

Pruitt, L., & Vanegas, M. (2015, Winter). Urbanormativity, spatial privilege, and judicial blind spots in abortion law. *Berkeley Journal of Gender, Law & Justice, 30*(1), 76–153.

Reynolds, W. (Ed.). (2014). *Critical studies of Southern place: A reader*. New York, NY: Peter Lang Publishing.

Rutter, M. (2005). *Upstairs girls: Prostitution in the American West*. Helena, MT: Farcountry Press.

Sachs, C. (1996). *Gendered fields: Rural women, agriculture, and environment*. Boulder, CO: Westview Press.

Sharpless, R. (2012, Summer). "She ought to have taken those cakes": Southern women and rural food supplies. *Southern Cultures, 18*(2), 45–58.

Shenk, D., & Christiansen, K. (2009). *Social support systems of rural older women: A comparison of the United States and Denmark*. Retrieved from http://faculty.usfsp.edu/jsokolov/webbook/shenk.pdf

Shipka, D. (2010). Loretta Lynn: Writin' life. *The Online Journal of Rural Research and Policy, 5*(4), 1–15.

Sohn, K. (2003, February). Whistlin' and crowin' women of Appalachia: Literacy practices since college. *College Composition & Communication, 54*(3), 423–452.

Thomas, A. (2011). *Critical rural theory: Structure, space, culture*. Lanham, MD: Lexington Books.

Thomas, S. (1989). *We didn't have much but we sure had plenty: Rural women in their own words*. New York, NY: Anchor Books.

Valentine, G. (1997). Making space: Lesbian separatist communities in the United States. In P. Cloke & J. Little (Eds.), *Contested countryside cultures: Otherness, marginalization, and rurality* (pp. 109–122). New York, NY: Routledge.

Vogel, L. (2013). *Marxism and the oppression of women: Toward a unitary theory*. Chicago, IL: Haymarket Books.

Websdale, N. (1998). *Rural women battering and the justice system: An ethnography*. Thousand Oaks, CA: Sage.

Whatmore, S. (1988). From women's roles to gender relations: Developing perspectives in the analysis of farm women. *Sociologica Ruralis, 28*(4), 239–247.

CHAPTER NINE

Rural Spaces OF Longing AND Protest

TODD ALAN PRICE

RE-CONCEPTUALIZING PLACE AND IDENTITY THROUGH STRUGGLE: VIDEO CURRICULUM

During my time spent attending the University of Wisconsin-Madison, Curriculum and Instruction coursework included most significantly *Introduction to Video Production* (1990) co-taught by feminist post-structural scholar Mimi Orner and political activist Ahmad Sultan and *Teaching Film in the Classroom* (1991) led by critical postmodern educator, Elizabeth Ellsworth. Video screenings—along with readings, including *The ideology of images in educational media* (Ellsworth & Whatley, 1990)—would soon follow. The collective works of these excellent scholars imparted upon me many useful lessons, none more powerful than the idea(s) that moving images work as texts, no less so than the printed words in K-12 student's school books. Furthermore, texts are "aimed" at the center, marginalizing those on the periphery and providing rich insight into power; video and film reels in education and elsewhere, presented as *neutral* [author's italics], are in the obverse *contested sites* [author's italics] for interpretation, representation, ideology and power. I was impressed that courses and lessons such as these could be embedded in what appeared to me (remains so today) to be the otherwise conservative discipline of teacher education. My imagination was stirred by the potential uses of "non-static" media for social change. Video and film *in* education and *for* education, especially interviews and observation to produce the documentary form, became part of my undertaking and helped to form me. In sum, these formative curriculum theory experiences using video unsettled and extended my understanding of the conditional, situational and temporal features of place and identity.

This was a heady time for curriculum theorists and activists alike. My colleagues and I cut our teeth in protest of the "first" Persian Gulf War, *Desert Storm*, a conflagration that—while emergent in the early 1990s to much accolade—was confronted by a growing student, labor, environmental, and community action coalition in response. I recall, without irony, that this particular conflagration was accurately by my estimation, if not popularly, deemed to be the first video game war (Baudrillard, 1994).

I was encouraged early on by Mimi Orner to edit my small collection of video footage—assembled during my time as a Louisiana State University teaching assistant/lecturer traveling first to Nicaragua as an unofficial electoral process observer, and later to Cuba as a Literacy Campaign researcher. Over the years ahead I would produce work much as a freelance journalist.

My newfound interest was ultimately engaged through community access television. Therein an education director Cindy Coloni helped me to acquire the skills and the know-how to edit, title, and disseminate the (at the time) analog information into a crafted format, discernible for an audience' reception and interpretation. Video production became the means to an end, for "telling the story" of these collective social protest movements and showing (literally, on television) the results. Furthermore, I found video to be an essential tool for conducting educational research. Most significantly, however, my identity/our collective identities were formed in opposition to the stifling, political culture of imperialism. We targeted the university itself.

Subsequently, I became immersed in a literal video network with other videographers, artists, and activists who also found the means of capturing footage, representing themes, and playing with ideas for telling their own story ... to be compelling. I never lost sight of, due to my Curriculum Theory lessons in rural University of Wisconsin-Stout with Bill Reynolds, that *the world is a text* and "curricular texts" as Ellsworth was to impress ... are open to interpretation. Indeed, I/we were texts on which video and social struggle were inscribed.

DNR Where Are You?

On a warm summer day, I joined my colleague and video production companion Luciano and together we traveled to Lady Smith, Wisconsin, site of the Northern Woods mining struggle. This remote area in Rusk County was the stage on which various actors performed a drama between rural citizens concerned with saving their Flambeau River and operatives from the mining construction company Kennecott Rio Tinto Zinc. A London-based firm that sought precious metals, Kennecott's goal was to extract the ore by all costs. A small assembly of environmental activists resolved to challenge them. Thus, with VHS-C camera and tapes in tow—similar to the equipment I had used on a first video journey into Leon, Nicaragua—Luciano, myself and the activists gathered at a county park. One of the party, John LaForge of *Nukewatch*, led the group in a solemn ceremony. Afterward the group traveled down the road to the driveway entrance of the proposed mine. They resolved to put their bodies on the line and "take back the site."

Documented in the massive volume *The Buzzards Have Landed! The Real Story of the Flambeau Mine,* longtime, dedicated citizen activist Roscoe Churchill recounts—with the aid of his erstwhile ally and friend Laura Furtman—the fifty-year struggle against multinational mining interests. My small role in this effort came at the battle pitch wherein civil disobedience began. Luciano and I aspired to video record a portion of that struggle, the protests that would grow after the commencement of construction on the site. Extraction of the hoped-for precious metals of copper and zinc would be precariously close to—really within a stone's throw—the pristine Flambeau river, a precious tributary to the Chippewa river. This was the repository for the region's fresh water, what Roscoe called "liquid gold."

Churchill took copious notes along his long life in stubborn resistance, and Evelyn, his lifelong partner, wife, and "pal" collected and stored the newspaper articles, political letters to officials, natural studies, and general correspondences in this back and forth battle against the mining company. This enigmatic, deep ecology story of northern Wisconsin is meticulously described by Secretary of State Douglas La Follette (cousin of "Fighting Bob" La Follette, the archetypical champion of the "Progressive Era Movement") in a 1975 meeting with Roscoe. Secretary La Follette supports and encourages Roscoe to continue the local, grassroots movement needed to prevent the mining company's efforts at securing the land and the water:

> Some years ago, after I (Secretary La Follette) finished giving a talk in Milwaukee, a tall, thin fellow came up to me and said that he and his neighbors in the Town of Grant in Rusk County needed my help … I learned that this fired-up and rather colorful individual was an elementary school principal who had been raised on a farm close to where a giant corporation had discovered copper and gold. Little did I know that he, with his quiet unassuming wife Evelyn, were to become central figures in rallying their community and people across the state to say "No" to the development of the Flambeau Mine. (Churchill & Furtman, 2007 p. ix)

Several years later, we turn up at a critical turning point in the protest. Fast forward to this quiet struggle on that warm Summer day, as Churchill reports:

> When the protesters arrived at the mine site on July 10, 1991, the mining company was just starting to clear brush and put up a fence around its property. So what my friends decided to do was symbolically stop the fence from going up. There was no pushing or shoving

or yelling. Instead the protesters sat down wherever the next post hole was to be dug and quietly talked to the workers about why the fence shouldn't be built. (Churchill & Furtman, 2007, p. 529)

But as Roscoe was to say "there is a lot more to the story."

> Two reporters from a cable broadcast station, WYOU Community Television, Inc. of Madison, Wisconsin, had come to the mine site to videotape the demonstration, and they were still there when the sheriff arrived. The reporters, Todd Price and his friend who goes by the single name of Luciano, tried to continue filming as the arrests were made. But for some unknown reason, one of the deputies decided to interrupt them and ask for press credentials. And even though Price told the deputy that he and Luciano were producing a documentary for television, moments later Sheriff Meyer demanded that the two reporters surrender their tapes! (Churchill & Furtman, 2007, pp. 530–531)

The entire episode (which included our successful lawsuit in suing the Sheriff's office) is documented in video and in another excellent book, *The new resource wars: native and environmental struggles against multinational corporations* by Gedicks & LaDuke, (1993). It remains to this day a formative experience, guiding my understanding of nature as the last frontier and final resource, and the plight of environmentalists who are the last ones left standing in the face of global pillage and conquest … telling their story provides me with hope for the future of our environment.

Blue Jeans Nation

In the years following this formative experience, austerity was placed on rural areas. Especially devastating to the rural school districts were measures including the Qualified Economic Offer (QEO) and the freeze on local school board spending, or revenue caps, as succinctly described here:

> In 1993, the State increased its share of funding for public schools from 40% to 66%. In exchange for significantly increasing the dollars available for public schools, the legislature capped the ability of local school boards to raise revenue. The legislature created a formula, tied to per pupil expenditure, which has allowed spending to grow at a state-wide average of about 2.5% annually. The QEO was enacted simultaneously to permit school boards to control the largest piece of their budgets, teacher compensation (approximately 80% of a district's budget). (Najita & Stern, 2001)

To provide a broader picture of what measures such as these have done to rural communities, I opted to interview Mike McCabe a seasoned analyst and advocate for good government in the state of Wisconsin. His insight was that there were several lost opportunities to be rediscovered in rural locations.

Price: So let's outline broadly the *Blue Jean Nation* and the political problems you address, especially in relation to the rural community(s):

McCabe: Well what I've found is that there are just a large group of people—in fact I think it's the biggest single block of voters in America—who are feeling politically homeless. They don't feel as though either major party is working for them. And I think that those feelings are especially strong in rural areas. There is a tremendous amount of alienation that people are feeling, they don't feel that their community interests are being served, they don't feel their voices are being heard, they don't believe they're being represented. And they've grown estranged from both major parties but I think almost by default they've chosen to typically vote for the Republican Party because the Republican Party has marketed itself as the party of limited government. And they figure if government's not going to work for them then they'll just try to keep it as small as possible and keep their taxes as low as possible.

Price: Let's talk specifically about rural education. What do you see are some of the major challenges in relationship to the budget and the politics for rural K-12 schools? Do you see these as similar or different from those faced by urban and suburban K-12 school districts?

McCabe: I think the problems are actually more acute for rural school systems: the way school-funding works in Wisconsin has always put areas that are suburban and some of the urban areas in a better financing position than rural districts. The loss of school aid has really hit rural school systems particularly hard, the revenue controls and limits that have been put on local school district budgets have certainly pinched and sometimes severely pinched urban school budgets, but those school systems are much larger, they operate on a much larger scale. If you have to lay off a few teachers you may increase some class sizes you may hurt the quality of the program in an urban school district, but if you have to lay off a few teachers in a rural school system, that might mean ending a program altogether. And eventually when a rural school system's budget gets pinched as we've seen in Wisconsin, sometimes it even threatens the existence of a school or even the continued existence of the school district. So we've seen these consolidations of school districts so students are traveling much farther to get to school in some far away neighboring community and you've seen the loss of rural schools where those schools are no longer viable. They can't even afford to operate them. So the revenue controls and budget limits that have been put into place in Wisconsin have certainly hurt urban schools but because those schools operate on a much larger scale they're not vulnerable to closure the way that you see in rural areas.

McCabe: You know, I think the other thing that is not taken into account by our school funding formula is the geographic size of rural school districts. There aren't a lot of students, but those students come from a really large geographical area. So there are much higher transportation costs and if the funding formula doesn't permit for the continuation of all those buses running on all of those routes and allow them to meet those transportation expenses ... if they can't do that then they've got to take it out of programs, they've got to take it from somewhere else in their budget and that's where you end up facing a situation where a local school might have to consider whether it can even exist. And we're seeing all across the state ... we're seeing some rural schools just close. So yeah there is a problem in urban school districts for sure as their programs are being hurt, but you don't typically see an urban school close altogether and you see it commonly out in rural areas.

Price: Now let's turn to the University of Wisconsin system with things emerging even in the last several weeks. How are rural communities served by extension and cooperative systems, how are they faring? It seems there's these new cuts being considered, enacted with staff reductions, sharing of personnel ... all these things are on the table. What do you make of this and how does this bode for the future [of] higher education in rural areas?

McCabe: Well you know Wisconsin had the Wisconsin Idea for many years. Central to that Wisconsin Idea was that the boundary of the university should be the boundary of the state that the university system should push out into every nook and cranny of the state of Wisconsin. Its reach should be the entirety of the state. In recent years we've seen hundreds of millions of dollars in cuts to the university's budget. We've seen similar budgetary constraints for the vocational technical school system and other elements of the higher education system. And what that ends up doing is that it means there's greater likelihood that the university and other higher education institutions will become more centralized that there will be fewer campuses or fewer satellites. There will be less ability to reach out into the more remote rural areas and basically the message that they'll have to send is that "you're going to have to come to us, we're not going to be able to come to you."

McCabe continued: You know one of the fundamental fears of people in rural communities is if they, if their children go off to college, if they go off to a vocational technical school they might never come back. If they leave and go a couple hundred miles away to one of the bigger cities in Wisconsin, they'll never return to that small, rural town ... and [what] we're seeing is a significant brain drain, and what were really seeing is the loss of youth in a lot of these rural communities. The older generations are still there, the younger generations are vanishing. Well that's deadly to those rural communities; they're literally losing their lifeblood. Well one of the things that could help remedy that is if vocational training, higher education could be closer to those rural communities, if those institutions could go out to the people in rural areas rather than simply telling those people "you've got to come to us" that would be comforting to parents and grandparents in those rural communities who are

	afraid of losing their children and grandchildren. But it also would have a beneficial economic impact in those rural communities and help them thrive.
McCabe continued:	Everything that's happened in higher education has actually worked against the interests of rural communities. And that's something Wisconsin's going to have to come to terms with. We've got some dying rural communities, and the policies that have been put in place, educational policies are actually threatening the wellbeing of those communities, actually leading to the death of those rural communities instead of helping them to thrive.
Price:	That a very disturbing cultural trend … do you have any words to say in wrapping up?
McCabe:	I think in general we've just got to come to terms with the fact that you either invest in success or you pay for failure. You know there's a cost associated with not investing in rural communities, and not investing in education, whether its rural education or urban education. You end up with problems on the other end. Where you're dealing with intractable poverty, you're dealing with dying communities; you're dealing with trying to repair damage that's done because you didn't invest in success. That's an ethic that we need to rediscover here in Wisconsin and really across the country; we've got to do more investing in success rather than putting ourselves in a position of forever paying for failure.

Wisconsin Rural Schools Alliance

Among the other formative, rural voices, concerned with investing in and sustaining rural communities, is Kim Kaukl, executive director for the *Wisconsin Rural Schools Alliance*. Of the three interviews, Kaukl's was the most nuanced, and while he no doubt shared concerns about the policies and impacts that were hurting local, rural schools, he did find hope that returning to the local meant that the local was being forced to step up, or at least that appeared to be his hope. His interview follows:

Price:	So how have rural citizens both as a group or individually responded to the budget cuts and the consolidations?
Kaukl:	I think the biggest thing is you know it has been a real shock to the system, from the standpoint that with the continued cuts you've seen many rural schools either having to close buildings—outlying buildings—which means more bussing, you know in many cases for elementary kids because a lot of times that's where you kind of keep your large rural districts you kind of keep your [elementary schools] closer to your base of constituents and then everybody kind of comes together [in] middle school/high school in one location but so the little kids

aren't on the buses as much. Well it is getting to the point where it is hard to keep those outlying buildings open and duplicating services you know with custodians, secretaries, some of your special need areas like art and music, so that's one issue that's taken place and its caused, it has become very contentious ... it really causes some hard feelings amongst people. Even though when you look at the fiscal reality it is probably the best approach to take. But you know people are very tied to their local schools.

Kaukl continued: I think other areas that you've seen are cuts to some pretty ... strong areas for a well-rounded student and that usually comes in the areas of art, music, and some of your technology education, and business education areas. Those seem to be getting cut back further and further. To the point where it's just going to be the core subjects, unfortunately. But I would say on the positive side of things, many districts are operating through local support through referendums, operational referendums. Up in Northland Pines up around Eagle River in that area, they're going to referendum about every two to three years just for operational expenses and the local folks are supporting that. It's that local decision making.

Price: How do these rural families understand these challenges to the school funding?

Kaukl: They're getting out to support the referendum. But there's also the concern of the rising property taxes too ... the funding formula is so complicated. Even for people in education sometimes it's difficult to understand. And for the layperson out there trying to explain it sometimes, its head scratching ... the whole idea of vouchers many of the rural people don't think the vouchers are impacting them because they don't have voucher schools. And trying to explain to them the roundabout way that it will impact them by the shrinking of the pot of money that's out there, and try to get that word out. The other piece to that is when we explain to them ... that 1.6% of their property tax dollars were leaving their school district to go support an independent charter school in the urban areas. And that gets people rather riled up.

Price: So to paraphrase, you are saying—what otherwise appear to be urban reforms—vouchers, charters, are impacting their own pocketbook? Their own school system?

Kaukl: Correct. And try to get them to understand that you know right now at the rate things are going we're trying to fund two educational systems from one pot of money.

Price: Problems associated with public education in Wisconsin, [have] largely in the public imagination been exclusively almost confined to inner city, public schools ... something like, "well we've been pouring all this money into urban schools i.e. Milwaukee and we haven't seen demonstrably impacts coming out." Have you seen in your coffee shop conversations where people gather, any changes in that thinking?

Kaukl: I think that … we've been passing a lot of things for the inner city the urban/suburban areas without looking at the bigger picture, because one size doesn't fit all. And some of the things that are happening in the urban/suburban areas by making a law to help them, really has a negative impact on how we operate out in the rural areas. It takes some flexibility, and it ends up taking some flexibility away from the rural areas on how they operate and try to maintain quality programs. That's probably been the biggest frustration and as a retired principal myself it was like I understood why the law was made for the urban/suburban but they made it this one size fits all and it has this negative impact on the rural schools and ends up harming us instead of helping us. Where it helps maybe the urban/suburban but it harms the rural schools.

Price: That's a great insight. Could you give me an example or two about that just specifically that insight you had where a law that's set up to impact urban schools all of a sudden has unintended consequences for a rural setting?

Kaukl: I think the one that I see probably the most recent one is this referendum bill. Where it doesn't seem that the urban/suburban need to go to referendum as often because of their operating budgets are ready. But out in the rural areas just because our budgets are so small and with the revenue caps the way they are, that's a real example there, where we do need that [referendum] and we need that local support. And you know with Act 10 when they were taking all this money away from education they said well we're going to leave it up to local control so you can go to referendum. Well now they're kind of going back on that word and saying "no we don't want you to go to referendum now" because of property tax, so that would be one example I would say there. What we're seeing out in the rural areas are people are supportive of education and if we can show them that this is for operating and this is why, they're more than willing to support that even though it might cost them a little more in property tax because they want good quality schools.

Price: One thing I was curious about was with relation to teachers and what flexibility school districts have to hire the teachers they need. One consequence it appears that in Wisconsin the standards [for teachers] have been dropped/lowered for who can become a teacher. But at the same time rural schools need to use who they have, and they [the prospective teacher] might have some expertise in some other ways. I'm sure you are familiar with that.

Kaukl: I mean those are some of the things we've been dealing with you know making sure that the licensure is up to standards. And I know the last year [2015] there was a law passed for people in technical education and now they're [the state legislature] trying to expand that to all of the career technical education courses that are out there. There's a shortage but I'm not sure weakening license is the way to go. I think there are enough ways to go about it out there that you can find people, get them trained under an emergency licensure, to get to the point where they have all the quality things they need, and to keep education professional. The latest one—and here again, urban versus rural—is a large group of southeast superintendents came forward with this whole bill that they could train these folks if they had a bachelor's degree; they would train them and then put them in the classroom. While there again, urban/suburban have those resources, they have those extra layers in their central office to train people. Out in rural areas we don't have that. And my concern with that—and I voiced my concern—was "so you're in suburban school A" and they train you to be a business ed. teacher using their criteria. With that criteria now you become a fully licensed teacher. Ok, if this is what they're trying to do—it hasn't come to fruition yet, and I think there's going to be some major changes to it. But so you work at suburban school A for three years now you've got your full teacher's license, you can basically go anyplace but not have the same criteria that the other teachers in some of the other districts have had. So the last of them I heard of this whole piece was that you would only be certified in that one school district, that it wouldn't become transferable. But I think there again, I had to do it a couple of times in my career, there is plenty of opportunities out there to get these people licensed the appropriate way, without a lot of extra work and headaches if you just know the right resources, go to and use. And that was one of the things we offered at our conference this year. UW Oshkosh has a great flexible, extended license program, and they're really easy to work with, where you have to be on site take all of the classes, maybe a couple of weekends, things like that, and a lot of work on your own, and working in your school district. I think opportunities are there, and my goal has always been—unfortunately since Act 10— education hasn't been looked at as a profession, as professional as it was in the past, and it is not a destination a lot of people want to go into. By lessoning the standards to me that just makes us look worse. I think there are better ways to go about this and one of the things, one of our member schools out in Washington and along with second member schools is a program called *Teachers Rising*. It's kind of a teacher's version of FBLA, the *Future Business Leaders of America*, *Teachers Rising* is kind of the same thing, it's where we're taking young kids that are interested in teaching and working with them to get them in the classroom to work with teachers and get them really interested in the teaching profession. And eventually we're hoping it gets certification or recognition for them at the state level where they can transfer some stuff into the universities. It's just in its infancy right now, but to me that's a great way to continue to start growing our education program.

Price: Young talent too, right?

Kaukl: Yep, you hope, you know especially out in the rural area, you hope that you train them and they'll come back and work for you.

Kaukl
continued:
And I think the other piece that gets overlooked sometimes is and its starting to raise its head a little bit—people are starting to talk about it more you know since Act 10—with Act 10 it was supposed to save districts money, you know, when it comes to hiring teachers, and really what it has started to do its caused quite [a lot of] angst between districts. I lost two of my better teachers to two larger suburban districts because they could pay them more and give them better benefits. I couldn't offer the same amount.

Price:
That's a very interesting anecdote. We'd be remiss if we didn't talk about students and families in these rural communities. Without generalizing, and I'm including myself here, I'm imagining that there are some commonalities between what rural families face or deal with in trying to get their students, their kids educated, and their might be differences, because of changing demographics. What can you help me with here in terms of understanding how are students and their families facing similar challenges or different challenges?

Kaukl:
You know I think the biggest thing is making sure families understand the importance of education right now. And when we're talking post-secondary it's not always four year; it's four year and technical training. And you get out into some of the rural areas and you know a lot of the folks out there maybe all they do have is a high school education because they've gone into a family business or the work is staying on the farm, you know working and haven't really seen the expansion of what could happen if they go on to post-secondary. But I would also say with the post-secondary side too, you know even running a family farm anymore, if you don't go on to some post-secondary, the two-year accelerated ag program that UW offers or some courses at the technical school, it's hard to run a family farm without that background and training because everything is so high tech now. And it's getting that understanding. It's kind of like, you know, back 8 or 9 years ago what kids wanted to become is auto mechanics. And getting them to understand that auto mechanics wasn't just turning wrenches anymore; you have to have that computer and technology background, because everything has become so high tech. And I think we've gotten past that where they do understand that now. So the way it was ten, twenty years ago is a lot different and it is going to continue to be different. And I think the biggest piece is that we are living in a global society. Thinking outside your community and outside Wisconsin is a tough sell sometimes to folks and they don't always want to hear it either. So those are the biggest things, and when you go out and talk to folks in rural areas, I don't care what it is they want to make sure their kids are getting the best education in the area of their interest. Make sure the programs are there.

In sum, Kaukl's interview helps in reconceptualizing the curriculum in relation to rural, urban and suburban places and identities and poses a symbolic challenge for curricularists but a pragmatic one too. Contestations over power and practice amidst these troubled spaces in rural areas will also provide important lessons. Protests over who controls rural spaces, as well as urban and suburban spaces, will continue to emerge, however, as privatization of the commons continues.

No Vouchers Coalition

The *Milwaukee Parental Choice Program* (MPCP), now a quarter of a century old, was understood by 2007 to be failing. Yet the idea would make a triumphant and figurative re-turn several years later (Price, 2013; Price & Wittkopf, 2014). Ironically, the political aspiration appears to expand "choice" options to otherwise wealthy families whose children already attend private schools. Initially the program was intended to serve only low SES families; now with the launch of the *Wisconsin Parental Choice Program* (WPCP) the intention is to draw into the pool of potential voucher recipients, rural citizens. This paradoxically replays the scenario from the 1950s when vouchers were first employed in Southern states like Virginia to re-segregate public schools.

Pam Kobielus describes having returned to her childhood home to care for her elderly mother, and along the way becoming engaged in the battle against vouchers:

Kobielus: I graduated from Merrill Public High School in 1972, so I'm dating myself her now. I'm almost 62 years old, and when I returned to my hometown I happened to just in passing read an article, a short blurb in our local paper about the school board meeting to discuss declines in the budget and how they were going to address it, and they were considering cutting music classes. And having gone through the high school and enjoyed all the wide variety of courses that were available, I knew how important it was for the rural kids to have an exposure to not only the fundamentals of education but music, art, debate, athletics, all of these things that make a person well rounded and able to enter the workforce and work well with others. I had seen in private business where I spent my career the importance of having individuals who had a good solid education, who are able to think critically, and to be able to work well with others and seem to be able to contribute to private business. So I was a little concerned … I had read they were considering cutting music education and that concerned me a bit because having worked in private industry and also gone through school that had broad courses that were offered for the kids I knew how important having [an] educational foundation was to kids entering the workforce. So it was important because when you're in private business as I was for my career, you like to have applicants come who not only have a solid basis and foundation in reading, writing and arithmetic, but you want them to have an exposure to the world and be able to deal well with others, so it was important to me that I find out what was going on in our public schools.

Kobielus continued: So I just showed up at a board of education meeting and my concern was why are we cutting courses, what is behind this. And what I found is that the rural schools are dealing with the cards that they have been dealt by legislators who do not have an idea of how the schools are having to deal with these budget cuts.

Price: And when you went to the board meeting, that might be a place to follow up, what were other people saying about it and were they interested in getting involved with your coalition?

Kobielus: Yes, there was one other party there that spoke about the issue. Now that might be because the board meetings are held right after the dinner hour and in rural areas its different than it was when I went to high school fifty years ago. When I went to high school you had a lot of parents, stay at home moms who were active in the PTA who could go to a lot of these meetings. That's not the case anymore, you have two working parents they have jobs they've got to you know take their kids around to organizations and things after dinner, do their homework, all of that so they don't have the time that they had to be involved and no one understands what is going on in their local community. And the newspapers have done a terrible job of communicating what is happening to rural school budgets and how the schools have to deal with these budget cuts. So the other party that was at the board meeting was also a retiree, it was a husband and a woman who were active in their church and new that church schools were interested in getting public money to support their churches. And they opposed that. And that was my first exposure to vouchers. So I thought ... I better start looking into it and see what's going on.

Price: So that lends itself to the second [question] ... given that vouchers emerged in Milwaukee, an urban area, when and how did you and your peers in rural areas become aware of this "reform"?

Kobielus: There were other cities, small rural cities that were aware of vouchers. And when I found out that there were significant budget cuts that had been happening apparently over decades I started reaching out and trying to find the names of other groups like mine which formed after I found out about these other groups to say "what's going on." So I contacted a woman who lived in the nearby city of Steven's Point, and I said "please explain to me what these vouchers are and what is happening, because we don't have vouchers in our community right now. So why are you involved in this and what's the big deal?" And she gave me the numbers in her community what had happened once vouchers came into their rural community. And she gave me the numbers that showed the dollar amounts that were being transferred out of her public school budget to support privately run for profit charter schools and/or religious schools. And since in rural communities we basically don't have private schools, the money is almost entirely in our rural schools being drawn out of our public school budget into the religious schools to support the religious schools existing student base. So what that means is one dollar that comes out of the public school budget that supports 9 children that 1 dollar is going into a private school to support 1 child. Now I have a unique situation in that I am a product of both a religious school and a public school. But my concern—and both schools are fine, they are great—but my concern is that the state constitution was written to support youth taxpayer dollar money to support public schools that accept everybody. And they are open to review and accountability to the taxpayer. That is not true in private schools. So my taxpayer money should be used to go to support public schools that are open to everybody. So that was my introduction to vouchers and the more that I read about it, the more I learned. Again the local media was not very good at explaining to the rural residents the impact that legislation in Madison could have on their rural schools even though legislation started out to be with the urban areas, primarily Milwaukee and Racine. It was starting to have an impact on rural schools. And let me give you an example of how that impact happened.

Kobielus continued: Over the last several years, in Merrill, my public school district, there was $262,000 taken off the top of the public school budget to go to support voucher schools. Not even vouchers schools in our rural community but 23 voucher schools that were in Milwaukee and Racine. Our group after it had formed did a survey of our members and the public at large and discovered that the public did not understand that monies were being taken off of the top of rural public school budgets to support voucher schools in Milwaukee and Racine in the urban areas. Now the school boards were dealing with that in every way that they possibly could in rural areas. They have been consolidating locations. They have been increasing class sizes. They have been taking every possible step, cutting teacher pay, making teachers pay more for their health insurance, but they're to the point now where all of the possible cuts and cost savings measures they can take have been taken. And now with the cap coming off of the voucher limits, more and more existing religious schools, primarily religious school students can accept vouchers which means even more money taken off the top of public school budgets. And now the public schools are faced with making changes that are harmful to 90% of the kids that are in grades K through 12.

Price: When you talk with the folks in your community—people at coffee shops, wherever they may gather, restaurants, anywhere else—how are they generally understanding the relationship between the expansion of vouchers and the decline in funding for rural schools?

Kobielus: There is a segment of the populating that understands that this is ... really is attacking public school kids. And that's 90% of the kids in Wisconsin. The people who understand that are extremely, extremely upset with what is happening in Madison. They were so upset, that all of these various groups in rural Wisconsin—when the legislators were talking about lifting the caps—they responded to Madison in mass, with phone calls, and e-mails and letters, objecting to and opposing vouchers moving into the rural community and the legislature said "oh no that's not our intention at all, we won't be doing that" ... but foot in the door [they said] "we'll just offer 1000 vouchers, that's all, we have no intention of going any further than those 1000 vouchers." So the 1000 vouchers were introduced and the next thing you know, they said "well, we're going to start lifting the cap on vouchers" and then again, the small segment that understood this was very upset and very opposed to it. And they said, "well don't worry, because these schools— we understand that there is no accountability there—so we will put in measures to make voucher schools accountable." Then we should have no objection. When they passed it they passed the taking the cap off of the voucher program and they had absolutely no measures of account-ability. So it's really like a Trojan Horse that has come in to the rural community. They introduced it slowly, they promised accountability, then they lifted the cap without accountability and now it's a free for all. Because basically now we will start seeing huge transfers of public taxpayer money from public schools to subsidize our private schools, which are basically, primarily religious schools.

Price: That lends itself very well to our last question here. So what I've been getting at with this is—having been a researcher myself on the first Milwaukee Parental Choice Project (MPCP) years ago—problems associated with public education have largely been, in the Wiscon-sin public imagination, exclusively confined to the inner city public schools. Now rural schools are coming under consideration and so what does this portend in your estimation given the consolidations, school closings, and external threats from these alternatives (vouchers and charter schools).

Kobielus: It is a path to destruction of publicly run, public schools. And sets up the scenario for legislators to step in and say ... "you are failing" "you can no longer run your public schools" "we are bringing in privately run, for-profit operators and they will run your schools." And because it is a privately run, for-profit concern, you the community will no longer have any input into how your schools are run, and how your children are treated because now they are put into a corporate environ-ment. And that is not what public schools were established to be.

Kobielus continued: I'll give you an example, in Rhinelander which is just several miles up the road from my hometown, they are faced now with a budget cut that will if they cannot raise local additional funds in a public referendum from local taxpayers they'll have to eliminate all extracurricular activities. I mean can you imagine going to a school and having no athletics? Closing an elementary school, closing a secondary school, eliminating all paraprofessional staff, continuing to reduce any benefits to teachers, of course this will cause difficulty attracting and retaining teachers to rural communities. Maintenance budgets cut, technology budgets cut, reducing or eliminating community art, [physical education] programs, I mean it's horrendous. But those are the choices that face rural communities because the legislators have not been listening to the rural residents.

Price: What are you seeing that is needed for rural families? You started to talk about the economic situation, what other needs do you see?

Kobielus: We have started to do research that has ... I mean we have talked to our legislators, and our legislators weren't listening to our small groups that were aware of what was going on. And we have started to document now that no matter what we tell our legislators they are ignoring us. So what I'm starting to see is that the only way that this can be reversed and our public schools protected is if we vote out the legislators who are not listening to rural communities. All the rural communities want is a return of the state taxes they paid to the state in the form of aid to the local communities that paid those taxes. What's happening is those state taxes are going to the state but they are being redistributed to corporations and to wealthy people in the form of tax cuts for very wealthy people and wealthy corporations. We want those dollars that we paid in taxes returned to our local communities. And the only way to do that is to have legislators who will fight for our rural communities and for the return of our state taxes to our local communities. So our efforts are now focused on exposing any legislators who are voting against rural public schools and for vouchers and taking it to the ballot box. Because they have an agenda, they are moving forward with their agenda, they're not listening to the voters so the voters have to say "if you don't listen to us, if you don't support our public schools, we will get legislators who do."

Price: You sent [information] that showed the declining enrollment in religious schools in Merrill. Can you just say a few words about what that means to you?

Kobielus: Well, one of the things that the legislators have said is that budgets for public schools in rural communities need to be reduced because enrollment is declining. And I know that the population of our community hasn't changed over basically fifty years. I thought well that's strange. But I looked up the actual numbers on the state web site as reported by both public schools and private schools and went through the calculation of over a fourteen-month period, to see what are the enrollment trends. Are we really losing population in rural communities? Are we really losing students, what's going on here? The shocking thing I found was the population was basically stable in communities. But what had happened over a period of thirteen years was that *the enrollment trends in public schools had shifted significantly from religious schools to public schools.* And what we found in our own community is that religious school participation had basically tanked. It had fallen depending on the school, twenty five percent, thirty three percent, fifty percent in the religious schools. It had actually increased in the public schools slightly. So it wasn't that school participation over all was declining, it was that private school participation was declining. And the decline mirrored a decline in church membership rates. Which makes sense; if your church membership goes down, the number of students that you have participating in your school also goes down. And that's not a public taxpayer problem.

Price: that's very helpful, a good way to speak to that graphic [declining enrollments in religious schools].

Kobielus: It's kind of the elephant in the room, and I can say this being both a public and a private school student. But it would appear that vouchers in rural communities are really—if you look at the numbers—are a taxpayer-funded bailout for privately run and/or religious schools. And the community knows that our research shows that even if you've attended public/private schools, public support for funding religious schools is extremely low. And that's true even in a community that has a very, very high church membership.

Indeed, as Kobielus warns, we might better appreciate that rural spaces are increasingly challenged by what Rob Helfenbein lucidly and incisively describes as "the urbanization of everything" (Tozer, Gallegos, & Henry, 2011). This process is in tandem with the neoliberalization and globalization of everything public (Harvey, 2005), of post-colonialism (Andreotti, 2011), and of epistemicide (Paraskeva, 2011). The loss in signification of the special place that rural communities occupy is apparent as residents grow older and the collective memory grows dim. Kobielus aims to reignite a rural sense of pride and resistance.

RURAL DEMOCRACY STRUGGLE(S)

As explained herein, rural Wisconsin has moved into the middle of the noble story of public education, rather than residing at the periphery, and it is fitting to recall the past rural role in the foundational moorings of the common school (Tyack, 1974). Educational reform in the present privileges the urban school, but that story needs to change, to be retold, contextualized within rural settings. Each interview suggests as much, that rural spaces must become sites where citizens reclaim their place and identity. Kaukl outlines the problem well, the dwindling school funds and the challenge of urban-led, one-size-fits-all approaches to educational problems that hamper and harm rural school districts. Kobielus warns that unless citizen activists push back against voucher expansion, public schools will cease to exist.

In essence, neoliberalism dominates education reform, imagines the entire world down to the school district merely as a commodity. Of the central function of knowledge, this worldview only values transfer and exchange. Neoliberal conditions exude toxic waste for rural areas and school districts where tradition and community are often portrayed as standing in the way of progress. Even more paradoxical is that progressivism and progressive education ideas drew initially upon the values and qualities of rural living and rural schools. In other words, progressivism is ironically being slowly dismantled in the place/state of its origin, all in the name of progress.

I attempt to describe, through an admittedly disjointed lived experience (graduate student, research assistant, professor and freelance video journalist) a longing for the pristine and uncluttered rural experience as I've imagined and experienced it: of belonging, community building, and small "d" democracy. I likely share this sentiment with others (critical educators, curricular activists) and in opposition to the penultimate narrowing of the curriculum toward commoditization and commodification. Through video and examining the rural stories, I instead offer insights for rethinking education in a new light, with a different tone, and toward an undetermined yet hopeful, rather than pre-determined, utilitarian end.

This essay does not reify a dichotomy of urban vs. rural, but problematizes it slightly, by showing how, specifically, the reduction of education to "choice", begun solely in the urban area of Milwaukee, is now spread to the periphery, the rural areas of Merrill, Richland Center, and Trempeleau. This process means that the "fight" to save public education is now being picked up most ardently by rural activists, like Pamela Kobielus and in the form of, for example, *Blue Jean Nation* and Mike McCabe who argue that Wisconsin is losing its identity as a progressive state when the place of the country school in the rural area declines. This essay has been an attempt to recover through stories past and present of the central place of rural "sentimentalities" … the fire in the belly to counter neoliberal dismantling of the progressive tradition and the progressive idea for Wisconsin … for education, school and society.

REFERENCES

Andreotti, V. (2011). *Actionable postcolonial theory in education*. New York, NY: Palgrave Macmillan.

Baudrillard, J. (1994). *Simulacra and simulation*. Ann Arbor, MI: University of Michigan Press.

Churchill, R., & Furtman, L. (2007). *The buzzards have landed! The real story of the Flambeau Mine.* Webster, WI: Deer Trail Press.

Ellsworth, E. A., & Whatley, M. H. (1990). *The Ideology of images in educational media: Hidden curriculums in the classroom.* New York, NY: Teachers College Press, Teachers College, Columbia University.

Gedicks, A., & LaDuke, W. (1993). *The new resource wars: native and environmental struggles against multinational corporations.* Boston, MA: South End Press.

Harvey, D. (2005). *A brief history of neoliberalism.* Oxford: Oxford University Press.

Luke, C., & Gore, J. (1992). *Feminisms and critical pedagogy.* New York, NY: Routledge.

Najita, J. M., & Stern, J. L. (2001). *Collective bargaining in the public sector: The experience of eight states.* Armonk, NY: M. E. Sharpe.

Paraskeva, J. M. (2011). *Conflicts in curriculum theory: Challenging hegemonic epistemologies.* New York, NY: Palgrave Macmillan.

Price, T. A. (2013, July). Taxpayer funded voucher schools for the wealthy. *People's Tribune.* Retrieved from http://peoplestribune.org/pt-news/2013/07/taxpayer-funded-voucher-schools-for-the-wealthy/

Price, T. A., & Wittkopf, S. (2014, October 24). How publicly subsidizing private schools is destroying community schools. *Counterpunch.* Retrieved from http://www.counterpunch.org/2014/10/24/how-publicly-subsidizing-private-schools-is-destroying-community-schools/

Tozer, S., Gallegos, B. P., & Henry, A. (2011). *Handbook of research in the social foundations of education.* New York, NY: Routledge.

Tyack, D. B. (1974). *The one best system: A history of American urban education.* Cambridge, MA: Harvard University Press.

PART THREE

Experiences OF THE Rural

CHAPTER TEN

Who Am I?

Cultural Identity in Rural Schools

PRIYA PARMAR

I remember wholeheartedly resenting White people … but at the same time wishing so badly to be White! … I was ashamed of my ethnic background, so much so that I wanted to be White. To be White meant you were accepted and "normal."

—PRIYA IN THE 7TH GRADE

Growing up in a small, rural town in central Pennsylvania for the first nineteen years of my life with very little cultural diversity and attending a school system that adopted a monocultural approach to teaching had a profound effect on my self-esteem and with the way I viewed myself. It wasn't until years later that I reluctantly—and embarrassingly—shared the thoughts expressed in the epigraph to one of my professors in graduate school when asked why I was pursuing graduate studies in education. While enrolled at The Pennsylvania State University pursuing undergraduate and graduate studies, I slowly opened up to a few friends about some of my experiences in school. But it wasn't until writing my doctoral dissertation—in my late-twenties—that I worked up enough courage to put in writing the difficulties I faced with my own identity growing up as an East Indian girl in a predominantly white, rural town in central Pennsylvania. And it wasn't until 2009 when I finally memorialized my story in the form of a published academic book (Parmar, 2009) that I revealed for the first time my personal struggles with schooling to my parents and siblings. It is due to my personal experiences in school as an impressionable, marginalized young girl that inspired me to embark upon a career in education working with pre- and in- service teachers to promote inclusionary practices that value and recognize the voices and experiences of students from marginalized communities.

The purpose of this chapter is to argue for a reconceptualized pedagogical vision of multiculturalism by re-envisioning multicultural education programs in *all* American schools that includes an awareness or critical consciousness of one's place and social identity as shaped by mainstream, dominant ideologies that move students from a place of alienation, marginalization, and hopelessness to a space that allows students to maintain their ethnic, cultural, and socioeconomic identities. The teaching and recognition of student identities from this wider lens transforms technocratic teaching practices to ones where students feel valued, respected, and included and which ultimately, inspire strong sense of self identity and respect for differences. Identity, as we know, is a complex and multilayered construct influenced and shaped by a number of factors. My intent is to broaden the scope of multiculturalism so it is not only studied from a monocultural lens, which can be detrimental to both white and non-white students attending schools in rural communities. This chapter starts with my personal narrative (shared elsewhere) illustrating the implications of how experiencing racial tension and loss of identity at a very young age, coupled with the general feeling of being invisible by my teachers and the school's curriculum, played a key role in my childhood development. It should be noted that I spent the majority of my life (nineteen years) growing up in a rural environment, followed by eleven years in suburbia, and the last fifteen years in metropolitan New York (Staten Island and Brooklyn). Albeit anecdotal, my story is far from an anomaly if we examine the scores of urban and rural students who feel socially marginalized, excluded, or invisible based on racial, cultural, ethnic, class, gender, or sexual identity. My assertion applies not only to students in urban areas, but more so to the overlooked, seemingly homogeneous population of students attending rural schools if examining race, class, culture, identity, and economic issues. To that end, I briefly dispel the myths and assumptions of rural education and argue for teachers in rural schools to rethink their definition, and ultimately practice, of multiculturalism. The chapter concludes with offering a renewed vision of multiculturalism from a critical pedagogical perspective, or more specifically what is known as *critical multiculturalism*. I write "renewed vision" because critical multiculturalism is a theoretical construct that has long existed in the fields of Cultural Studies and Critical Theory, and has been researched and practiced in urban and suburban schools, but not nearly implemented enough in rural schools in the United States.

MY STORY

Excerpted with permission from Sense Publishers: Parmar, P. (2009) *Knowledge Reigns Supreme: The Critical Pedagogy of Hip Hop Artist KRS-ONE*. Rotterdam: Sense Publishers.

I was raised in a small, rural, predominantly White town in central Pennsylvania. My family was one of approximately four minority families of color in the entire town. My being "different" from my peers was not addressed nor even mentioned in the classroom. Individual teachers would occasionally engage in private conversations with me, showing interest in my culture and ethnicity, but these conversations were never brought to the attention of the entire class or addressed in the curriculum in a critical or just manner. I now realize that because my teachers failed to address issues of race, ethnicity, and culture in any way on a regular basis, their oversight or failure was a disservice not only to me but to others as well.

Elementary school was a piece of cake. I excelled in all the core subjects and enjoyed attending school on a daily basis. I fondly remember most of my elementary teachers and reminisce about the days in which I was eager and willing to participate in class discussions and activities. I took on many leadership roles inside and outside the classroom and was unafraid to challenge authority, but always in a respectful manner.

By the time I graduated to junior high school, in the 6th grade, I remember being unusually tall for my age, reaching heights well beyond many of my female and male counterparts. I recall having a huge crush on Matthew, a fellow classmate and friend, whom I felt, genuinely liked me, but ironically, constantly called me out of my name. On a daily basis, Matthew would address me by calling out my cultural origin: [East] Indian. But rather intentionally, he failed to pronounce the word, Indian, correctly. Instead, he placed emphasis on the first letter "I" using a long sounding "i" rather than the correct short "i" sound. Phonetically, it sounded like, "Ayn-dee-in". Sometimes he would repeat the "Ayn" syllable several times before saying the word in its entirety. As I previously stated, I felt that Matthew genuinely cared for me, as a friend, despite addressing me by a racial epithet. I did not feel it was mean-spirited because of the way in which he said the word; it was expressed in a non-malicious, fun-natured, friendly manner. I do not believe he intended any harm or disrespect (although it was indeed disrespectful), but more importantly, I do not think he was fully aware or understood the effects of what such name calling entailed. Although he reminded me that I was "different," I still felt like I belonged. However, I started to feel slightly self-conscious and even a little embarrassed for being so noticeably and awkwardly different (physically tall and lean). I'm not certain whether my 6th grade teachers were aware of Matthew's innocent name-calling; if they were, they did not address it. Nor did I address it to my teachers … or parents.

My "difference" was made painstakingly clear by fellow classmates during my 7th grade year, particularly by three White male students who were repeating the 7th grade … twice. As in most junior high schools, my 7th grade cohort changed classrooms and teachers depending on the core subject being studied. My math, science, and health teachers were strict and somewhat authoritarian in their teaching style. They demanded, and were granted, respect from their students; therefore, it was rare to see any disruptions or classroom management problems in their classes. My social studies, English, and home economics classes, on the other hand, were taught by teachers who had virtually little or no control of their students. It was in these three classes, but mostly in social studies and home economics, that I was relentlessly ostracized and openly teased and taunted by the three White males mentioned above. I was called damn near every racial slur known to African Americans, Native Americans, and Eskimo-Americans. Any racial or ethnic references to Asian Americans or South Asians (East Indians) in particular were never revealed simply due to the boy's ignorance of my cultural and ethnic background. The students may have had an excuse for being ignorant or uneducated about my ethnic background, but the ignorance displayed by certain teachers was not so easily excusable. The teachers were, I believe, guilty of failing to include thoughtful discussions on race, ethnicity and other multicultural issues. My physical features, besides being unusually tall, certainly identified me as being East Indian— or so I thought. Rather than using the strength and courage I once had when challenging authority in my elementary school years, or using my height as a weapon of defense, I sheepishly cowered to the boys intolerable behavior, remaining silent, often times staring at the ground while the hurling of insults continued day after day. I regret being so weak and fearful of defending myself. On the other hand, I refused to break down and cry in front of the boys or the rest of the class. I felt strong in the sense that, by restraining myself from showing any tears or emotions, I was prohibiting the boys from gaining satisfaction or pleasure in witnessing a break down. I remember wholeheartedly resenting White people ... but at the same time wishing so badly to be White! I also remember blaming those students who teased me and not the real culprits, the teachers, for condoning racist and hateful treatment of their students.

The verbal abuse continued religiously for nearly seven months in the three classes mentioned above but never in the hallway or cafeteria during lunch. Ironically, the teasing occurred only when there were teachers present. And the teachers said nothing, allowing for a divisive and unsafe environment. Not one disciplinary action was taken when racial slurs were maliciously spouted from the hateful mouths of my classmates. Instead, the teachers addressed the act of disrupting the lecture by simply asking the boys to get back to work or requesting they pay attention to the lecture, thus outright ignoring the content and maliciousness of the remarks. The teasing was not innocent like that of Matthew. I could feel the hatred and viciousness of the words once they left their lips. I could see in their eyes the detestation and disgust they had for me. They loathed me simply for my outward, physical appearance—for being me. Their words were meant to penetrate and to hurt. And they were successful.

I refused to inform my parents of the abuse I was subjected to for fear of them getting involved (in fact, my parents would not be privy to my school experience until I was in my early 30s). I was raised in an extremely loving and caring home but I was deathly afraid that once my parents were made aware of the teasing, they would immediately contact the school and if the boys were reprimanded, the teasing would somehow become worse, extending to the unguarded hallways and cafeteria lunchroom. I felt the verbal abuse may lead to physical harm within the isolated confines of the hallway. I remained silent for the duration of the abuse and was actually very good at hiding any signs of emotion. At home, I acted "normal" revealing no hint of trouble in school. As I reflect back though, I was embarrassingly passive, simply sitting in class taking it, ignoring the remarks, unable to find the strength and courage to fight back. My personality—my being—had changed. I was no longer confident, outspoken, or willing to engage in classroom discussions as I had in the past. Instead, I felt vulnerable, insecure, and extremely self-conscious of my very existence. I was ashamed of my ethnic background, so much so that I wanted to be White. To be White meant you were accepted and "normal." After all, my environment ranging from school to community population was White. The school curriculum and mainstream media appeared to revere Western European leaders, figures, and heroes. The disregard and degradation of my culture was made strikingly evident by the fact that the entire sub-continent of India was studied for precisely two 45 minute class periods in my social studies class. The two days we covered my home country, I intentionally faked an illness to my parents so I would not have to attend school. I was afraid the boys would finally learn of my ethnic background when pictures of "my people" were revealed to them in the social studies textbook we were assigned to read. I was convinced that the long list of racial slurs would be never-ending and the torture would continue more than ever.

Apparently, the constant disruptions in class were unbearable to some of my other classmates as well. A female student, who happened to be friends with the boys, was the only student with enough courage to report the misbehavior to the school's guidance counselor, a gentle and kind elderly White woman. I remember that day like it was yesterday. The guidance counselor called me into the main lobby area of the guidance office. In the lobby, not in her office, she informed me that she was made aware of the disruptive behavior and name calling from the three boys. She continued to explain that she spoke to the boys and reassured me that the teasing will cease to continue. Apparently she threatened them with some sort of disciplinary action if their taunting continued, so ultimately only a warning was given as a means of discipline. The counselor asked if I knew why the boys teased me. I deliberately stood silent. She picked up on my cue and explained that the reason the boys teased me was simply because they liked me; it was their way of expressing their affection towards me. She explained that young males, in general, due to their inability to communicate feelings and emotions with kind, caring words, resort to name calling and teasing in order to attract the attention and affection of the female they were infatuated with. I stared at her in disbelief, thinking to myself, "Do you think I'm some kind of fool??? You expect me to believe they desired me and wanted my affection??? No, they despised and hated me with a passion!!!" While nodding my head in agreement like the naïve little girl she must have thought I was, the only words that came pouring out of my mouth was "okay, thank you" only because I was so anxious to get the hell out of there! The "explanation" took no more than five minutes.

I left the guidance office and rushed to the girl's restroom. The female student from my class happened to be in the restroom as I entered. She told me she had had enough of the teasing and since our teachers lacked any sort of integrity or agency to discipline the boys, she was compelled to report them to the guidance counselor. I thanked her and proceeded to the privacy of one of the restroom stalls. Once safely inside, I finally, for the first time throughout this torturous ordeal, shed what felt like endless mounds of tears—tears that were deeply buried and locked away for months. I was filled with enormous gratitude to my fellow classmate who put an end to months of persecution. I was also grateful to the guidance counselor for forcing the boys to stop, regardless of the rationale given to me for their actions. I felt such an overwhelming sense of ease and relief, as if the weight (of stress and loneliness) I was carrying on my shoulders were at last lifted! I felt like a new person, but one that allowed the teasing to penetrate so deeply that it left scars and fears that would take months and years to overcome.

The remainder of my time in the public school system was relatively (and thankfully) free of drama—and trauma. I did not experience any more incidents of public humiliation or persecution. However, the seven months of ridicule played a tremendous role in shaping who I was to become and how I felt about myself. I continued to feel vulnerable when any attention was given to me in a public forum. I remained silent during class discussions simply because I felt I had nothing important to contribute. It was "safe" to remain voiceless and undetected. Essentially, I felt my opinions would seem worthless and valueless. I was timid and shy, reluctant to take on leadership roles—a far cry from my childhood experiences in elementary school.

As I am continuously reflecting on my educational experiences, I realize now that I utilized other forms of coping mechanisms when dealing with marginalization and exclusion. I credit much of my strength for coping with my treatment at school to the music I listened to. I used music as an outlet and as a safe haven into which I could escape to feel safe and powerful. I realize now that this escape into music helped me release all of the built-up, negative anger that was brewing inside. The lyrics of the songs I listened to were empowering and liberating; the beats were ener-gizing, giving me strength to stay calm and sane in the face of cruelty and ignorance. I immersed myself into listening to songs that resonated with my experiences. I found so much solace and comfort in music that it was enough to hide my pain from my friends and family.

Beginning in the fall 1990, while attending [undergraduate studies at] *The Pennsylvania State University, University Park main campus located in the suburban town of State College, PA., I was pleased with the large class sizes.*[1] *Many of the introductory-level general education courses required of all Penn State students easily enrolled up to 200 students. I felt safe and invisible in these lecture-style classes that often met in huge auditoriums. Fear of being called upon had nearly diminished, until I was forced to take classes in my major, elementary education, which were smaller in size. I successfully conquered my fear of public speaking but it did not come easy. In fact, it was a long, difficult struggle complete with sleepless, anxiety-filled nights prior to major presentation dates. I felt distressingly self-conscious in the presence of large groups; my nervous and shaky voice was one indicator of such anxiety. The trembling of my hands was another.*

The social experiences and friendships I cultivated at Penn State helped me regain cultural and ethnic pride I so desperately needed. Student population at University Park main campus was large in size (approximately 40,000 students enrolled at the time), but small, and segregated, in terms of minority population. I had a diverse circle of friends, but strangely enough found myself connecting more to African Americans and Latinos, rather than my fellow East Indians. In fact, I was quickly embraced by many members of the African American community more so than by members of my own culture. I had the feeling that East Indians felt uncomfortable approaching me either because I looked "too American" or conversely because I was "not Indian enough", that somehow I was being untrue to my Indian roots. I also realize my own responsibility in not taking initiative to approach them for reasons of my own. Another assumption I made for the lack of friendships I had with my fellow people was because I associated with other minority groups, mainly African Americans and Latinos. I base these feelings on the many ignorant, and at times racist, remarks I heard from some East Indians about the company I kept when they actually did approach me, as well as the countless stares I received when I was with my African American and Latino friends. I want to emphasize that my feelings are founded on assumptions I made based from my own personal experiences and are not meant to be reflective of all East Indian people.

My friends and I shared stories about our cultures, families, and experiences growing up. We shared similar stories about being marginalized or experiencing some form of racial or prejudicial treatment. I was finally able to reveal [some of] *my personal story to people who could relate to the pain and suffering I had experienced as a youngster in school. I was also able to relate in some ways to the pain and suffering they had experienced as a result of prejudicial treatment. As a result, my self-esteem and cultural pride slowly resurrected within me due to the friendships, and particularly, strong women of color I surrounded myself with. Leading by example, my girlfriends exhibited pride and confidence and as a result, they taught me to challenge and resist dominant standards when it conflicted with my own standards.*

My college friends were deeply embedded in Hip Hop culture, in other words, most of them were Hip Hop—it was their identity, their being, their lifestyle. With my relatively light exposure to the culture, mainly the rap and break-dancing elements from Dewayne [African American male friend originally from Brooklyn, whom I met in high school], *my experiences during my college years introduced me to the other elements of the culture not so often recognized in mainstream society. The entire lifestyle and culture that permeated the Hip Hop world resonated with me to the point that I embraced Hip Hop just as easily and quickly as my friends embraced me. The more I learned about the culture and the more I listened to the music, the more*

I was fascinated by it. My deep appreciation of rap music in particular and its personal meaning for me were my rationale for exploring its texts [in my subsequent doctoral dissertation and 2009 book].

Upon enrolling in the Cultural Studies Program at the graduate level (Master's and Doctoral Programs) at The Pennsylvania State University, I was given the opportunity to study, reflect, and share the effects my K–12 schooling experiences had on me. I realized that I could use Hip Hop culture and any of its elements, as an educational tool to empower others. Partly, I discovered the potential of the rap element as an educational tool when I took several courses from prominent professors in the field of Cultural Studies who opened my eyes to how media, power, control, representation, and production affect nearly every facet of our social, political, and economic life. It was very disappointing but enlightening in graduate school to learn about, and to be exposed to, the harsh realities and hidden truths about these and other Cultural Studies issues that had not been previously presented to me in my academic career. I understood how hegemony operated within society and education and how it contributed to my own sense of self. Ultimately, I developed a consciousness that made me painfully aware of the social, cultural, and political structures that valued the dominant culture at the expense of marginalized ones. I began to question the purpose of education. Was it to truly educate students and produce active citizens or was it to school students on knowing their place in society? Or were certain demographics of students educated while others were simply schooled? Sadly enough, I felt my real education had just begun in graduate school, with the realization that my K–12 schooling was just that—I was schooled by a technocratic, hegemonic system that produced passive and complying citizens that furthered the interests of the dominant culture. I was indoctrinated to act in prescribed manners, instructed in a way that discouraged me from asking questions or challenging textbooks; in fact, the textbooks were used as tools to sell so-called truths, as the final authority on what was right and wrong, what was centralized and marginalized, or excluded altogether, and ultimately, what was valued and devalued. It must be emphasized that I do not place sole blame or responsibility of the crisis I experienced on the educational system alone. There were many contributing factors that assisted in my struggle with identity, including my own sense of responsibility and that of my family; however, I do contend that the public schools I attended played an influential role in shaping my identity as well as my perception of others. I venture to say that my experiences are not isolated ones and that many students across the nation have experienced similar feelings of marginalization, exclusion, and denigration as a result of being schooled.

RURAL EDUCATION

It still amazes me today how being teased and ridiculed for seven *months* in the seventh grade has profoundly affected and completely obliterated the seven *years* of confidence and general contentment I felt about myself in my earlier school years. Those seven months changed me. That change, however, fuelled a desire in me to pursue a career in education working with pre- and in- service teachers addressing marginalized and excluded voices through curriculum development, language and (critical) literacy, and multiculturalism from the lens of critical theory and critical pedagogy. Before making a case for a critical approach to multiculturalism, or critical multiculturalism (Kincheloe & Steinberg, 1997; May & Sleeter, 2010; Steinberg & Kincheloe, 2001), I want to dispel some common myths and assumptions about rural schools and briefly address how multicultural educational programs are perceived and implemented.

When envisioning the landscape of rural America, one may conjure up images of the "country" remote, isolated geographic regions comprised of monocultural white people who are self-sufficient, engaged in agriculture or a related field, and economically advantaged as compared to their metropolitan counterparts. Although the definition of rural is multidimensional, it is usually characterized by the U.S. Bureau of the Census by population size of fewer than 2,500 residents. According to the USDA's Economic Research Service (July, 2015), in 2014, 46.2 million, or nearly 15 percent of U.S. residents lived in nonmetropolitan counties making up 72 percent of the landscape in America. According to the last U.S. Census report (U.S. Bureau of the Census 2010) rural communities are home to a growing number of subcultural groups, with Hispanics leading the numbers, followed by Native Americans, African Americans, and Asians. Rural counties tend to have higher rates of poverty than metropolitan counties with rates varying significantly based on regions. For example, from 2010 to 2014 it was estimated that 42.7 percent of the nonmetro population lived in the South. However, of that population, the poverty rate was at a staggering 21.7 percent, as compared to an estimated 15 percent in the region's metro areas (USDA ERS, 2015). States with the most severe poverty are found in the Southeast, including the Mississippi Delta, Appalachia, and on Native American lands as well as in the Southwest and North Central Midwest (ibid). In 2014, the USDA (November, 2015) reported 36.9 percent African Americans in nonmetro areas living in poverty, followed by 33 percent of American Indians and Alaskan natives, and 27.5 percent Hispanics. The poverty rate for whites in nonmetro areas was reported at 15.5 percent in that same year (ibid). Although rural America is often associated with farming and agriculture, other industries such as forestry and mining exist as well. Residents with limited education (high school degree) are often employed in low-wage jobs in the service and manufacturing industries.

Much of the educational research and literature on multicultural education ranging from program and curriculum development to pedagogical strategies focuses on implementation in urban and suburban schools, thus overshadowing its importance in rural schools, deeming rurality as invisible or marginalized, and perpetuating harmful stereotypes (Reed, 2010; Weis, 1988; Yeo, 1999, 2001). To illustrate by way of example, it is of little surprise that pre- and in- service teachers with whom I teach (at CUNY-Brooklyn, NY) place significant importance on multiculturalism as a major priority when developing their pedagogy. Before I introduce the theoretical concept of critical multiculturalism to students, I ask them to define what multiculturalism means to them and to reflect on their own teaching practices and/or P-12 educational experiences of how multiculturalism was taught. The most common definition of multiculturalism I receive is that it is a study or celebration of cultural differences of *mainly* minority cultural groups while also recognizing that diversity includes the study of race, class, gender, ability, language, and sexual orientation. Most of my students also view the inclusion and study of diverse ethnic groups as part of their definition of what they perceive as a "true" (pluralist) multicultural education program. This includes but is not limited to the often neglected study of African and Afro-Caribbean cultures, as well as Italian-, Jewish-, and Irish- American histories. This is not a surprising revelation since many of my students identity is tied to one of those groups (and other groups not listed). Their exposure to diverse cultures, ethnicities, languages, and religions in their many forms (e.g., dress, food, customs, signs/symbols, celebrations, festivals, parades) by virtue of living in an urban environment also helps promote the importance of multiculturalism. Consequently, many students have expressed a desire to include marginalized or excluded cultures and ethnic groups as part of their own teaching of multiculturalism.

When reflecting upon their own P-12 education, most students report that multiculturalism is generally taught from a simplistic or assimilationist approach, or what multicultural scholar James Banks (1993) refers to as the *contributions* or the *additive* approach to multicultural education. It is at these reductionary levels that students express their desires to include multiculturalism into their own teaching because that is how they were taught. The "contributions" of mainstream ethnic heroes are studied, the celebration of holidays and ethnic foods are introduced, units, themes, and concepts have been "added", and race, class, and gender differences—not their similarities—are emphasized without making significant changes to the mainstream curriculum, which is heavily patriarchal- and Eurocentric dominated. Additionally, students have reported multicultural education as being generally relegated—and taught in limited scope—to the social studies, English, art and music content areas.

So, does multicultural education hold similar importance and priority for school personnel in rural schools as it does for urban educators? The research in rural education suggests it does not, and it is even less relevant if (pre- and in- service) teachers and administrators perceived their student populations to be monocultural and small in size (Ayalon, 2003; Reed, 2010; Yeo, 1999, 2001). If school population was large and diverse, administrators tended to be more supportive of multiculturalism but limited it to address linguistic and racial diversity and often times linked race with culture (Yeo, 1999). Research analysis of several reputable multicultural textbooks conducted by Ayalon (2003) suggests that the failure to include the voices and histories (place) of rural communities marginalizes and excludes their perspectives, thus contributing to the feelings of irrelevancy towards multiculturalism amongst rural practitioners.

CRITICAL MULTICULTURALISM

The push for a more *critical* approach to multicultural education is not a foreign concept to scholarly research grounded in the tradition of critical theory evolving from the Frankfurt School of Social Research in 1920s Germany (Freire, 1973; Kellner, 2000; Kincheloe & Steinberg, 1997; May & Sleeter, 2010; Sleeter, Grant, & McLaren, 1995). While differing levels or taxonomies of multicultural approaches to education has been referenced and practiced in urban and suburban school contexts for some time now (Banks, 1993; Kincheloe & Steinberg, 1997; May & Sleeter, 2010; Steinberg & Kincheloe, 2001), very little research exists connecting a critical multiculturalism to rural schools and communities (Yeo, 1999). As Ayalon's (2003) analysis suggests textbooks on multicultural education that lack place and localized histories of rural perspectives must be affirmed. Beyond the failings of textbooks, teachers in rural schools must be open to viewing multiculturalism as more than simply limiting it to racial, linguistic, and religious diversity.

Critical multiculturalism values and appreciates the complexities that the study of culture entails. The term "culture" in the curriculum must be expanded upon to include more than the study of "high" culture and instead, viewed as shifting, hybrid, and pluralist, thus allowing for the inclusion of localized, rural histories and contributions that are often marginalized or excluded altogether. Critical multiculturalists work with students to reveal power dynamics, to challenge hegemony, and to raise questions of inequalities that include whiteness promoted as the norm and the privilege that results from it. Such an analysis targets the subtle ways racism works to shape consciousness and produce identities that results in the cultural reproduction of the dominant group's values, beliefs, and ideologies. This process of enculturation may lead to loss of self/identity and an unconscious, internalized hatred of one's culture, language, and dialect. In other words, critical multiculturalism is committed to challenging traditional curricula that values particular forms of knowledge, language, and experiences familiar to those that are privileged, or what French sociologist, Pierre Bourdieu refers to as "cultural capital" (Parmar, 2009, 2011).

Legitimizing privileged cultures and devaluing less privileged ones tends to silence and ignore large groups of students, their families, and communities because their personal histories and experiences are generally not valued or affirmed. Critical multiculturalists work to transform the curriculum by starting on a microlevel in helping students position themselves to the social worlds around them, and then moving to a macro-analysis of making connections between personal experiences and larger societal problems. Culture in this context is seen as a form of social and cultural critique because it includes diverse historical perspectives, examination of social inequalities, and identification of structural exclusion, all of which are crucial when including insidious and often ignored forms of racism, classism and privilege.

This critical view of multiculturalism and culture acknowledges that differences exist based on social and economic injustices and includes discussions about "whiteness" that empowers white students without promoting ethnocentrism and white supremacy. The acknowledgement of white privilege and how it operates in shaping identity are important elements of the success of critical multiculturalism. To ignore whiteness studies as part of a multicultural education program is to deny white people of the rich and diverse ethnicities and histories that exist within "white culture". As a result, culture and ultimately, ethnicity, does not apply to whites, only to people of color, thus limiting the study of culture in a multicultural program to minority groups. Implications can be detrimental to poor or working class white students who have been conditioned to view themselves—or their whiteness—as an invisible norm, thus ignoring how classism in the context of historical and economic injustices have worked against them in their everyday social and political lives.

A critical multiculturalism that includes the study of whiteness from multiple perspectives of class and ethnic identification requires teachers to acknowledge their role in the school institution and to examine their own position and thinking within and in relation to the power structures of society. A reconceptualization of the curriculum is necessary in that our definition of culture is expanded and validates and legitimizes a wide range of perspectives and experiences. This includes the study of our own students' histories, cultures, and experiences, many of whom are currently marginalized in the traditional monocultural curriculum. Centering marginalized knowledge helps students understand how privileged knowledge, experiences, and histories have been constructed and considered standard or the norm, thus insidiously shaping their own identities. A critical consciousness of one's position in society in relation to the larger social context provides opportunities to question and critique power relations and calls out social and economic injustices. Critical multiculturalism requires teachers to move beyond the safety zones of instruction, to take risks in not knowing where some lessons may lead, and to acknowledge that they do not have all the answers in an effort to embark upon an authentic learning experience with their students. Such risks transform the classroom to an empowering learning environment by engaging students and helping them view schools as a relevant and meaningful part of their lives. It develops a critical consciousness in students that enable them to function in the modern world, and just as important, it creates a more balanced, egalitarian curriculum giving students opportunities to be agents of social and political change. Critical multiculturalism structured around personal, social, cultural, economic, and political interests builds a sense of community and belonging, as well as brings the notion of democracy back into the classroom.

NOTE

1. Upon graduation of high school in 1988, I actually attended Clarion University for one year (1988–1989), took the following year off due to personal and financial reasons, then transferred to The Pennsylvania State University beginning fall 1990.

REFERENCES

Ayalon, A. (2003, Fall). Why is rural education missing from multicultural education textbooks? *Educational Forum, 68*(1), 24–31.

Banks, J. (1993). Approaches to multicultural curriculum reform. In J. Banks & C. Banks (Eds.), *Multicultural education: Issues and perspectives.* Boston, MA: Allyn & Bacon.

Freire, P. (1973). *Education for critical consciousness.* New York, NY: Seabury.

Kellner, D. (2000). Multiple literacies and critical pedagogies: New Paradigms. In P. Trifonas (Ed.), *Revolutionary pedagogies: Cultural politics, instituting education, and the discourse of theory* (pp. 196–221). New York, NY: Routledge.

Kincheloe, J., & Steinberg, S. (1997). *Changing multiculturalism.* Buckingham: Open University Press.

May, S., & Sleeter, C. (Eds.) (2010). *Critical multiculturalism: Theory and praxis.* New York, NY: Routledge.

Parmar, P. (2009). *Knowledge reigns supreme: The critical pedagogy of Hip Hop artist KRS-ONE.* Rotterdam: Sense Publishers

Parmar, P. (2011). Towards new epistemological possibilities: The critical complex epistemology of hip hop culture. In R. Brock, C. Mallot, & L. Villaverde (Eds.), *Teaching Joe Kincheloe.* New York, NY: Peter Lang.

Reed, K. (Winter 2010). Multicultural education for rural schools: Creating relevancy in rural America. *The Rural Educator, 31*(2), 15–20.

Sleeter, C., Grant, C., & McLaren, P. (1995). *Multicultural education, critical pedagogy, and the politics of difference.* Albany, NY: SUNY.

Steinberg S., & Kincheloe, J. (2001). Setting the context for critical multi/interculturalism: The power blocs of class elitism, white supremacy, and patriarchy. In S. Steinberg (Ed.), *Multi/Intercultural conversations: A reader* (pp. 3–30). New York, NY: Peter Lang.

U.S. Bureau of the Census. (2010). *2010 Census Summary File 1.* Retrieved January 10, 2016 from http://www.census.gov/prod/cen2010/doc/sf1.pdf

USDA ERS. (2015, June 15). *Population and migration: Overview.* Retrieved January 10, 2016 from http://www.ers.usda.gov/topics/rural-economy-population/population-migration.aspx

USDA ERS. (November 30, 2015). *Poverty Demographics.* Retrieved January 10, 2016 from http://www.ers.usda.gov/topics/rural-economy-population/rural-poverty-well-being/poverty-demographics.aspx

Weis, L. (1988). *Class, race, & gender in American education.* Albany, NY: State University of New York Press.

Yeo, F. (1999, Fall). The barriers of diversity: Multicultural education & rural schools. *Multicultural Education, 7*(1), 2–7.

Yeo, F. (2001). Thoughts on rural education: Reconstructing the invisible and the myths of country schooling. In S. Steinberg (Ed.), *Multi/Intercultural conversations: A reader* (pp. 511–526). New York, NY: Peter Lang.

CHAPTER ELEVEN

A Memoir OF Littleville School

Identity, Community, and Rural Education in a Curriculum Study of Rural Place

RETA UGENA WHITLOCK

I am a product of rural schooling in a place called Littleville, Alabama. I have a sense of pride in it. I have a Ph.D., have published, have traveled all over the world. I chair a department in one of the largest universities in the state of Georgia. I am successful according to most any metric that is used to measure success. In this essay I recount my experiences going through the school, yet this is not an exercise in nostalgia for nostalgia's sake, nor a progress narrative of outmigration. From my accounting, it is my hope that the school as an anchor of the community will emerge, as a place-within-a-place. This essay, a curriculum study of rural place, extends existing conversations on rural education, specifically the effects school closures have on communities. My narrative takes up the span of years where my story and the school's intersect, 1969–1977, and speaks to intersections of identity, intergenerationality, schooling, and rural community—all contextualized in a place that no longer exists and possibly never did. Littleville School closed in 1994 after 56 years in operation, a casualty of the wave of school consolidation in that began in the 1980s. "We might as well not *have* rural education research," declare Howley, Theobald, and Howley (2005, p. 1), "… that fails to center itself on rural cultures and ways of engaging life." That, ultimately, is the goal of this narrative, to center autobiographically on rural culture in one engaged life—mine.

Littleville School was the central fixture in the small incorporated town in Colbert County, Alabama. The school was closed in 1994 and its corpse deteriorated over the course of two decades, until in 2015, it was burned and grazed by the local volunteer fire department. The debris and field stones that made up its exterior were buried in a mass grave dug on the site. I will suggest that its deterioration parallels, as research suggests is a trend, that of the town itself. To capture a setting of place and/in time, I will set my own story against my father's nostalgic attempts—through storying the place over the years—to hold onto a past and more than a past. If for me this small rural community school symbolizes the stagnation that overlays the community, for Daddy it seems to re-place him in a simpler place in time. History has, after all, shown us that times, places and people, were never simple in 1954, his Golden Age. Likewise, I argue, just as there doesn't exist a simpler, happier time, the taking account of place—school, community, region—will not automatically yield a denouncement of it. As with my previous analyses of religion, condemnations that are unexamined and predetermined are as much sentimentality as nostalgic frolics can be. The self is complicit in institutions and communities and places, and the conversations about them must uphold the same complexity with which we consider the self-in-relation. That, too, is part of this essay. I realize that goal is ambitious and that I will not all accomplish all of it in this space, but it is my ultimate destination.

BEING RURAL

Howley et al. (2005) speak of the term "rural meaningfulness" in rural education research, a rural way of knowing in keeping with Kincheloe and Pinar's "epistemology of place" (1991, p. 10). As a Southern writer who writes about the South, I am aware of the need to confront and grapple with the myth of Southern exceptionalism—with a larger extension toward U.S. exceptionalism. The same, as a rural Southerner, goes for confronting one's own rural lifeworld (Tieken, 2014, p. 5). I do not seek to isolate rural and South from each other in my work. They are too inextricable to my experiences and identifications. Ironic, then, that the question, "What does it mean to be Southerner"—one that sociologists have attempted to address for decades, can also be asked of rural folks. Beyond, of course, demographics information. Curriculum scholars, myself included, have also offered generalizable qualitative traits of Southerners—who are wildly diverse: having a sense of place, storytellers, heightened experience of the natural environment (Casemore, 2005; Kincheloe & Pinar, 1991; Whitlock, 2007, 2013). I begin with the assumption here that rural dwellers share some of the same traits, especially a sense of place. As Tieken (2014, p. 5) points out, many rural scholars feel that "feeling rural" (that which feels rural *is* rural) should actually define rural. Tieken extends the thought that the "meanings inherent in rural lives" define those lives as rural.

> "Rural," then, is a matter of the commonplace interactions and events that constitute the rural "lifeworld," a value mostly overlooked by the media and academia, and a significance impossible to quantify. This understanding, shared by many of the residents of rural

communities, is tied to place; it provides a geography-dependent sense of belonging. Rural, in this conception, is not simply a matter of boundaries. It constitutes one's identity, it shapes one's perspectives and understandings; and it gives meaning to one's daily experiences. This identity, this shared and place-dependent sense of rural belonging, gives rural its significance. (p. 5)

Incidentally, as I research for any new project, I find the book I wish I had written. For this project, Mara Casey Tieken's *Why Rural Schools Matter* (2014) is that book. She describes a study, conducted in portraiture that deeply examines relationships in and across two rural communities for "a more authentic understanding of rural schools and rural communities ..." (p. 31). Through the stories, contextualized by the communities' schools, she captures stories, voices, and lessons central to locating "the realities beyond the myths." The carefully—and to me lovingly and beautifully—crafted stories of Delight and Earle, Arkansas, one community predominantly White and the other predominantly Black disrupt what Tieken identifies as two competing myths that dominate thinking about rurality. Rural places are either "backwoods, backwater, and backward" (think *Deliverance*) or idyllic—with an "uncomplicated simplicity, with some sort of lost *golden age*" (p. 7) (think *The Waltons*). Or both (think Faulkner). And in the poignantly honest stories Tieken locates the drama of local and state politics and their effects on rural schools that lead to consolidation and closure.

The U.S. government has offered several designations of rurality based on economic designations. Howley and Howley (2010, p. 38) have condensed these to three community types: (1) durable-agrarian communities, (2) resource-extraction communities, and (3) suburbanizing rural communities. Based on their descriptions, Littleville is considered a resource-extraction, starting out as a mining town and growing up around the railroad that was built in the late 1880s. Daddy knows where the old quarries are located. The town remained after the last ore was extracted. So technically, Littleville is a resource-*extracted* community, what remains after the earth was literally drilled out from under it. The first school house was a log building built in 1908 for the children of mine and railroad workers, store and boarding house owners, and farmers. It was covered in white clapboard, as evidenced in a picture taken around 1911, which shows my great-great grandfather, John Kirkland, and his two daughters, Grace and Geneva. Grace's son, William, would marry Nettie B, shown with three of her siblings in another picture. Seven of eight of my grandmother's siblings had attended the old school located on a wagon trail where the First Baptist Church stands today. By the time the baby, Janelle, had arrived, the new school was under construction along Jackson Highway, a military road that Jackson and his troops traveled to get to the Nachez Trace. That school was built in 1938 as a WPA project.

Recent research on rural education explores relationships between the schools and community, and important to my essay here, the relationship between effects on the community when its local school closes. This research yields important insights into what it means to be and feel—to believe oneself to be—rural. For example, Theobald and Wood (2010, p. 18) contend that rural dwellers learn to be rural, and in spite of diversity of identities or intellects and navigating the social and cultural, etc., "all rural dwellers are nevertheless recipients of the messages from the dominant culture regarding what it means to be rural." This is the interesting part: "Though some may possess the ability to dismiss the messages, the very act of dismissing them becomes a part of the identity an individual builds" (p. 18). If it is my contention, then, that Littleville School shaped my identity, or rather, helped me negotiate and navigate the identifications I took on, where does *that* process intersect with the process of dismissing negative stereotypical messages of what it means for me to be rural?

CURRERE OF THE RURAL

How can we make meaning of rural schools and education if we do not make meaning of the lives—told, drawn, and communicated by them—of rural people? I draw no generalizations here, offer no list of qualities, characterizations, or values common to rural people. I will leave that to the sociologists. I tease out my own rural meanings from my own partial, contingent, contextualized, incomplete narrative. Mindful of the autobiographical methodology of currere (Pinar & Grumet, 1976), I examine regressive, progressive, analytic, and synthetic moments to complicate conversations on rurality and schooling, while bringing rural education conversations into curriculum theory. "It promises," promises Pinar, "no quick fixes" (2004, p. 4). This meandering narrative of identity, school, and community engages in the slow remembering and re-entering the past, where I might "meditatively imagine the future ... in order to understand more fully, with more complexity and subtlety," my submergence in the present (Pinar, 2004, p. 4). I thus intentionally become "temporal" (p. 4). This essay takes the form of a series of re-memories, scenes that come to me as I show how the past, present, and future live in one another. My scenes are illustrations of my "past existential experience as 'data source'" (p. 36). The snapshots are framed by current literature on rural education, which, in turn, guides my theorizing. In what immediately follows, I will briefly explain how I employ the school as character, inter-related and engaged with me in autobiographical snapshots as clear as the snapshots I reference to punctuate my storying.

The Regressive Moment: Returning to the Past. The narrated experiences as I remember them and set them down are examples of my entry into the regressive moment. I think of remembrances as memoir, since they are based on personal knowledge and are an accounting. While with some introspection it is not much of a stretch to see how the past infuses the present and future, it is a challenge to see this particular present engages meaningfully with the past in which it co-habits.

The Progressive Moment: Imagining the Future. "The future inhabits the present," writes Pinar. Lived experiences of time-in-place hold a queering of the narrative, thus disrupting the examining act of the school as a nostalgic, romanticized, fixed in that same place and time. While local memories of place illustrate shapings and relationships between community, identity, and school (DeYoung & Howley 1992, p. 8; Tyack, p. 11), what meanings might be made that extend into "imagine possible futures" too late for Littleville School, but critical for self and community?

The Analytic Moment: Examining the Past and Present. This moment is a mindfulness of the present, a deep engagement with daily life, rather than an "ironic detachment from it." Daily life means here an intense grappling with the above relationships in terms of my own experiential knowledges. I seek, in a phenomenological move, to find "distantiation from past and future functions to create a subjective space of freedom in the present" (Pinar, 2004, p. 36).

The Synthetical Moment: Reentering the Lived Present. I grapple with questions of how rural meaningfulness is inscribed upon me, and how is it written in such a way to interact and relate to my gendered queerness. This is a moment of "intense interiority" (Pinar, 2004, p. 37), in which questions are posed as the embodied Other takes a look around. How do my rural identifications—and queer(ed) identities—inform conversations about schooling in rural place? Schafft and Jackson (2010, p. 11) state emphatically that "place *matters*," emerging in a complicated network of "paradoxical, provisional" and incomplete discourses. No rural idyll; rural stories speak to resiliency and complexity of "being" rural. Place does matter. I am marked by a place that is in-between and in decline, and that decline is itself marked by the closure of its school, the school that nurtured and grew me. Next, I will frame my curriculum study of place within a seminal work that continues to ground how I think about place, Kincheloe & Pinar's *Curriculum as Social Psychoanalysis: The Significance of Place*.

Place matters; *Place* matters; place *matters*. No matter which word is emphasized, the implication is the same. Kincheloe and Pinar declare simply, "The endurance of place perpetuates hope, not in the static, conservative sense that romanticizes and mythologizes, but in an emancipatory, hopeful sense that accentuates significance, and tragedy …" (1991, p. 7). Place is partially defined by a its "embedded temporality" (p. 8); looking at place is looking at place-in-time. And, looking at time, in my autobiographical work, is set in place. Therefore, a curriculum theory treatment of rural schools that is infused with and grounded in place looks at rural place with renewed historical consciousness. It rejects and dispels stereotypes of the "naturalness" (p. 10) of rural place by contextualizing it by its varied contexts, identified through remembered storying. Distinctive rural ways of knowing shape an "epistemology of place" (p. 10) that has at its center historical awareness expressed in particularity and localism. Kincheloe and Pinar point out that Southern localism "involves a tendency to think of communities as distinct from one another and to prefer one's own" (p. 12). This view is consistent with qualitative research on rural community, and the challenge is to extend thinking of the particular toward social transformation. Place-based autobiography can employ the local and particular to, as the authors state, "confront the meaning of the given world, reject it, reformulate it, and reconstruct it with a social vision that is authentically the individual's" (p. 21), squarely embedding currere into epistemologies of place. Autobiographical work, like mine, that lay claim to having a *sense of place*, becomes imbued with an "intensified focus on sensation" revealed by the particularity of that place (p. 22).

SELLING CLOSURE

More than any of the churches in the community, the school was used for social functions; some were sponsored by the school—donkey basketball and the Halloween festival, for example. Others were not, the Saturday evening gospel singings, which my family did not attend because we were members of a non-instrumental congregation and these quartets were accompanied by a piano. In the late 1940s, when Daddy was at Littleville School, and then again in the late 1970s, the town put on a "womanless wedding" for a fundraiser. The first of these, performed before I was born, was part of my childhood lore of place, a mythology told and re-told through laughter by Daddy. I witnessed the later performance—with several cast members who had been in the original nearly thirty years before. Daddy recreated the role of the "singing uncle." Brock Thompson has described in superb detail the spectacle of the womanless wedding as "cross-dressing, comedic gender inversion in folk drama" (2013, p. 20). Within the context of politics of performance, he suggests these performances, which took place throughout rural areas from about the 1940s through the 1970s, are "built upon the visible and performed difference of gender and class," with a "general mockery of the uneducated hillbilly" (p. 22) a common theme. Womanless weddings also served as an acceptable stage for displaying masculinity and Whiteness (in Whitlock, 2013, p. 28). I won't describe it here but I could. It was memorable fuel to Daddy's nostalgia, allowing him to perform and shine; the days were glory days—for both him and Littleville.

Each year school children—then as now—had school pictures taken in the fall. When my parents were there—from 1948 to 1957—the school produced a yearbook, first called *Villager*, then *The Hornet*, after the mascot when the school grew large enough to form sports teams. By the time I got there in 1968, the school had long since stopped sponsoring a yearbook, but my parents kept four of their old ones. As a child I scoured through them—as I do to this day; writing now, they are tangible artifacts of the school. As we go through, they can name their schoolmates—those alive and dead. In the oldest, 1949, Daddy sits among the other third graders; he points out the white sweatshirt that was handed down from his pal Skipper. During those years, he tells me, times were hard. That was when his daddy plowed with a mule for fifty cents a day. My daddy looks much like he does today, his little face leaner but the grin is the same. Yet only the name by my mother's school photo identifies her to me at first; then I see her in the eyes and freckles.

Rural schools have been consolidating and closing since before I went to Littleville School. Reports from the Committee of Twelve, appointed by the National Education Association, mention the "rural school problem" (DeYoung & Howley, 1992; Tyack, 1974) as early as 1896. Tieken reports that from 1910 to 1960, "one-or-two-teacher schools dropped by 90 percent" (2014, p. 17). For a hundred years, experts have sought the "one best system" (Tyack, 1974) of educating America's young. In 1959 Conant declared that "the most outstanding problem in education was the small high school, and that the elimination of small high schools would result in increased cost-effectiveness and greater curricular offerings" (qtd in Bard, Gardener, & Wieland, 2006). Most small high schools are in rural areas, and so were susceptible to forced consolidation. Of this wave of consolidation in the 1980s, Bard et al., note that it was, "considered successful by some because no one in the literature had challenged the research that bigger schools gave a more quality education."

In their monograph, *The Political Economy of Rural School Consolidation* (1992), DeYoung and Howley, describe and "interpret distinctive features" of rural schools and analyze political and economic reasons historically provided to justify school consolidations. I selected their paper at first for context; it was written two years before Littleville School closed for good. I had hoped it would give me insight as to the political winds that blew the doors shut, and it did. The political excuse was and is that it is cheaper to put students in consolidated schools. Politicians sell this excuse with the enticement of access to greater resources, such as computer labs and extra curricular activities. DeYoung and Howley bluntly note the "intentional concealment" of political motives:

> Astute readers will already have recognized our underlying interpretation—that social, political, and economic circumstances provide more compelling explanations of school consolidation than the advertised curricular, pedagogical, or administrative benefits. We think the latter arguments—tiresomely repeated in the current round of school closings— actually serve to conceal the social, political, and economic agendas intended to change the behavior of the affected parties (communities, parents, and students). (p. 15)

And, again, in what is no surprise to those of us who follow educational policy and politics, the authors point out that almost none of the districts that forced consolidation documented improvements that they alleged would result from closings.

They did not report them because they did not evaluate for them (p. 16). In what I see as a Foucauldian move to explain theories of citizenship relevant to rural communities, they note the paradox of the state: that while it must mediate raced, classed, and gendered inequalities, it must at the same time "secure a productive economic system based on the progressive accumulation of wealth, and hence, on inequity" (p. 23). It is in the interest of the state, therefore, for economic development to become not plans and policy but ideology. Once people have embraced the ideology, "it obfuscates and opposes many alternative social interests less clearly associated with economic growth and consumption and with the ceaseless imperative to accumulate capital" (p. 39). And finally, according to the authors, when ideology becomes "common sense," it is legitimated by the people and they support initiatives and policies that are in the interest of the state, "regardless of the direction in which their true interests may lie" (p. 40). This explains why the U.S. South votes overwhelmingly candidates into office in spite of continued economic downsizing, outsourcing, plant and school closings, de-regulated trade, and opposition to universal health care. We vote against our own self-interest to support profit, no matter what the cost to us.

PHOTOS

Abandoned stone buildings dot the countryside of North Alabama. I remember looking at them from the back seat car window as a child, roofs caved in, windows broken, overgrown with weeds and saplings. Schools like these—Spring Valley, New Bethel, Underwood—dated back to the turn of the 20th century. Family lore—this time from Mother—held that Littleville had been the proposed site of the high school to be built on our side of the county. The sitting superintendent, whose name both of them spoke with great distain, lived Colbert Heights, a neighboring un-incorporated farm community that lacked many resources and amenities Littleville had. But because he had lived in Colbert Heights, it got the school. The location of the high school was an early lesson in educational politics, and clearly one I have never forgotten. This one decision would have lasting effect on Littleville, both school and town, that is felt even today. A high school would have the life blood of feeder schools from half the rural county to keep it alive. Predictably, as the community stopped growing, over the years, Littleville School reduced the number of grades it served; from grade 9 in the 1950s to grade 6 in 1993. It was just a matter of time till it vanished altogether. No wonder they spit out his name, which I refuse, in their honor, to mention here.

In the 1950 *Villager*, the first in which Mother and Daddy appear together, Mother is in her class photo. The child in this picture, Wonnell, a good country name picked by a neighbor, had not yet taken on the features of the face most and earliest familiar to me. Despite the black and white photo, my mother's freckles shown. Seven years later in *The Hornet*, she notes her accomplishments on the inside cover: co-Captain cheerleader, Class President, 4-H Club. There is a candid shot of her, this time a 15-year old maturing eighth grader, three years before she would start working at the local café to help her widowed mother make ends meet, three years before she and Daddy noticed each other. I recognize her in this picture. She is standing in front of the one of the school's old stone walls wearing a floral skirt, bobby socks, and loafers. Behind her is a young man—not my daddy—curly headed, blue jeans and checkered shirt, both of them perfectly indicative of the 50s. He holds bother her wrists, arms around her; she is in a pose I describe as flirtatious. They both smile into the camera. I looked him up in the class photos. He was a "senior" ninth grader, Thomas Robison, whose photo caption read, "Elvis Presley's Twin."

I have fewer photos of Daddy at school. Unlike Mother, Daddy's candid "shots" are in the stories he tells; for her, I have to make up the stories. One of Daddy's strongest memories is being in the Kiddie Band. Littleville School had no band program, but it did in the 40s and 50s have a very competent music teacher, Miss Wagnon. She, like Miss Dove, was the stuff commanders were made of. In the 1950 *Villager*, there is a picture of that year's Kiddie Band, with my mother in it. In 2007, the local paper, the *Franklin Free Press* came to the Littleville Senior Center, where my mother is director, and interviewed the seniors about the recollections of Littleville School. Both my parents are quoted in the human interest story, and Daddy talks about the Kiddie Band. He goes on to mention other stage performances—glee club, talent shows—remembering them, it is apparent, as though they happened seven—rather than seventy—years ago. "Kids don't realize it, but school is the best time of their lives," my mother told the reporter (Franklin Free Press, p. 12)

The 1949 *Villager* has a good shot of the school; the building is the original structure, before the addition of the gym, lunchroom, or portable buildings that housed the Special Education classes. The large auditorium—focal point of the building—is pictured left, and was where all assemblies were held. It also served for awhile as the basketball court until the "new gym," as it was called for thirty years, was added. When I was there we still gathered in the auditorium for assemblies, lines from the old basketball court still visible beneath our metal folding chairs on buffed wood floors. The entrance to the auditorium was to its right, three heavy green doors from which protruded a concrete pad. Across the front of the building were two classrooms, the main entrance, and the principal's office.

The building itself was L-shaped, with classrooms along the front, back, and sides. By the time I attended, one classroom had been made into a library. In the mid 1960s the gym, lunchroom, and classrooms for first and second grades were built. These classrooms, behind the main building and facing the softball field, was where I spent the first two years at Littleville. Between the main building and the new gym was the Head Start trailer purchased with President Johnson's Head Start funds. I had gone to Head Start for 8 weeks in the summer of 1968. That was the summer Robert Kennedy was assassinated and the rest of the country was restless—but not North Alabama. Birmingham and Tuscaloosa were far away and Governor Lurleen Wallace was keeping George's legacy alive as he ran for President. None of this mattered to me: I had started to *school*. From the moment I walked into the trailer, I was in love with school. And with *the* school. Very few children in the area at that time went to kindergarten—which were privately owned and charged tuition. To be honest, I do not remember a thing about the curriculum that summer. I remember that I instantly loved my teacher—a trend that was consistent as I transferred another love that could not speak its name to almost every woman teacher I ever had. I still remember the smell of materials—fresh construction of the trailer that had been hauled onto the school property to prepare young children for first grade.

Growing up, Daddy would tell about performing on the stage. By his seventh grade year, 1953, he had graduated from Kiddie Band to the glee club. That same year, as an "underclassman," he was voted the school's Most Talented. He remembers writing his name on one of the backstage walls before a performance. For as long as I went to Littleville, I would search every board on every wall to find his name, to find the mark that he had been there. I never did. I suppose it never occurred to a child searching to connect her father's childhood with her own that a name scribbled in pencil by a little boy thrilled to go on stage stood little chance against twenty years and several coats of paint. In April 1994 after the closure was announced, the community held a reunion for all former students, which was, essentially, the community itself. Generations of families with the school, as well as blood, in common. As we, my mother, daddy, brother, and I, walked around the auditorium for the last time, Daddy told the story once more, looked at the stage, then headed for one of the stage door entrances on either side. I followed, knowing without needing to be told where we were going. He pointed to where, nearly thirty years before, he had written his name.

I have written a good deal over the years about growing up a child who would embrace a lesbian identity as an adult in relation to the contexts of the South and fundamentalist religion. But the little tomboy girl who loved her school and her teachers and her *Jungle Book* lunchbox had no language for it yet. What I can say is that I was a queer child in a rural school, a smart girl who was the beneficiary of educational initiatives in the late 1960s and 1970s, from Head Start to Title IX. New photo: my school picture in the gym, from my scrap book. This class picture is in full 1970s color. I wonder if every queer grownup looks back like I do to her childhood to look for signs I should have seen. I do see a few. For starters, I fell utterly and completely in love when I was twelve years old with my teacher, Miss Renwick.

Inasmuch as I can conceptualize pre-adolescent desire—the wanting and wanting to be that overtakes, I desired her. She was from New England and had an air of sophistication—the first I had seen in a real, live woman. The way she spoke and dressed, the experiences she told us, places she had been—all of these made her distinct to me. I could not construct a single narrative that would place her in Littleville, Alabama, so she seemed as un-fitting as I was. To my pre-teen way of thinking, she was here, and she was mine, and that is all that mattered. Looking back, I blush when I recall how I behaved like a smitten adolescent. I talked about her incessantly, lingered after school just to talk with her. Our 1968 Impala was more times than not the lone car in the parking lot, my mother sitting, waiting. I took pictures of her; I took pictures of her car. It is cliché and predictable to say she brought the world to me, but that is what happened. I had never met anyone *not* from North Alabama; moreover, had never thought of myself in terms of life beyond there.

However, in 1974, I had neither the maturity nor vocabulary to articulate any of this. What I told my mother, sitting in the parking lot feeling as though she were losing her child, but to what she did not know, was that I wanted to be a lawyer and live in Boston. Now when I look back at this child driven by inexplicable wanting, the other significant face is see is not that of a well-spoken young New Englander who would likely had rather been anywhere but Littleville, Alabama, but that of another young woman, auburn hair now flecked with gray, body thickened by child birth, freckles still there but faded. Mother sat alone in a parking lot waiting for me, afraid at my rebellion. She still recalls that I wanted to live in New England, the only desire I could name. Years later, when I left Alabama for Louisiana and a doctorate, through tears she told me, *We always knew you'd grow up to leave.*

TAKING LEAVE

Miss Renwick was not the first teacher to invite me to look beyond the town's borders. From the time I made the "red bird group" in second grade—the first time students were tracked for aptitude in 1970—I was educated to leave. My teacher, Mrs. Fowler, talked to me about what a wonderful place college was and even brought me brochures so that I could see the mystical, foreign place for myself. I was enamored. Two years later, my parents were advised to enroll me at an advanced school based on my grades and test scores. They did not tell me at the time—which they were right not to do—no doubt because they expected me to beg to go. They declined, they told me later, because the advanced school was "in town." I have always thought that it was as much by virtue of it being there—the place, city, citified—rather than any extreme hardship of money or transportation, which there was sure to be—that led to their decision, one I am convinced contributed significantly to my identity construction.

Studies report the pattern in rural school education of teachers "raising" their students to get out, resulting in the rather vulgarly termed "brain drain" of rural communities of their best and brightest (see Hektner, 1995; Tieken, 2014). Based partly on an increasingly global economy, shrinking world community, and privileging urban and suburban educational values. Students leave and seldom return. Howley and Howley (2010, p. 46) note that "prominent rural scholars have suggested that rural schools are the principal institutions in which young people learn *authoritatively* to leave rural places." They go on, to me disturbingly, to report, "In Appalachia we have often worked with educators in resource-extraction communities who regard the local place as somewhere to leave" (p. 46). I was one of those students who left, and although I did not return, Littleville never leaves me.

In his 1995 article, When Moving Up Implies Moving Out: Rural Adolescent Conflict in the Transition to Adulthood, Hektner explores the influence of community contexts of adolescents about their plans for adulthood—where they will live, what careers they will choose, etc. He notes a prevalence among rural youth "of a potential conflict between the perceived importance of staying close to parents and … moving away from their area" (p. 3), which manifest in feelings of emptiness and anger about their future plans. Although, it should be noted, as the author disclaims, that the sample was taken from a nonmetro area outside of Chicago, an area that does not identify itself as rural. Hektner keeps the term *rural* to differentiate it from non-rural, that is, urban or suburban. While this is a long way from Littleville, the premise is the same: kids who live beyond cities, beyond suburbia, feel the conflict when we consider our options. Economic, academic, cultural opportunities on the one hand and family, familiarity, local culture, *home* on the other. This is, of course, generalized and not applicable to all rural youth, but it is, according to Hektner, a historical trend of outmigration.

Among the factors Hektner reports that influence adolescents' desire to stay is one particularly relevant to my essay: "the existence of strong intergenerational networks, which serve to transmit shared values and attitudes" (p. 4). Hektner mentions a paradoxical context of "leaving, but staying rural" in which adolescents who do leave seek out "small-town" communities; however, "For high-aspiring youth, such a preference would be nearly as likely to lead to a conflict in future desires as staying in the home town, given the limited range of opportunities in most rural areas" (p. 4). Howley and Howley (2010) make a more startling claim, that "Schools facilitate out-migration, in part, by shaping *identities* that willingly embrace departure" (p. 46). Rural knowledges, traditions, cultures are experienced as loss, even as students aspire to standards set outside of rural place. They write,

> Children from impoverished rural families are doubly burdened by this scheme. Schooling denies them identification with the (bad) places ehere they are and simultaneously excludes them from the (good) places they hear about in school. Exceptions are rare indeed. …

Middle-class rural students learn to aspire to a permanent elsewhere, but youth from impoverished familiies are confined to a place they learn from their schooling is *no place to be*. (p. 46)

Howley and Howley finally note of outmigration, "In the end, there will be no rural place to which young people might return …" (p. 47). By age 7, I was identified as a "high aspiring youth" and educated to "willingly embrace" my departure.

What if, rather than a conflict, this desire—to leave, but stay rural—were reframed as a tension, one that might be stretched and worked and manipulated without the pressure and expectation of resolution? In this light, I have found that I resolve this tension—of staying or going, betraying either myself or my place—not by hypothesizing the staying or going, but by realizing that Littleville never really leaves me. Whether I am in Finland or Fifth Avenue, I am never far away. Schafft and Jackson (2010, p. 9) note the tension over rural community identity that is "framed principally at the interstices of the local and the global," tensions that involve how rural people negotiate our identities within societal discourses that "ignore, dismiss, or denigrate" [sic] the rural. I find that it is not particularly difficult to "feel country (rural)" in New York, but when others notice that I am, assumptions go immediately into play. Perhaps it is this sort of "sense of place" Southerners consistently report feeling. Littleville is for me, then, an interstitial space that lies phantasmagorically between past and present, here and anywhere, time and place. It is everywhere and nowhere. I embrace it, feel a fondness for it in many ways, and since I do not necessarily need to be *not there*, Littleville rests comfortably close to me.

During my research I called Daddy, helping Mother at the Senior Center, where she is Director, whether Mrs. Ann Wells, school principal when the school closed, was well enough to talk. Today she is well in her 90s. He gave me her number—hollered at her neighbor playing dominoes and asked how Mrs. Wells was doing. Then he said, Ann's the one who called and told us you were acting up because you were bored and we needed to get you out of that school. Now, I had always thought my parents worked so hard to help me get into RHS was my worrisome pleading to join the band I had fallen in love with. I was wrong; it was this call. He said, you were staying in trouble and we didn't know what was going on. Mrs. Wells said it would "be her job" if word got out to the principal that she had called us.

I did not finish junior high at Littleville School; I left one year before I would have finished 8th grade, in 1977. The leaving was pivotal, and it is a space of intersection between my father's experience and my own. It was in his retelling of this that I saw him cry for one of only two times in my life. I wonder whether my own telling of it can capture the intimacy, a generational bridge—the slow decaying of the place itself. For many of the texts I have read in preparation for writing this chapter have noted the relationship between the decline of the community and the closing of a school—the life blood of both dries up, breaking a generational community tie. I am attempting to capture that moment when it happened in one particular family, mine, in a reckoning of time, place, and identity.

Local children whose parents did not want them to attend Littleville School found loopholes in district lines and went to the city school in the neighboring town, Russellville. That meant they would feed into Russellville High School rather than my district's high school, the interloper Colbert Heights High School, which was about as rural as it gets. Before CHSS had been built, children in Littleville, an in-between place, could attend a city school on either side of the county. My daddy had attended RHS, while Mother went to Deshler High School. I have very early memories of Daddy talking about how miserable he was from the moment he started high school, he could still name those teachers and classmates who had been kind—and those who had not—to the country boys. For instance, he remembered the young red-haired woman who had helped him register for his first classes; she was the daughter of the principal. When I started to RHS in 1977, she was my algebra teacher, and Daddy told me of her kindness. And, whether she remembered him or not, she showed me that same kindness when I related the story to her. He and his buddies from Littleville clung together, sharing and extending their sense of community into this city space to lessen the not-fitting, the out-of-placeness of the terrible unfamiliar. One or two of the "smart kids" were able to find their place in academics to fit in.

Daddy remembers the school principal telling the 1958 graduating class that if he could ever do anything for them, they should come see him. This is a very Southern stock-phrase which essentially means goodbye and good luck. Daddy remembered it, though, and by the time I was in junior high, that principal had become superintendent. Daddy packed me up in the car to go see him. I wanted to go to Russellville for the band. Even though the CHHS band director had worked tirelessly teaching us to play music to build the high school band program by feeding into it. In the summer of my 7th grade year, I saw the RHS Marching 100. I thought they were beautiful in their sleek black and gold uniforms. Their hundred members plus covered a football field, very different from our rag-tag group of forty-three mostly elementary and junior high beginners. I have not longed for anything so much as to be in that band. Not before then or after. Daddy went one morning to the superintendent's office to remind him of his offer 20 years earlier. And probably because no former student had taken him up on it in all those years—especially one of the country kids—Mr. Courington found a loophole. I was allowed to enroll. It was not until forty years later Daddy told me of the shame he had felt when, later that year I told them they ought to get a new car. After band practice, there was Mother, waiting for me in the same 1968 Impala—now out of style in 1978. It brought feelings he felt as a kid from Littleville twenty years before—feeling un-fitting and un-seen by the city kids. I was now one of those city kids. Not even our car was good enough, he told me through tears. The great irony here is that in spite of having a city education, I did not move up nor out of North Alabama. I succumbed, as I name it now, to gender expectations. I got married at age eighteen—no college, no leaving—and had children, and became a school teacher. Thinking now of Hektner's research on resolving conflicts whether to stay or go (1995), I wonder sometimes how different this narrative would have been if I had gone on to that small rural high school built on a patch of farm land.

CONCLUSION

The town of Littleville changed during the recession of the 1980s. The four main industrial job sources—three that had contributed to the post-War boom in North Alabama—shut down because of outsourcing. This left its citizens, formerly employed—as my parents had been—by the makers of Lee jeans, Reynolds Metals, Robbins Rubber and Tire, and Ford Motors, left only with low-paying, low-skilled, non-union jobs. The area also felt a "ripple effect" brought on by the farm crisis of the 1980s (Bard et al., 2006). The lucky ones, like my parents, had worked in these factories for long enough to retire with benefits, so their lifestyles did not change much. It was a town that slowly, and nearly unnoticeably to most people, lost its children. With declining numbers, the little district succumbed to the consolidation movement of the 80s. Around the same time economic markets and demographic patterns shifted, *A Nation at Risk* came out, which has been identified as the driving force behind school reform in the 80s (Bard et al., 2006). The threat of "risk" allowed the federal government to mandate that states initiate accountability measures such as performance standards, testing, and teacher requirements ("High Quality Teachers," in *No Child Left Behind*). But, accountability does not ensure quality; accountability only assures accounting.

The first mention of closing Littleville School was in 1977—the year I left. In an article from the *Florence Times*, Alabama Board of Education Surveyors recommended closing five rural schools in Colbert County due to falling enrollment, limited program offerings, and cost per students—all of which support research on rural consolidation. The article states, "Enrollment at Littleville Elementary also falls below the recommended Average Daily Attendance (ADA), but with the closing of Underwood [school] and transfer of grades 1–4 to Littleville, the enrollment would increase enough to meet requirements, the survey said" (*Florence Times*, 1977). In 1986, the School Board the first phase of a bailout plan was revealed by Superintendent Roger Moore: Littleville's seventh- and eighth-grade students would be transferred to Colbert Heights (*Times Daily*, March 1, 1986). The *Times Daily* reported Superintendent Moore's decision to keep the school open for the 1989–1990 school, although enrollments continued to drop, by now dipping to a total of 120 students in grades K-6. In 1993, so few students were enrolled in 5th grade, those remaining students were moved to Colbert Heights Elementary. The vote to close Littleville School took place at the School Board in Tuscumbia on Thursday, July 8, 1993. By 1994, the year it was finally closed, enrollment was down to 84 in grades 1–4 and 6 (*Times Daily*, 1994).

In 1994, the city purchased the property, promising the townspeople that the building would be kept alive by using it regularly for various community functions. They promised, and for a year or so, it seemed that they tried. The local Jaycees held a Halloween festival for the neighborhood kids, and the whole building was turned into a spook house. Few additional cobwebs were needed for effect. Slowly, though, the city council began having a hard time finding enough uses for the old place. Here and there a board went up over a broken window. The new gym, once a community showpiece, was now showing its age, paint peeling, metal windows rusting. In 2010, the city admitted defeat and sold the dilapidated school to one of the councilmen for scrap lumber. One Saturday, he was alone inside ripping up planks on the old wood floors when he had a massive heart attack and died instantly, the last life the old school would ever change.

In the summer of 2015 the Littleville Volunteer Fire Department had the unique opportunity for a practice drill. The town council had voted to demolish the shell-place where the majority of them had been students. Daddy showed me a picture Mother had taken of him, back to her, looking down at the smoldering rubble, head down, hands in pockets, a stance I had seen many times. Come on, he said, I'll show you the last of it. When I got out of the pickup, there was nothing to see. The bulldozer had buried everything that was left. How strange, I thought, that they even buried all the stones that were its exterior walls. I thought about the verse in the Bible where Jesus says, *But he responded, Do you not see all these buildings? I tell you the truth, they will be completely demolished. Not one stone will be left on top of another* (Matthew, 24:2, New Living Translation). Over there, Daddy said, you can still see the smoke. We walked over to where the old auditorium had been—Kiddie Bands, band practice, class plays, the stage behind which my dad had marked the date of his being there—and rising up out of the red earth was a curl of smoke. I waited for you, it said, as I smelled the last of the burning memory, sorry that I had taken its physical presence for granted.

Tieken's meticulous portraits draw the lives of communities and how these are inextricable from their local schools. When the schools close, the communities suffer loss—but the loss experienced by communities are felt individually in the people who voice the stories. The loss of its school "permanently diminishes the community itself, sometimes to the point of abandonment" (Tieken, p. 22). Economically and socially, communities are dependent upon their schools, and when they close, the effects are devastating to those communities. One irony is that the same government reform that promised unrealized economic advantages to communities in exchange for consolidation is the reform that led to closure with communities "slowly and quietly disappearing after" (Tieken, p. 27). Time and again, studies show spirals of decline (p. 62) in which it is hard to tell which closed first, businesses or the school. "If there is a road sign, there is a school ... or there was," Tieken notes (p. 160). And where there are schools, there are signs of life. It is the other road signs that are disturbing—the road signs "without much else" (p. 160), where schools have closed and communities have dried up. Schools sustain communities in ways that no other organizations do—not even churches. Littleville School constructed local histories in the lives of its students, and in those storied lives, constructed its own. While I agree, from my own autobiographical analysis, with Jackson in her Foucauldian analysis of rural shooling (2010, p. 91) that "the idea of unity in a community is a fiction—a constructed condition of discourse," I recognize a life cycle between communities and schools that also constructs sites of historical consciousness from which transformation might occur. Loss creates spaces for the interior work of the synthetical moment; it is the site of possibilities for transformation.

I plan to continue my curriculum studies of rural place. I'm not sure why it took me so long to come to this topic, only giving it serious consideration when Bill Reynolds asked me to write for his book. I have, after all, written about Southern place for more than a decade. I believe I have been myopic toward my home town—anchored for over a half century by its school—too close to it to see how we clung to one another. The work here is a beginning, for there is so much that has remained unquestioned and unnamed. For example, I only uncovered the Google Newspaper archives of the local newspaper accounts surrounding the closure as I was wrapping up the piece. There was no time to discuss the political implications and public reactions beyond what I included here. One important discovery is directly related to the disclaimer about the absence of a discussion of race in this piece. I discovered two articles from the *Times Daily* that brought race directly into discussions having to do the closure. The first, from 1993, Racism, Betrayal Charged in Vote to Close Schools, states that Superintendent Moore had heard charges of racism for eight years, "I'll continue to hear it and I don't agree with it," he said. The second, Racial Balance Routine Locally, Area Officials Say, is from May of 1994, following the closure, that lists, forty years after Brown v. Board, the percentage of minority students in area schools. Only one school had zero percent: Littleville School.

I would like to look more at historical contexts as they related to school and community. A great deal was going on in Alabama and the South from 1938 to 1994, and yet as a student I was hardly conscious of any of it. I wonder how conscious the community was—since, whenever I go back, I go back in time, as though nothing much affects the sensibility of the place. I am interested in exploring local historical, political, social, and religious contexts to help me understand more of how "power and privilege combine, within discourse, to produce place identity" (Jackson, 2010, p. 91). My studies have webbed outward—or rather backward—to my genealogy, because a history of my ancestors is a history of Littleville itself. All roads, for them, led to here, so as I learn about the place, I am constructing my own historical contexts. I have also undertheorized queering place through the lens of queer identity. That, too, is a part of the continuing work, and I will approach it by holding my father's story up to mine and looking for intersections. Oncescu's recent study of community resiliency when its school closes finds that the school anchored the community's different generations by cultivating inter-generational interactions and connecting different generations in the community (2014, pp. 14–16). I realize I could spend the rest of my life looking at one place; I think that may be what a "Curriculum of Place" is for me.

CODA

I called my parents yesterday, happy to be able to tell them I had been writing on "The Littleville Piece." I told them I wanted to sit down and turn on the recorder and capture more of their stories. Told them I still want to contact Mrs. Wells to hear about the closing from "the inside." Daddy said: "You know, not long ago, I was down at the store, and I ran into Mr. Wagnon, who used to be the principal at Littleville. He was a fine man; a fine looking man. Member of The Church [of Christ, my parent's denomination]. I introduced myself to him and told him I had been a student when he was there. So then he looks at me and says, 'Well, let me ask you something, Gene. Why in the world did y'all just sit back and let them put the new high school out in that cow pasture. Littleville had the water works, and was incorporated, and sits right here on the highway. Y'all just let 'em do it.'" Then Daddy said, "I thought a minute and said, "Mr. Wagnon, I reckon nobody cared. They didn't know what it would mean, and they didn't care." And then he said to me, "And the people that did care—well, they're all about dead now. Including us." And he finished, "I'll tell you one thing though: when a town loses its school, it's in trouble. It's done." I could not have said it better myself.

REFERENCES

Bard, J., Gardener, C., & Wieland, R. (2006). National Rural Education Association report rural school consolidation: History, research summary, conclusions, and recommendations. *The Rural Educator, 27*(2), 40–48.

Casemore, B. (2005). *The language and politics of place: Autobiographical curriculum inquiry in the American South.* Dissertation. Retrieved February 10, 2016 from http://etd.lsu.edu/docs/available/etd-11162005-131958/unrestricted/Casemore_dis.pdf

DeYoung, A., & Howley, C. (1992). The political economy of rural school consolidation. *Viewpoints.* Retrieved from ERIC on February 1, 2016.

Florence Times/Tri-Cities Daily. Surveyors Recommend Closing Five Colbert Schools. March 27, 1977. Retrieved February 27, 2016 from https://news.google.com/newspapers?nid=1842 &dat=19770327&id=uyUsAAAAIBAJ&sjid=D8cEAAAAIBAJ&pg=1692,3939487&hl=en

Franklin Free Press. (2007, February 7). Memories of Littleville school still delight alumni. *2*(6), p. 12.

Hektner, J. (1995 Spring). When moving up implies moving out: Rural adolescent conflict in the transition to adulthood. *Journal of Research in Rural Education, 11*(1), 3–14.

History and Remembrances of Littleville, Alabama. (1984). In A. McCollister (Ed.), Produced by the Northwest Alabama Council of Local Governments.

Howley, C., & Howley, A. (2010). Poverty and school achievement in rural communities: A social-class interpretation. In K. Schafft & A Youngblood Jackson, (Eds.), *Rural education for the twenty-first century: Identity, place, and community in a globalizing world.* University Park, PA: The Pennsylvania State University Press.

Howley, C., Theobald, P., & Howley, A. (2005). What rural education research is of most worth? A reply to Arnold, Newman, Gaddy, and Dean. *Journal of Research in Rural Education, 20*(18), 1–6.

Kincheloe, J., & Pinar, W. (Eds.). (1991). *Curriculum as social psychoanalysis: The significance of place.* Albany, NY: State University of New York Press.

Oncescu, J. (2014). Creating constraints to community resiliency: The event of a rural school's closure. *The Online Journal of Rural Research and Policy, 9*(2), 1–30.

Pinar, W. (2004). *What is curriculum theory.* Mahwah, NJ: Lawrence Erlbaum.

Pinar, W., & Grumet, M. (1976). *Toward a poor curriculum.* Dubuque, IA: Kendall/Hunt.

National Education Association. *Report of the committee of twelve on rural schools appointed at the meeting of the national educational association.* Chicago: University of Chicago Press, June 28, 1896.

Theobald, P., & Wood, K. (2010). Learning to be rural: Identity lessons from history, schooling, and the U.S. corporate media. In K. Schafft & A. Youngblood Jackson (Eds.), *Rural Education for the Twenty-First Century: Identity, Place, and Community in a Globalizing World.* University Park, PA: The Pennsylvania State University Press.

Thompson, B. (2013). Drag and the politics of performance. In *Queer south rising: Voices of a contested place* (pp. 19–41). R. U. Whitlock, Ed. Charlotte, NC: Information Age Press.

Tieken, M. C. (2014). *Why rural schools matter.* Chapel Hill, NC: The University of North Carolina Press.

Times Daily. Deficit Claims Schools, Jobs; Board Criticized. March 1, 1986. Retrieved February 27, 2016 from https://news.google.com/newspapers?nid=1842&dat=19860301&id=YWEeAAAAI-BAJ&sjid=msgEAAAAIBAJ&pg=3150,6783&hl=en

Times Daily. Littleville school to stay open. May 5, 1989. Retrieved February 27, 2016 from https://news.google.com/newspapers?nid=1842&dat=19890505&id=v1geAAAAIBAJ&sjid=LsgEAAAAIBAJ&pg=2725,505720&hl=en

Times Daily. Littleville school: Faculty say small-campus closeness lingering to end. April 24, 1994. Retrieved February 27, 2016 from https://news.google.com/newspapers?id=AkseAAAAIBAJ &sjid=DccEAAAAIBAJ&pg=1130%2C3406847

Times Daily. Racial balance routine locally, area officials say. May 18, 1994. Retrieved February 27, 2016 from https://news.google.com/newspapers?id=EE8eAAAAIBAJ&sjid=JccEAAAAIBAJ &pg=3423%2C2570904

Times Daily. Racism, betrayal charged in vote to close schools. July 9, 1993. Retrieved February 27, 2016 from https://news.google.com/newspapers?nid=1842&dat=19930709&id=L4EgAAAA-IBAJ&sjid=ascEAAAAIBAJ&pg=1420,1107972&hl=en

TimesDailycom. Councilman's death a loss for town, mayor says. November 22, 2010. Retrieved February 28, 2016 from http://www.timesdaily.com/archives/councilman-s-death-a-loss-for-town-mayor-says/article_bd8bab68-9ee7-54f7-beed-063b372d2422.html

Tyack, D. (1974). *One best system: A history of urban education*. Cambridge, MA: Harvard University Press.

Whitlock, R. U. (2007). *This corner of Canaan: Curriculum studies of place and the reconstruction of the south*. New York, NY: Peter Lang.

Whitlock, R. U. (Ed.). (2013). *Queer south rising: Voices of a contested place*. Charlotte, NC: Information Age Press.

Youngblood Jackson, A. (2010). Fields of discourse: A Foucauldian analysis of schooling in a rural, U.S. Southern Town. In K. Schafft & A. Youngblood Jackson, (Eds.), *Rural education for the twenty-first century: Identity, place, and community in a globalizing world*. University Park, PA: The Pennsylvania State University Press.

CHAPTER TWELVE

Nowhere TO Somewhere

RANDY HEWITT

> Autobiography is an architecture of self, a self we create and embody as we read, write, speak and listen. The self becomes flesh in the world. Even when authentic and learned, it is a self we cannot be confident we know, because it is always in motion and in time, defined in part by where it is not, when it is not, what it is not. The self who welcomes the dawn is a self constantly expanding to incorporate what it fears and resists as well as what it desires. The self who rows with golden oars is a self constantly contracting, losing its gravity so it may rise, expansive toward the sky. Full of tears and full of laughter may we teach and may we learn; may we become gods of our own lives, servants to others.[1]

I got my first teaching job during the 1991–1992 school year on the Navajo Reservation at 5,307 feet up on the Colorado Plateau. My assignment was to teach 10th grade English at a public boarding school located on a federal compound, operated by the Bureau of Indian Affairs. The school served as the heart of a remote community 85 miles south-southwest of the Four Corners Plaque and 104 miles north-northwest of Gallup, NM, both by way of US 191, a road that runs from the Mexican border up the edge of and into the middle of nowhere. We were in the middle of nowhere.

It didn't start out this way, though. We actually thought we were going somewhere. Our tattered Rand McNally put us out close to Albuquerque, Flagstaff, Denver, Death Valley and Vegas. These places existed to us only in newspapers, movies, and cartoons. My wife, the daughter of a career Marine, had lived in Jacksonville, Florida and Algiers, Louisiana but she hadn't really been nowhere neither. She, at least, had experienced the kind of liberal education one receives by virtue of people from parts as diverse as the Bronx and Walla Walla coming together to form "the few and the proud." At 25 years old, I had been as far east as Myrtle Beach, as far west as Atlanta. Through high school, I had gone to watch the Shrine Bowl every year in Charlotte. This is not to say that I was sheltered.

I grew up to three generations of white trash, "lint-head" who didn't have a pot to piss in nor a bed to slide it under. What we did have was a stubborn pride in a puritan work ethic and in the fact that we were clean and fed every night. We also possessed demons of failure that typically torture the poor. I had witnessed my father batter my mother, always over money and always taunted by the implication that he was a "no-count-son-of-a-bitch" who couldn't provide for his family. Once his rage destroyed his external world, it ricocheted inward as he banged the sound and fury into the wall with his head until it bled. I had watched my grandfather spend the last ten years of his life slowly dying of blood loss through a hole he had drank into his stomach with vodka. He consumed it daily to sedate himself from coughing out 30 years worth of cotton dust. On the day we buried him, my grand-mother told me that he was always bitter that she had been promoted to weaving supervisor over him and the rest of the men. When it was all said and done, the vodka dulled his sense of emasculation, and, more importantly, I would imagine, the fact that after 30 years of working their assess off, none of them would do no better than warping and weaving thread for a meager living. The "mill-hill" had various ways of reminding us of this latter sense. And whether through pills or paint, through stealing or simply giving up, we all found ways to endure the futile, and usually to the effect of debasing ourselves even more.

Fortunately for me, I escaped this fate through a serendipitous stroke of mis-fortune. Early one summer Tuesday, my father was hauling 11,000 gallons of fuel in a gasoline truck and was run over and killed by a county trash truck. Insurance money moved us from Victor Mill to Victor Heights, but don't let the name change fool you. We moved only a mile and a half away from the mill and the railroad tracks. The same demons of class that circulated our heads before moved with us. But, the slight change in context and contacts led me to college seven years later where I met my wife over a shared tab of window-pane. No, we weren't sheltered; we were just a young couple who never had nothing, never been nowhere.

The 1969 film *Easy Rider* captured the best of what she and I knew of the American Southwest. And now, we were Captain America and Billy The (With) Kid on our way to find what was pure about America. Naïve? Certainly, though more like ignorant than anything else. We both shared the image of Native Americans as depicted by Iron Eyes Cody in the 1971 Keep America Beautiful campaign.

Having stepped thru the windowpane several times together already, we started to develop an emergent idea of "various ways of knowing" and of sub-uni-verses with their own temporal orders, as William James would later identify for us in *The Principles of Psychology*. Once on the other side of this windowpane, all human beings were merely forces of chemistry and physics animated right before our eyes. The idea that human beings are merely part of this universe and not set over or against it represented to us the core of Native American beliefs and magnetically, we were drawn to this "homegrown" idea.

We became political. Courses in U.S. History had pointed up to us that the government and greed muscled the Native Americans to inhospitable lands. *Mother Jones* reported about rallies to free the political prisoner Leonard Peltier, and when Neil Young sang "And I know she's living there/And she loves me to this day/I still can't remember when/Or how I lost my way," we both conjured up the image of old Iron Eyes Cody crying for a dying earth spirit prostituted for the unquenchable thirst for profit, patronized and demeaned in the name of progress. All of the above coalesced with the questioning of our own taken-for-granted assumptions about class, race, and gender in capitalist America. To our minds, we had come from the subaltern and, therefore, it was our duty to find our philosophical and political voice for those who had been shut-up and forgotten about. So, when Jack Nicholson tells Dennis Hopper in *Easy Rider* that "it's hard to be free when you are bought and sold in the marketplace," I intended, as a teacher in an Indian school, to open up a space in which the Navajo could voice their experience and be free. I guess you could say that we left the wee hours of South Carolina naively idealistic, just the sort that untested commitment to abstractions and exuberant youth create.

It was during our crawl up US 191 that "somewhere" changed to "nowhere." Once we turned off of Interstate 40 at Chambers, Arizona, we left any semblance of civilization familiar to us. In fact, between Lubbock and Gallup, the rural morphed into the plain barren, and now we had turned off from barren straight into the extraterrestrial. Apparently, somewhere up on the surface of the Colorado Plateau, we were to build our young little family. The feeling that we had just made a terrible mistake grew exponentially with every bloated, dead horse and dried-up cow carcass we passed. Suddenly, the warnings from a dear friend who knew someone who knew someone who lived and taught on the Rosebud Reservation looped through my mind. "They're drunk about half the time," "somebody is always getting shot," and "you will get lice, you can be certain of that." Not that any of these things were new to me at all. Drunks, gunshots, pool-hall cold-cocks were standard operating practice where I came from. But, I didn't need to move 1,800 miles into the middle of nowhere for that. Of course, our friend was a shit-talker and we knew this. It turns out that, with the exception of the alcoholism, none of the warnings applied. Though, on our initial approach up through this high desert, it was hard to imagine anybody living out here at all, and if, in fact, somebody did live out here, it wouldn't surprise me any if he or she drank. This is not to say that we didn't appreciate the natural beauty of the place. The wind-whipped mesas and the solitary red-rock buttes stood as ancient monuments to geologic time against a Sadie Blue sky. The beauty of this odd place counterbalanced the sense of anxiety its isolation generated and kept us occupied the 90 miles until we turned onto the road for the school compound, right past a Fina Mart that sold gas, fishing lures, and hamburgers. Three mangy dogs, one with a plastic milk jug stuck over its head, patrolled the parking lot. Several Navajo men wearing quilted flannel jackets in 96° weather stood post-like in random, illogical spots while tourists stopping for gas maneuvered around them. Once we got to the school, I was to meet the assistant principal, Mr. Ronnie Hunter, with whom I had discussed teaching assignment, housing and moving plans the prior week.

School had already started the second week in August, at the end of which, I had heard from a university professor and lead resume reference, Mr. Hunter had called inquiring as to my availability for a teaching job. The professor told me that the conversation was strikingly brief. The only thing Mr. Hunter wanted to know was if I was the sort of person who sticks by his commitments. He wanted to know if I would stay out there for a full year. In fact, this is the only question asked of my three other references as well. They all thought it strange that a principal of a school in a place and culture quite foreign to mainstream America wouldn't want to know something about a candidate's philosophy of education, his abilities as a classroom teacher, his understanding of subject-matter, his classroom management style, his knowledge and understanding of Native American culture in general and about the Diné in particular. My major professor was so uncomfortable by the dearth of questions that he asked and answered them for Mr. Hunter. Mr. Hunter's comment was, "Great, thanks for answering my question." My professor hung up concerned about where he was sending me. But, after all, I had long hair and a straggly goatee that I refused to cut out of principle, which already had disqualified me from jobs for which I had been seriously considered "a hire." Plus, we had a young daughter and had every intention of having more, so, "until I came to my senses," he advised me to "take it and see what happens." By Tuesday of the following week, Mr. Hunter called me and I told him that I would take the job but that it would take me at least the rest of the week to gather the wherewithal to move across the country and then about three days to get there. "Take what time you need, within reason." He said that they would be expecting us on Friday, August 23rd and would have a house ready for us by the time we got there. 24K, a house, and "take what time you need" getting to your first ever professional job for which you use your mind rather than your muscle? To a young, poor couple living in a trailer, 24K amounted to a small fortune, and moving from rural South Carolina to anyplace Arizona seemed like going from nowhere to somewhere.

We walked into the school at 1 pm on the Friday, just like we said we would. The Navajo women who appeared to be office clerks greeted us with nods and blank faces. After telling a Ms. Yazzie who I was and what I was doing there, she directed a young student to summon Mr. Hunter by pointing down the hallway with a quick purse of her lips, a practice I came to see as common. The girl took her time carrying out the direction. She dropped off a folder at another desk down the hallway, talking briefly with the lady there, chatting with another girl, probably another student, with long jet-black hair spilling over a devil-head Ronnie James Dio t-shirt, black eye-shadow and thick black lipstick. After giggling for the better part of two full minutes, the metal-head pursed her lips back at us standing there, which jarred the messenger's memory about her task. She had returned to her post behind the front office desk for a full 10 minutes before a white male who looked to be late 50s came to greet us. He was wearing a pristine white cowboy hat, a black long-sleeve western shirt, jeans, and black cowboy boots. I would come to see that heavy metal and western wear were the preferred styles here, regardless of age and gender.

Mr. Hunter shook our hands and pinched the little one on the cheek, winking the entire time we spent talking to him. He said that he had moved here from Oklahoma 30 years ago, married a Navajo woman, had two daughters of his own. He said that we were probably anxious to get settled, so he was ready to show us to our house if we were ready to "skedaddle on out of here." As he was saying this, a middle-aged Navajo woman wearing a beautiful sliver and turquoise necklace over a purple, crush-velvet shirt emerged from down the hallway and handed him a folder, then turned her head at us and quickly pursed her lips. This apparently meant something to him because he said, "Oh yeah. I guess you will want to get paid, don't you." The paperwork inside included several U.S. Department of The Interior, Bureau of Indian Affairs forms, numbered and lettered in bureaucratic fashion, a W-4 form, a contract, and a liability waiver. Fittingly, a box on the contract labelled "Geographic Location" was filled in as "Isolated." Mr. Hunter told me to fill this stuff out and give it back to Ms. Tsosie while he called somebody on the phone to see what house had been assigned to us. His exchange with whoever was on the other end didn't sound too promising. Mr. Hunter hung up and said that the housing maintenance department hadn't identified a house for us, which was "good anyhow 'cause now you can pick between one close to the school or one at the back of the school compound." We chose to be closer to the school. He fished around in a drawer, retrieved two sets of keys and then told us to follow him over to the house, which was in a cul-de-sac, right around the corner from the school and in one of several sections of similarly built, stucco-plastered, dirt-colored, government-issued, single-family housing, all set upon red sandstone with no tree nor plant in sight. My wife was impressed. She had lived in base-housing for much of her life and, despite the lack of green, she liked that each house had a yard and a garage. She and I had lived in apartments and a trailer together but never in a house, and now we had one with a garage! We had made it. However, our excitement was short-lived. Once inside, Mr. Hunter flipped on a light switch only to prove what he had feared: no electricity. However, the water was on, and we discovered that we had central heat and air, which brightened our spirits greatly. Mr. Hunter just shook his hat, bemused.

Now don't get too carried away. It's Friday and nothing can be done about the electricity until Monday at best. I don't know if you noticed this yet, but we can get real hot during the day this time of year. So that air conditioning will be of no use until you get electricity. You might want to come stay with me until you can get your power on.

We immediately thanked him for his kindness but we weren't about to go stay with strangers with a baby who is up at all hours of the night. It simply would be too uncomfortable for us to do that, which he understood just fine. He told us where we needed to go on Monday to get the power cut on and gave us directions to his house if it got too hot for us. Then, he left us to ourselves until Monday, at which point I would see him at school.

We made it through the three nights but barely. The temperature outside was still 86° at 10:30 pm. Fortunately, the temperature fell off greatly around midnight, which allowed us to fall asleep, only to be awakened by four wild horses carrying on in the front yard. (It took us just one trip up to the Fina Mart to find out that the Navajo let their animals roam, which was a serious, even fatal, problem for drivers who happened along a cow standing in the middle of the road at night.) By 10 am the next day, we had driven the 110 miles back to the nearest place to return the moving truck, which was Gallup, and made our way back through to Chinle, a town of about 4,000 people 13 miles away from our new home.

Chinle served as a supply hub for people living within a 50 mile radius and for hikers, backpackers, and sight-seers going down into Canyon De Chelly, a small-scale version of the Grand Canyon. At the time we were there, Chinle had a Bashas' grocery store, a newly opened Burger King, a hardware store, two motels, and two sit-down restaurants, one attached to each of the motels. There were local tribal offices there, several elementary schools, two junior high schools, and Chinle High School. On our way back from returning the moving truck, we stopped at the grocery store to buy food items that didn't need to be refrigerated. On the edge of the parking lot was a small flea market comprised of Navajo arts: kachina dolls, paintings, silver and turquoise jewelry. Our little one, like us, had been sitting in a car all day and had just started walking, so we thought that this would be a good time to let her move around and we could get to know something about the people of our new place. Several Navajo girls came out to see the baby and hold her hands while she walked around, picking her up every so often just to show their age. The adults, however, didn't seem so impressed nor cordial. One lady who stood behind a table displaying beautifully intricate jewelry looked at us stone-faced when my wife asked her a question about the craft work. Thinking that the woman didn't hear her, my wife asked again, and again, a blank stare as if she had never asked a question at all. Perhaps the woman didn't speak English or perhaps she didn't want to converse in English, which certainly put us at a disadvantage because we were crippled with knowing only one language. When my wife asked one more question about price, the woman, stone-faced and looking dead at us, turned her back, signaling all deals were off. We attributed this behavior to some idiosyncrasy of the woman's. It turns out that a woman selling pottery and one selling rugs exhibited similar shunning behavior. By the end of the day on Monday, we took this type of behavior toward us personally.

I went to school early Monday morning to find my room, check resources, and pick up my class rosters. I already knew that I would have five class periods of 10th grade English and could see that there was a mix of portable classrooms and several buildings comprising the school campus. I would be in one of the portables. In fact, all English, math, science, and social studies classrooms were in the portables. P.E. was held in a stand-alone gym and on two athletic fields that transitioned immediately from discernable, raked baseball diamond to rocky high desert. Music, art, and shop had their own building next to the gym, and drama took place in a stand-alone library. There also were two dormitories, a cafeteria and the administration building. Ms. Yazzie handed me the keys to the classroom but told me that the official rosters of students wouldn't be complete until after the fair and rodeo season. She also gave me a binder with a cover page titled *The Navajo Way*. I wasn't sure what to do with this binder, as she gave me no instructions, though I politely took it and then went off to find my portable.

I had a corner portable, one closest to the road into the school and the closest to my house. It was very clean, with a chalk board and five rows of seven arm-rest type desks, with chrome baskets underneath. I had a metal desk at the front. The room was bare of any resources whatsoever. About sixteen students filed into my "homeroom." Students scurried across the red dirt court-yard to get to their portables. I propped the door open and stood on the steps to greet students as they come in. Most saw me standing there but didn't make eye contact as they went into the room. There was no bell system, so I guessed that a "gentlemen's agreement" on schedule and time management was the practice. I entered and introduced myself, pointing to my name, which I had already written on the chalk board. Two girls, one with a warm expression and extremely groomed, long, black hair, whom I recognized as my next door neighbor, along with her friend, who, it turns out, wasn't a student at the school at all, sat up front, smiling attentively. The rest of the students looked down or sat sideways in the desks, peaking at me through hair covering their eyes, whispering to their friends seated next to them. Their unwillingness to make eye-contact or to respond directly to any question I asked to the group was unnerving. I was to take attendance and make whatever announcements were put into my school mailbox each day. However, on my first day, there were no announcements and no official attendance form to fill out. I asked the group how attendance is typically taken at the school. They grew silent to hear what I was saying but no one answered. After waiting several seconds, I said, "No? Nobody knows?" A boy sitting sideways in the back followed my question with something in Navajo to a nearby classmate, at which point both boys snickered, quickly looking at me to see if I noticed, and I did. I didn't take offense; I was simply looking for a response to my question. I asked about the attendance again, directing the question at the two boys more so than the entire class. This seemed to suggest to them that their secret joke had somehow emotionally affected me, which fueled several more under-the-breath coded comments. So, I walked over to the one who had initiated the banter and asked him directly if he knew something about attendance. This evidently embarrassed him. His face quickly turned serious, his torso pivoting back under the desk properly, his chin going down to rest on the back side of his hands, which were overlapped and resting on the desk. He wouldn't answer me. I asked the girl who was my neighbor what his name was and she looked at him as if to say, "I'm sorry for doing this," and then reluctantly said, "Kevin." I told Kevin my name and asked if he had a sheet of paper I could have. Without looking at me, he said, "-elp," neither a "yes" or a "no." So, I waited but he kept his head down. Seeing that he wasn't going to cooperate, I said "thank you" to him, which he repeated in a mocking but damn good impression, inviting the class to laugh as I turned and walked back to the front. My neighbor, who was laughing herself, produced a sheet of paper. I passed it around and instructed the students to sign in. As the sheet was circulating, two boys and a girl swung open the door as if to say "surprise," again drawing laughter from the class. Ignoring my "Hello, how can I help you," they rushed to the back, one sitting on the top of the desk facing a girl with whom he was familiar, the other two holding their exaggerated "surprise" expressions to muscle failure. They had barely taken their seats when students from other portables begin pouring out, which had a contagious effect on my homeroom. All filed out hurriedly except my neighbor. She said that she was in the next class too, that is, first period. I collected the attendance sheet from a desk and went to open the door for the next class. Everyone had simply written their first names.

I only had 12 students in my first period class. About eight filed in on time, again passing by without eye contact, spending the entire class looking down, playing with their hair or fingers, or simply laying their heads down on their desks. We could all see out the window that students were still milling around outside five, ten minutes past when a bell should have sounded, which was behavior that continued and was accepted over the entire year. Two of those many students walking around outside bounced up my stairs and rumbled into my room, looking around like they had just woken up and didn't know where they were. They didn't take seats but didn't approach me standing there either. "Can I help you," I asked. Shy to a crippling point, one said, "We are here." "We're not absent," the other boy said. "Okay, that's fine," I said, "just take a seat." Both looked around the room at mostly empty seats, confused by too many choices. "We just want to make sure you say we are here," one boy finally said. I looked to my neighbor for help. She said something to them in Navajo, to which one responded. Again with a warm smile,

Lorie told me that the boys were in my homeroom and wanted to make sure I marked them in attendance for the day. "Oh," I said, looking back at them, causing them to blush at Lorie. "Okay, no problem," I said, shaking my head affirmatively. "Okay," they responded, smiling, then turned and busted out the door, punching each other on their way down the steps and running off.

Students' time awareness and management became an issue, at least for me, in every class. Once students were in the classroom, they stayed put for the most part, unless they needed to go to the bathroom or if they suddenly became ill. In these cases, they would just get up and leave, regardless of my or any other teacher's pass policy, which seemed silly to them. But, getting students into the classroom on time was as frustrating as herding cats. From the first day of class to my very last one there, somebody or several somebodies were always showing up late for class, sometimes ten minutes late, other times ten minutes before class was over, never with an official excuse and usually without a personal one either. And, true to form, two students came fifteen minutes late to my first period class, during which I was introducing myself, my hobbies, and what we could look forward to doing in 10th grade English for the year.

Since there was no official English department, and no specified or pre-determined English curricula for the four grades, I was left to my own devices as to what to do for the year. Later on in the week, the 12th grade English teacher, who served as our subject-area leader by default of seniority, and I met to talk through what we each were going to do. I had intended to use Native American literature as the foundation for the course, with a heavy emphasis on writing. My colleague said that we didn't have any of that material in storage. Then I would just follow what the curriculum that was standard in South Carolina at the time: a foundation of 19th and 20th century literature, a review of grammar and mechanics, and an emphasis on writing. When I told him this plan, he laughed and told me that we have this material but I might find that I will have to temper my expectations quite a bit. He said that 12 grade English is supposed to focus on the 20th century novel but said that he will be lucky if they read an entire novel before the Christmas break. "God forbid, don't let them take the books out of the classroom. They won't bring them back." I didn't tell my colleague that he was cynical and short-changing the students out of a meaningful education but I think he could sense that I felt this way because he followed up his words of advice with, "But you do whatever you think is right." Since I had five classes of the same prep, and hadn't had a chance to rummage through the storage room before my first day, I basically introduced the class to what English II would entail. We were going to read, write, read, and write. I also wanted to set them to work right away. Once I had introduced myself and explained some of my interests, I instructed the students to do the same. Each class fell silent and just stared, not directly at me but at some spot either beyond me or at each other. They seemed dumbfounded that I had asked them to do anything at all. "Does everyone have paper and something to write with," I asked, trying to prod them along. Someone in every class responded with "elp" and then sat there still staring. I had no paper and only four extra pens in my bag. I asked if someone would be so kind as to give paper to those who didn't have it. Despite every student receiving paper, it turned out that a good portion of each class, at least 20%, left without turning anything in. And those who did wrote three to five sentences that were, again for the most part, non-sensical. Don't get me wrong. Each class had two or three academically inclined students who could and did accomplish the tasks I asked them to carry out. The vast majority of students, however, mostly constructed simple sentences, of which the ideas entailed often were not connected or related even in an implied sense. Writing was something we needed to work on.

My fourth and fifth period were lunch and planning, respectively. On that first Monday, I went into the storage room and found a large amount of texts, from Earth science to physics, algebra to geometry and U.S. history. I settled on Thornton Wilder's *Our Town*, a play underscoring the idea that humans should cherish the present in light of the ephemeral nature of existence, a theme that resonated with me personally. Ms. Yazzie had told me to expect between 35 and 50 students and I had figured that 40 copies would work just fine. We would read in class and I could allow students to take the books home in alternating fashion when necessary. I also took a stack of grammar texts as well, since elements of grammar and mechanics would be just as important as elements of fiction. I carried the books back to my room in three trips, leaving a good 40 minutes of my planning period to read through *The Navajo Way* binder Ms. Yazzie had given me.

The first half of the binder described the Navajo people (Diné), their customs, ways of seeing the world, their history as descendants of people who migrated over the land-bridge from present day Siberia into Alaska. The material also provided a history of the Navajo Reservation, which students as well as teachers referred to as "The Rez" but the Navajo more formally referred to as Navajo Nation (Dinétah). The binder also provided some general demographic information, all based on U.S. census data. The poverty rate among the Navajo was 38%; the unemployment rate was 50%, with the largest number of workers in construction, mining, education and health services, and the arts. The second part of the binder outlined our education mission and goals. The aim of our instructional endeavors was to prepare Navajo students to be 21st century global, economic citizens. We were to do this basically through a process of deculturalization. They were not to speak Athabaskan except in their Navajo Studies class, which every student had on his or her schedule. English was the official language of instruction. We were to encourage cooperation through competition. Sports and clubs should play a prominent role in their extra-curricular life. Of course, the imperialism was implicit in paternalistic language. The aim wasn't to create a context whereby Navajo students would develop the intellectual skills and habits necessary to understand their lives, their experience as sacred souls on the Earth; it was to foster habits, values, skills necessary for them to become global citizens, seemingly defined only in economic terms. Now, I wouldn't read Herbert Bowles' and Samuel Gintis' *Schooling in Capitalist America* for another three years, but my intuition based upon my own experience of schooling suggested this meant that we were to sort and them prepare Navajo students to take their place in a newly de-regulated economy. I couldn't have articulated the idea then but in hindsight, such an aim made no sense at all, unless students were planning on moving off their sacred land 232 miles to Albuquerque, or 170 miles to Flagstaff, or 312 miles to Phoenix. Unless farming, rodeo performing, working in the uranium or coal mines, painting, weaving, and silverwork, or herding sheep were included in a 21st century economic blueprint, then this whole educational enterprise I now was a part of was a charade. And while it is true that Wilder's play had something to say about the human condition, I suddenly saw it and all the other literature in that storage room as insidious tools of the Overseer, of which I now was one. Two boys fighting each other to be first into my 6th period class shattered the overwhelming feeling that I was an agent of cultural destruction, and I snapped back into my role as Mr. Hewitt before a live, trickling –in audience.

Both 6th and 7th periods were roughly similar to the first three: non-responsive students, late students, poorly written to no essays. One difference, though, was that I had three clean-cut full grown men in my last period class, who by posture and statement, let me know that I wasn't going to intimidate or push them around. Their cowboy hats, boots, and large belt-buckles made them appear puffed-up and bigger than they actually were. In a way they were cute. While appearing tough, all three dressed and looked alike, as if they had coordinated their attire the night before. Climbing up the stairs together, the biggest of the boys stood tall a foot away from me, his cowboy hat nearly touch my forehead.

"You the teacher?" He asked.

"Yes, my name is Mr. Hewitt and I teach 10th grade English."

The big boy turned to the other boys when he heard my name.

By 2:30 in the afternoon, the bureaucratic routine called school had drained their attention and taxed their patience. One girl, who would wear the same Nirvana shirt every day, asked, "Why we need to do this at all … what did you say your name was?"

"Mr. Hewitt," I returned.

"Who-it! She said, mimicking me with an exaggerated "oo" sound. This then became the cue for several of the boys in the class to make owl sounds, drawing laughter at me first and then collecting it themselves as the class focus turned to the silliness of their antics. While the three cowboys laughed, they did so reservedly and went back to writing their introductions, seeming annoyed that the foolishness had gone on too long. Mr. Hunter came in, smiled, and looked around as if he were checking to make sure certain students were in class, nodded to himself, then walked to the back and sat down next to the three cowboys. This did have somewhat of a cooling effect on the groups, though I wish it hadn't. At least I got some energy off of them, even if it verged on mutiny. Some completed their work quickly, then put their heads down. Others just looked out the window without getting out paper and pencil at all. I went around to each student who didn't have writing materials out to see if I could help them get started but this worked only temporarily. I convinced them at least to get paper out and try, even if they didn't know what to say. Occasionally, these same ones would glance to see if Mr. Hunter was watching and then hold the pencil to the paper, poised to write something, if only something would come to their minds. I instructed those who couldn't think of anything to write down a favorite tv show, a movie, a band, song lyrics that described them. This went on for a good 30 minutes. "I don't know what to write." "Mr. Hunter, write this for me." "This is stupid, Who-it." At 3:20, Mr. Hunter, who had been talking to students throughout the period, got up and went out. Five minutes later, all of the students got up and left, even though it wasn't 3:30, the time at which the day was finally over. And for whatever reason, this five minutes early knock-off time applied to everybody the entire year.

On their way out, students place their work on my desk, repeating "Who-it, Who-it" as they left. The three cowboys stayed seated, finishing up their work. I went to hold open the door and found Mr. Hunter on the steps. He quietly said that my last class had several students of concern in it and that he would pop in from time to time to see if they were behaving themselves. I asked about the three students with the cowboy hats still sitting in the room. He told me that they were the very ones he had come to check on. Two of them were brothers, though you wouldn't have known it by looking at them. Titus was the bigger one and was older than his brother Jimmy. Titus should have been out of school already, Mr. Hunter explained. "Tracy is the cousin. The brothers' mom and dad were killed four years ago in a car wreck. A herd of cows standing in the road."

I went back in the room to find the three on their way out. The toughest repeated "Who-it" several times. I responded with "Titus, Titus." This seemed to surprise him as he turned with a slight smile as he existed the door. It would come to be that Titus was my best ally.

The next day I distributed copies of *Our Town* and true to the 12th grade English teacher's prediction, most of these copies vanished from the face of the Earth. I found several laying around the campus, one in a trash can, one out on the bleachers. A dorm counselor gave several back to me when he saw me and a staff member of the cafeteria came by my room in December with a few copies of *Our Town* and *Lord of the Flies*, which I also distributed, determined to make reading the foundation for the class. Not only did the books disappear but expecting students to read out-loud in class and then discuss the meaning of what they had read became pointless. Those students who demonstrated grade-level reading ability simply found reading out-loud in class sophomoric and boring; others who spoke in broken English to start with found the activity assaulting to their self-esteem. I tried reading to them, which held their attention but it didn't translate into reading on their own. On one of our family "get-aways" to Albuquerque, I bought a copy of Richard Erdoes' and Alfonzo Ortiz's *American Indian Myths and Legends*, assuming that these stories would appeal to them. They listened politely but then claimed, "That's not how the story goes, Who-it!" Great. This was an invitation for them to tell me how the story goes but they wouldn't do it. They would just look at each other and smile as if they were part of a club that I had no way of understanding by the very nature of who I was. And this spiritual separation, the feeling that they considered me another form of creature, the sense that I couldn't be trusted, the feeling that I represented to them something despised grew stronger as the days grew shorter.

I read *To Kill a Mocking Bird* and *Animal Farm* to them, which took us up through the last week in October. Plot, setting, characterization, symbolism, point of view wasted their time and made them mad. "Just read the story, Who-it!" The pigs ruling the rest of the farm animals wasn't so much a classed society as it was a story about "some bad-ass pigs forming a gang." Thus, a critical examination of such rhetoric as, "all animals are equal, but some animals are more equal" just led to silence. I showed them the movie versions of the books I read to them. Again, they felt relief that I required something passive instead of asking them to discuss anything. But, if I stopped the movie to make a thematic point or if I asked them an open-ended question about what they would do, for instance, if they were an animal ruled by another group of animals, they would shake their heads at the interruption or respond with a dismissive "nuthin." I thought the question about being ruled by other animals a good metaphor for discussing race but they would tisk and shake their heads as if to say, "There he goes again." The sense of separation from them was the same sense I got when I first read through the binder Ms. Yazzie had given me on the first day of class and the same sense was demonstrated right before my eyes on my first Friday there.

Powwow took place in the gym on the last Friday of every month. Students made a grand entry wearing a variety of beautifully elaborate native dress, apparently dancing out the sacred spirits to a steady rhythm beat on large and small-framed drums. While the pageantry and symbolism inspired awe, I noticed that many of the students wore Megadeth, Slayer, or Pantera t-shirts underneath their feathered costumes. A few students in the ceremony stuck out their tongues like Gene Simmons, Kiss's demon, and flashed el diablo signals with their hands to their friends in the bleachers. These students wore the costumes of two kinetic

forms: the ancestral form of mythical wisdom and the commodified form of preda-
tory capitalism. Oral history as performance transferred the first; MTV channeled
thru the common areas of the dorms carried the second. Perhaps, as I would come
to see over the course of the year, I was not so much despised by the students for
who I was as an individual as I was not trusted for what I represented to them. The
kids instinctively knew that I had no way of understanding that which I didn't live,
just as they didn't have the means to explain to me the contradictions they lived.
I recognized early, on that first Friday, that I had entered into a cultural rift so
convoluted, so old, and so engrained that I felt not only out of place, but helpless. I
also knew that being a white, civil servant of the U.S. Government explained why
I felt like a despised misfit in a land of misfits. In fact, the entire operation represented centuries of ideological and material colonization of native people, and I
suddenly wanted to go home. But, of course, I couldn't; we didn't have no money.

The immediacy of everyday, practical concerns obstructed the empathy I felt
toward the students' situation. A full month of no pay added to my frustration.
Ms. Yazzie had told me on the first day that my pay could be delayed by one
pay-period due to the fact that my paper work had to go to Washington, D.C. to be
processed. In 1991, there was no such thing as the internet or email, at least for use
by the general public. All correspondence with the U.S. Department of the Interior
was conducted by telephone or through the U.S. Postal Service. Information on all
official forms needed to be in hardcopy form, thus sent through the mail. At the
end of my first pay-period there (we were paid every two weeks), I didn't receive
a pay check. Okay, unfortunate for me but this was expected. However, I didn't
receive a pay check for the second time in a row, and now I had a problem. The
moving van, its gas, plus a little over $1000 in extra cash had drained my wife's
parents of all emergency help they could offer. Ms. Yazzie had no idea what could
be wrong. Mr. Hunter said that the school mail went out at the end of every week
and speculated that my paperwork simply got misplaced and, therefore, delayed.
By this point, this was a labor issue to me and I became furious that I was being
taken advantage of, whether from incompetence or willful neglect, it didn't matter
the reason. I didn't up root my family to come all the way out into nowhere for
nothing. And I told him so, pacing back and forth like a caged animal. Mr. Hunter
tried to claim me down by offering to lend me money until mine came. As I saw it,
taking a loan from him was just one more debt I had to pay with the money I had
yet to receive. The place was simply getting to be too much. Students coming late
to class and their consistent resistance to anything related to effort became onerous
to deal with and to understand. For example, I was asked to coach the junior varsity
football team. Now, I had played and excelled at football from the time I was seven
years old until I graduated high school. I knew football intimately well and had
played with the discipline and intensity of a middle linebacker. The Navajo students, however, showed up to practice late, some there on time, others straggling in

30 minutes, 20 minutes, sometimes five minutes before practice ended. And their attitude toward the sport I took so seriously was nonchalant. In games, 225 Ibs. tackles would switch positions with 120 Ibs. quarterbacks so that each could have a turn throwing or running the ball. They would cheer when the opposing team scored on them. I didn't get it. I was missing something. At one point in the middle of the season, I told Mr. Hunter that I couldn't coach the team any longer. The constant search for players to get to practice, the non-competitive nature of their play all made for an exercise in futility. As expected, Mr. Hunter had some perspective on the matter.

"Well, as far as time goes," he explained,

> they will make it to practice when they finish doing whatever it is they are doing before practice. You see, the Navajo are sheep herders by tradition. It's time to go on and do something else when the herd gets from one place to the next. So, when they finish eating or sleeping or watching tv, they will get to practice. And too, look where the hell you are. There ain't much else out here but each other and each other is all they got. These people put a premium on cooperation, not competition. They are not going to compete with the very people they have to depend on. And this holds true for everything they do. Place and people shape each other, son. There's more important things out here than football.

Place and people shape each other. If I had to be honest with myself, this wasn't my place nor my culture. It wasn't any battle I wanted to fight. Once I accepted this, I had to accept that we were leaving here at the end of the year. This also meant that I had given up on the students as well. I reconciled myself with being a quitter, at least temporarily, by claiming that every teacher out here had done the same thing when they gave up having any expectation. They just couldn't admit the conclusion to themselves. Yet still, I had to maintain some semblance of dignity as a person, one snared in a place that couldn't claim me and that I couldn't claim as my own. The Navajo weren't the misfits; I was.

Eudora Welty has written insightfully about the function of place in fiction that is instructive to what Bill Pinar has called "the architecture of the self." Welty writes,

> Unlike time, place has surface, which will take the imprint of man—his hand, his foot, his mind; it can be tamed, domesticated. It has shape, size, boundaries; man can measure himself against them. It has atmosphere and temperature, change of light and show of season, qualities which man spontaneously responds. Place had always nursed, nourished, and instructed man; he in turn can rule it and ruin it, take it and lose it, suffer if he is exiled from it, and after living on it he goes to it in his grave.[2]

A racialized mill-hill literally divided by a railroad track nursed, nourished, and instructed me—that is, constructed me. I started first grade in 1971 as only the third class to integrate my elementary school, which was across the railroad tracks in the black neighborhood called Sunnyside. Most Americans typically think of school integration as black students bused into schools with a majority of white students. However, I, along with all the other kids on my side of the tracks, went to a poorly-funded elementary school in working-class Sunnyside. How I came to a deeper understanding of race through class is simply too long to tell. However, attending a predominantly black school as a white minority quickly disabused me of any idea I may have had about inherent superiority based on my skin color. This lesson was omnipresent. I stammered and stuttered with the "Buzzards" reading group, while many of my black classmates soared with the "Eagles." I struggled to count with my fingers, while Kenny, Vicky, Lisa, and Matt could add and sub-tract quantity in a moment's glance. My clothes were often stained, worn, and slept in for the fourth night in a row, which was a point of ridicule. And where it really mattered to me, in physical activity, my physical size, speed, and strength caused my black counterparts to look me up and down contemptuously and exclaim, "Bitch, please!" Crying to my father was of no use. He gave no shelter to "yellow-bellied quitters." And I sure as shit wanted my own father's love.

> They got it just as hard as we do. They work for fucking pennies, struggle to keep their lights on, their babies fed, and their shit from being repossessed. On top of that, they got to work twice as hard as anybody else to earn respect just because of the color of their skin. You can lay down and quit or you can prove their asses wrong. Best you prove their asses wrong.

Saying this and doing this certainly wasn't the same thing. My black classmates, particularly my fellow athletes, weren't giving me nothing, especially because I was white. They forced me to earn, by quality of performance, every bit of adulation I received. What I learned from my black peers was that excellence is about process, about taking the little bit of nothing one has and turning it into something, despite obstacles. Hell, the entire African American experience stands as a testament to this. "Making something out of nothing," though, comes with no instructions; it's trial and error that forces one, due to the consequences that return back, to trust and fine-tune one's qualitative sense, to know by feel, by rhythm of the quales at work on and though a body. This is not to say that this qualitative sense was a sole possession of black people or that all black people exhibited this sense. This is just my partic-ular experience of some who did. Plenty of white people on my side of the tracks lived by this sense as well. Its root source lies in the blues of the downtrodden but its funk grows out of the invincible determination not only to survive but to prevail. I'm referring here to a class mentality that registers the call of tribulation with a response of "I'm here motherfucker, you best be ready." Tony Bolden has pointed out that this funk "bespeaks a kinetic epistemology" and flows like an electrical charge across an electromagnetic field.[3] The kinship I felt toward the people of Sunnyside had less to do with race directly than it did with a common attitude toward tran-sitory, unstable, and volatile forces that dominated our shared experience of place.

Despite what my whiteness may have represented to the Navajo, it wasn't at my center. And once I reclaimed this center, the better I felt about myself out there in someone else's place. I no longer worried about what they thought of me and my culture, or my skin tone. Whatever their call, my response was from another funky place all together. This doesn't mean that I changed my mind about leaving. This doesn't mean that the students began reading and writing according to federal standards. Their silent resistance towards the covert form of forced assimilation called schooling left many academically paralyzed. But I came to understand the students better in the context of the place that shaped them.

During this same period, I coached wrestling, a sport that I excelled at in high school. This was an opportunity to participate in something I enjoyed but wrestling with the students also allowed them to see me in my element and in another light, looser, less confined by the rules and restraints of our bureaucratic statuses. Not only did they come to respect my balanced control of physical force but, more importantly, they came to see that I cared about them as people, as human beings. I cared that Titus's uncle was dying from kidney failure due to the effects of uranium and radon from a decade of mine work. Other wrestlers or their family members suffered from birth abnormalities, leukemia, lung cancer, and various sorts of blood disorders. If the kids needed something, food, a coat, shoes, a ride, I did my best to meet their demands. And I would like to think that my constant harp on the importance of basic, functional literacy made some impact on them.

My wife and I left this place two weeks before school was over. She was now eight months pregnant with our second child and we needed to be back someplace where we had familial support. I left knowing that I hadn't found the pure at all. I had given up on this quest almost as soon as I got here. But, this remote place in the American Southwest pointed up to me where I was not and what I was not. I may not have found anything pure but I did discover the authentic.

NOTES

1. Pinar (1994, p. 220).
2. Welty (2002, pp. 94–95).
3. Bolden (2008, 15).

REFERENCES

Bolden, T. (2008). Theorizing the Funk: An introduction. In T. Bolden (Ed.), *The Funk Era and beyond: New perspectives on black popular culture* (pp. 14–29). New York, NY: Palgrave Macmillan.

Pinar, W. F. (1994). *Autobiography, politics and sexuality: Essays in curriculum theory 1972–1992.* New York, NY: Peter Lang Publishing.

Welty, E. (2002). *On writing.* New York, NY: Random House.

CHAPTER THIRTEEN

Liberatory Consequences of Sharecropping and Rural Education in the South

DERRICK M. TENNIAL

Over the past few years, I have become the "family historian" as I have been called upon numerous times to collect information to write the obituaries (funeral programs) of deceased loved ones. The obituary is very important in African American culture and serves a genealogical blueprint and final testament that reveals or conceals the intimate details of a person's life. I learned the significance of the obituary from my maternal grandmother, McQuilla Cole, who kept a small green metal file box near her bed that contained important documents such as birth certificates, school report cards, insurance policies as well as the obituaries of loved ones—many of whom died before I was born. Growing up, I would periodically go through that box and read the obituaries; I was fascinated by the lived experiences of the deceased and would often go to my grandmother to fill in the details that I thought were missing. My mere curiositydeveloped into a love of family history, which coupled with my ability to write, all but cemented my position as the "obituary writer."

As I age, the patriarchs and matriarchs of my family are dying giving way to a new generation. Unfortunately, in recent years, I have penned the obituaries of my paternal grandmother, my paternal great-uncle, my maternal great-grandmother, and my paternal great-aunt. Recently, while writing my paternal great-aunt's obituary, I took of note of a trend as it relates to education amongst my deceased family members. (a) They were educated in rural Northern Mississippi or rural Southwest Tennessee. (b) None them completed their high school education. (c) All of their educations were impacted by the sharecropping system.

Reflecting upon my dissertation, *Unto the Third and Fourth Generation: Kaleb Norris' Stories of Generational Poverty and Inequality in the South* (2008) that explored the affects of educational, political, and public policies across five generations of my family, I was reminded of a quote I used from an article regarding education that stated, "the history of education for African-Americans is not a story of liberation and prosperity but one of struggle and disappointment ... education, as we know it, was never intended to have liberatory consequences for African-Americans" (Lynn, 2010, p. 116). As I thought about these four relatives, some of the last who came of age in the "New South" during the Great Depression and the Jim Crow era, I began to wonder did education, rural education, in its simplest form, have any liberating consequences for them? How does rural education in the Northern Mississippi and Southwest Tennessee look today?

After the Civil War, the institution of slavery was replaced with the sharecropping system. During slavery, the plantation was a highly centralized system operating as one unit. The owner or a designated overseer controlled every aspect of plantation life from the crops planted to the capacities in which the slave labor served. However, under the sharecropping system, the plantation operated as a decentralized unit divided into small plots of land, which were leased on a yearly basis to individual families. Instead of living in former slave quarters, the individual families lived on their tract of land. Each family was responsible for planting and harvesting the crops designated by the landowner. The landowner advanced the sharecroppers farming supplies and equipment; in return, the sharecroppers repaid the landowner with 33% to 50% of the crop and kept the remaining portion to do with as they willed. My family, like many other African American families, had no other economic means to make a living as African Americans were prohibited "by law or custom from other almost all other full-time jobs" (Iceland, 2012, p. 81) designated as a "White man's job."

The sharecropping system proved beneficial to the landowners and detrimental to African Americans. Sharecropping failed to liberate African Americans from the agricultural job market nor did it provide opportunities for African American land ownership and control as both remained firmly clinched in the fists of rural southern and northern White investors. Like slavery, African Americans remained under the authority of the landowners or the owners' overseers, managing the sharecropping system in a manner similar to the plantation system, keeping the "true power" under the control of the landowner and the suppliers. Many African American sharecroppers were uneducated (in the formal sense of the word) in that they could not read or write. As a result, many landowners and overseers cheated them out of their crops and profits, falsely leading sharecroppers to believe that instead of making money and getting ahead, they were more in debt at the end of the harvest season. The landowners would keep "accurate" accounting of the sharecropper's debt. The sharecropper would then hope that enough money would be made the next season to pay off the outstanding debt. However, the sharecropper never got ahead and remained indebted to the landowner. As a result of their indebtedness, their socioeconomic mobility was severely restricted by laws that imposed severe penalties and jail time for breaking their sharecropping agreements with the landowners, thus perpetuating a cycle of poverty and economic dependence on the landowner. The sharecropping system proved to be nothing more than slavery—without physical chains.

> Sharecropping, ultimately, failed to secure for freed people a strong enough economic base from which they could establish a political foothold. The economic and political vulnerability of black sharecroppers … rendered them effectively powerless in the political arena, unable to promote their economic interests and protect their civil rights … Freed people agreed to sharecropping … because southern whites managed to close off to them other possibilities, including employment opportunities outside of agriculture. (Royce, 2010)

The most damaging and damning aspect of the sharecropping system for African Americans in the New South was that the de-emphasis of education. African American education, particularly in rural areas, was under funded. Many areas in the rural South "double" taxed *themselves* in order to fund education. In addition to paying property taxes, many African American citizens (who could afford it) took on the burden of financing the "public school" out of their own pockets. "Black teachers, parents, and citizens taxed themselves for school improvement costs, and this practice became increasingly difficult as poor rural communities experienced the Great Depression" (Anderson, 1988, p. 176). "Studies of southern school finances for the period demonstrated that school offices were reluctant to appropriate money for school houses and teachers for black children, expanded virtually no funds for school maintenance, repair, supplies, and transportation" (Anderson, 1988, p. 176). As a result of the lack of funding from state and local authorities, many African American public schools provided an inferior education. Also, some southern states adopted policies requiring a specific attendance rate at African American schools. If the attendance rate fell below a certain level, then the school was closed and funding diverted to other "more deserving" White schools. School attendance in African American schools was a problem—not only because of the inclement weather that would prohibit the students from walking the long distances to school—but also because many families depended on the children to plant and harvest crops, do other chores, and care for younger siblings. The family's livelihood and survival depended on all its members. As a result, when having to make a choice between education—which was not providing the basic needs of food, shelter, and clothes—and working to put food on the table, a roof over their heads, and clothes on their backs, education and schooling became less or unimportant by default.

In 1837, when the idea of universal education for elementary-aged children was introduced to American society by Massachusetts Secretary of State Horace Mann, it was heralded as "the great equalizer." Education was supposed to make "Americans" of the children and bridge the gap between the rich and the poor, the privileged and the underprivileged, and the advantaged and disadvantaged. However, African Americans (and other minorities) were excluded from the concept of education. As mentioned, "the history of education for African-Americans is not a story of liberation and prosperity but one of struggle and disappointment … education, as we know it, was never intended to have liberatory consequences for African Americans" (Lynn, 2010, p. 116).

As a writer and researcher, the challenges presented to me each and every time I have to write an obituary is how do I make meaning of the lived experiences of the dearly departed? In this particular instance, as I reflect upon the lived educational experiences of these relatives, how I do interpret their rural educational experiences? Did education, in its simplest form, have any liberating consequences for them?

My paternal grandmother, Helen Lindsey, passed away three days after her 79th birthday in September 2011. Her birthday is September 11. In her obituary, I wrote:

> She grew-up during the Great Depression and the Jim Crow Era in the farming community. … and experienced the hardest of times. Foregoing a formal education, she went to work at very early age to help her family, which was customary in those days, toiling from sun-up to sun-down, picking cotton and performing other farming chores. This hard work continued into adulthood as Helen had children of her own: Linda, Robert Earl, Johnny Lee, Lurlean, Nina Pearl, and Rennie. As machinery replaced manual labor on the farm in the early 1960's, Helen went to work in a flower nursery, where she worked very hard and received little pay—less than a dollar an hour. She once told of how she had to work in the coldest weather conditions—putting Kroger plastic bags on her hands and feet just to keep warm. Her hands, legs, and feet became visibly riddled with arthritis as a result of the strenuous, back-breaking work.

I did not really begin to understand my grandmother's story until I interviewed her for a family history project during my senior year of high school. It was then that what I seemingly always knew was validated—that she had little formal education. Four years later, I saw her print her own name with verbal prompting. I knew that she could not read, but I was astonished that she could write. I learned that she did attend a nearby primary school, but the growing demands of the family and rural sharecropping life forced her to quit altogether. As the oldest girl, she was tasked with helping her parents take care of her younger siblings and working the land to help the family survive.

"Helen," as I called my grandmother, was a kind and gentle woman, who did not have the opportunity to take full advantage of the even subpar rural education system due to the fact that the sharecropping system kept her economically suppressed and culturally contained in Northern Mississippi. Her educational story is not one of liberation and prosperity, but it is a story void of education that denotes lifelong struggle. "We had a hard life. All we could do was make it from day to day," she once told me with pain and sadness in her eyes as she reflected. In her obituary, I concluded:

> Although she worked hard and never achieved fortune or fame, Helen was rich in the things that matter most. She had the love, respect, and admiration of her family and friends. She believed her children were indeed a blessing and an inheritance from Lord, and she rejoiced as her family grew to include grandchildren and great-grandchildren whom she cared for and encouraged to do great things in life.

Just like my grandmother, my great-uncle Clyde Lee, my grandmother's elder brother, who passed away in January 2015, grew up sharecropping and did not have the opportunity to complete his formal education. As the oldest male and "head of the family," a title he wore with pride in later years, he too had to quit school in order to work the land to help support the family. However, Clyde Lee learned to read and write. The ability to read and write in the African American rural southern community during this time Uncle Clyde Lee came of age set him apart from the masses and automatically made him a community leader as he had what other African American perceived (although limited) was a "White man's education." After farming automation ended sharecropping, Uncle Clyde Lee acquired a position with the Coca Cola Bottling Company. He retired after 31 years of service without missing a single day of work. A very intelligent man, who served for many years as a deacon and trustee in our family church, he was unable to realize and develop his full potential as the educational system along with sharecropping hindered his socioeconomic mobility. In spite of his limited formal education, Uncle Clyde Lee taught his children the importance of education. In fact, he made sure that each one of his children graduated high school and earned college degrees.

At Uncle Clyde's funeral, amongst the sea of Black faces was one White face. It was the same one of two White faces that I remembered from my great-grandmother's funeral some 16 years earlier. I soon learned from the obituary (program) that this White gentleman was W.C.—the son of the property owner on whose land my family were sharecroppers, whom my father told me my great-grandmother Lurline served as his wet nurse and regarded as a son. This was the same man, a lawyer and a judge, who was called upon when legal issues arose in the family—a man whom I never formally met. W.C. spoke genuinely and eloquently about my great-uncle and how he admired, respected, and loved my great uncle. He described him as his best friend whole growing up whom he followed everywhere and from whom he had learned so much. After the funeral, I did some research on my "family member" W.C. and discovered that he is a 13th generational southerner, who is very well respected in the Southwest Tennessee community, for whom education as it *was intended* did have liberatory consequences, perhaps bought and paid for by the sweat from the brow of my great-grandparents, my grandmother, my great-uncles, and other relatives including my father Johnny who lived and worked on his family's former plantation.

The sharecropping and limited education opportunities affected my maternal family as well. My maternal great-grandmother, Connie Mae Cole Faulkner Atkinson, affectionately called "Granny," passed away in November 2011. She was born to sharecropping parents in rural Southwest Tennessee. I recorded this in her obituary:

> Connie Mae Cole was born on Monday, September 20, 1920, and raised in rural Southwest Tennessee. The only child of James and Beatrice Cole, she lost her mother at the tender age of 18 months and was thereafter raised by her father and her grandparents James and Allie Cole alongside her first cousin Mary Lou Payne whom she regarded as a sister. She attended Geeter School, and though quiet and shy, Connie Mae excelled. Her favorite subject was reading, and she enjoyed reading the Bible.

Granny attended Geeter School, which is the one of the oldest schools in Southwest Tennessee. The present day school still sits on land deeded to the county by the widow of Jackson Geeter, a former slave who served in the Union Army during the Civil War, to establish an elementary school to serve the African American children of that rural area (Ford, 2010). Coming from a smaller family, the demand for Connie Mae to work and take care of the family was not as great (unlike that of my paternal grandmother and great-uncle). She was able to enjoy school and completed the elementary grades. I interviewed her as well for a project on my family during my senior year in high school. Granny vividly remembered the names of her teachers, who lived in the same community and attended the same church. She recalled that education and the overall care of children was a community effort that extended beyond the school as teachers were regarded as extension of the parenting unit. Granny even recalled the curriculum she learned as a student at Geeter School. She once told me, "We learn to read from the Baby Ray Book," akin to the Dick and Jane (Primer) Books produced from the 1920s through the 1940s. Granny was fortunate to complete Geeter School; however, that was the extent her formal education as there was not an African American high school available in the rural area. She lived her entire life—married twice and raise four children—not too far from the area where she born.

The educational experience of my paternal great-aunt Laura Mae Tennial Raiford, who passed away in July 2015, mirrored that of my paternal grandmother and great-uncle (mother's side). I wrote these words in her obituary:

> Saturday, April 20, 1916, will forever be recorded in history as the day Laura Mae Tennial made her triumphant entry into the world. Born in the farming community

of Northern Mississippi, she was the first of Bruce and Bernice Taylor Tennial's eleven children. As additional children were born into the family, Laura Mae grew up quickly, performing chores and other duties that came with being a member of a sharecropping family. However, the demands of planting and harvesting crops did not prevent her from receiving a formal education through the Marshall County Schools. Learning to read at an early age developed into a lifelong passion. Laura Mae read daily, and her favorite book was the Bible ... She was a student under her mother, who taught her how to be a nurturing homemaker. Laura Mae used what she learned when she left on a wagon with a mule and cow tied behind to create a loving and enduring home with her husband, Sherman Harrison Moore Raiford, whom she married in 1936. God blessed their union to include thirteen children. Her success of a wife, mother, and homemaker can be seen in the lives of family.

Aunt Laura Mae was one of the strongest people I have ever known. Still at age 97, she had a handshake that would bring any man, woman, or child to their knees. From her mere conversation, one could tell that she was a highly intelligent, well-read woman. Like my maternal great-grandmother, she was able to take full advantage of the limited educational opportunity available in her rural area (unlike my paternal grandmother and great uncle) as education beyond the elementary grades was nonexistent in many rural communities. Even though there are no certificates, diplomas, or degrees lining her walls, the education Aunt Laura Mae received from mother allowed her to become a skilled baker, gardener, quilter, and canner, who promoted formal and technical education amongst her children and grandchildren, many of whom completed high school, college, and/or have successful careers in law, medicine, business, transportation and logistics, etc.

As a writer and researcher, the challenges presented to me each and every time I have to write an obituary is how do I make meaning of the lived experiences of the dearly departed? In particular instance as I reflect upon the lived educational experiences of these relatives, how I do interpret their rural educational experiences? Did education, in its simplest form, have any liberating consequences for them? Although my great-uncle and great-aunt were able to be leaders within their local community and church, the rural education or lack thereof they received and the sharecropping system kept them economically suppressed and culturally contained. They lived as they had been born.

What must be done to ensure that education—whether urban or rural—has liberating consequences for African Americans? For education to liberate African-Americans, we must educate our children about family history, healing the wounds of the past. Learning about their family's history, generational struggles, and cultural history will provide a sense of self-worth and social consciousness (Kozol, 1991, 2005). It will awaken them first to the plights of their own race, culture, and community. "Practices that promote racial pride may be associated with better cognitive and socioemotional outcomes to the extent that they foster positive self-esteem in the child" (Caughy, O'Campo, Nettles, & Lohrfink, 2006, p. 1221).

(b) We must address economics issues. We cannot depend solely on traditional or public education to educate our children. We must teach economic principles to students that allow them to critique the economic system and policies in their community, city, state, nationally, and internationally. We can do nothing to change our family's sharecropping past, but we certainly can learn from it in order to enhance the future. (c) Finally, we must push our children to achieve academically in order to increase number of high achieving, culturally-relevant socially productive African-Americans. We must expose our children to life outside of their rural community. I am not referring to traveling to other parts of the country or world, but I am referring to traveling to other parts of the region in which they live. We must show them that an entire world exists beyond the rural community in which they live. They must be exposed to other cultures and communities. Exposure will open the door to new worlds and encourage the current generation of students in my family and other African-American students in generational poverty to "… reach unparallel levels of success … despite tremendous odds." (Nieto, 2011, p. 33). Also, exposure to things outside their community will teach students to be more socially conscious—encouraging literary skills and social interaction to be successful (Kozol, 1991, 2005). Education (in the traditional sense) may not have had liberatory consequences my grandmother, great-uncle, great-grandmother, and great-uncle's generation, but it can have liberatory consequences going forward.

REFERENCES

Anderson, J. D. (1988). *The education of blacks in the south, 1860–1935.* Chapel Hill, NC: The University of North Carolina Press.

Caughy, M. O., O'Campo, P. J., Nettles, S. M., & Lohrfink, K. F. (2006). Neighborhood matters: Racial socialization of African American children. *Child Development, 77*(5), 1220–1236.

Ford, H. (2010). *More Davids than Goliaths.* New York, NY: Crown Publishers.

Iceland, J. (2012). *Poverty in America.* Los Angeles, CA: University of California Press.

Kozol, J. (1991). *Savage inequalities.* New York, NY: Crown.

Kozol, J. (2005). *The shame of a nation: The restoration of apartheid schooling in America.* New York, NY: Crown.

Lynn, M. (2010). Race, culture, and the education of African-Americans. *Educational Theory, 56*(1).

Nieto, S. (2011). *Affirming diversity: The sociopolitical context of multicultural education.* New York, NY: Longman.

Royce, E. (2010). *The origins of southern sharecropping.* Philadelphia, PA: Temple University Press.

Tennial, D. (2008). *Unto the third and fourth generation: Kaleb Norris' stories of generational poverty and inequality in the south* (Doctoral dissertation). Retrieved from http://digitalcommons.georgiasouthern.edu/cgi/viewcontent.cgi?article=1477&context=etd

CHAPTER FOURTEEN

Rural Education
IN Wisconsin

DANIEL R. PAULSON

OUR PLACE

Northwestern Wisconsin is a beautiful, region rich in natural resources, wildlife, and vast woodlands, prairies and abundant waters. Driving to school I pass through one of a number of a woods and wetlands area which is a state owned public hunting area with no hiking trails or cross country trails here—just woods and wetlands with "logging" roads. I, like so many others, have encountered deer here, one of which bolted onto the road and put its shoulder into the front fender of my car then trotted off into the woods as if to say "stay out of my place." This keeps local body shops in business.

During Thanksgiving week this road is a parking zone and sounds like a "war zone" when deer hunters quest for the "trophy deer" out at their "shacks" with lots of blaze orange, ammunition and liquor. At school the "hunting teachers," have their hunters' preseason breakfast. School boards debate whether to close the school during deer hunting because a large percentage of the students and teachers will be absent, out in their deer shacks for the week. The hunters' organizations are powerful in Wisconsin forcing the Wisconsin Department of Natural Resources to maintain a herd of trophy deer for hunters; other recreational, wild life and environmental issues are secondary. Governor Scott Walker signed Senate Bill 338, which protects hunters from being disturbed, into law at the Wisconsin Bear Hunters' Association 52nd Annual Convention (Walker, 2016).

Guns are a significant part of the culture in rural Wisconsin and communities have hugely popular gun shows which can be held at the schools on a weekend because it's the largest indoor space in the community. Gun raffles are quite commonly held to raise money for the local organizations such as the volunteer fire departments and even high school trap shooting teams. Most households and all farms have guns, usually at least three: a shotgun, a small caliber rifle for shooting varmints and a large caliber deer hunting rifle.

The newest high school sport in Wisconsin is Clay Target shooting. The Wisconsin High School Clay Target League (WSHSCTL), claims to be the fastest growing high school sport in Wisconsin with an anticipated 1,200 participants in grades 6–12 and 50 teams in the spring 2016 league (Wisconsin State High School Clay Target League, 2016). Unlike most sports, there are two seasons for this sport: one each in the fall and spring with competitions between schools and a state championship tournament. The sport is patterned after the Olympic trap shooting competition and all competitions are held at gun ranges which have a trapshooting field with shooting stations and a trap house (WSHSCTL, 2016). According to the organization's website:

> The purpose of the Wisconsin State High School Clay Target League is to attract students to participate in shooting sports … This is accomplished by providing a safe, comfortable, positive team environment that enhances a student athlete's character and personal growth through safe, educational and socially acceptable involvement in shooting sports. (WSHSCTL, 2016)

Students are very enthusiastic about the "sport" but must have their own guns and ammunition which can be quite costly. The league has no trouble gaining sponsors from gun manufacturers and retailer: Cabela, Winchester, Browning, Benelli Armi SpA and SKB. With the guns costing anywhere from $500 to $1500, it is estimated that in 2015 trap teams will be spending over $5 million. The gun manufactures and the NRA are excited about this new group of youth who will spend a lot of money over their lifetimes and become gun rights advocates. Deprez (2015) described a 16-year-old shooter, who wore a T-shirt with a falsely ascribed Thomas Jefferson quote, "Free men do not ask permission to bear arms," as being not interested in guns or the 2nd Amendment until the league came to his school and recruited a team. Deprez (2015) quotes Dennis Taylor, a NRA member and manager with the Wisconsin Trapshooting Association, "These kids are going to be future legislators, and they're going to get in there and know the truth about weapons." To date, no injuries or deaths have been reported during trap shooting league events. Range safety is paramount for these groups; educating students about the gun violence epidemic is not.

Gun tragedies do happen. One Sunday in early November, a teenage boy was cleaning his deer rifle in preparation for deer hunting when it discharged. The bullet went through the bedroom wall into another bedroom and struck one of our 1st grade girls, killing her. In Wisconsin there are often two or three deaths each year from guns during hunting season.

As I continue along my drive to school I pass farms, some of which are small family farms and a few are large corporate farms. Even with the economic problems and the decreasing numbers of small farms, farming is an iconic part of every rural community. It is very difficult to be a dairy farmer with the fluctuation in prices, and it is very difficult to find people who will work long hard hours for minimal pay and no benefits. In class one day a girl Google Mapped her farm for me which showed massive barns and pens where over 300 head of cows are in a milking cycle that goes on around the clock. She said that she sometimes works in the barns with the "Mexicans." Even though we think of farms as being iconic of rural life, the number of students who live on farms is a small percentage of the student population even in rural schools.

Every farm needs laborers to do the hard work with the long hours needed to tend the animals, to do the field work and maintain the buildings and machinery. The pay is low with no benefits because many small farmers are just getting by financially and cannot afford to provide health insurance for their help. Farmers often are able to provide housing on the farm, usually an old trailer house or the old farm house which helps the farmer with worker reliability. As a consequence, increasingly, even in Northwestern Wisconsin, you will find farm laborers that are undocumented immigrants, mostly Mexican. The children in these families attend the schools and often need special attention with English as a Second Language (ESL) or with handicapping conditions. ESL programs are rare in small rural schools. Their numbers are not large in most rural school districts but they generally are welcomed into the schools. Many teachers give these children the special attention they need without special programming on the part of the schools. Parents often do not have driver's licenses and in the current atmosphere wish to keep as low of a profile as possible, yet it is common for the teachers of these children often reach out to the families. The children of these undocumented laborers who are born in the United States are in need of a passport in the event that they are deported. There are many teachers helping these families with these processes and connecting them to county social workers to provide for their needs. Wrap around services often happen informally and through the extraordinary efforts of teachers in small rural schools. This is a manifestation of the sense of community found in these small rural schools. Though the efforts of these teachers is not unique to rural schools, it is more significant given the isolation of these families in rural areas. A number of Agriculture Education teachers have begun teaching Spanish agriculture vocabulary to their students so that they are better able to communicate with these Hispanic farm laborers (E. Bartz personal communication, February, 8, 2016).

NATIVE AMERICAN STUDENTS

Native Americans students are struggling in public schools with high drop-out rates and under achievement. In Wisconsin the relationships between Native American communities and the dominant Non-Native culture has been strained at times over treaty rights and has contributed to this problematic situation. In 1983 the 7th U.S. Circuit Court of Appeals (La Coute Oreilles Band of the Lake Superior Chippewa Indians vs Voigt, 1983) affirmed that "Chippewa Indian" tribes had the rights granted to them in the 1837 and 1842 treaties which give them the right to practice their traditional spring spear fishing of walleyes to the great consternation of non-Native anglers feeling that this would destroy the fisheries. Fish counts have disproven this accusation but walleye are considered a "trophy" fish in Wisconsin and Minnesota and are highly, and sometimes exclusively, sought by many anglers. As a result, there were protests and racial taunting. Over the 30 some years since the Voight Decision the protests at the boat landings are fading into history but sometimes one can hear a few individuals attribute their fishing woes to tribal spearing.

In 1989, the Wisconsin Legislature passed Act 31, as a result of the controversy over the Voigt Decision, which mandated instruction in the history, culture and tribal sovereignty in both K-12 schools and in teacher education programs. Schools are required to create curriculum for students in grades 4–12 in giving students an understanding of different value systems, cultures and human relations particularly in regard to African Americans, Hispanics, and Native Americans. They are also required to teach Native American studies at least 3 times throughout a student's K-12 career and must maintain instructional materials which appropriately reflect diverse cultures (Bird Bear, 2016).

Northwestern Wisconsin is home of the Lake Superior Chippewa Indians with sub nations consisting of the St. Croix Band, the Lac Courte Oreilles Band, Lac du Flambeau Band, Red Cliff Band, Lac Vieux Desert Band and the Bad River Band. Their educational efforts involve Head-Start programs and a tribal school run by the Lac Courte Oreille Band (LCO). They also help provide a school liaison or coordinator in school districts that have tribal communities. Not all of the school age youth on the LCO Reservation attend the tribal schools as 555 of them attend two neighboring schools. It does have 330 students in the LCO K-12 School with another 28 in a K-5 Ojibwe Language Immersion school (Waadookodaadin). The LCO Reservation does have a community college with an enrollment of 250 (Wisconsin State Tribal Initiative, 2016).

The St. Croix Band's 11 tribal communities are spread out in 4 counties whose children attend local school districts which have a tribal liaison staff member who works to provide communication between the school and the parents of the community, as well as to provide assistance to the students. The main Native

American cultural activity at school is an annual pow-wow where the Native American students from the school dance in traditional native attire depending upon the style of dances they do. For example, I had students who were Grass Dancers and Jingle Dancers.

The literature and personal experience have found that barriers to educational success for Native American students are racism and oppression, and difficulty in identity formation (Trujillo & Alston, 2005; Welsh, 2008). While overt racism is rare, it nonetheless is perceived and remembered from a not too distant past. It is easy to see at times an alienation paradigm at work where a Native American student will have difficulty negotiating the Native American culture and the dominant Anglo culture in the schools. It has long been known that a key to breaking the alienation paradigm is to build a bridge between the cultures. The work of the Native American school-community coordinators in these schools has focused on bridging this gap. I spent a lot of time in their office listening to their suggestions and insight about how to help the students I worked with and how to involve the parents and grandparents of my students. One thing they taught me was that Native American students' learning styles are more group oriented with experiential and cooperative learning projects being more effective and attuned to their culture.

They were teaching me about culturally responsive teaching (Gilbert, 2008; Kea, Campbell-Whatley, & Richards, 2006; Pewewardy & Hammer, 2003) which is a set of dispositions towards the learners rather than a set of lessons in Native American culture and history. Pewewardy and Hammer (2003) state,

Native studies courses can help, overcoming ethnocentric outlooks is hard work and must be viewed as an ongoing process. Teachers must learn to be reflective practitioners and develop observational, empirical, and analytical skills necessary to monitor, evaluate, and revise continually their respective teaching styles.

Bergstrom, Cleary, and Peacock (2003) interviewed 120 Native American students who gave some examples of the qualities teachers had that helped them: having cultural knowledge, using encouragement, having high expectations, being flexible, being interested in students, listening and understanding, being open minded, being respectful, using multiple approaches to teach, and having patience. To this end, the teaching of Paulo Freire is compelling. Engaging Freire's mode of teaching creates a dialogue between cultures that validates the lived experiences of Native American students and counters the alienation that many Native American students feel in a "banking" model of teaching where they are lectured and given verbally abstract immediate attempts at new skill acquisition (Shimek, 2003, p. 32). Because of the culture and community life of the Native American students, they will often find education alien to their existence, such as when the "teacher talks about reality as if it were motionless, static, compartmentalized and predictable" (Freire, 1984, p. 57).

> Through dialogue, the teacher-of-the-students and the students-of-the-teacher cease to exist and a new term emerges: teacher-student with studentsteachers. The teacher is no longer merely the-one-who-teaches, but one who is himself taught in dialogue with the students, who in turn while being taught also teach. They become jointly responsible for a process in which all grow. In this process, arguments based on "authority" are no longer valid; in order to function authority must be on the side of freedom, not against it. (Freire, 1984, p. 67)

Native American culture and heritage are a part of Northern Wisconsin and offer unique understandings of the woods, prairies and waters of our region within the region there are teachers who demonstrate a passion and commitment to learning about and understanding this culture and heritage. One such teacher, a science teacher who is a regionally recognized naturalist and birder, has taken it upon himself to learn the very difficult Ojibwe language to the level of conversational fluency. It is important to recognize and celebrate within the education community when a teacher does have passion for understanding and learning of the Ojibwe culture. This teacher's passion and compassion for the culture is remarkable but, it does not signify a commitment by the school district as a whole to validate the culture and traditions of the Native American Students who are a part of the school's community.

Teachers' attitudes and dispositions are crucial but they need not be experts in Native culture to provide an inclusive atmosphere in their classrooms. When a Native American student can walk down the halls of the school and see, on its walls and in a number of its classrooms, anything that acknowledges or honors Native American culture or heritage it sends a powerful signal to all that this is a respected element in our community. As one Native student commented in the Bergstrom et al. (2003) study, "Last year, I had one teacher, Mr. S. He was a history teacher, and I like usually don't like my history teachers 'cause they never teach anything about Native Americans. I walked into the room, and all I saw on his walls were pictures of Native American people. And I think, 'Okay, I'm going to like this guy.' And then, when we got to Native American subjects, I think he spent about four weeks. … I liked that guy, he was pretty nice. And the weird thing about it was, he'd always ask me after he said something if that was right."

AGRICULTURE EDUCATION

In the land of woods, prairies and waters, the Agriculture Technology program has a powerful place in connecting students to the land and community. The Wisconsin Department of Public Instruction (DPI) classifies technology education with a set of academic standards that includes "courses of high-quality academic content and technical competencies which focus on programs of study to prepare students for successful college and career readiness" (Wisconsin Standards for Agriculture, Food and Natural Resources, 2013, p. 8). At the middle and high school levels the program includes "three distinct and crucial elements—rigorous academic and technical skill attainment, work-based learning and Career and Technical Student Organizations" (DPI, 2013, p. 15). In the case of Agriculture Education, the Career and Technical Student Organization is the Future Farmers of America (FFA), which is different from the after school 4H programs that often evoke an image of young boys or girls raising a cow or pig taken to the county fair to be judged and then sold.

FFA tells us that it "makes a positive difference in the lives of students by developing their potential for premier leadership, personal growth and career success through agricultural education" (FFA, 2016). Their vision statement is: "Students whose lives are impacted by FFA and agricultural education will achieve academic and personal growth, strengthen American agriculture and provide leadership to build healthy local communities, a strong nation and a sustainable world" (FFA, 2016). The organization prides itself on some of its most notable participants such as President Jimmy Carter, Willie Nelson and Rick Perry.

Putting students on a tractor is in most schools a thing of the past. Interest in traditional production agriculture is declining just as the number of farms is declining, but FFA is strong with 19,000 students in 255 chapters in Wisconsin where students are showing interest in alternative forms of agriculture that "you wouldn't typically associate with farming—law, public policy, entrepreneurship and bookkeeping" (Runyon, 2014). Runyon (2014) reported "A greater number of students are interested in organic farming methods, grass-fed beef and cage-free eggs."

Each year the FFA holds a National Convention, which the New Jersey Department of Agriculture claims is the "world's largest youth convention" (New Jersey Department of Agriculture, 2016). The tensions and conflicts within the agriculture community are reflected in their convention. The 2015 National FFA Convention and Expo, held in Louisville, Kentucky, was described in various ways depending on one's view point. Ward (2015), a Wisconsin farmer and former FFA member, noted that the

> National FFA Convention introduction looks more like an MTV video, the First Lady makes reference to the importance of agriculture by "planting a garden," and the USDA Deputy Secretary Krysta Harden is moved to tears by an inner city FFA chapter in "Philly." I begin to wonder what direction is the nation's largest youth agriculture organization heading?

Another perspective on FFA conventions described the "Feed the World" convention slogan was presented by "flashy, digital, draconian and utterly Orwellian interactive displays and mountains of corporate schwag" (Greenhorns, 2014). According to Greenhorns (2014), and other organic farm groups, the convention shows the "FFA is turning these next-inline farmers, agriscientists, ag teachers and farm sympathizers into successful leaders, fierce entrepreneurs, and good Samaritans … for Big Ag."

FFA and 4H have ties to large agribusiness corporations like Monsanto, Zoetis, Cargill, Dow, Syngenta, and Elanco (Greenhorns, 2014). Monsanto provides scholarships and grants to participants of 4H and FFA. Monsanto's America's Farmers Grow Ag Leaders, is administered by the National FFA Scholarship Program, but FFA membership is not required (Monsanto Fund, 2016).

An alternative perspective that is not often considered by FFA curriculum, if at all, is presented by Eggert (2015) when he states that

> I dream of a day when parents, politicians, economists, CEO's bankers, mining and logging companies and others make their decisions based upon an authentic ecological consciousness, including an understanding and full appreciation of a broad spectrum of environmental values that allow ecosystems to be sustainable, healthy and whole. (Eggert, 2015, p. 16)

He calls this approach "Meadowlark Economics" to highlight and contrast the effects of efficient agricultural haylage practices. At one time farmers were told to plant wind breaks and to have smaller fields that would resist the ravages of wind erosion so common in the droughts of the 20th Century. Current agriculture technology, such as no-till or chisel plow soil preparation, have mitigated the erosion problems, so farmers are now advised that it is more efficient to cut down those trees and have larger, open fields and to plant fence to fence. Farmers green cut hay rather than let it mature and dry in the fields so now hay is cut earlier in the season and fed green to their animals or stored that way. This practice has been devastating to meadow nesting birds because the earlier harvesting does not allow the newly hatched birds to mature enough to leave the nests before the choppers come across the fields. Eggert (2015) states,

> Despite their sweet song, these birds have no voice economically or politically. They represent a "zero" within our conventional economic accounting system. We don't even buy birdseed or build birdhouses for Meadowlarks. Their disappearance would not create even the tiniest ripple in the Commerce Department's spreadsheets that are supposed to measure our standard of living. (p. 4)

In the FFA's efficiency-technology-entrepreneur model, a student might learn about the following set of concepts about the management of the school forest (Eggert, 2015, p. 17):

- The monetary value of wood products (including export earnings), incomes for loggers, truckers, and sawmill workers.
- Logging will lead to increased sales for equipment, including manufacturing jobs.

- Logging will increase in each of these companies' short term profits.
- Logging will create short-term increase in corporate stock prices, adding value to stockholder portfolios.

In contrast to this model, the Meadowlark Economics model as applied to forestry, which is practiced by the Menomonee Indian Reservation in Wisconsin (Johnson & Johnson, 2012), would teach the students the following concepts about a school's forest (Eggert, 2015, p. 18):

- It is a habitat for endangered plants and animals.
- It needs to be maintained as a "living classroom" enabling students and scientists to study a healthy ecosystem.
- It is a source of beauty, inspiration, and spiritual sustenance.
- Old-growth forests protect and create new topsoil, prevent excessive run-off of rainwater and help recycle nutrients more efficiently than clear-cut forests.
- Old-growth forests sequester atmospheric carbon which helps stabilize Earth's climate.

In one very small school district the Ag teacher, who with her husband farm and milk 40 cows, offers a wide variety of 15 different courses in grades 6 through 12. These include courses in wildlife and natural resources, plant horticulture, veterinary science, equine science, ag science, food science, leadership and ATV and snowmobile safety as well as introductory survey courses for middle school students. The program has numerous field trips to fish farms, meat processors, farms, sawmills, and agribusinesses. The school has a school forest that is awaiting a selective cutting of trees after which they will rebuild the trails. They also have a prairie that they burn, as it happened naturally keeping the trees and brush from growing in it. The teacher collaborates with the science teacher working with students on projects for the school science fair.

ONE ROOM SCHOOLS

It is well documented that schools play a central role in rural communities. Salamon (2003) studied community change in six rural farm towns in Illinois in 1995. Economic and population changes had created a new social fabric in these towns located in productive agricultural areas that lacked social and economic attachments to the areas. In addition, Salamon (2003) argues this new social fabric causes agrarian communities to become post-modern in nature, where lives are fragmented, attachment to land is seen as personal property or as an investment, and where the agrarian social fabric and values are being transformed. A large wooded area across the road from my house is owned by people from out of the state who use it as a private hunting area. This is not uncommon.

On my journey to school I pass three buildings that were once one or two room schools. In 1912 Grant County, Wisconsin, for example, had 15 high schools, five first-class-graded schools, five second-class-graded schools and 201 one-room schoolhouses (Wisconsin Historical Society). Each township had its own school for about 15 elementary students. The rural one room school is still a psychological and mystical presence in our area.

I have a friend who attended a one room school house for the first 9 years of her schooling during the 1960s. Her school was a small rural neighborhood school serving about 21 children in grades K–8 who were in walking distance to the school. The building consisted of one large classroom, a small library room with shelves on both sides and a window at the end which was always cold in the winter. The school had no running water and was heated by an oil stove. The restrooms were out back. Water was brought to the school each morning by the closest neighbor and was put into a galvanized metal keg with a spigot at the bottom for drinking. To wash their hands, one student would ladle water from the keg onto another student's hands over a waste water pail. The desks were the kind with an ink-well and were arranged in three sections throughout the room. The smallest desks were on the right side of the room, the middle sized desks in the middle, and the large desks, for the 7th and 8th grade students were on the left side of the room. It was a very big deal for the students when they were old enough to move from one size desk to the next.

The area where these schools were located is in the bluffs and coulees region along the Mississippi River, an area of high ridges and valleys that lead down to the river. The towns are located on the river. The students who attended the school were all within walking distance and they all lived on farms on a "ridge." There were other small schools in the district; one a few miles away in a valley had two rooms, another ridge school was exactly the same as the one my friend attended. Although the community was tight knit, it was very open and welcoming to new students, who were few and far between. There was a "school board" but their duties appeared to be mainly concerned with the maintenance and day to day functioning of the school. Once in a while the "Superintendent" from the town would visit the school. He is remembered as a big man who smelled of onions, who would walk the rows of desks looking at the students' work and occasionally ask a student to read to him.

This school was the focus of the community. Parent teacher conferences were not individual meetings between a student's parents and the teacher, but rather a social event. The parents would come to the school and view the students' work which was displayed around the room, after which the parents would sit down and play cards and eat. The Christmas production was also a community gathering. The fathers would build a raised platform for a stage and run wires for the curtains and backdrops. They even had homemade spotlights. The children would put on the Christmas play and at the end Santa would come in the back door with a bag of candy and an apple for each child. Then the parents would play cards. For days after these community events the school smelled of tobacco smoke.

The teacher was an older woman who drove to the school from town. She was there all of the 9 years my friend was at the school and was considered strict and assigned home work every night. To my friend, it seemed as if there were a law that required that mathematics be taught before 10:30 each day. If you were in trouble you might find yourself under teacher's desk. If you had difficulties learning or if the teacher had an issue with you, there was little help or recourse. Once, when the regular teacher broke her hip, a younger substitute teacher stepped in for a few weeks. This woman had young children of her own and lived on a farm so she understood the lives for her students. She did not assign homework since she knew that they all had chores to do when they got home each afternoon. The students felt like they were on a vacation.

The teacher worked with the younger students first and then the older students in succession for each subject except for music and art. Thus, everyone heard and saw the teacher's lessons for each group. It gave the younger students exposure to the concepts and vocabulary of the advanced material while also giving the older students a review of things they had been taught in the past. It was an informal looping of the curriculum for all of the students. The older students tutored the younger students, especially in reading. Tutoring sometimes became an escape from a lesson or subject the older students didn't like. Each student had a clear understanding of what they needed to learn because they saw the total curriculum. They all new that they had to have mastery of multiplication by the end of the third grade. The curriculum seemed to be very traditional with a lot of grammar, phonics, and diagramming of sentences. The school had a piano and the teacher used it every day to teach the children songs. There were big maps on rollers, a picture of George Washington and all of the traditional iconic one room school things that are in local museums today. "Weekly Readers" on Fridays were their current events lessons. The library was stocked by the teacher with books, with Laura Ingalls-Wilder's "Little House on the Prairie" series being one of the most well-worn. Once in a while old books were given to students which became prized possessions.

The community and the children were very close knit. There were no cliques or subgroups. Competition was almost shunned. The students were mostly Catholic and they prayed before lunch. They played hard and spirited games on the playground but without much rivalry or bluster. My friend said that she did not even notice the clothes of her classmates until she entered the high school where clothes mattered. The farm, school, church, and 4H was the focus of their lives. They all participated in 4H. They all worked on their family's farm. They all went to the same church.

THE NEW RURAL EDUCATION

Prior to 1963, rural school districts were under the supervision of County Superintendents. Then the school bus made it possible to transport children to the graded town schools efficiently. As the transition from the country one room schools to the town school districts progressed, role of the County Superintendent became unnecessary and the Wisconsin Legislature decided to replace the county superintendent with Cooperative Educational Service Agencies. Wisconsin is divided up into 12 Cooperative Service Agencies with 8 CESAs having the majority of the rural school districts. The legislature intended the CESA's to provide a service unit between the State Superintendent and individual school districts to provide leadership services and coordination of services for school districts, including such programs as curriculum development assistance; school district management development; coordination of vocational education; and exceptional education, research, special student classes, human growth and development, data collection processing and dissemination, and in-service programs (CESA 7, 2016).

Wisconsin adopted the Common Core State Standards (CCSS) under authority of Article X of the Wisconsin State Constitution (State of Wisconsin, 2010). CCSS have been very controversial under Governor Scott Walker. In Wisconsin, opponents to the Common Core have been aligned with the "Tea Party Republicans" in the state (Richards, 2014) who have rallied grass roots support at events like the one sponsored by the Republican Women of Waukesha County in 2014. The Milwaukee Journal Sentinel (Laasby, 2014) described the rally where,

> a University of Wisconsin-Oshkosh professor, Duke Pesta outlined what he considered the "dangers and threats" that the Common Core standards pose on the educational system, liberties and Christian values. Pesta called the Common Core standards "socialism" funded by leftist lobbyists, including Bill Gates.

In July of 2014, Governor Scott Walker asked the Wisconsin State Legislature to repeal Common Core and replace it with "standards set by people in Wisconsin" (Richards & Marley, 2014) but no action was taken.

When the State adopted the Core Curriculum Standards the CESAs were thrown in action to help school districts implement the new standards and align their curriculum to the assessments that would measure the academic achievement on those standards. For example, CESA 9 states that their work with the

CCSS "creates and organizes educator resources through the lenses of innovation, effectiveness and equity. We do this to promote ... standards-based teaching and learning. In essence, we create, curate and communicate the CCSS to Wisconsin" (CESA 9, 2016).

In conjunction with the adoption and development of the CCSS, the State Superintendent of Instruction began work on an Educator Effectiveness System (Department of Public Instruction, 2016). This system was piloted and implemented state wide with legislative authority (WI ACT 166) in the 2014–2015 school year. CESAs again became the focus of implementation with CESA 6 developing a model that is replicated throughout most of the state. This model is a "turnkey" teacher evaluation that has "research based standards, with rubrics and indicators" The program has professional development for "deep understanding of accountability concerns and research-based strategies". It provides information at the individual, school, district and regional levels so that there can be "data-driven, standards based professional development" (CESA 6, 2016).

The CESAs serving most rural districts in Wisconsin provide support and services to rural school districts that is centered on a standardized approach to developing curriculum, instruction and teacher evaluation. Rural school districts that wish to develop curriculum and instruction specific to their place and community are not going to find much support or resources from their CESAs. Individual districts are always free to develop their own curriculum and do not have to follow or purchase the curriculum and instruction services from their CESAs.

TREE-STANDS IN THE WOODS

Often one finds that individual teachers, with a vision and a passion, will do great things to bring together the school, the community and its environment. It is difficult to find a whole school district that has this focus and passion on their community and sense of place. One school district appears to exemplify this community-environment-school relationship. It is a very small school district with 382 students and covers 85 miles of rivers, rolling farmland and forest. The elementary, middle and high school are under one roof with 37 professional staff and 21 support staff. The school boasts that it has a computer to student ratio of 1 to 1 with many classrooms having SMARTBoards. The school is also able to provide classes in Agriculture, Family and Consumer Sciences, Band, Choir, Spanish, Business and Technology Education. The school has a school forest and a school garden. One long time teacher describes the school as:

> The school is one of main attractions in the town, and we get a lot of open enrolled students because we are "small", and truly get to know the students and families. Many classes visit the local bank, store, sheet metal plant and nursing home for learning opportunities,

and to learn from others. Our elementary students walk to the nursing home with their costumes on to "parade" for the residents, and they are given a candy treat. We also walk over to sing Christmas songs for the residents. It is a great way for the young and the old to interact with each other.

The community comes together to support projects and events at the school. A few years ago it was a dream to have a nice baseball field, so a group of parents got together and started fundraising to earn money for the project. We now have a beautiful baseball field within walking distance from the school. Improvements are still being made to it and it is being maintained.

Our latest project has been a community fitness center. The school had some money that needed to be spent on something that would benefit the community, so it was decided to build an addition onto the school, move our weight room equipment up out of the lower level in the high school, and re-locate it to the fitness center. We also have some cardio machines, along with space in the room to hold our "overflow" after school activities, such as dance class for younger students, or wrestling practice. Community members are able to purchase a one-year membership for a very small fee.

Our third grade students have an annual craft fair, which is wonderful to see. The students make craft items to sell, and people can also donate gently used Christmas/winter items. The third grade students run most of the sale themselves with some adult supervision. The project is worked into many curriculum areas, and they need to apply for their jobs they wish to have as well as interview for them. Some jobs are greeters, security, shopping helpers, wrapping station, cashiers and stockers. They take their jobs very seriously! The items are priced from a quarter to five dollars. Students bring their money to school and shop at their assigned class time.

The money that is raised is counted carefully, and the students work together to decide where to donate it. Most years they give some to the town food pantry, but other causes have been the town park and a children's hospital in a nearby city. They keep a portion of the money to help pay for their trip to the science museum in the spring, but most is donated after they discuss and vote in their classroom. (L. Hamernick, personal communication, February 3, 2016)

In the land of water, woods and prairies, the school's connections to its waters, woods and prairies should be a major influence in the curriculum and identity. Lieberman and Hoody (1998) studied a number of outdoor education programs and presented ways of integrating the environment as context for learning. In Northwest Wisconsin, a number of rural districts have school forests that enjoy a large variation in utilization. To help schools develop outdoor education programs and better utilize school forests, prairies and waters, the University of Wisconsin-Stevens Point has the LEAF program which has registered over 25,000 acres of school forest land, and is integrating learning in and about Wisconsin's forests into K-12 schools. Its mission is to provide the knowledge, skills, and ways of thinking necessary to sustain our forests and communities (LEAF, 2016). Research on outdoor education indicates it creates a sense of place and attitudes, increases academic performance and child development, and is healthy and fun. The program tries to promote the core values of dependence and connection to the Earth, forests systems support all life, forests can be managed sustainably, and healthy communities are dependent on engaged and informed citizens (LEAF, 2016).

A number of schools have developed school forest programs, but one school district has demonstrated what is possible in developing and utilizing a school forest (Amery School District, 2016). This school district has a school forest program that features a lake, prairie, and woods. The students have constructed trails, a picnic shelter, a floating dock, planted hundreds of trees, replanted 18 acres of native prairie, relocated an Osprey nest and installed a remote camera for viewing from the middle school. They also have a school forest logo and mascot named "Bandit the Raccoon". Trail head and trail markers were constructed and put in place by the Boy Scout Troop. They have raise thousands of dollars through student activities and grants for the development of this total school program. The outdoor learning activities are found in all of the curricular areas in the school.

MCDONALDIZED SCHOOLS

The prevailing, dominant forces in rural education tend to create small rural schools that are indistinct, examples of some generic core curriculum, test defined effective schools with test defined teaching excellence. The state report cards for schools in Wisconsin does not give any distinctive information about the schools—only tables of test scores that glorify a "McDonaldized" rural educational system. School athletics do little to differentiate one school from another other than a school's "colors," a team logo and a nickname.

When I walk into a small town school that has a sense of community it is readily apparent immediately inside the doorway. In the wall I see a big built in aquarium with fish that came from the river that runs by the school with informational displays telling me the name of the fish and information about the fish as well as the names that the kids have given them. Further on down the hall I see a television on the wall with a live feed from a local farm that is showing a barn with calves asleep in their pen. A sign tells me the name of the calves, how old they are and other information about them. Further on down the hall I see students gathered around a computer monitor that is showing some deer in the school forest. One of the students tells me that they have a camera on a deer trail that they have been studying for some time identifying specific deer and noting their frequency and direction of travel. They have mapped the deer trail and are studying their habitat, movement and eating patterns. They click an icon that changes the television view to an eagle's nest in a tree by the river. I see on another wall a display that features the local business of the month with information about this business's economics (products, sales, resources, wages paid, taxes, etc.) kinds of jobs and skills utilized by the employer and a web link for more information that was put together by the 6th grade class and the high school social studies/economics class. There is a local history display put up by the middle school history class which features information about a logging railroad that was in this area from 1880 to 1912. In the library they have a diorama depicting the town in the 1930s with a model railroad showing connections to neighboring towns that are long gone. I see a mural that depicts a local farm from the early 1900s on one wall. On the wall near the high school science class is a display about counting frogs with charts and graphs explaining the results of years of counting and data collection. Another wall mural depicts Native Americans who inhabited the area before the settlers, spear fishing on the river.

The school training room has not only student athletes but also senior citizens on the treadmills and bikes with student trainers assisting them with their fitness program. At lunch senior citizens eat in their own area of the cafeteria but once in a while a student will join them for conversation or to get information about a report where the teacher requires not only literature research but also personal interviews with non-family members. The middle school students also have to create a website for a community family or business that is available only on the school's network. They often visit the local nursing home to chat with their friends who they also build a website depicting the lives and community history of these special people. The school forest has an outdoor classroom that is busy year round with science projects, art projects, writing projects and even music in the woods. The mathematics classes have studied probability and data analysis of data from hundreds of samples and studies from the woods and waters around the school as well as the geometry and mapping of the land. They do math problems submitted by parents and community members from the farms and businesses in the community as well. Some high school students are helping some small businesses with their accounting.

I also see a large trophy case with awards and trophies from not only the athletic teams, bands, dance teams but also from academically oriented awards for robotics, mathematics, science, writing, geography, history and the proverbial spelling bees. The athletics are very important for this community and the school but they do not dominate the school and community relationship. The student athletes do well and are highly supported in all sports regardless of the win-loss statistics by the school and the community. In the fall the school sent the cross country team to the State Championship Meet with a rousing pep rally. Currently the school's basketball team has not had a "winning" season but nobody is discouraged and attendance is still high for their games. Some students have to compete in multiple school teams in both boys' and girls' sports such as hockey, softball, lacrosse, swimming. The community support for the athletic programs is reflected in the local newspapers and attendance at athletic events.

CONCLUSION

Place-based pedagogies have been alluded to and present throughout history. Elfer (2011) traced the place-based pedagogies from Aristotle to Dewey. Dewey's emphasis on educating the "whole child" in the context of the child's "lived experience" is credited with the philosophical foundation for current place-based pedagogy. Dewey states (1938)

> One consideration stands out clearly when education is conceived in terms of experience. Anything which can be called a study, whether arithmetic, history, geography, or of the natural sciences, must be derived from materials which at the onset fall within the scope of ordinary lifeexperience.

Woodhouse tells us (2015, p. 30)

> An educational process that helps the learner to understand the ecological and cultural dynamics of a specific place, its people, and the community those people share in that place as well as to understand how to participate in maintaining community will be an education for sustainability imbedded in a place-based pedagogy. An education that is place-based can accommodate the diversity that various contexts present. A place-based pedagogy allows for content and process that is explicit to the ecological and cultural dynamics of that place, the people, and the ecological and sociological processes that created and sustain that community.

In this discussion of rural education in Wisconsin it has been noted that in certain schools and classrooms teachers are taking the lived-experiences of their students in the family, community and environment into a curriculum and pedagogy of place. Dewey (1938) tells us

> A primary responsibility of educators is that they not only be aware of environing conditions, but that they also recognize in the concrete what surroundings are conducive to having experiences that lead to growth. Above all, they should know how to utilize the surroundings, physical and social, that exist so as to extract from them all that they have to contribute to building up experiences that are worthwhile.

Dewey goes on to say that this is work above and beyond the effort need to teach from a set standardized curriculum. Teachers who intuitively understand that students are more engaged and curious when presented a place-based pedagogy have taken it upon themselves in most cases to provide this to their students. They do so most often with little or no support from educational systems that are focused on standards based learning and assessment. Some schools have begun to embrace the communities and the environments but they are islands in the "MacDonald" like sea of rural education.

REFERENCES

Amery School District, (2016). *Amery school forest.* Amery, WI: Amery School District. Retrieved from http://www.amerysd.k12.wi.us/community/schoolforest.cfm

Bergstrom, A., Cleary, L. M., & Peacock, T. (2003). *The seventh generation: Native students speak about finding the good path.* Charleston, WV: ERIC Clearinghouse on Rural Education and Small Schools.

Bird Bear, A. (2016). *First steps: Explore essential understandings.* University of Wisconsin, School of Education. Retrieved from http://education.wisc.edu/soe/about/resourceservice-units/student-diversity-programs/american-indian-curriculum-services/why-act31/first-steps

Cannon, A. P. (1981). *Wisconsin legislative innovations.* Retrieved from https://books.google.com/books?id=f_4QAQAAMAAJ&pg=PA11&lpg=PA11&dq=Wisconsin+Outdoor+recreation+act&source=bl&ots=n-fA8GKziS&sig=ud8tX2jQSTGPuZ8qFoU9-OlM6Xo&hl=en&sa=X&ved=0ahUKEwjRzN7E4-3KAhXsw4MKHZkAAuQQ6AEITjAI#v=onepage&q=Wisconsin%20Outdoor%20recreation%20act&f=false

Capital Times. (2009, June 5). *State trails now a legacy to Aldo Leopold.* Capital Times. Retrieved from http://host.madison.com/news/article_fed70e34-b46a-517a-94ce366453d16382.html

CESA 6. (2016). *Effectiveness project.* Retrieved from http://www.cesa6.org/services/ep/index.cfm

CESA 9. (2016). *Common core state standards Wisconsin.* Retrieved January 11, 2016 from http://www.cesa9.org/programs/ccss12814.cfm

Deprez, E. (2015). *U.S. high schools embrace shooting as hot new sport.* Retrieved from http://www.bloomberg.com/news/articles/2015-07-09/making-guns-cool-high-schoolsembrace-shooting-as-hot-new-sport

Dewey, J (1938). *Experience & Education. New York, NY: Kappa Delta Pi.* (Kindle Location 379). Free Press. Kindle Edition.

Eggert, J. (2015). *Meadowlark economics (revised): Exploring values for a sustainable future.* Bradenton, FL: BookLocker.com, Inc.

Elfer, C. J. (2011). *Place-based education: A review of historical precedents in theory & practice.* Retrieved from https://getd.libs.uga.edu/pdfs/elfer_charles_j_201108_phd.pdf

FFA. (2016). *What is FFA.* Retrieved from https://www.ffa.org/about/what-is-ffa

Freire, P. (1984). *Pedagogy of the oppressed.* New York, NY: Continuum Publishing Corporation.

Gagnon, D., & Mattingly, M. L. (2012). *Beginning teachers are more common in rural, high-poverty, and racially diverse schools.* Retrieved from http://scholars.unh.edu/cgi/viewcontent.cgi?article=1172&context=carsey

Gilbert, W. S. (2008). *Impact of culturally based teaching on student academic and social development.* Campaign for High School Equity (CHSE) Congressional Briefing: Culturally Based Teaching: A Model for Student Success. Alliance for Excellent Education. Retrieved from http://www.highschoolequity.org/events/congressional-briefings/

Greenhorns. (2014). *Greenhorns report on the national FFA convention.* Retrieved from https://thegreenhorns.wordpress.com/2014/11/24/greenhorns-report-on-the-national-ffaconvention/

Hatch, K. L. (1913). *Types of agricultural schools in Wisconsin* (Wisconsin Research Bulletin No. 40). Madison, WI: University of Wisconsin, Agricultural Experimental Station. Retrieved from https://books.google.com/books?id=kKwzAQAAMAAJ&pg=RA4PA46&dq=Wisconsin+research+bulletin+40&hl=en&sa=X&ved=0ahUKEwivdeklb_KAhVGwiYKHUJ8CqoQ6AEIHTAA#v=onepage&q=Wisconsin%20research%20bullet in%2040&f=false

Howley, C. B., Howley, A., & Yahn, J. (2014). Motives for dissertation research at the intersection between rural education and curriculum and instruction. *Journal of Research in Rural Education, 29*(5), 1–12.

Johnson, C., & Johnson, B. (2012, Spring). *Menomonee forest keepers.* Washington, DC: American Forests. Retrieved from https://www.americanforests.org/magazine/article/menominee-forest-keepers/

Kava, R. (2015). *Charter schools.* Madison, WI: Wisconsin Legislative Fiscal Bureau, Informational Paper 27. Retrieved from https://docs.legis.wisconsin.gov/misc/lfb/informational_papers/january_2015/0027_charter_scho ols_informational_paper_27.pdf

Kea, C., Campbell-Whatley, G. D., & Richards, H. V. (2006). *Becoming culturally responsive educators: Rethinking teacher education pedagogy.* Retrieved from http://glec.education.iupui.edu/equity/Becoming_Culturally_Responsive_Educators.pdf

Kemp, S. (2016, January). *A perfect storm.* Retrieved from http://www.wasb.org/websites/wisconsin_school_news/File/2016_JanFeb/perfect_storm_JanFeb _2016.pdf

Laasby, G. (2014, February 22). *Wisconsin event helps rally opponents of Common Core Standards.* Retrieved from http://www.jsonline.com/news/education/wisconsin-eventhelps-rally-opponents-of-common-core-standards-b99210818z1-246713001.html

Lac Courte Oreilles Band of Lake Superior Chippewa Indians v. P Voigt, 700 F. 2d 341 (1983).

LEAF. (2016a). *About the LEAF program.* Stevens Point, WI: University of Wisconsin-Stevens Point. Retrieved from http://www.uwsp.edu/cnrap/leaf/Pages/about_us.aspx

LEAF (2016b). *Outdoor education—research summary.* Stevens Point, WI: University of Wisconsin-Stevens Point. Retrieved from http://www.uwsp.edu/cnrap/leaf/SiteAssets/Pages/School-Forest-Research/Outdoor%20Education%20Research.pdf

Lieberman, G. A., & Hoody, L. L. (1998). *Closing the achievement gap: Using the environment as an integrating context for learning.* Ponway, CA: Science Wizards. Retrieved from http://www.seer.org/extras/execsum.pdf

Mack, M. D., McFaul, S., & Slack, A. (2011). *Wisconsin rural school teachers 1880–1950.* Retrieved from http://people.uwec.edu/MACKMD/documents/rural_sch_teach_0504_new.ppt

Maheshwari, S. (2015). *Gun sellers have high hopes for high school shooting leagues.* Retrieved from http://www.buzzfeed.com/sapna/why-gun-sellers-want-shooting-to-be-morefun#.lanQ4bG5j

Monsanto Fund. (2016). *America's farmers: Grow ag leaders.* Retrieved from http://www.monsanto-fund.org/grants/grow-ag-leaders/

New Jersey Department of Agriculture. (2016, January). NJ FFA Association State Activity Guide. Retrieved from http://www.jerseyageducation.nj.gov/agriculture/ag_ed/ffa/activity/nationalffa-convention.html

Pewewardy, C. D. (1994). Culturally responsible pedagogy in action: An American Indian magnet school. In E. R. Hollins, J. E. King, & W. C. Haymon (Eds.), *Teaching diverse populations: Formulating a knowledge base.* Buffalo, NY: State University of New York Press.

Pewewardy, C. D, & Hammer, P. C. (2003). *Culturally responsive teaching for American Indian students.* Retrieved from http://files.eric.ed.gov/fulltext/ED482325.pdf

Richards, E. (2014, March 5). *Common Core 101: A primer to separate education fact from Fiction.* Retrieved from http://www.jsonline.com/news/education/common-core-101-aprimer-to-separate-education-fact-from-fiction-b99214588z1-248604151.html

Runyon, L. (2014, April 10). *No plows, cows, sows: Not your (Grand) father's youth Farm group.* Retrieved from http://www.npr.org/sections/thesalt/2014/04/10/298890213/no-plowscows-sows-not-your-grand-fathers-youth-farm-group

Salamon, S. (2003). Newcomers to old towns. Chicago: University of Chicago Press. [Upscale suburbanization: Prairieview, pp. 74–92]

Shimek, R. (2003). *Racism, education and the American Indian student* (Masters Thesis), Menomonie, WI: University of Wisconsin-Stout. Retrieved from http://www2.uwstout.edu/content/lib/thesis/2003/2003shimekr.pdf

State of Wisconsin. (2010). *Wisconsin adopts common core state standards* [News Release] DPI-NR 2010–75 B. Retrieved from https://www2.ed.gov/programs/racetothetop/phase2-applications/amendments/wisconsin.pdf

Trujillo, O. V., & Alston, D. A. (2005). *A report on the status of American Indians and Alaska Natives in education.* Retrieved from http://www.nea.org/assets/docs/HE/mf_aianreport.pdf

Walker, S. (2016). *Governor Scott Walker signs legislation to protect hunters, fishers, and trappers from interference.* [News Release]. Retrieved from http://walker.wi.gov/newsroom/press-release/governor-scott-walker-signs-legislation-protect-wisconsin's-hunters-fishers

Waller, R., & Barrentine, S. J. (2015). Rural elementary teachers and place-based connections to text during reading instruction. *Journal of Research in Rural Education, 30*(7), 1–13.

Ward, M. (2015, October 30). *Am I a fuddy-duddy or has FFA gone urban?* Retrieved from http://farmprogress.com/blogs-am-i-fuddy-duddy-has-ffa-gone-urban-10336

Welsh, C. A. (2008). *Making science education meaningful for American Indian students: he effect of science far participation.* Retrieved from https://conservancy.umn.edu/handle/11299/47736

Wisconsin Department of Public Instruction. (1998). Wisconsin's model academic standards for environmental education. Retrieved from http://dpi.wi.gov/sites/default/files/imce/standards/pdf/envired.pdf

Wisconsin Department of Public Instruction. (2013). *Wisconsin standards for agriculture, food and natural resources.* Retrieved from http://dpi.wi.gov/sites/default/files/imce/cte/pdf/ag_standards.pdf

Wisconsin Department of Public Instruction. (2016a). *Academic standards.* Retrieved from http://dpi.wi.gov/standards

Wisconsin Department of Public Instruction. (2016b). *Currently operating charter schools.* Retrieved from http://dpi.wi.gov/sms/charter-schools/current

Wisconsin Indian Education Association. (2016a). *Overview.* Retrieved from http://www.wiea.org/index.php/About/

Wisconsin Indian Education Association. (2016b). *2016 WIEA conference details.* Retrieved from http://www.wiea.org/index.php/Conference/Details/

Wisconsin State Tribal Initiative (2016). Retrieved from http://witribes.wi.gov

Wisconsin State High School Clay Target League. (2016a). *About us.* Retrieved from http://wiclaytarget.com/about-us/about-trap-shooting/

Wisconsin State High School Clay Target League. (2016b). *Join Wisconsin's fastest growing high school sport!* Retrieved from http://wiclaytarget.com/2015/09/18/join-wisconsinsfastest-growing-high-school-sport/

Woodhouse, J. (2015). The ecology of the education for sustainability paradigm. *Thresholds in Education, XXXVIII*(1) 29–33.

CHAPTER FIFTEEN

Rural IN A Different Caye

Listening to Early School Leavers About the Importance of Place

BEVIN ETHERIDGE

Educational research in small, "developing" nation-states is primarily driven by the neoliberal imperatives of international development agencies that require both measurable outcomes and favor quantitative research. With equity and access as primary goals, the focus of most research is limited to assessing whether poorer populations and rural communities are participating in the educational system and "catching up" academically. Although over half of Belize's population live in rural areas (World Bank, 2015), research agendas are similar to metropolitan-based scholarship elsewhere which often ignores the relationship of specific rural places to education (Howley & Howley, 2014). While equity and access are both justifiable and worthwhile goals for education everywhere, educational research and policy, albeit sometimes unintentionally, can result in silencing the people whom schools serve and rendering the places in which schools exist invisible.

Following Lefebvre (1991), I consider place not simply as a geographic location, but also as a socially produced space in which social inequalities are embedded, reproduced, and contested through everyday practices. In my research with early school leavers[1] concerning their perspectives on school, its purposes, and their reasons for leaving it, place emerged in different and unexpected guises. Although the primary focus was on what early school leavers had to say, this was situated in the wider historical, sociocultural, and economic context in order to better understand their perspectives. Because this work is located on what will be referred to here as Paradise Caye,[2] a small caye in Belize that is both rural and a popular tourist destination, it not only has a unique relationship to global "flows" of people and capital (Appadurai, 1996, 2014), but also offers insight into different ways rural people, schools, and places articulate. This chapter will examine two ways in which place influenced early school leavers' beliefs about and experiences of school in significant ways. In so doing, I hope to show how both the specificity of places and the attitudes of youth toward schooling are fundamental to any deeper understanding of educational issues, particularly in scholarship that not only takes place in, but claims to be *"for* rural communities"(Corbett & White, 2014, p. 26).

INTRODUCTION TO BELIZE

As a former British colony and the only Central American nation with English as its official language, Belize is considered both part of Central America and the Caribbean. Although originally home to the Maya, and located geographically within Central America, the diverse makeup of races and ethnicities primarily from the two regions lends itself to this dual designation. Following the Spanish and then British incursion into what is now Belize, the earliest immigrants included African slaves—often brought by way of Jamaica, the Garinagu—of both African and Arawak descent originally from St. Vincent, and the various groups of Maya— fleeing oppression in neighboring countries. Achieving the right to self-govern in 1964 with formal independence following in 1981, Belize maintains strong ties to Britain, who—along with the UN, supported its right to sovereignty in the face of territorial claims made by Guatemala.

Bordered in the east by the Caribbean Sea, in the north and northwest by Mexico, and in the south and west by Guatemala, Belize has a total area of 8,867 square miles, roughly the size of Massachusetts and twice the size of Jamaica. As of September 2015, Belize's total population was estimated at 370, 300 (Statistical Institute of Belize [SIB], 2015). Today Belize still has the lowest population density in Central America with 15 people per sq. km. of land area and 54% of the population living in rural areas (World Bank, 2015). Many Belizeans consider themselves to be of "mixed" ethnicity. Reflecting this, the *Belize Population and Housing Census* of 2010 allowed respondents to indicate their membership in up to two ethnic groups (SIB, 2013). Those who considered themselves Latino/Spanish/ Mestizo were by far the largest ethnic group at 52.9% followed by the Creoles at 26%. Together, the three Mayan groups—the Kek'chi, Mopan, and Yucatec—are 11.3%, with the Garinagu representing 6.1% of the total population. Other ethnicities include Asian, Black/African, Caucasian (Mennonites and ex-patriots primarily from the US and Canada), East Indian, Hindu, and Lebanese (SIB, 2013, p. 19).

Belize's economy has traditionally been based on agriculture and fishing with marine products, sugar, citrus, and bananas being the chief exports. Tourism in Belize began around the 1960s but was not actively developed until the 1980s.

It is now Belize's primary industry and has surpassed all expectations with a record-breaking 1.2 million tourist arrivals in 2014 (Humes, 2015). Discoveries of oil in Belize beginning in 2006 have also added to the GDP growth, however production has recently been decreasing. Expansionary policies in the 1990s and early 2000s, including privatizations, borrowing, and budget deficits provoked a debt crisis that resulted in restructuring the debt in 2007 (Halcrow Group, 2010, p. 27). Belize struggles with a large trade deficit and has one of the largest debt to GDP ratios (79.6% debt in 2014), which hinders it fiscal spending. The combination of "heavy foreign debt burden, high unemployment, growing involvement in the Mexican and South American drug trade, high crime rates, and one of the highest HIV/AIDS prevalence rates in Central America" are all major concerns for Belizeans (Central Intelligence Agency [CIA], 2015).

EDUCATION IN BELIZE

Education in Belize is seen by many as both the gateway to a better future on an individual level, as well as the key to a more socially cohesive and economically competitive citizenry. Prior to and after Belize's independence, the importance of both secondary and tertiary education has become established and tied, as in many other post-colonial nations, to nation-building aims. However, as Crossley and Tikly (2004) have noted, many of these educational systems at the "so-called periphery of the global economy and politics" have been shaped within their particular colonial encounter. Policymakers must grapple with the "colonial legacy on the one hand whilst simultaneously engaging with the demands posed by rapid globalization on the other" (Crossley & Tikly, 2004, p. 151).

Formal education in Belize emerged as a partnership between various churches and the state, whose respective original intentions of imparting morals and having a "well-disciplined labor force" coincided (Bennett, 2008, p. 3). State policy toward education was generally laissez-faire, and for the most part, education was the purview of the churches. Eventually the colonial government, and later the post-independence government of Belize, took a leading role in primary schools. The goals of both improving primary school and making it accessible to all Belizeans fit well with international agenda, which for a long time only focused on "basic education" at the primary level (King, 2007, p. 379). In Belize, school attendance is mandatory until the age of 14 or upon completion of primary school. While primary school is tuition-free, there are associated expenses, such as school fees, additional books (dictionaries, religious books, etc.), and uniforms.

The colonial legacy of education in Belize is perhaps more pronounced at the secondary level. Because the purpose of secondary school was originally to serve the upper echelons of society, state involvement at the secondary level progressed at a much slower rate than that of primary (Bennett, 2008). In contrast to primary schools, the state's role in secondary schools remained limited for a long time to the granting of scholarships. Gradually, both secondary and tertiary took on a greater importance for the government, particularly around the time of independence until the present, as both were seen as the key to future development and nation-building.

Reflecting the assumptions and goals embedded in international agendas since the 1990 World Conference on Education for All at Jomtien, Thailand (King, 2007), international aid for education in Belize was traditionally limited to the primary level. Thus, until recently, international education policy continued the state's original hands-off policy toward secondary schools, neglecting the growing concern among Belizeans for investing in post-primary education (Crossley, 2008, p. 247). This is reflected today in both the distribution and quality of secondary schools, with Belize City in particular having more schools overall, as well as most of the prestigious schools. The majority of secondary schools in Belize are not tuition-free, and along with associated costs shared with primary schools such as uniforms and school fees, secondary schools have additional expenses such as significantly higher book fees, food, and in some cases, transportation.

EDUCATIONAL POLICY AND CURRENT REFORMS

Influenced by larger global trends of neo-liberalism, public and social policy discourses often explicitly link education to development and economic goals (Apple, 2000; Spring, 2009). Underlying the link between education and development in Belize is human capital theory and its promises of economic competitiveness and social cohesion in the "global knowledge economy" (McGrath, 2010, p. 237). This view implicitly positions the nation as a whole in the early stages of an unproblematized *telos* of modernity (Ferguson, 2005). Along with the development paradigm that situates small nation-states like Belize on track but "not yet" at the pinnacle of development, policy discourses also emphasize the urgent need to address issues of poverty and crime, often looking to education as the panacea. Educational policy in Latin America, and Belize is no exception, has centered around two goals since the 1980s—reforming educational systems and targeting poorer populations to help with their educational needs (Bonal, 2007). While both represent important goals, the implicit value-laden hierarchy of development embedded in such educational research and reform parallels those same metropolitan-based reforms of rural schools which deem place irrelevant to educational issues. Thus, just as rural education scholarship has drawn attention to the fact that metropolitan-based reforms often prioritize equity and access over "appropriateness" (Atkin, 2003; Corbett & White, 2014), educational reform in Belize has also focused on the twin goals of equity and access without paying attention to the way schools "fit in" with certain places, particularly from the different perspectives of their inhabitants.

Annually published documents of educational statistics in Belize feature the urban and rural as primary categories of comparison, consistently showing students from the rural areas performing below those in urban settings. In addition to underperforming on national assessments, youth in rural areas often live far from schools, limiting their access to schools beginning as early as preschool (Ministry of Education and Youth [MoEY], 2012a, p. 8). The current five-year education reform plan, the Belize Education Sector Strategy (BESS) (MoEY, 2012a), created in partnership with the Caribbean Development Bank (CDB), laid out three main policy objectives for the MoEY's reform agenda. These goals, applicable to all levels of education, were: (1) increasing equitable access, (2) improving the quality and relevance of education, and (3) strengthening governance throughout the sector with an emphasis on increased student achievement. The goal of equitable access in the case of secondary schools involved a joint project with the International Development Bank (IDB) to refinance secondary education in order to distribute government funds more equitably to schools. To further alleviate the financial obstacle to accessing secondary school, the MoEY also provides free bus transportation for rural students to attend schools. The relevance of education, as defined by the MoEY, is directly tied to the educational system's ability to "produce the level and type of human capital required for broader social and economic advancement" (MoEY, 2012a, p. 29).

Increasing secondary completion rates is seen as the key to reaching the larger goal of expanded and more equitable access to secondary school. With higher fees, and in most cases tuition, secondary schools represent a larger financial commitment on the part of the parents and sponsors than primary school. While one might assume that the financial burden of tuition in secondary school would deter many students from continuing on to secondary after primary, this is not the case. From 2011 to 2014, transition rates from primary to secondary ranged between 82% and 90%—remarkably high transition rates given that high school is neither free nor compulsory (MoEY, 2015). However, many of these students will eventually leave school prior to completion—an issue focused on in the BESS and noted by the fact that only 57% of an incoming class was still enrolled by the last year of high school[3] (MoEY, 2012a, p. 10). As stated in the BESS (MoEY, 2012a), it is assumed that the main reform objectives focusing on quality and relevance of the curriculum, increased governance and accountability, as well as the clearance of financial obstacles to secondary school will together increase high school completion rates. Reforming the financing of secondary education, it is further speculated, should "change attitudes" toward dropout and repetition (MoEY, 2012a). Responsibility for lowering dropout rates is placed primarily with the schools, whose administrators and teachers "need to better understand the causes and put in place actions to address them" (MoEY, 2012a, p. 25). The plan is to "maximise the incentives" for schools to reduce repetition and dropout (MoEY, 2012b, p. 4). Hopes for the reforms are high, as stated on the MoEY's website, "Over time, this reform will put an affordable high school within reach of all Belizean children. It will also lead to increased enrollment rates and lower dropout rates—and fight crime, violence and poverty" (MoEY, 2013).

While national ministries of education seek new ways to hold schools accountable for their students' successes and failures, they too are held accountable by the various international agencies that help design reform plans and lend money to implement them. The need for measurable outcomes in project evaluations favors quantitative research over qualitative, and in the case of students leaving school prior to completion, there is little to no attention given to understanding either the early school leavers' perspectives on why they left school or the larger sociocultural and economic context. Furthermore, the issue of early school leaving is assumed to be a problem that rests entirely between the school and the student—an assumption that ignores the fact that students have a relationship to the school, the places they inhabit, and their larger sociocultural and economic context. Assuming that reintegration programs, creating higher quality schools, and even making schools more affordable will lead everyone back to school ignores not only the complexity of the issue, but also the early school leavers' perspectives, which often tell a different story.

MY ROLE AS RESEARCHER

As a researcher I had both insider and outsider status, having lived approximately two and a half years on the caye by the time I began my research and elsewhere in Belize for many years. I also taught full time for one year at the local high school, what I refer to here as Paradise High School (PHS), prior to beginning my research. Fifteen of the 21 participants attended PHS, six of whom were former students of mine. Having the opportunity to teach gave me insight into the inner workings of the school, as well as the particular ways in which education fit in with daily life on the caye. My research interests emerged from witnessing and knowing students within PHS who left school for reasons that did not seem reducible to financial burden. Because of the unique setting of the caye, I wanted to understand better how these early school leavers saw the purpose of school in their lives, as well as how they experienced school and why they left. By the time I began my research, I had stopped teaching and thus neither the participants nor myself had any direct affiliation with the school. Furthermore, the fact that I was not an "island insider" most likely made it easier for some of these stories to be shared.

As "exiles of school," early school leavers have often had the opportunity to critique and reflect on their experiences, as well as more interest and less restraint in sharing their opinions (Fine & Rosenberg, 1983). This discussion of the way in which place emerged in the perspectives of 21 early school leavers residing on Paradise Caye is based on qualitative research conducted utilizing semi-structured interviews and a follow-up survey based on themes which emerged in the interviews. Researchers, educators, and policymakers can learn from early school leavers' perspectives, not only about issues of early school leaving, but also youth-centered views of school experiences and the purposes of school in Belize. This is not to suggest however, that their voices are all that we need to attend to, but rather that they are a crucial part of the picture. As Nieto (1994) has pointed out, "nobody has all the answers, and suggesting that students' views should be adopted wholesale is to accept a romantic view of students that is just as partial and condescending as excluding them completely from the discussion" (p. 398).

While the focus here is primarily on the perspectives of early school leavers, these are situated in their sociocultural, economic and historical context. Taking a critical, dialectical approach, this research is not founded on any notion of determinism—economic, historical or otherwise, but rather begins from the understanding that "individuals navigate lives in 'limit situations' (Freire, 1982; Martín-Baró, 1994). People negotiate, conform, and resist structural constraints within a specific set of historic moments, unequal power relations, and the everyday activities of life" (Weis & Fine, 2013, p. 224). Social structures and human agency exist within a dialectical relationship, and thus people are not simply acted upon or constrained but their actions may intentionally or unintentionally reproduce or alter the social structures. As McLaren (2003) has emphasized, "dialectical theory attempts to tease out the histories and relations of accepted meanings and appearances, tracing interactions from the context to the part, from the system inward to the event" (p. 193). Thus, the "role of critique" can be envisioned as "the excavation of the wider structural forces—and the unequal social condition—that configure the various worlds we observe and write about" (Comaroff & Kim, 2011, p. 173).

IMAGINING THE RURAL

Rural education scholars often make a point of distinguishing between the way in which rural communities are imagined by others and what they actually are. Green and Reid (2014), following Lefebvre (1991) and Soja (1996), explained how "the rural must be understood as both real and imagined" (p. 77), and as Corbett (2013) has discussed, "there are as many imaginaries as there are people with imagination" (p. 2).

As a category, "rural" is first and foremost an official one, constituted in its difference from the urban. Employed by nation-states and statisticians, rural as a category encompasses many places, at the same time that it eradicates and erases their incredible differences. Research and reform in rural communities is often aimed at "improving" rural schools (Howley & Howley, 2014; Howley, Howley, & Huber, 2005) without any regard for the places, the multiple "rural ways of being and living" that Howley and Howley (2014) refer to as the "substantive rural," or the way in which these inform education (p. 36). Rural places and their schools are often imagined, as Corbett and White (2014) described, as a "residual space," not only geographically located outside of the city, but also spatiotemporally removed from modernity and postmodernity (Corbett & White, 2014, p. 27). Similar to development discourses in international contexts, the rural is often perceived to be located near the beginning of a teleological progression, implying both that rural places need to and eventually will, with help from those more developed, become like their more modern benefactors. As Balfour, Mitchell, and Moletsane (2008) explained, "ideas of rurality are concerned with space, isolation, community, poverty, disease, neglect, backwardness, marginalization, depopulation, conservatism, racism, resettlement, corruption, entropy, and exclusion" (p. 97).

Rural scholars often orient their scholarship toward showing the relevance and merits of specific rural places to educational issues and the community due to their own positioning against metropolitan-based reforms and research. A central focus in many rural education studies is the relationship between a specific rural place, the people living there, and education. People in rural places are attributed with having a salient attachment to place (Budge, 2006) and often a sense of loss (Kelly, 2009) as rural exodus for cities is common and their places are abandoned or transformed. Corbett (2007) has described how for many in rural places formal education often means having to leave for work elsewhere. As Budge (2006) explained, there are no universal characteristics of rural schools or communities, but they are often similar in both their strengths and in the challenges they face.

PARADISE CAYE

Paradise Caye is a small caye—approximately 5 miles long by 0.15 to 1.2 mi. wide and about an hour away by boat from the mainland. At the time of the 2010 census, the caye had a population of less than 1,800, however it is now estimated to be around 2,300. Many people who inhabit Paradise Caye today can trace their roots back to the Caste Wars in the Yucatan beginning in the 1840s, and Mestizos have been the dominant ethnic majority on the caye for over a century. In the 1970s, there were eight main family localities in which large kin groups lived. As Sutherland (1998) explained, "identification with a family name, participation in a family support network and acquisition of land on [Paradise Caye] are closely connected" (p. 40). Set amidst rich lobster beds, Paradise Caye had a local economy based primarily on fishing lobster and conch. In 1960, a fisherman's cooperative was created which brought economic success to the caye residents. Not only was wealth equitably distributed, according to Sutherland (1998), but those "who were willing to work and had some family support system in place could do extremely well" (p. 33).

Tourism began in the 1960s, first with a visiting professor and various students, and then in the 1970s with those backpacking along the "Gringo Trail" through Mexico, Central, and South America (Jackiewicz & Govdyak, 2015; Sutherland, 1998). Many families supplemented their income with one or more hotels, restaurants, bakeries, bars, and rental houses (Sutherland, 1998). As tourism grew more in economic importance and lobster fishing became less lucrative, tourism became the mainstay of the local economy. Both the social and physical landscape has changed considerably over the last 40 years. Tourism and its associated employment opportunities has drawn to the caye many people of varying ethnicities and backgrounds—Garinagu, Chinese, Maya, Central American immigrants, and many "ex-pats" from Europe, Canada, England, and the United States. Reflecting global flows of people particular to the caye (Appadurai, 1996, 2014), two categories of distinction among caye residents are Belizean/non-Belizean and islander/non-islander, with the non-islander status originally, although arguably less so today, referring to those who began arriving after 1980 (Sutherland, 1998, p. 37).

Physically, the caye has also transformed. Not only are there roughly 90 or more hotels to meet the demand for lodging by tourists, but also realtors aggressively market land to foreign buyers at prices that are out of reach for many Belizeans. As Jackiewicz and Govdyak (2015) noted, there are divergent views on the future of the caye, with some lamenting all of the development. In one interview with a local realtor, Jackiewicz and Govdyak (2015) related that Paradise Caye was described as about 80% Belizean, but locals "are starting to sell and cash out" (p. 33). However, given that tourism provides jobs and is the mainstay of the economy, there are also many residents who are not planning on moving anywhere. Furthermore, the locals and long-time ex-pats have a vested interest in maintaining the "laid-back," local atmosphere in juxtaposition to the more developed neighboring caye. Not only is it in sync with the traditional pace of the caye, but also the easygoing atmosphere is an integral part of the caye's image and attraction as an "authentic" tourist destination. As Fløysand and Jakobsen (2007) described, not only do outsiders have a role to play in the commodification of a place, but so too do "insiders," both as producers of the images and as "target consumers" (p. 209). According to Rainer (2016), "consumption-orientated restructuring of specific rural areas around the globe can be conceptualized as a particular form of an emerging global countryside, characterized by increasing transnational flows of ideas, capital, and people" (p. 105). New and starker social divisions have arisen as "global spaces" have merged with "local particularities" (Rainer, 2016, p. 115). Some locals have access to resources to capitalize on the opportunities in tourism and others do not.

Although people in urban and rural places face many of the same challenges, one way in which these challenges tend to differ is in intensity (Balfour et al., 2008). For instance, access to resources such as social services is often "absent or inaccessible in rural areas, owing to distance, poor transportation, and neglect" (Balfour et al., 2008, p. 98). In the case of Paradise Caye, many residents of lower socioeconomic status are confined to the social services available on the caye. Resources available on the caye are few—just one primary school (although in 2015 a new private primary school opened), one secondary school, one small library, a health clinic with one doctor, a post office, and a police station. For many social and educational policymakers working within the native category of modernity, Paradise Caye would be considered "underdeveloped" (Sachs, 1997). Resources such as health care and other basic infrastructure to meet the needs of local residents pale in comparison to the increasingly upscale, small hotels and restaurants, as well as the expensive diving and sailing trips geared toward tourists.

Considering a rural place in both its specificity and in its multiple socioeconomic and historical relations and connections, however, is necessary to avoid oversimplified understandings of a place. As Corbett and White (2014) explained:

> The idea of the rural remains important precisely because of the way it is both connected and different from the burgeoning urbanising landscapes of the contemporary world. As Lefebvre (1992) has shown us, capitalism transforms space in ways that are complex, specific and dynamic. The rural was never a space apart from the mainstream of capitalisms; rather, it is intimately caught up in the way that people and place are defined, organised, exploited and moved. (pp. 27–28)

Ironically, tourists flock to the caye because of its characteristically "laid-back"— dare I say "underdeveloped" atmosphere that emanates an "authentic," local feel. Maintaining this image is also of primary importance to sustaining the local economy. In terms of its connections with global flows of capital and people in the form of tourism, Paradise Caye is certainly not forgotten. Nevertheless, while globetrotting tourists come and go daily by boat and air, and local and foreign tour operators, as well as restaurant and hotel owners cash in, prior to 2008, there was not one secondary school on the caye. The only way to attend secondary school before PHS opened was either by living with extended family away from home, or the more expensive alternative of commuting daily by boat. Thus, secondary schooling was, for the most part, only an opportunity for the children of wealthier families. One has to wonder if this is not the manifestation of an educational policy discourse that ties the purpose of education to economic development. Paradise Caye, with its strong, local tourist economy, may not have seemed like an educational priority given that it is not difficult to obtain a job in tourism. In this respect, Paradise Caye *was* forgotten, particularly when it came to the plight of the youths' educational futures.

Thus, there may be some places like Paradise Caye, but not *exactly* like it. And for this reason, and because there are always multiple ways of imagining a place, I agree with Green and Reid (2014) concerning all educational studies, rural or otherwise:

> To focus, rather, on what happens in this school, or that one, in this place or that one, is to insist on specificity, on the particularity and complexity of situated practice(s). An understanding of the specificity of place displaces the metro-normative assumption of a unitary rural "Other." (p. 87)

PHS opened as a private, non-governmental high school (although the school receives some government aid) in response to the need expressed by the community members, particularly parents, for secondary education to be made available on the caye. Although the school's tuition was slightly higher than most secondary schools, it was still less than it would be in total for a student to commute daily. In line with their philosophy of serving all high school-aged youth in the community, administrators have consistently made concerted efforts to secure work-study positions, scholarships, and sponsors for those students who are unable to pay for school.

Common assumptions about why students leave school in Belize include academic and financial difficulties, as well as notions about families of out of school youth not valuing education. As a former teacher and resident of Paradise Caye, none of these assumptions about why the majority of students left school seemed to ring true. The perspectives of the early school leavers provided much needed insight into the more complex reasons for early school leaving. The following discussion looks at two ways in which place emerged to influence the perspectives of early school leavers regarding beliefs about the purposes of school and school experiences. While these themes are not presented here in their entirety, the following discussion should illustrate the necessity of attending to both the specificities of places and the perspectives of rural youth in educational research and policies.

BELIEFS ABOUT THE PURPOSES OF SCHOOL

Similar to other rural education research, place emerged with respect to early school leavers' beliefs about the purpose of education in their lives. Although not limited to these influences, both the colonial remnants of an elitist secondary school system and the larger global tourist economy in which the caye is a destination shaped these beliefs in a unique way. PHS was the only option for post-primary education for many caye residents, however it was still situated, and as such, judged within the wider set of secondary schools throughout the country. All but three participants expressed the desire and motivation to attend secondary school initially, however many would have preferred to attend a different, more prestigious school. The perception of school legitimacy significantly affected beliefs and experiences of school, illustrating the need to consider perspectives of rural youth with respect to schooling.

Early school leavers also related education's purpose to their own beliefs about the social relations and economic opportunities both in their immediate local context and the country as a whole. For most participants the purpose of high school *in general* was to obtain the high school diploma, and get what was continually referred to as an "office job." Although many participants discussed how more advanced degrees were necessary to get an office job, they often qualified this with the observation that even then, no job was guaranteed. As Luis explained:

> … but I think it's kinda waste of time because you know, um, well no really a waste of time but most people come out of like UB [University of Belize] and I think they no even have a job. So I just come out of Third Form and I'm on my, my foot right now then. And I never gone, I never went to Sixth Form or anything like that. (Etheridge, 2015, p. 235)

Thus, although school's purpose was strongly tied to eventually getting a job in an office, there was doubt as to whether even a higher credential would help one gain employment. Complementing this doubt was the belief that getting a job was often based on one's social connections.

Unlike studies which recognize a rural exodus of youth to more urban areas for employment (Corbett, 2007; Howley, Harmon, & Leopald, 1996), because of the unique relations and global "flows" of capital and people that define Paradise Caye, many early school leavers felt they would be able to stay and survive economically without a high school diploma (Appadurai, 1996). Currently, most hotels, restaurants, tour operators, and gift shops on the caye do not require a high school diploma. Beliefs relating to the purpose of school and the usefulness of the diploma on the caye were, for the most part, directly related to the local tourism-based economy and the types of jobs available in the formal and informal sector. Because school's purpose was tied to getting a job in an office, the lack of such office jobs also added to the seeming irrelevance of high school. Furthermore, the easygoing lifestyle of the caye, the ability to rely on family, and not needing a lot to live on influenced beliefs about school. As one participant explained:

> You can either … do underhanded stuff or you can do stuff like … work 'cause there's lots of restaurants and bars you can work at if you don't want, if your goal is not to go off to a different place and …' cause a student was there one time I forgot his name, he said that why should we be sitting down in here spending our money to go to school when we could be out there doing a job, making money and that's when I found out that he stopped school. (Etheridge, 2015, p. 233)

The economic trajectory of the nation as a whole is tied to tourism in multiple policy documents, including those in education in which it is often postulated that education will be increasingly essential as the market in tourism continues to grow. Paradise Caye, where tourism accounts for the majority of all jobs, offers a glimpse of the relationship between education and a tourism-based local economy. Because of Paradise Caye's lack of office jobs and the fact that most hotels, restaurants, bars, and tour companies do not require a high school diploma for work, many felt that high school was unnecessary. While these beliefs may not have been the reason for leaving school, knowing that it would not be difficult to obtain a job without a high school diploma made leaving school more justifiable.

Ironically, although early school leavers took into account the larger social and economic context of their own schooling opportunities, the way in which employment is obtained, the reputations of schools and the validity of different credentials, educational policymakers and researchers rarely focus on either the perspectives of rural youth or the way in which places articulate with particular schools and educational issues. Rather, educational policy often locates the issue of early school leaving as a problem of either the school or the student, making it an issue of school reform, rather than one that extends into and beyond local places.

Corbett's (2007) work has shown the role that education plays in the exodus of young people to more urban places and as a complement to this, Kelly (2009) has demonstrated how rural education is "premised on loss" (p. 1). Kelly's (2009) work draws attention to the more neglected affective aspects of the ambiguous relationship between rural places, their schools and the people whom they serve. Kelly (2009) explained:

> For whether one stays in or leaves a rural area (and the oscillations of mobility and tran-sience are rarely so simply demarcated), indeed, regardless of geographical place attention to such affective dimensions, what William Pinar (1991) calls "a social psychoanalysis of place" (p. 165), can reap rich insights into both the challenges and possibilities for educa-tion and/in rurality. (p. 1)

In Paradise Caye, although no exodus of people has taken place, nor did any sense of loss come up in the perspectives of early school leavers, tourism devel-opment has brought with it rapid physical and social transformations. Although many businesses are locally owned, there are increasing numbers of wealthy ex-patriots investing in land and businesses. There was an absence of complaints concerning tourism and the changes in Paradise Caye by early school leavers, although in small ways the recognition of the need to have control over one's own businesses and lives emerged. Some early school leavers related education's purpose to the tourist economy as giving one the ability to not get "cheated out of your money" and to become like one of the locals who own their restaurants and other businesses.

Instead of accepting the amorphous notion of "economic development" as the ends of education, social and educational policymakers and researchers should consider these desires of early school leavers for ownership and control of their businesses as indexing unequal power relationships that need to be explored. Although Belize has the third highest income per capita in Central America, this hides the giant income disparity between the rich and poor (CIA, 2015). Particularly because places like Paradise Caye are marketed to visitors as homogeneous, romanticized, and often static "imaginaries," it should be the duty of both rural education scholars and one of the main purposes of school anywhere to lay bare the global and local connections and relations of capital in which places and people are made and remade. Thus, instead of uncritically linking education's purpose to economic development—either at the national level or at the individual level in the form of "office jobs," educational scholars, policymakers, and schools, in conjunction with youth in and out of school, should explore what exactly economic development looks like, how wealth is distributed, and what forms development should take in that particular place. As Mishel and Rothstein (2007) have discussed, "the biggest threats to the next generation's success come from social and economic policy failures, not schools. And enhancing opportunity requires more than school improvement" (p. 35). Educational policy and reform that considers early school leaving as the result of an issue between the school and the student alone assumes that youth are myopic, and somehow not able to understand or interested in the larger educational system and socioeconomic context as a whole. Although policies directed toward making schools more equitable and accessible are worthy and necessary goals, engaged and motivated students are not a direct result of such policies, nor does school reform alone prevent people from leaving school.

SOCIAL RELATIONS IN THE COMMUNITY AND EXPERIENCES OF SCHOOL

Investigating the local or even the larger socioeconomic situation is not enough to understand the meanings education has for people or why people do the things they do, in this case leave school early. Although many early school leavers' beliefs about school's purpose were shaped by the larger socioeconomic context, their leaving school cannot be reduced to these beliefs. Rather, there were many varied and complex reasons that these particular earlier school leavers gave for leaving. In contrast to the previous discussion in which beliefs about school were informed by the wider local and national socioeconomic context, school experiences were in many ways shaped by the social relationships that existed within the community and carried over into the school. I will briefly discuss some ways in which aspects of the social relations in the community affected school experiences, which in combination with other factors, affected the non-completion of high school.

As Nespor (2008) has pointed out, although often conflated, place is not the same as community. By employing the term community I do not intend to uncritically connote either a sense of "boundedness, intimacy, connection, intergenerational stability, and lack of internal division" (Nespor, 2008, p. 478) or the opposite. Rather, by beginning from the perspectives of early school leavers and situating them in their historical, sociocultural and economic context, I hope to show the ways in which communities are experienced differently. School experiences, as described by the early school leavers, were not cut off from social relations outside of the school, and often reflected and reinforced social divisions. In many ways, school experiences were influenced by the fact that most people knew everyone and their families outside the school context.

Unlike those who attended high schools off of the caye, those at PHS often mentioned both favoritism and discrimination based on who they and their families were in the community. Not only did people know each other from childhood, but also many found that their reputations were hard to shake. Because of the small size of the community, reputations in primary school travelled with students into high school, as exemplified by one young woman, who expressed that she felt unfairly labeled as a "bully." Assuming the impression her teachers had of her in primary school was communicated with her secondary school teachers, she explained:

> … I think that they already put their mind 'cause I know some of the primary school teachers went there and said oh well you don't have to take all that from Tiffany' cause she's really disrespectful, and she's this, and she's so negative. (Etheridge, 2015, p. 200)

Concerns about favoritism and unfair disciplinary practices were brought up by many of the students, as one young woman explained:

> … 'cause they have kids that go and they smoke at the back of the school there and I don't see anything ever happen to them. N'even a demerit they get for doing stuff at the school like that. But other than that they pick on other people for other stuff that isn't even wrong and they give you a demerit and the ones that do wrong they don't get anything so I don't find that fair so that's just, I didn't find that fair … (Etheridge, 2015, p. 178)

A few participants brought up their desire for having teachers from somewhere else besides the caye. This was thought to be a remedy to favoritism and unfairness concerning who was disciplined. When asked what Linda would change if she was the Minister of Education, she mentioned that she would get better teachers that treat students with respect. For Linda, they would be from:

> … far away because they find teachers that is from the caye and then they have favoritism with the people … I would find teachers from far that the children don't know and they can't only be picking on certain people for stuff because they know you, they know

your whole life because they live here so they're gonna pick on you for every little stuff ... (Etheridge, 2015, p. 178)

Furthermore, the small size of the community meant that anonymity was impossible, and personal lives were often very soon public. Thus, having a counselor who was not from the caye was also an expressed need, so that students could feel comfortable talking about their problems. In both primary and high school, teachers brought up personal issues about a participant's family in front of other students. As one participant described, "They had this time that me and my teacher we got in a little argument and she start bringing up stuff about my mom that I didn't think was appropriate for the class to know about so ..." (Etheridge, 2015, p. 178).

Here, place, and particularly the small size of the community, emerged as a defining factor in the way social relationships in the community were played out and experienced in the school. Learning about this resulted from beginning from the standpoint of early school leavers, a group normally left out and thus silenced in educational research. Although the voices of early school leavers are not always welcome, their perspectives can illuminate aspects of schooling that would often be left in the shadows if researched from a different perspective. As Steinberg and Kincheloe (2010) have reminded us, "to establish a working democracy, critical theorists make use of voices and perspectives that have been traditionally excluded" in order to tell "suppressed stories" (p. 145). Drawing on feminist theologian Sharon Welch's emphasis on the "power of difference," Steinberg and Kincheloe (2010) explained, "Communities gain great moral strength when they are based not on consensus and homogeneous values but on a solidarity that validates and employs this power of difference" (p. 145).

CONCLUSION

In Belize, most research that informs educational policy at the national level centers on statistics such as test scores, repetition, and dropout along familiar lines of difference such as gender, rural/urban, and districts, for example. Educational policymakers and those researchers working toward the implementation of certain metro-normative, neoliberal policies often neglect the way in which particular places are intertwined with education and hold specific meanings for people. As this chapter has shown, however, extricating the particularities of place from studies in education ignores the context that shapes experiences of and beliefs about education. Taking into account the larger socioeconomic, cultural and historical context invites a vision of school, following Nespor (1997), as "an intersection in social space, a knot in a web of practices that stretch into complex systems beginning and ending outside the school" (p. xiii).

Qualitative research that is grounded in cultural, historical, and socioeconomic relations of a place, attending to the meanings that education in that particular place have for people, can often contribute answers to the tricky *why* questions. In this regard, policies, which usually locate the causes of leaving school early between the school and the student, could benefit from rural education scholarship in which specific places and the meanings that they have for their inhabitants are central. For early school leavers on Paradise Caye, beliefs about the purposes of school and school experiences were informed by the local and wider socioeconomic context—particularly the way one obtains a job and one's own social network, as well as the historical context of an unequal secondary school system. Beginning research from the standpoint of those most silenced, the early school leavers, gives those serious about making schools appropriate, (Corbett & White, 2014) "placed resources" (Blommaert, 2002, in Balfour et al., 2008, p. 103), more thorough insight into the articulation of place, schooling, and people. Just as many educational policymakers and researchers have much to learn from rural education scholarship's emphasis on place-specific studies, rural education scholars should also seek to include the normally silenced voices of rural youth, and in particular early school leavers. Not only will this complicate the homogenized view of community that is criticized in some rural education studies (Nespor, 2008), but also it will honor the ideal of researching *for* rural communities (Corbett & White, 2014, p. 26)—particularly those living and experiencing life in schools.

NOTES

1. For purposes here, leaving school prior to graduating from high school with a diploma will be referred to as *early school leaving* and "dropouts" will be called *early school leavers* (Clandinin, Steeves, & Caine, 2013). This term does not have the negative connotations which "dropouts" has and honors the fact that there are many different reasons for leaving school. Early school leavers are not intended to be seen as a homogeneous category.

2. Although I utilize a pseudonym, I am also aware of Green and Reid's (2014) point that both anonymization of places and the 'disclaimer' about generalizability in qualitative research reflect the "metro-normativity of educational research, and fail to acknowledge that the material and affective dimensions of place cannot be factored out of any understanding of it." (p. 89). I fully acknowledge the paradox of following 'protocol' in terms of protecting the anonymity of places and yet at the same time, focusing on the importance of specificities of places in educational research.

3. This is based on the 2009/2010 data, the latest available at the time the BESS (MoEY, 2012a) was written.

REFERENCES

Appadurai, A. (1996). *Modernity at large: Cultural dimensions of globalization.* Minneapolis, MN: University of Minnesota Press.

Appadurai, A. (2014, July 1). Arjun Appadurai. *Globalizations, 11*(4), 481–490. doi: 10.1080/14747731.2014.951209

Apple, M. W. (2000). Standards, markets, and curriculum. In B. M. Franklin (Ed.), *Curriculum & consequence: Herbert M. Kliebard and the promise of schooling* (pp. 55–74). New York, NY: Teachers College Press.

Atkin, C. (2003). Rural communities: Human and symbolic capital development. Fields Apart. *Compare, 33*(4), 507–518.

Balfour, R. J., Mitchell, C., & Moletsane, R. (2008). Troubling contexts: Toward a generative theory of rurality as education research. *Journal of Rural and Community Development, 3*(3), 95–107.

Bennett, J. A. (2008). *Education in Belize: A historical perspective.* Belize City, Belize: The Angelus Press.

Bonal, X. (2007). On global absences: Reflections on the failings in the education and poverty relationship in Latin America. *International Journal of Educational Development, 27*, 86–100. doi: 10.1016/j.ijedudev.2006.05.003

Budge, K. (2006). Rural leaders, rural places: Problem, privilege, and possibility. *Journal of Research in Rural Education, 21*(13), 1–10. Retrieved from http://jrre.psu.edu/articles/21-13.pdf

Central Intelligence Agency [CIA]. (2015). *The world factbook.* Retrieved from https://www.cia.gov/library/publications/the-world-factbook/geos/bh.html

Clandinin, D. J., Steeves, P., & Caine, V. (2013). *Composing lives in transition: A narrative enquiry into the experiences of early school leavers.* Bingley: Emerald Group.

Comaroff, J., & Kim, D. K. (2011). Anthropology, theology, critical pedagogy: A conversation with Jean Comaroff and David Kyuman Kim. *Cultural Anthropology, 26*(2), 158–178. doi: 10.1111/j.1548-1360.2011.01093.x

Corbett, M. (2007). *Learning to leave: The irony of schooling in a coastal community.* Halifax: Fernwood Books.

Corbett, M. (2013). Improvisation as a curricular metaphor: Imagining education for a rural creative class. *Journal of Research in Rural Education, 28*(10), 1–11. Retrieved from http://jrre.psu.edu/articles/28-10.pdf.

Corbett, M., & White, S. (2014). Why put the 'rural' in research?. In S. White & M. Corbett (Eds.), *Doing educational research in rural settings: Methodological issues, international perspectives and practical solutions* (pp. 26–32). London: Routledge.

Crossley, M. (2008). The advancement of educational research in small states. *Comparative Education, 44*(2), 247–254.

Crossley, M., & Tikly, L. (2004). Postcolonial perspectives and comparative and international research in education: A critical introduction. *Comparative Education, 40*(2), 147–156. doi: 10.1080/0305006042000231329

Etheridge, B. (2015). *Early school leavers in Belize: Perspectives on school experiences, the purpose of school and why they left.* (Doctoral Dissertation). Retrieved from http://scholarworks.boisestate.edu/td/1040

Ferguson, J. (2005). Decomposing modernity: History and hierarchy after development. In A. Loomba, S. Kaul, M. Bunzl, A. Burton & J. Esty (Eds.), *Postcolonial Studies and Beyond* (pp. 166–181). Durham, NC: Duke University Press.

Fine, M., & Rosenberg, P. (1983). Dropping out of high school: The ideology of school and work. *Journal of Education, 165*(3), 257–272.

Fløysand, A., & Jakobsen, S.-E. (2007). Commodification of rural places: A narrative of social fields, rural development, and football. *Journal of Rural Studies, 23*, 206–221. doi: 10.1016/j.jrurstud.2006.09.012

Green, B., & Reid, J. (2014). Social cartography and rural education: Researching space(s) and place(s). In S. White & M. Corbett (Eds.), *Doing educational research in rural settings: Methodological issues, international perspectives and practical solutions* (pp. 73–99). London: Routledge.

Halcrow Group (with Decision Economics and Penny Hope Ross & the Belize National Assessment Team). (2010, August). *Belize country poverty assessment, final report.* London: Halcrow Group.

Howley, C. B., Harmon, H. L., & Leopald, G. D. (1996). Rural scholars or bright rednecks? Aspirations for a sense of place among rural youth in Appalachia. *Journal of Research in Rural Education, 12*, 150–160.

Howley, C. B., & Howley, A. (2014). Making sense of rural education research: Art, transgression, and other acts of terroir. In S. White & M. Corbett, (Eds.), *Doing educational research in rural settings: Methodological issues, international perspectives and practical solutions* (pp. 33–72). London: Routledge.

Howley, C. B., Howley, A. A., & Huber, D. S. (2005). Prescriptions for rural mathematics instruction: Analysis of rhetorical literature. *Journal of Research in Rural Education, 20*(7). Retrieved from http://www.umaine.edu/jjre/20-7.pdf

Humes, A. (2015, January 13). Belize sets records in tourism arrivals. *Belize Breaking News.* Retrieved from www.breakingbelizenews.com

Jackiewicz, E. L., & Govdyak, O. (2015). Diversity of lifestyle: A view from Belize. *Yearbook of the Association of Pacific Coast Geographers, 77*, 18–39. doi: 10.1353/pcg.2015.0007

Kelly, U. A. (2009). Learning to lose: Rurality, transience, and belonging (a companion to Michael Corbett). *Journal of Research in Rural Education, 24*(11). Retrieved from http://jrre. psu.edu/articles/24-11.pdf

King, K. (2007). Multilateral agencies in the construction of the global agenda on education. *Comparative Education, 43*(3), 377–391. doi: 10.1080/03050060701556331

LeFebvre, H. (1991). *The production of space.* Oxford: Blackwell.

McGrath, S. (2010). The role of education in development: An educationalist's response to some recent work in development economics. *Comparative Education, 46*(2), 237–253. doi: 10.1080/03050061003775553

McLaren, P. (2003). *Life in schools: An introduction to critical pedagogy in the foundations of education* (4th ed.). Boston, MA: Pearson/Allyn & Bacon (Original published in 1989).

Ministry of Education, Youth, and Sports [MoEY]. (2012a, March). *Education sector strategy, 2011–2016: Improving access, quality and governance of education in Belize.* Retrieved from http://www.moe.gov.bz

Ministry of Education, Youth, and Sports [MoEY]. (2012b, March). *Education sector strategy 2011–2016: Summary framework.* Retrieved from http://www.moe.gov.bz

Ministry of Education, Youth, and Sports [MoEY]. (2013). *Secondary Education Reform.* Retrieved from http://www.moe.gov.bz/index.php/secondary-education-reform

Ministry of Education, Youth, and Sports [MoEY], Policy, Planning, Research and Evaluation Unit [PPRE]. (2015). *Abstract of educational statistics 2014/2015.* Retrieved from http://www.moe.gov.bz

Mishel, L., & Rothstein, R. (2007, November 1). Schools as scapegoats. *Education Digest: Essential Readings Condensed for Quick Review, 73*(3), 32–39.

Nespor, J. (1997). *Tangled up in school: Politics, space, bodies, and signs in the educational process.* Mahwah, NJ: Lawrence Erlbaum.

Nespor, J. (2008). Education and place: A review essay. *Educational Theory, 58*(4), 475–489.

Nieto, S. (1994). Lessons from students on creating a chance to dream. *Harvard Educational Review, 64*(4), 392–392.

Rainer, G. (2016). Constructing globalized spaces of tourism and leisure: Political ecologies of the Salta Wine Route (NW-Argentina). *Journal of Rural Studies, 43*, 104–177. http://dx.doi.org/10.1016/j.jrurstud.2015.11.007

Sachs, W. (1997). *The development dictionary: A guide to knowledge as power.* London: Zed Books.

Soja, E. W. (1996). *Thirdspace: Journeys to Los Angeles and real-and-imagined places.* Oxford: Blackwell.

Spring, J. (2009). *Globalization of education: An introduction.* New York, NY: Routledge.

Statistical Institute of Belize [SIB]. (2013). *Belize Population and Housing Census 2010: Country Report.* Belmopan: Statistical Institute of Belize.

Statistical Institute of Belize [SIB]. (2015). Statistics of the nation. Retrieved from http://www.sib.org.bz

Steinberg, S. R., with J. L. Kincheloe (2010). Power, emancipation, and complexity: Employing critical theory. *Power and Education, 2*(2). Retrieved from www.wwwords.co.uk/POWER

Sutherland, A. (1998). *The making of Belize: Globalization in the margins.* Westport, CT: Bergin and Garvey.

Weis, L., & Fine, M. (2013). A methodological response from the field to Douglas Foley: Critical bifocality and class cultural productions in Anthropology and Education. *Anthropology & Education Quarterly, 44*(3), 222–233. doi: 10.1111/aeq.12023

World Bank. (2015). *Population density (people per sq. km of land area).* Retrieved from data.worldbank.org/indicator/EN.POP.DNST

CHAPTER SIXTEEN

Dumbing Down THE Fly-Over State

The Scape-Goating of Education in Oklahoma

JENNIFER JOB, KRISTI DICKEY, SUSAN KIRK, JUSTIN McCRACKIN, AND GINA MORRIS

America's education system is currently undergoing a systematic assault on its status as a public good, led by a conglomeration of neoliberal entrepreneurs, venture philanthropists, and the government entities that cater to both (Kohn, 2012). Media organizations portray America's schools as failing, parroting political messages, contrary to significant evidence otherwise (Watkins, 2012). "Reformers" have developed a complex system—stemming from the power of No Child Left Behind—of ranking, assessment, and punitive grading systems designed to defund and discredit democratically-run schools. This system replaces locally-designed curriculum with corporate programs and tests, and public administrations with private for-profit businesses. Recent media attention on seemingly-stagnant Program for International Student Assessment (PISA) rankings and National Assessment of Educational Progress (NAEP) scores have convinced much of America that its public schools are just not serving its children, and charter school companies are being hailed in the media and by politicians as the wave of the future. In addition to news reports that laud the work of groups like KIPP and Stand for Children, popular films such as *Waiting for "Superman"* and *The Lottery* are furthering market reforms of schools.

However, there are a handful of states that have resisted this trend, and they are suffering a number of consequences. In 2014, Oklahoma made the decision to withdraw from the Partnership for Assessment of Readiness of College and Career (PARCC), a group of states who have agreed to use common assessments to evaluate student progress, typically made by major testing corporations such as Pearson. Quickly thereafter, the legislature repealed its implementation of the Common Core State Standards. This pushback against market reforms has made for strange bedfellows—an alignment of progressive education thinkers who see the Common Core as a gateway to neoliberal education reform, and Tea Party neoconservatives who see the Common Core as a product of big government (specifically President Obama's big government). Prior to these decisions, Oklahoma tended to fly under the radar, gliding at the bottom quarter of education efficacy rankings but not typically seen as examples of poor education quality as with Alabama or Mississippi.

The decision to withdraw from the Common Core carried political consequences that caused Oklahoma to garner new media attention. As Berliner and Glass (2014) explain, the public perception of education is reliant on a number of myths that combine to paint a picture of a system in crisis, only fixed by large-scale, government-sanctioned neoliberal reform. Several of these myths—including the belief in a silver bullet that can "fix" all of America's schools, and the idea that mastery is only exhibited on standardized tests—were publicly flouted by Oklahoma's decision. This chapter argues that in response, national attention has been given to a narrative of Oklahoma's education system, despite localized efforts to the contrary (e.g., Schoonmaker, 2012), as one of Bible-Belt-induced ignorance.

While mainstream media (e.g., national and state newspapers, magazines, and online publications) work to further the agenda of neoliberal reform in education by creating an oversimplified and often false narrative, grassroots media (e.g., blogs and local websites) have provided a counter narrative that seeks to address the issues that are central to Oklahoma's education struggles while pushing back against market reforms. This chapter looks to use a comparison of both types of media coverage of Oklahoma's P-12 education in order to deconstruct the current narrative of this system as uncaring about education. The chapter concludes with recommendations of how teachers and other public pedagogues might use this division to advocate for positive change.

THE FRAMING OF EDUCATION ISSUES ALONG NEOLIBERAL LINES

The Oklahoman, one of two newspapers Oklahoma has that provides statewide coverage, published an editorial in April of 2015 about the Oklahoma School of Science and Math. The article began with this paragraph:

> It says something about the state of education in Oklahoma that local officials will fight tooth and nail to prevent closure of even the worst performing school site, but far less energy is expended regarding the loss of one of the state's best schools: The Oklahoma School of Science and Math. (Achievements of Oklahoma, 2015, para. 1)

This one sentence makes the assumption that Oklahoma's school officials are actively working to protect terrible schools, one of the key myths perpetuated by neoliberal reformers (Berliner & Glass, 2014). The media has cast Oklahoma as fighting against high standards and excellence through "mediocrity" discourse and the proliferation of biased ranking systems, serving to push a neoliberal agenda.

Leveraging The Mediocrity Discourse

In 2015, the *Oklahoman* published an article by Jennifer Monies that accused Oklahoma's schools of "settling for mediocrity." The same paper also published an interview in January of the same year with Janet Barresi, Oklahoma's superintendent under Governor Fallin's first term who lost to Tea Party candidate Joy Hofmeister in 2014. The article quoted Barresi as calling Oklahoma's education system "abysmal," "mediocre," and "broken," and spent considerable space quoting the latest Quality Counts report raking Oklahoma 48th in America in education. This is typical of a media discourse of Oklahoma's system as mediocre.

Often this discourse is directed squarely at teachers, framing them as greedy and lazy. The Associated Press covered the 2015 Oklahoma Educator's rally as solely about teacher pay and the reduction of standardized testing, and highlighted how schools were closing so teachers could attend. No mention was made about the conditions teachers are working under. The *Oklahoman*, in an editorial about the same rally, accused teachers of being anti-reform and "skipping work" (What will doubling, 2015), and in another editorial called the rally about a "cause" rather than a "plan" (Oklahoma education rally should, March 29, 2015). This language is used to undermine teacher organizations as well, as articles in the *Tulsa World*, Oklahoma's other statewide newspaper, repeatedly referred to the Oklahoma Educators Association as a "union" regardless of the fact that it is illegal for the Association to collectively bargain for teachers, and then went on to quote several state representatives' comments on why the OEA should have less power (Hoberock, 2015). Articles seeming to be pro-teacher are cloaked in neoliberal discourse. Two May 2015 articles in the *Oklahoman*, one headlined "Top students and educators deserve respect" and the other "Academic excellence is a year-round goal," promote competitive systems, only rewarding the "top" teachers (Boren, 2015; Wheelock, 2015). Oklahoma's teachers are also held responsible for poverty by the media in articles claiming, with no evidentiary support, that education is the answer to getting kids out of poverty (e.g., Education is Crucial, 2015).

The same discourse is seen in both state and national media after Oklahoma was thrust into the spotlight by its repeal of the Common Core State Standards (CCSS). The Common Core State Standards were initially a state-led effort through the National Governors Association Center for Best Practices and the

Council of State School Officers to develop college and career readiness objectives that would provide common expectations across the nation (CCSSI, 2010). The standards were to be informed by the "state standards already in existence; the experience of teachers, content experts, states, and leading thinkers; and feedback from the public" (CCSSI, 2010, para. 2). However, the process was quickly co-opted by corporations, from the Walmart executives who sat on the steering committee to the information trips and workshops for the designers that were led by Pearson (Job, 2012). Teacher input and public feedback appeared to get lost in the process, and major testing companies began to develop curriculum and testing packages for the standards before they were made public, to the extent that it is "Common Core" has become synonymous with "testing" in the public discourse. Finally, President Obama's "Race to the Top" initiative included as a criterion that states must adopt the Common Core State Standards in order to receive the award. The narrative of the standards turned from that of a state-led initiative to one of federal government and corporate control, and states that had previously supported the standards turned against them.

In Oklahoma, state political leaders, most of whom are Republican, pressured Governor Mary Fallin to reject the standards in 2014, decrying federal intrusion (Associated Press, 2014; Green & Willert, 2014b; Paxton, 2014; Strauss, 2014b; Stop Common Core in Oklahoma, [ca. 2013]; Turner, 2014). Fallin complied, despite the fact that she was the chair of the National Governor's Association committee in charge of the Common Core. Fallin said, "President Obama and Washington bureaucrats have usurped Common Core [sic] in an attempt to influence state education standards" (Green, 2014a), following the party line of framing the standards as federal intrusion into state issues. However, media coverage did not follow suit. When the bill to repeal the CCSS was being considered in the summer of 2014, the *Tulsa World* published an article entitled "Schools superintendent candidates have opinions on Common Core" (Archer, 2014b), giving the viewpoints of the state superintendent candidates. The article began by describing CCSS as "ensuring that all students are subject to the same benchmarks and that children get a deeper and more rigorous education" (para. 1), before calling efforts to keep the CCSS in place "a losing battle" (para. 3). Oklahoma was positioned as being against those "rigorous" standards. The *Oklahoman* also invited national opinions, publishing an editorial from the former governors of Alabama and Georgia urging Oklahoma to stay the course (Perdue & Riley, 2014). The paper published a statement from the U.S. Secretary of Education, Arne Duncan, calling the repeal "politics" and a reducing of standards that is "bad for kids" and "bad for the country" (Green, 2014b). *The New York Times* called Oklahoma's repeal a step in the wrong direction and a misunderstanding of what kids need (Ellenberg, 2015). NPR highlighted districts that refused to leave the CCSS and the difficulty Oklahoma is having in writing replacement standards (O'Donoghue, 2014), and only quoted one teacher's thoughts on the repeal: "I was sick to my stomach. I cried" (para. 3). Without providing any context to the corporate root of the CCSS and how it related to the abundance of standardized testing students faced, the media's implication was clear: Oklahoma's decision was wrongheaded and backwards.

The Common Core was not the only issue in the past year to bring Oklahoma negative national attention. After repealing Common Core, the Oklahoma legislature continued the fight against national standards in the form of AP History classes. House Bill 1380—sponsored by Rep. Dan Fisher (R)—would have prevented state funding for any AP history classes, and it listed primary and secondary resources that should be used for the class instead (Conlon, 2015). The issue for many Republicans stemmed from the recently revised framework of the AP U.S. History class. Some conservative groups pointed to unfavorable references, such as "President Reagan's 'bellicose rhetoric'" (Hartmann, 2015, para. 6), as proof that the College Board's curriculum lacked political neutrality. However, the effort was not framed by the media as one of academic debate or a fight for local control. *The Tulsa World* ran an editorial entitled "Effort to Ban AP History in Oklahoma is Ignorant" in which the author assured Republicans that the new framework was not "a secret left-wing plot to inculcate American youth with seditious ideas, just a hard class for bright kids" (World's Editorial Writers, 2015, para. 9). *Inside Higher Ed,* a nationally-read education population, mocked Oklahoma for calling the repeal an emergency (Flaherty, 2015), and *The Guardian,* an English newspaper ran an editorial entitled "Sorry, Oklahoma. You don't get to ban history that you don't like" (Thrasher, 2015).

What little positive national attention occurs is undermined by media discourse. A Tulsa-based news company used the struggle for approval on H. B. 1657 to claim "establishing a progressive program in a conservative state wasn't that easy; some say he snuck it into law" ("Oklahoma's pre-kindergarten," 2013). This implied Oklahoma conservatives are unwilling to accept progressive programs, regardless of benefits to citizens, while advancing the theory that liberals in Oklahoma must "sneak" beneficial legislation past conservatives. Suzy Khimm (2013, para. 3) reported in *The Washington Post* that, "Oklahoma's universal pre-K initiative is particularly striking coming from a deeply red state with a limited budget. The expanded pre-K access was slipped into a bill." Nicholas D. Kristof (2013, para. 1) wrote in the *New York Times,* "Liberals don't expect Oklahoma to serve as a model of social policy. But, astonishingly, we can see in this reddest of red states a terrific example of what the United States can achieve in early education." Deborah Phillips states, "If it can happen in Oklahoma, it can happen everywhere" (Sanchez & Turner, 2014, para. 39). Herman (2009) notes this wordplay as the "mainstream media carrying out their propaganda service on behalf of the corporate and political establishment" (p. 27).

Ranking Oklahoma as a "Failing" State

In 2013, Oklahoma students measured in the bottom 20% of the nation's scores in National Assessment of Educational Progress [NAEP] assessments for reading and math. NAEP originated in 1962 under Federal Commissioner of Education Francis Keppel and consultant Ralph Tyler as a report on the progress of America's students (NAGB). Currently, NAEP assesses reading and math scores biannually at the 4th and 8th grade level in all states.

Oklahoma's national rank of 40th does not reflect positively on Oklahoma's public schools, and it is a rank quoted frequently in the media by publications such as *Oklahoma Watch, The Wall Street Journal, and The Washington Post,* to highlight how poorly Oklahoma educating its students (Alger, 2015; Robson, 2015; Rubin, 2015). However, a closer look at the actual scores is revealing. Table 16.1 shows the range of scores for each exam.

Viewed within the context of national scores, Oklahoma's ranking does not seem quite as negative; the range of scores for each subject and grade level is too narrow to reveal major differences occurring within instruction and learning. A fourth grader in Oklahoma is only four points behind her national counterparts in reading, and only two in math, out of hundreds of points available. Statistics, while numerically accurate, do not reflect a valid portrayal of Oklahoma's public education. Statistics become a form of discourse that, without the exchange of contextual information, can be skewed. Ranking Oklahoma's public education in the lowest 20th percent of the nation is an example of discourse without relevant context. Statistical language provides the shadow within which power is hidden. Lather (2012) tells us that data "disallows what cannot easily be counted in a way that profoundly shapes what counts as science" (p. 1023).

Education Week has developed its own ranking system, Quality Counts, that places Oklahoma as 48th in the nation based upon three criteria: chance for success, school finance, and K-12 Achievement (Education Week Research Center, 2015). The American Legislative Exchange Council, a group that operates on "a common belief in limited government, free markets, federalism, and individual

Table 16.1. NAEP Rankings 2013.

Grade/Subject	OK Score	National Avg. Score	Range
4th Reading	217	221	26
4th Math	239	241	24
8th Reading	262	266	29
8th Reading	276	284	36

Source: NCES (2013).

liberty" (ALEC, 2015) and has a number of U.S. Senators and Representatives on its board, has released its own education ranking. This scale is measured by state academic standards, whether school choice is offered, the size of the charter school program in place, whether online schools are available, and how it perceives "ineffective" teachers are handled (Ladner & Myslinski, 2015). Oklahoma is ranked 41st. ALEC's report card was published in newspapers nationwide.

Oklahoma's public school image is negatively portrayed by statistical ranking, which displaces expertise and empowers mandates from afar (Taubman, 2009); ranking negates the social movement for equity, using economics to undergird authoritarianism and enforce restructuring of social and institutional architecture (Watkins, 2012). It perpetuates a hierarchal system that dehumanizes people by reducing them into categories of data. Marion Namenwirth (as cited in Lather, 2012) makes this point: "Scientist firmly believe that as long as they are not conscious of any bias or political agenda, they are neutral and objective, when in fact they are only unconscious" (p. 1022). The media then leverages this unconsciousness to further a neoliberal agenda. For example, Oklahoma received national attention when President Barack Obama, at his 2013 State of the Union Address, proclaimed Oklahoma was a state that made it "a priority to educate our youngest children" (State of the Union Address, 2013). Oklahoma House Bill 1657 created "half-day and full-day early childhood programs" (H. Res.1657, 1998). The President, among others, touted Oklahoma as a model for the nation ("Oklahoma's pre-kindergarten," 2013). This is not reflected in the rankings, and yet no one thought to question how a state with such a progressive program would rank so low.

MEDIA REFRAMING AS NEOLIBERAL AGENDA

In order to understand the effects of the media's neoliberal discourse in misframing Oklahoma's education system, one must first understand Oklahoma's characteristics as a state.

Issues Oklahoma Faces in Education

Oklahoma's population and geography create a unique setting for a state-controlled education system. The state is predominantly rural, with two major urban areas, Tulsa and Oklahoma City that are more than three hundred miles away from the isolated Panhandle area. These cities comprise 25% of Oklahoma's total population of 3.85 million people. Nearly 10% of Oklahoma's population is Native American. The median household income is $8,000 below the national median, and 17% of Oklahomans live below the poverty line (U.S. Census Bureau, 2015a, 2015b).

The major industry in the state is oil, and high school graduates make more money working high-risk oil rig jobs than they would as college graduates. The relatively high poverty levels in the state, combined with rural districts that are so far removed from state resources, create challenges in state oversight of education and increase the emphasis on local governments.

Because of the privileging of local control, there are 584 school districts governed by locally-elected school boards and superintendents, and there is little collaboration amongst the districts. Communication between school districts and the Oklahoma State Department of Education relies on technology due to the distance between the capitol and the outermost reaches of the state, occurring via phone, e-mail, and texting rather than in-person meetings. Districts contact their legislators, and legislators hold meetings within their districts to educate the public on changes, atomizing the process rather than centralizing it.

In Oklahoma, state financial support for education has been historically mixed. In 1990, Oklahoma educators rallied in support of HB 1017, landmark legislation that brought about reduced class sizes, equitable distribution of funding, and uniform state standards (Oklahoma Policy Institute, n.d). By 2014, many of the bill's provisions were greatly reduced (Green, 2015), and unfunded state mandates became the norm. Between 2008 and 2014, lawmakers' cuts to Oklahoma's education funding were the deepest in the nation (Mai, 2013) and occurred despite an increase of 40,000 students (Oklahoma Policy Institute, 2014). Additionally, because surrounding states offer significantly higher teaching salaries, educators now commonly commute across state lines, creating a critical teacher shortage in the state (Archer, 2014a; England, 2015). Local communities have stepped in to support their schools, and private foundations, including the Foundation for Oklahoma City Public schools and the Oklahoma Foundation for Excellence, have formed to fund education initiatives; however, Oklahoma's students still struggle. A recent study found that four out of ten Oklahoma students are required to take at least one remedial class upon entering college (Kemp, 2014).

Schoonmaker (2012), in her study of an Oklahoma elementary school, discusses the importance of education reform that is targeted to the particular student needs, and examples of this can be seen throughout Oklahoma. A commitment to its youngest learners has led the state to be one of only three in the nation to offer free, universal prekindergarten, proving to be a national model for high-quality preschool programs (Gormley & Phillips, 2005). Ninety-eight percent of districts offer Pre-K programs (Willert, 2015b), and a 2013–2014 annual review conducted by the National Institute for Early Education Research found that 76% of four-year-olds in Oklahoma attended Pre-K, far above the national average of 29% (Willert, 2015a). Due to these state level decisions, Oklahoma sets itself apart from other states with larger education budgets.

Additionally, pockets of excellence stemming from a culture of local responsibility is evident throughout the state (Schoonmaker, 2012). Howe Public Schools, a district located in southeast Oklahoma, provides students with experiences beyond those they would normally receive in their small, rural community through the use of technologies that serve to counteract the significant poverty and remoteness of the area (Miller, 2014b). Crutcho Public Schools faces an urban environment riddled with "gangs, violence, drugs and poverty" (Miller, 2014d, para. 13); nonetheless, the district is making a difference in the lives of urban youth through application of grant monies that allow for 1:1 laptops, extended school days, Saturday school, and summer classes (Miller, 2014d). Scenarios such as these are not uncommon in Oklahoma due to the state's unique demographics and its significant number of school districts—the focus is on individualized improvement based on the district's needs, not statewide mandates of reform.

Reframing of the Issues to Fit an Agenda

Thus, the two greatest challenges that Oklahoma faces are a lack of funding and hundreds of districts that are distrusting of anything that seems like a top-down mandate. However, as described above, the media have reframed these issues into an over-simplified narrative of "just not trying." This narrative is accomplished by depending on a neoliberal philosophy of market reform and well as a perpetuation of educational myths and assumptions that support that philosophy (Berliner & Glass, 2014). A recurring myth is that high standards equal high performance, seen repeatedly in the media's discussion of the Common Core. Watts (2014) in an editorial in the *Oklahoman*, writes that under Oklahoma's pre-CCSS standards, only 25% of eighth-graders showed proficiency in math and only 29% in reading. No discussion is made of how funding, poverty levels, teacher support, or parental involvement contribute to those numbers; the assumption is that Oklahoma has low standards for its students. Other myths are also repeated throughout the mediocrity discourse: Oklahoma teachers are lazy, Oklahomans are ignorant and backwards, and business leaders are sorely needed to improve education in the state.

A closer look at the ranking systems the media rely on uncovers both misdirection of educational issues and several political agendas. Returning to *Education Week's* Quality Counts ranking, we see that Oklahoma starts the race behind other states. The "Chance for success" criterion includes parent education, parental employment, parents who are fluent English speakers, family income, NAEP scores, graduation rates, preschool enrollment, postsecondary degrees and adult income (Education Week Research Center, 2015). Thus, even if a state is working to improve education, it is automatically scored lower for its prior generation's characteristics. "School finance" examines the relationship between district funding and local property wealth and per-pupil expenditure, but there is no other data considered, and the ranking does not make clear how funding affects schools. Contextual data in this report would add depth to rank. For example, Table 16.2 shows how top-ranked Massachusetts compares to Oklahoma in per capita income, pupil/teacher ratio, and total teachers. Massachusetts spends twice as much per students as Oklahoma, and Oklahoma's per-capita income is significantly lower than Massachusetts, providing less revenue for its schools, but none of that is explained when newspaper headlines shout Oklahoma's 48th place rank.

Table 16.2. State Profiles: Education and Income.

State	Total Teachers	Pupil/Teacher Ratio	Per Capita Income	Poverty Threshold	Per Pupil Expenditure
MA	70,636	13.5	$35,763	$27,376	$14,262
OK	41,775	16	$24,208	$27,376	$7,690

Source: NCES, State Profiles, State Education Data Profiles (2013).
U.S. Census Bureau, Poverty Threshold: based on family of four (2015b).

ALEC's ranking is significantly biased towards a neoliberal political agenda, discounting Oklahoma's specific educational needs. ALEC gives each criterion an A-F grade, and each high grade Oklahoma received was directly connected to a neoliberal philosophy. Oklahoma received a B- in policy after instituting a A-F grading systems for its schools, removing nearly all barriers to online learning and homeschooling, and relaxing the rules for opening charter schools. However, ALEC graded Oklahoma's charter school laws at a C for not allowing charters outside of major city centers, giving no consideration to the fact that many of Oklahoma's districts have only two or three schools; opening charter schools would decimate those districts. Oklahoma's "digital learning" grade from ALEC was a D+, due to Oklahoma's prior restrictions on allowing virtual charter schools.

The outcome of these discourses has been twofold. First, Oklahoma has consistently turned to neoliberal reform efforts that rely on data collection and an increased load of standardized tests. For example, so as to avoid more negative attention, Oklahoma has passed two significant laws in the past three years that align with reform efforts—the ranking of schools A-F (drawn from Florida's program) and the Teacher and Leader Effectiveness law requiring teachers to be evaluated by student test scores through a Value Added Model (OSDE, 2015c). These laws were passed due to pressure from the U.S. Department of Education—working closely with reformers (Watkins, 2012)—regardless of the fact that both the A-F rankings and Value Added Model had shown poor results in other states (Kohn, 2012). Second, a larger space in the state's media has been devoted to promoting charter schools and business relationships with education, two elements of market reforms that lead to the privatization of public schools. Monies' article, quoted above, called for businesses to become more involved in education, and in the first half of 2015, the *Oklahoman* devoted four editorials in favor of an initiative called "For the People: A Vision for Oklahoma Public Education," an effort to fix the problem of "education and business communities operating at odds" (Hime, 2015). A Google News search of "Oklahoma charter school" shows over 8,000 stories in the first six months of 2015.

While the power of neoliberalism seems to be a recent occurrence, Chomsky (2009) describes its roots in the foundation of our country and constitution. The framers of the Constitution had a belief in the capability of the wealthy to govern, and Chomsky quotes Madison's determination of how power should rest in the "more capable set of men," "the wealth of the nation" (p. 24). The general public, on the other hand, was identified as "ignorant vulgar ... unable to manage [government's] reins" and "the only serious danger" to order (quoted by Chomsky, p. 25). These are the roots of neoliberalism, which places the market above all other public goods, and thus those who run the markets in charge of major decision-making. This value system of relegating the public to Lippman's "bewildered herd" (Chomsky, 2009, p. 25) supplies one explanation for why Americans look to billionaires such as Bill Gates and Eli Broad to reform our public education system rather than the public itself.

Watkins (2012) describes the "corporate intrusion" (p. 25) into public education, "interjecting themselves into the policymaking processes as never before." One of the goals of neoliberalism is to privatize all that is public and make it subject to the market, and this corporate intrusion is a step in that direction. Standardized testing has transitioned from a spot-check of America's schools to a powerful industry unto itself, driving every aspect of education from curriculum to teacher certification to which students receive help or not. There is little to no oversight, Watkins argues, and the wealthy are driving vast changes with impunity. This movement is not currently being publicized in mass media, and people are ignorant to the real purposes of education "reform." They do not know the extent to which corporations are driving the education system.

However, this agenda is only fulfilled if those who push back against it are positioned as harmful to public education, and the media plays its part in that positioning. The word "reform" is carefully chosen by advocates of neoliberalism and repeated ad nauseum by the media until the word is inextricable from the movement. As Herman (2009) notes:

> "Reform" is the classic of word revisionism in the service of those in power, transforming from meaningful institutional and policy changes helpful to the afflicted and weak to move away from the welfare state and toward free markets, thus helping the afflictors and strong. (p. 28)

The genius of using the word "reform" is that it positions anyone against this "reform" as in favor of the status quo. The status quo, as the media has told Oklahomans, is 40th in NAEP scores, and 48th overall in the nation in education. Rather than being able to emphasize the good of public education and argue against an agenda that includes privatization and profiteering, anti-reformers are forced into a binary position of defending a system that is perceived as failing. Rather than blaming education problems on funding, which is a correctible variable, the blame is put on the system itself (e.g., public control of education through standards, democratic management of teachers, and eschewing business involvement).

The perception of an education system as failing is critical to the ongoing neoliberal overhaul on public schooling (Kohn, 2012). The reframing of educational issues has assured that a blind eye is turned to the effect poverty has on schooling. Rather than highlighting that schools without students in poverty consistently outrank other countries on the Programme for International Student Assessment (PISA) test while schools with high rates of impoverished students lag behind (Ravitch, 2013), newspapers report aggregate scores and crow about America's dismal education performance (Strauss, 2013). Even more effective in furthering the agenda is that states respond to reform pressure with policies that turn successes into failures (Kohn, 2012).

A clear example of this reframing is in the Oklahoma A-F report cards for its schools. In February 2013, Howe Public Schools—the rural district known for technological excellence—was described by Supt. Barresi as being, "… truly at the forefront of the most dynamic learning in the state" (Miller, 2014b, para. 4). By October of the same year the district garnered an F grade on the state report card and the distinction of being in the bottom 5% of Oklahoma (Miller, 2014c). Similarly, Crutcho—the district dealing with significant issues of poverty and violence—went from being flaunted as one of the State Department of Education's great successes to being portrayed on the nightly news as the worst district in the state due to their test results (Miller, 2014d). This is because the Oklahoma grades are based entirely on one criterion: standardized test schools. "Bonus points" may be earned through attendance rates and rate of students' taking advanced courses, but the grade is an amalgam of test scores read in various ways: improvement of the bottom 25%, overall improvement, and performance (OSDE, 2013a). As Strauss (2014a) noted in her blog The Answer Sheet, standardized tests are essentially problematic when used to evaluate teachers and schools. She argues that the testing regime schools are facing forces are inherently biased against poor and diverse communities, and they often have poor validity in showing students' mastery of the curricula. However, they do achieve the neoliberal end of convincing the public that schools are failing. Oklahoma law mandates that the grades schools receive on the A-F system must be prominently displayed in the entrance of the school, and the grades are published yearly in the media (Franklin & Mills, 2014). Rather than seeing these cases as proof that the neoliberal policies are flawed, they are instead being taken by the media as evidence that reform efforts must be redoubled; the state is now participating in a longitudinal data system to track teachers from their SAT scores in high school through their college performance and into their careers, attempting to standardize performance even more (OSDE, 2013b).

GRASSROOTS MEDIA PUSHBACK AS PUBLIC PEDAGOGY

Despite the overwhelming neoliberal media narrative, public voices in Oklahoma—in the form of what we term as grassroots media (e.g., personal blogs, petitions, and public presentations)—refuse to be silenced in this fight against a neoliberal agenda. For the purposes of this discussion, we define grassroots media as publications from public individuals and democratic groups. There has been a growing trend of "astroturfing"—the attempt to create an impression of widespread grassroots support when in actuality the backers of a policy or product are corporations or single individuals (Bienkov, 2012). Stand for Children is one such organization; the group sells itself as a grassroots parent group instead of a corporate reform lobbyist that has taken $5.3 million from the Gates Foundation (Barkan, 2012). Grassroots media grows from teachers themselves, as well as the children and parents in Oklahoma's schools. Negative discourse and statistical rankings reduce the perceived value of Oklahoma's public education, but Oklahomans continue to give voice to education as a freedom of democracy they will not release. Local standards, the professional voice of educators, and grassroots support from the public coalesce to distinguish Oklahoma's public education.

In Oklahoma, deconstructing the common sense assumptions surrounding neoliberal doctrine (Lipman, 2012) takes place through the use of social media. Authors of edublogs swork in tandem to oppose those undermining public education and they garner hundreds of thousands of views in the process. Rob Miller, an assistant superintendent in Sand Springs, Oklahoma, has been blogging about neoliberal attacks on the education system in Oklahoma for years. His posts reach thousands of Oklahomans. He works to undermine the narrative being pushed by neoliberal legislators, such as when he revealed in his blog that the lawmaker criticizing the educators' rally at the capitol earns approximately $38,000 plus per diem for a four-month legislative session, in contrast to the state's beginning yearly teacher salary of $31,600 (Miller, 2014a). Richard Cobb, an Assistant Superintendent of Public Instruction in Moore, Oklahoma, blogs because after he had been asked to participate in the drafting of the No Child Left Behind Waiver (a requirement of states who were not meeting annual yearly progress mandates to explain how Oklahoma was going to improve), he realized that he was "just there as window dressing," as the waiver had already been written by the Foundation for Excellence, a proponent of market reform (Cobb, 2014a). Cobb's blog, *OK Education Truths*, has featured posts about the importance of educators discussing funding with legislators, the Common Core State Standards, high-stakes testing, third grade retentions, A-F Report Cards, and the VAM-esque portion of a newly reformulated Teacher and Leader Evaluation system—all of which are being used to destabilize public education in the state (Cobb, 2014a).

Other edublogs in Oklahoma fulfill Ayers' (2012) call to "ask how we might engage, enlarge, and change our lives" (p. 5), Claudia Swisher publishes a blog called *Fourth Generation Teacher*, in which she most recently discussed teaching during the massive teacher shortage Oklahoma has experienced (2015). *Excellence in Mediocrity* is a blog written anonymously by an Oklahoma City middle school principal, and much of it is devoted to encouraging teachers to become politically involved. And *Blue Cereal Education* is another anonymous blog by a Tulsa teacher who writes often about elements of education that are disappearing due to the focus on standardized tests, such as creativity and empathy (Dolph and Lana Break the Rules, 2015). As lawmakers and media perpetuate myths that threaten public education (Berliner & Glass, 2014) Oklahoma educators are advancing a crusade intent on protecting public schools.

The arching theme amongst these bloggers is that the fight against neoliberal reforms is not one that is already lost. Watkins (2012) contends that elected officials today are unapologetic in their use of "unilateral decision making" (p. 15) dependent on neoliberal myths, and these bloggers expose neoliberal reforms as doing little more than inaccurately representing schools and showcasing poverty (Cobb, 2014b) while noting the ways in which innovative districts go from being touted as instructional exemplars to being portrayed as failures within a matter of months. These educators are following the footsteps of more nationally-recognized bloggers such as Diane Ravitch and Valerie Strauss, both popular writers who work to unpack the context of the reform movement and expose its weaknesses.

Other teachers in Oklahoma have also courageously taken action to illuminate issues surrounding the undemocratic nature of the quest for accountability and its negative effects on students (Apple, 2012; Kohn, 2012), and they are working to gain the public eye. In 2014, the *Tulsa World* reported that Tulsa Public Schools, "a statewide model for Oklahoma's Teacher and Leader Effectiveness system" (Eger, 2014a, p. 1), would be the first district to use the results of unwieldy and confusing student surveys in annual performance evaluations. This new "empirically robust" teacher evaluation model soon proved to be a source of contention among educators (Tulsa Public Schools, n.d., p. 1). Tulsa first-grade teachers Nikki Jones and Karen Hendren made national headlines when they refused to administer the student survey, as well as the Measured Academic Progress assessment (MAP), which had been chosen by the district to be one determining factor in evaluating teacher effectiveness (Eger, 2014c). In an open letter to the parents and guardians of their students—a letter that was republished in Valerie Strauss's blog (2014c)—Jones and Hendren bravely explained why they felt the mandated survey was a violation of families' privacy, and listed details explaining the demoralizing effects of the MAP (of which over 85% percent of their students failed and were subsequently labeled *at-risk*) on classroom instruction (Eger, 2014b).

Jones and Hendren's courageous actions were applauded by many education activists, including former U.S. Assistant Secretary of Education Diane Ravitch, who hailed them as heroes "defending the rights and childhood of their students" (Ravitch, 2014, para. 2). John Thompson, lobbyist and award-winning historian and teacher, specifically noted in his blog *Living in Dialogue* TPS' acceptance of money from the market-reform-advocate Gates Foundation (Thompson, 2014) in developing the evaluation system, and mused whether Superintendent Ballard, who had staunchly opposed abuse by standardized testing in the past, was now comfortable with "his part of the bargain" (Thompson, 2014, para. 9). Ravitch, referencing Thompson's blog, posed this question to her readership: "Will Superintendent Ballard listen to his professional ethics or the Gates Foundation?" (2014, para. 9).

Students and community members have also begun to take the public stage in defense of their education. When Jenks High School student, Moin Nadeem, read that State House Bill 1380 could cut funding for Advanced Placement history courses, he didn't hesitate to challenge the bill by creating a petition to ensure that it would never become law (Delatorre, 2015). The Change.org petition garnered over 36,000 supporters before the public outcry by teachers, parents and students caused enough pressure that the bill was withdrawn (Song, 2015). Linda Hampton, president of the Oklahoma Education Association, credited the publicity with the "shift in momentum" (Song, 2015, para. 15). Through the efforts of many to combat the political attack of education in Oklahoma, the bill's sponsor, Rep. Fisher, removed the bill from the House saying, "We're trying to fix the bill … It was very poorly worded and was incredibly ambiguous, and we didn't realize that, so it's been misinterpreted … We're very supportive of the AP program" (Habib & Krehbiel, 2015, para. 3). The bill has not resurfaced. Additionally, hundreds of students and their parents have joined the United Opt Out movement protesting standardized testing usage in the state. Blogger Rob Miller, who at the time was a principal of Jenks Middle School in Jenks, Oklahoma, spoke out publicly in 2013 about the harm the testing load was doing to the students. He educated parents on their rights to opt students out of testing, and in the spring, half of the parents in the school opted their children out (Archer, 2013). The Oklahoma state Parent Teacher Association president, Jeffery Corbett, followed Miller's lead, encouraging parents to refuse standardized tests for their children and providing information on how to do so on the Oklahoma PTA website. An

Oklahoma City news station interviewed Corbett specifically about field testing (which only provides results to the state and testing companies, not the teacher), and quoted him as saying, "We believe parents have the right to make informed decisions regarding whether or not their child provides unpaid research to the billion-dollar testing industry" (State PTA Wants, 2015).

Informed, articulate advocates for the integrity of meaningful education absent of the neoliberal accountability that shackles teachers and students to test scores have a responsibility to counter the narrative that schools are failing our children. We can learn valuable lessons from the many Oklahomans who are still making a valiant effort. As Kohn (2012) writes, "Ultimately, we must decide whether we will obediently play our assigned role in helping to punish children and teachers" (p. 93).

CONCLUSION: TURNING GRASSROOTS MEDIA INTO PUBLIC PEDAGOGY

Despite what appeared to be widespread support for the bravery of the Tulsa teachers, both Jones and Hendren became casualties of the neoliberal policies, sacrificing their jobs on the "altar of accountability" (Kohn, 2012, p. 90). In an April 2014 *Teach with a Voice* blog post by Jones, she wearily describes what she recalls as "the most difficult trial in my career" (Jones, 2014, para. 3) and writes, "I knew at the end of the day that they would choose testing over children or good educators. I knew that a lot of the people who held the power to save me would cower. It's simply the nature of the system" (Jones, 2014, para. 4). Neoliberalism "thrives on a culture of cynicism, insecurity and despair" (Giroux, 2010, p. 486), and Jones' blog post reiterates the feelings of hopelessness that the pedagogy of neoliberalism has imparted upon our best and brightest educators. Jones reported plummeting teacher evaluation scores and the feeling of no longer being welcome in her own school, along with the news that her colleague (Hendren) was leaving to teach abroad, and that she (Jones) was looking for a new position. Her resignation with Tulsa Public Schools was reported June 1 (Tulsa Board of Education, 2014).

Clearly, not all Oklahoma administrators have bowed to media pressure in favor of the neoliberal agenda, and not all media is devoted to furthering that agenda. *The Tulsa World* provided space for Sand Springs, Oklahoma, Superintendent Lloyd Snow to be publicly vocal that his school district administered only the tests that were required by the state and expressed the importance for advocating for the repeal of the requirement of quantitative measures on teacher evaluations (Eger, 2014d). Snow stated that he believed that the opposition from teachers such as Tulsa educators Jones and Hendren was inevitable, and was quoted "… it wouldn't take a whole bunch to have those two become 200. Teachers are not on board with this—they were uninvited to the conversation about assessments. My view: This is just the tip of the iceberg" (Eger, 2014d, p. 5).

However, the vast majority of the media narrative about Oklahoma continues to coalesce around the idea that the state just does not care about education, and as long as it does, Oklahoma will continue to make policy in reaction to it. The Oklahoma edublogs named in this chapter have a regular readership in the hundreds; *The Answer Sheet*, Valerie Strauss's blog, has a readership of a few thousand. There is an opportunity for public intellectuals (Giroux, 2004) to "denude dominating public pedagogies" (Sandlin, Schultz, & Burdick, 2010, p. 3) by working to lessen the impact of media furthering market reforms and strengthen the visibility of grassroots media to act as a public pedagogy in itself—a transitional space of learning for public engagement. If educators believe that public education is the "ground of democracy" (Ayers, 2012, p. 5) with a goal of equity and opportunity for all, then they must be willing to act as public intellectuals, claiming spaces to share counternarratives such as those provided by online blogs, petitions, and other grassroots media. The growth in popularity of social media platforms provides spaces that were previously unavailable to these counternarratives, and they must be utilized to their fullest extent. We also must share widely stories of teachers like Jones and Hendren, and the parents who opt their children out of testing. These are not just actions, they are statements that claim a "refusal to believe, or be complicit, in a corporate-run system of education that hurts children" (McDermott, Robertson, & Johnson, 2014, p. 52), and grassroots media can make these statements heart. The privatization of America's schools may not be a foregone conclusion, but media voices need to be raised to carry that message to the public.

REFERENCES

Achievements of Oklahoma science-math school justify its funding. (2015, April 12). *The Oklahoman*. http://newsok.com/article/5409111.

ALEC. (2015). *History*. Retrieved from http://www.alec.org/about-alec/history/.

Alger, V. (2015, January 11). Education's no dollar left behind competition. *The Wall Street Journal*. Retrieved from http://www.wsj.com/articles/vicki-alger-educations-no-dollar-left-behind-competition-1421017161

Apple, M. W. (2012). Foreword. In W. H. Watkins (Ed.), *The assault on public education: Confronting the politics of corporate school reform* (pp. ix–xiv). New York, NY: Teachers College Press.

Archer, K. (2013, October 2). Jenks school administrator encouraged testing 'opt out' movement, state says. *Tulsa World*. Retrieved from http://www.tulsaworld.com/news/education/jenks-school-administrator-encouraged-testing-opt-out-movement-state-says/article_660d0498-2bda-11e3-a58c-001a4bcf6878.html

Archer, K. (2014a, January 20). Oklahoma teacher need reaches crisis point. *Tulsa World*. Retrieved from http://www.tulsaworld.com/news/education/oklahoma-teacher-need-reaches-crisis-point/article_5dddfa51-1e26-598c-b489-5d3884cd354b.html

Archer, K. (2014b, June 2). Common Core draws criticism from state superintendent candidates. *The Tulsa World*. Retrieved from http://www.tulsaworld.com/news/2014_elections/common-core-draws-criticism-from-state-superintendent-candidates/article_d3e4827e-275a-5ffa-9d5b-9ded7db55a0c.html

Associated Press. (2014, June 6). Common Core repeal in Oklahoma signed by Governor Mary Fallin. *CBS News*. Retrieved from http://www.cbsnews.com/news/common-core-repeal-in-oklahoma-signed-by-governor-mary-fallin/

Ayers, W. (2012). Challenging the politics of the teacher accountability movement: Toward a more hopeful educational future. *Occasional Papers Series 27*. Bank Street College of Education.

Barkan, J. (2012). Hired guns on astroturf: How to buy and sell school reform. *Dissent Magazine*. Retrieved from https://www.dissentmagazine.org/article/hired-guns-on-astroturfhow-to-buy-and-sell-school-reform

Berliner, D. C., & Glass, G. V. (2014). *50 myths & lies that threaten America's public schools: The real crisis in education*. New York, NY: Teachers College Press.

Bienkov, A. (2012, February 8). Astroturfing: what is it and why does it matter? *The Guardian*. Retrieved from http://www.theguardian.com/commentisfree/2012/feb/08/what-is-astroturfing

Boren, D. L. (2015, May 10). Top students and educators deserve respect. *The Oklahoman*. Retrieved from http://archive.newsok.com/olive/APA/Oklahoman/PrintArticle.aspx?mode=text&href=-DOK%2F2015%2F05%2F10&id=Ar10203

CCSSI (Common Core State Standards Initiative). (2010). *About the standards*. Retrieved from http://www.corestandards.org/about-the-standards/

Chomsky, N. (2009). Preface to the myth of the liberal media: An Edward Herman reader. In D. Macedo & S. R. Steinberg (Eds.), *Media literacy: A reader* (pp. 24–26). New York, NY: Peter Lang.

Cobb, R. (2014a, March 31). Today's rally (and why The Oklahoman hates it) [Web log post]. Retrieved from https://okeducationtruths.wordpress.com/2014/03/31/todays-rally-and-why-the-oklahoman-hates-it/

Cobb, R. (2014b, September 21). A gentle reminder: Poverty matters [Web log post]. Retrieved from https://okeducationtruths.wordpress.com/2014/09/21/a-gentle-reminder-poverty-matters/

Conlon, K. (2015, February 19). Oklahoma bill would make AP U.S. history history. *CNN*. Retrieved from http://www.cnn.com/2015/02/18/us/oklahoma-ap-history/

Delatorre, M. (2015, February 18). Oklahoma student starts petition to keep AP U.S. history courses. Retrieved from http://kfor.com/2015/02/18/oklahoma-student-starts-petition-to-keep-ap-u-s-history-courses/

Dolph and Lana Break the Rules [weblog, no author]. (2015, September 9). Retrieved from http://bluecerealeducation.com/blog/dolph-lana-break-rules

Education is Crucial in Lowering Poverty Stats. (2015, May 19). *The Oklahoman*. Retrieved from http://archive.newsok.com/olive/APA/Oklahoman/PrintArticle.aspx?mode=text&href=-DOK%2F2015%2F05%2F19&id=Ar00800

Education Week Research Center, The. (2015, January 2). A fresh approach to ranking states on education. *Education Week*. Retrieved from http://www.edweek.org/ew/articles/2015/01/08/a-fresh-approach-to-ranking-states-on-education.html?intc=EW-QC14-LFTNAV

Eger, A. (2014a, November 16). TPS teachers questioning use of K-12 student surveys on their performance evaluations. *Tulsa World*. Retrieved from http://www.tulsaworld.com/news/education/tps-teachers-questioning-use-of-k--student-surveys-on/article_6a7cf9ca-aa77-54b4-998c-0c3e17ff3905.html

Eger, A. (2014b, November 18). Read letter from Tulsa first-grade teachers detailing concerns about testing, student surveys. *Tulsa World*. Retrieved from http://www.tulsaworld.com/read-letter-from-tulsa-first-grade-teachers-detailing-concerns-about/pdf_adb3a8ba-342e-5917-8841-6734cef149da.html

Eger, A. (2014c, November 19). Tulsa teachers refuse to give student tests; Superintendent: That's not an option. *Tulsa World*. Retrieved from http://www.tulsaworld.com/news/education/tulsa-teachers-refuse-to-give-student-tests-superintendent-that-s/article_849d923d-d4db-5757-bdfa-ba5014220b85.html

Eger, A. (2014d, November 24). Two teachers' refusal to give tests puts their jobs at risk, but they say it's worth it. *Tulsa World*. Retrieved from http://www.tulsaworld.com/homepage2/two-teachers-refusal-to-give-tests-puts-their-jobs-at/article_a3b1005b-09c2-555f-9a5d-39eaeb497205.html?mode=story

Ellenberg, J. (2015). Meet the new Common Core. *The New York Times*. Retrieved from http://www.nytimes.com/2015/06/16/opinion/meet-the-new-common-core.html

England, A. (2015, June 30). A 12 minute commute to Texas is costing Oklahoma students their future. *Stand for Children Oklahoma*. Retrieved from http://stand.org/oklahoma/blog/2015/06/30/15-minute-commute-texas-costing-oklahoma-students-their-future

Flaherty, C. (2015, February 23). Whose history? *Inside Higher Ed*. Retrieved from https://www.insidehighered.com/news/2015/02/23/oklahoma-legislature-targets-ap-us-history-framework-being-negative

Franklin, D., & Mills, C. (2014, September 17). Oklahoma school report card: More schools receive an "F." KFOR News Channel 4. Retrieved from http://kfor.com/2014/09/17/oklahoma-school-report-card-more-failing-grades-than-last-year/

Giroux, H. (2004). Cultural studies, public pedagogy, and the responsibility of intellectuals. *Communication and Critical/Cultural Studies, 1*(1), 59–79.

Giroux, H. (2010). Neoliberalism as public pedagogy. In J. A. Sandlin, B. D. Schultz, & J. Burdick (Ed.), *Handbook of public pedagogy: Education and learning beyond schooling* (pp. 486–499). New York, NY: Routledge.

Gormley, W. T., & Phillips, D. (2005). The effects of universal pre-k in Oklahoma: Research highlights and policy implications. *The Policy Studies Journal, 33*(1), 65–82.

Green, R. (2014a, June 6). Fallin repeals Common Core. *The Oklahoman*. Retrieved from http://archive.newsok.com/olive/APA/Oklahoman/default.aspx?Reader=http%3A%2F%2Farchive.newsok.com%2Fdefault%2Fclient.asp&Id=0&d=2015-07-31&r=none&c=bc46a943a0e98e5c-debd4a17cdd76368#panel=document

Green, R. (2014b, June 10). U.S. Education Secretary Arne Duncan says politics led to Gov. Mary Fallin's Repeal of Common Core academic standards. *The Oklahoman*. Retrieved from http://newsok.com/article/4898745

Green, R. (2015, April 28). Primary tenets of historic 1990 Oklahoma education bill not being met. *The Oklahoman*. Retrieved from http://newsok.com/primary-tenets-of-historic-1990-oklahoma-education-bill-not-being-met/article/5414235

Green, R., & Willert, T. (2014, June 5). Fallin signs bill repealing Oklahoma Common Core Standards. *The Oklahoman*. Retrieved from newsok.com/fallin-signs-bill-repealing-oklahoma-common-core-standards/article/4888114

H. Res. 1657, 46 Leg. (1998). Retrieved from http://webserver1.lsb.state.ok.us/cf_pdf/1997-98%20ENR/hB/HB1657%20ENR.PDF

Habib, N., & Krehbiel, R. (2015, February 19). Oklahoma lawmaker says he will pull back controversial AP history bill for rewrite. *Tulsa World*. Retrieved from http://www.tulsaworld.com/newshomepage1/oklahoma-lawmaker-says-he-will-pull-back-controversial-ap-history/article_3f733d69-f450-5b72-af81-696142327df3.html

Hartmann, M. (2015, February 18). Why Oklahoma lawmakers voted to ban AP U.S. history. *New York*. Retrieved from http://nymag.com/daily/intelligencer/2015/02/why-oklahoma-lawmakers-want-to-ban-ap-us-history.html

Herman, E. S. (2009). Word tricks and propaganda. In D. Macedo & S. R. Steinberg (Eds.). *Media literacy: A reader* (pp. 27–35). New York, NY: Peter Lang.

Hime, S. (2015, June 26). OSSBA director: Creating a new vision for Oklahoma public education. *The Oklahoman*. Retrieved from http://newsok.com/article/5429915

Hoberock, B. (2015, March 9). Legislation unfairly targets teachers, education group says. *The Tulsa World*. Retrieved from http://www.tulsaworld.com/news/legislation-unfairly-targets-teachers-education-groups-say/article_12348ae3-660b-53ed-9322-63b4151b2ff7.html

Job, J. (2012, November). On the rise of Pearson (oh, and following the money) [weblog]. Retrieved from http://teacherblog.typepad.com/newteacher/2012/11/on-the-rise-of-pearson-oh-and-following-the-money.html

Jones, N. (2014, April 27). To die alone on the hill … or not. [Web log post]. Retrieved from https://teachwithavoice.wordpress.com/2015/04/27/to-die-alone-on-the-hill-or-not/

Kemp, A. (2014, September 2). Many Oklahoma students start college taking remedial classes. *NewsOK*, Retrieved from http://newsok.com/article/5337902

Khimm, S. (2013, February 14). Is Oklahoma the right model for universal pre-k? *The Washington Post*. Retrieved from http://www.washingtonpost.com/blogs/wonkblog/wp/2013/02/14/is-oklahoma-the-right-model-for-universal-pre-k/

Kohn, A. (2012). Test today, privatize tomorrow: Using accountability to "reform" public schools to death. In W. H. Watkins (Ed.), *The assault on public education: Confronting the politics of corporate school reform* (pp. 79–96). New York, NY: Teachers College Press.

Kristof, N. D. (2013, November 9). Oklahoma! Where the kids learn early. *The New York Times*. Retrieved from http://www.nytimes.com/2013/11/10/opinion/sunday/kristof-oklahoma-where-the-kids-learn-early.html?_r=1

Ladner, M., & Myslinski, D. (2015). State education rankings. ALEC. Retrieved from http://www.alec.org/publications/report-card-on-american-education/

Lather, P. (2012). The ruins of neo-liberalism and the construction of a new (scientific) subjectivity. *Cultural Studies of Science Education, 7*, 1021–1025.

Lipman, P. (2012). Neoliberal urbanism, race, and urban school reform. In W. H. Watkins (Ed.). *The assault on public education: Confronting the politics of corporate school reform* (pp. 33–54). New York, NY: Teachers College Press.

Mai, C. (2013, November 4). Local and federal government funds don't compensate for state cuts to K-12 education. *Center on Budget and Policy Priorities*. Retrieved from http://www.cbpp.org/blog/local-and-federal-government-funds-dont-compensate-for-state-cuts-to-k-12-education

McDermott, M., Robertson, P., & Johnson, R. (2014). *An activist handbook for the education revolution: United Opt Out's test of courage*. Charlotte, NC: Information Age Press.

Miller, R. (2014a, April 2). With No Due Respect [Web log post]. Retrieved from http://www.viewfromtheedge.net/?p=2687

Miller, R. (2014b, April 7). Howe exceptional! [Web log post]. Retrieved from http://www.viewfromtheedge.net/?p=2702

Miller, R. (2014c, April 8). 'Howe' the A-F did this happen? [Web log post]. Retrieved from http://www.viewfromtheedge.net/?p=2689

Miller, R. (2014d, May 10). The shameful treatment of Crutcho public school [Web log post]. Retrieved from http://www.viewfromtheedge.net/?p=3128

National Center for Education Statistics [NCES]. (2013). NAEP State comparisons: 4th grade reading scores. Retrieved from http://nces.ed.gov/nationsreportcard/statecomparisons/withinyear.aspx?usrSelections=0%2cRED%2c0%2c0%2cwithin%2c0%2c0

O'Donoghue, J. (2014). What Common Core repeal looks like in Oklahoma, NPR reports. *NPR*. Retrieved from http://www.nola.com/politics/index.ssf/2014/12/common_core_repeal.html

Oklahoma's Pre-kindergarten Program Now a Model for Nation [Video file]. (2013, April 1). Retrieved from http://www.kjrh.com/news/oklahomas-pre-k-now-a-model-for-nation

Oklahoma Policy Institute. (n.d.). *House Bill 1017, What's That?* Retrieved from http://okpolicy.org/house-bill-1017

Oklahoma Policy Institute. (2014, April 17). *Investing in education is key for growth and job creation.* Retrieved from http://okpolicy.org/fact-sheet-investing-education-key-growth-job-creation

Oklahoma Education Rally Should offer Plan, Not Platitudes. (2015, March 29). *The Oklahoman.* Retrieved from http://newsok.com/article/5405186

Oklahoma State Department of Education [OSDE]. (2013a). *Text of proposed rule submitted for final adoption.* Retrieved from http://ok.gov/sde/sites/ok.gov.sde/files/documents/files/210-10-13-22%20A-F%20Adopted.pdf

Oklahoma State Department of Education [OSDE]. (2013b, April 30). *State longitudinal data system grant.* Retrieved from http://ok.gov/sde/state-longitudinal-data-system-grant

Oklahoma State Department of Education [OSDE]. (2015a). Retrieved from http://www.ok.gov/sde/

Oklahoma State Department of Education [OSDE]. (2015b, July 9). *Oklahoma granted ESEA extension waiver.* Retrieved from http://www.ok.gov/sde/newsblog/2015-07-09/oklahoma-granted-esea-waiver-extension

Oklahoma State Department of Education [OSDE]. (2015c). *TLE Value-added measures (VAM) frequently asked questions.* Retrieved from http://www.ok.gov/sde/documents/2014-03-07/tle-value-added-measures-vam-frequently-asked-questions

Paxton, S. (2014, November 26). Oklahoma fights back after feds pull education funding over Common Core. *Fox News.* Retrieved from http://www.foxnews.com/us/2014/11/26/oklahoma-fights-back-after-feds-pull-education-funding-over-common-core/

Perdue, S., & Riley, B. (2014, June 4). Former governors: Oklahoma shouldn't repeal Common Core. *The Oklahoman.* Retrieved from http://newsok.com/former-governors-oklahoma-shouldnt-repeal-common-core/article/4879980

Ravitch, D. (2013, December 5). Daniel Wydo disaggregates PISA scores by income [Web log post]. Retrieved from http://dianeravitch.net/2013/12/05/daniel-wydo-disaggregates-pisa-scores-by-income/

Ravitch, D. (2014, November 26). Will brave Tulsa teachers lose their jobs? [Web log post]. Retrieved from http://dianeravitch.net/2014/11/26/will-brave-tulsa-teachers-lose-their-jobs/

Robson, N. (2015, January 7). State ranks among the worst in education outcomes report. *Oklahoma Watch.* Retrieved from http://oklahomawatch.org/2015/01/07/state-ranks-among-worst-in-education-outcomes-report/

Rubin, J. (2015, May 22). A poster child for Common Core. *The Washington Post.* Retrieved from https://www.washingtonpost.com/blogs/right-turn/wp/2015/05/22/a-poster-child-for-common-core/

S. 48, 55 Leg. (2015). Retrieved from http://www.oklegislature.gov/BillInfo.aspx?Bill=sb48& Session=1500

Sanchez, C., & Turner, C. (2014, April 22). What exactly is 'high-quality' preschool? *NPR Ed*. Retrieved from http://www.npr.org/sections/ed/2014/04/22/304563233/what-exactly-is-high-quality-preschool

Sandlin, J., Schultz, B., & Burdick, J. (2010). Understanding, mapping, and exploring the terrain of public pedagogy. In J. Sandlin, B. Schultz, & J. Burdick (Eds.), *Handbook of public pedagogy: Education and learning beyond schooling* (pp. 1–6). New York, NY: Routledge.

Schoonmaker, F. (2012). *Living faithfully: The transformation of Washington School*. Charlotte, NC: Information Age Press.

Song, J. (2015, March 16). Oklahoma educators quash attempt to ban AP U.S. History. *NEA Today*. Retrieved from http://neatoday.org/2015/03/16/oklahoma-educators-quash-effort-ban-ap-u-s-history/

State PTA wants Oklahoma parents to opt out of standardized field tests. (2015, January 28). *News On 6*. Retrieved from http://www.newson6.com/story/27963940/state-pta-wants-oklahoma-parents-to-opt-out-of-standardized-field-tests

State of the Union Address. (2013, February 12). *ABC News*. Retrieved from http://abcnews.go.com/Politics/OTUS/transcript-president-barack-obamas-2013-state-union-address/story?id=18480069&singlePage=true

Stop Common Core in Oklahoma. [ca. 2013]. In *Facebook* [Community Organization]. Retrieved July 6, 2015, from https://www.facebook.com/stopcommoncore/app_190322544333196

Strauss, V. (2013, December 3). Key PISA test results for U.S. students. *The Washington Post*. Retrieved from http://dianeravitch.net/2013/12/05/daniel-wydo-disaggregates-pisa-scores-by-income/

Strauss, V. (2014a, April 22). 11 problems created by the standardized testing obsession. [weblog]. Retrieved from https://www.washingtonpost.com/blogs/answer-sheet/wp/2014/04/22/11-problems-created-by-the-standardized-testing-obsession/.

Strauss, V. (2014b, June 2). How much do Oklahoma legislators hate the Common Core? This much. *The Washington Post*. Retrieved from http://www.washingtonpost.com/blogs/answer-sheet/wp/2014/06/02/how-much-do-oklahoma-legislators-hate-the-common-core-this-much/

Strauss, V. (2014c, June 5). Two more states pull out of common core. *The Washington Post*. Retrieved from http://www.washingtonpost.com/blogs/answer-sheet/wp/2014/06/05/two-

Swisher, C. (2015, September 14). Teacher shortage is real. No claim [weblog]. Retrieved from http://fourthgenerationteacher.blogspot.com/2015/09/teacher-shortage-is-real-no-claim.html

Taubman, P. (2009). *Teaching by Numbers: Deconstructing the discourse of standards and accountability in education*. New York: Routledge.

Thompson, J. (2014, November 21). Tulsa first grade teachers risk their jobs by opting out of tests. [Web log post]. Retrieved from http://www.livingindialogue.com/tulsa-first-grade-teachers-risk-jobs-protest-testing-mania/#comments

Thrasher, S. W. (2015, February 18). Sorry Oklahoma. You don't get to ban history you don't like. *The Guardian*. Retrieved from http://www.theguardian.com/education/commentisfree/2015/feb/18/oklahoma-ban-advanced-placement-history

Tulsa Board of Education. (2014, June 1). *Tulsa Public Schools agenda*. Retrieved from http://www.tulsaschools.org/1_Administration/_board_agendas/Agenda_150601.pdf

Tulsa Public Schools. (n.d.). *Tulsa Public Schools' teacher observation and evaluation system: Its research base and validation studies*. Retrieved from http://www.tulsaschools.org/4_About_District/_documents/TLE/Teacher_Eval_System_Research_Brief.pdf

Turner, C. (2014, December 30). Common Core repeal, the day after. *nprEd*. Retrieved from http://www.npr.org/sections/ed/2014/12/30/371654882/common-core-repeal-the-day-after

Turner, M. (2014, March 26). You guest it: Work in the classroom speaks louder than burning taxpayer dollars [Web log post]. Retrieved from http://www.ocpathink.org/post/you-guest-it-work-in-the-classroom-speaks-louder-than-burning-taxpayer-dollars

United States Census Bureau. (2015a). Poverty: Poverty thresholds. Retrieved from http://www.census.gov/hhes/www/poverty/data/threshld/index.html

United States Census Bureau. (2015b). State and county quick facts. Retrieved from http://quickfacts.census.gov/qfd/states/40000.html

Watkins, W. H. (2012). The new social order: An educator looks at economics, politics, and race. In W. H. Watkins (Ed.). *The assault on public education: Confronting the politics of corporate school reform* (pp. 7–32). New York, NY: Teachers College Press.

Watts, J. C. (2014, July 30). With our kids' education, state can't afford to settle. *The Daily Oklahoman*. Retrieved from archive.newsok.olive/

What Will Doubling the Size of an Oklahoma Education Rally Accomplish? (2015, January 13). *The Oklahoman*. Retrieved from http://newsok.com/article/5384055

Wheelock, B. (2015, May 10). Academic excellence is a year-round goal. *The Oklahoman*. Retrieved from http://archive.newsok.com/olive/APA/Oklahoman/PrintArticle.aspx?mode=text&href=DOK%2F2015%2F05%2F10&id=Ar10403

Willert, T. (2015a, January 7). Oklahoma public school students continue to perform poorly compared to other states. *The Oklahoman*. Retrieved from http://newsok.com/article/5382758

Willert, T. (2015b, May 12). Oklahoma's early education enrollment numbers rank near top in national report. *The Daily Oklahoman*. Retrieved from http://newsok.com/oklahomas-early-education-enrollment-numbers-rank-near-top-in-national-report/article/5418114

World's Editorial Writers. (2015, February 18). Oklahoma AP history class under fire for omitting 'American exceptionalism'. *Fox News*. Retrieved from http://www.foxnews.com/us/2015/02/18/oklahoma-ap-history-class-under-fire-for-omitting-american-exceptionalism/

CHAPTER SEVENTEEN

"It WAS THE river THAT taught ME …"

The Southern rural ecology as educative space

REBEKAH CORDOVA, ILLUSTRATED BY ERIN BOWERS

The goal of the educational researcher is to conceive of the many ways to answer these questions: How might we know what is educational? Of what will draw our attention to this matter?

When critically looking to the rural to understand or problematize that which provides education, or that which could be deemed educative, I concur with McLaren and Giroux (1990) when they acknowledge that "… very little writing exists that deals with critical pedagogy in the rural school, classroom, and community" (p. 154). Of course there is ample discussion of the rural, as in comparison to what is often described as "urban", but not necessarily as two-sides of the same coin, rather it is as if rural areas can better and more easily be characterized by the *absence* of urban characteristics.

Specifically when we review education research that focuses on urban education, these writings can often perpetuate a perspective on the nuanced ecology of the urban that either conflates geography with demography or essentializes it to the most difficult of spaces (see Milner, 2012; Watson, 2011)—however, when poised against these constructions, the rural takes on a sort of absence of character. It is often painted as a place devoid of significant storied experiences (other than those that encourage stereotypes)—a place that is overly simple and occupied by few people.

Kreitlow (1954), in one of the earliest attempts to define the rural as distinct, posits that quantitative geography is not the most apt foundation for education research, in that it is not in the number of people, or population, that define the rural, but in "the relationships between people and between people and the land" (p. 3). To further this point more recently, Coladarci (2007), discusses the primary way education research has yet to fully alleviate this issue of improperly honoring the rural context:

> … rural education researchers, in their reports and publications, typically fail to describe the context of their research in sufficient detail. … the images, scents, tactile sensations, and assorted inferences about the participants' lives, values, and sense of community are almost inescapable. Moreover, they are essential to this work, and often they are altogether missing. (p. 2)

In order to use a critical lens to detail these relationships between people and the relationships between people and the land, I chose to focus on the ways in which women, who have grown up in the rural South, conceive of the ways in which the rural has been as educative space. In other words, I have attempted to answer the original questions that education researchers face: How might we know what is educational in the rural setting and of what, within the relationship to the land, draws our attention to this matter?

Using transcripts from phenomenologically-inspired in-depth interviewing, what follows are three short illustrated vignettes, which attempt to produce what could be described as the "the images, scents, tactile sensations" associated with the "relationship between people and the land", or otherwise understood as the ways the rural ecology is perceived as educative space.

REFERENCES

Coladarci, T. (2007). Improving the yield of rural education research: An editor's swan song. *Journal of Research in Rural Education, 22*(3), 22–3.

Gruenewald, D. A. (2003). The best of both worlds: A critical pedagogy of place. *Educational researcher, 32*(4), 3–12.

Kreitlow, B. W. (1954). *Rural education: Community backgrounds.* New York, NY: Harper and Brothers.

McLaren, P. L., & Giroux, H. A. (1990). Critical pedagogy and rural education: A challenge from Poland. *Peabody Journal of Education, 67*(4), 154–165.

Milner, H. R. (2012). But what is urban education? *Urban Education, 47*(3), 556–561.

Roberson Jr, D. N. (2005). Lifelong learning in the county: A context of nature, community, and simplicity. *The Rural Educator, 27*(1), 29–40.

Watson, D. (2011). What do you mean when you say "urban"? Speaking honestly about race and students. *Rethinking Schools, 26*(1), 48–50.

Vignette One: Rachel

How I remember it, which might only be half-truth, I spent most of my daylight working hard to build a raft that would float on the river.

Finding just the right wood that had not rotted through.

The right way to overlap the twine I had found.

The right way to knot the rope my daddy had given me from his last cutting job.

And I would sit on the banks, next to my make-shift raft, watching the current flow. I would feel the cold water pushing against the mud that swallowed your toes over time.

When I grew weary of the task, I would set off to seek the purple of flowering thistles—they always grew along the dirt roads—tall and strong, with thorns that required attention.

I never knew loneliness in these spaces.

We would eat
Moon Pies and
drink Mountain Dew
at the gas station

in the back
of my daddy's truck and

listen
to other men talk mean
about the gypsies
who had made up camp
across from our land.

Loneliness came from people —

those who would drive by
at night

and shoot guns in the air
to scare
the world.

We didn't go to the school—

and we would hear about it from the church ladies, telling us that it was a sin to not attend, especially me since I was a girl

and shouldn't have been out and around with boys.

But my mother wanted us to learn from the land instead –

and on special days she would take me on long walks through the skinny tall pines, pointing out the places in the earth where things belonged.

Where the cycle of life and death was so clearly marked in the leaves and soil.

IT WATCHED OVER ME AS I GREW

My river was my place of quiet retreat ...

It was always there, soothing, rhythmic —a constant.

It was the river that taught me

strength
and
confidence

It watched over me as I grew.

As I made mistakes.

As I shouted to the world my proudest moments.

I told it all my secrets.

And at night—I would dream of paddling down my river just like Liza Lou.

And at night, we would read ...

about the courageous and crafty Liza Lou and her adventures outsmarting the Swamp Monster

by paddling down her very own river.

Vignette Two: Cara

I've lived in the South forever.

My parents are here, my grandparents are here. I remember our community as being very small—I remember that we would play from dawn to dusk. When they would yell our name out one time, a second time, but the third time it would be with our middle name, we knew then that it was time to come in.

Everything we did —
we were always teaching and learning.
We would be making our
own games up because it
was
easier to do things
like that. You know,
because we were poor —

We had this old
dirt road behind us
where we could follow
it out into the woods.

We got in the mud.
We built forts.
We had twigs and a
lot of pine straw.

We had this one tree that was
hooked to my fence
so we would put boards to make a stabilized seat
like it was a ship.
We would crawl up into the tree and I was the lookout.
I made a long paper telescope. I could see forever across the woods.

Those kinds of things helped me decide my love for building,
Because we lived in the country, we spent a lot of time teaching others.

But my favorite part of life was Round Lake.

Every day we were going down to the lake, playing in the water, catching minnows, we saw owls and bats that would come down around us.

Sometimes, there would be baby water moccasins hatching —

we would go down to the lake and play and they would be right there.

But I always come back to the lake in my mind … because that was my place to go for myself.

So whenever I didn't want to be found, I would go down to the lake and sit down on the bank.

It was my sanctuary.

It shaped the independent part I needed to have.
You get to know yourself when you have that kind of time.

Everybody needs that kind of place to go to build themselves.

A lot of people don't have that space if they aren't from the country.

Everybody needs that space.

GIRLS DON'T REALLY DO THAT SORT OF THING

YEAH WE DO

The country led me to …

the lake led me to …

to myself.

I remember …

one time I took my dad's fishing pole without his permission and I caught this big fish – I was so excited, but I was still a girl, so I dropped the whole rod and real into the water.

As a child, my dad—well—he had 2 girls.

I guess he thought girls couldn't do what boys could. And I'm the type of person who is going to do it anyhow – he was very old-fashioned.

After I dropped the pole in the water, I went back in a few days and I thought, I'm not gonna have something hold me back.

He would always say, "Girls don't really do that kind of thing." —and I was like, "Oh yeah, we do."

We still live here—and I want, for my daughters now, to figure stuff out on their own. When I was building and learning as a child, I always thought about my creations, "We could do this or that …" and "What can we add to this to make it better?" I can remember looking around in the woods and using what we found – because it was more fun that way.

When we found it ourselves, it was better—we could share it with the world.

When you create it and you are involved in it—it's yours.

Vignette Three: Letty

Growing up, I lived in a small southern country town – in a brick home.

But what I remember most is that I grew up around the river.

Behind my neighbor's house was a beautiful 300-foot hill of green grass – with a bulkhead on the St Johns River. The wind often blew off the water – it was peace.

When I was a small child, first starting school, I was scared of my teacher because she would yell – I remember that school made me nervous.

In my mind there is such a vivid memory—of when I was standing next to a little boy who had been bad, so my teacher went outside, got a switch off the azalea bush and hit him with it.

I remember being so close to him that when she hit him, she accidentally hit me too.

But after school,
I would go to the river.

When the tide was low,
my friends and I
were able to walk down

to the riverbed
and pick up rocks to
skip.

For us,
it was like
a treasure hunt
to find the
perfect flat smooth stone
that would produce the
6 to 7 splashes across
the water.

We learned from the river—it was a place we never outgrew.
We knew the tides and yearned to always find new ways
to explore the river as we got older.
Even now, 20 years later, I find peace in this same tranquil water.

CHAPTER EIGHTEEN

A Small Town
WITH Long Roads

Wyoming as a Post-Western Curriculum

MARK HELMSING

WHAT SHOULD YOU KNOW ABOUT WYOMING?

"What is one thing you think someone new to Wyoming should know about this place?" I pose this question as an icebreaker to my students during our first day in the teaching methods course I teach at the University of Wyoming. What has turned out to be a fascinating discussion prompt began as a simple way to break the ice and take roll; I had given the question no thought prior to asking it. In my first year, as a new member of the faculty recently arrived from Michigan, I began my first day with my students displaying my limited knowledge about Wyoming, which mostly included things I learned the previous week during a post-move-in road trip throughout the state to sightsee my new home. My students, given the charge that they could not repeat any previously stated responses, began with the obvious pearls of wisdom newcomers to Wyoming are quickly told by quasi-welcoming strangers: you need a four-wheel drive car, you need snow tires (a subject of much debate), you need a well-insulated, downy, thick coat (not a simple winter overcoat that would have gotten the job done for me in the Midwest); when you are inevitably stuck off the side of the road in a snowdrift wait for a passerby to dig you out (they always will one is told).

At some point as the sharing snaked through the horseshoe assembly of desks a student shifted the focus of sharing "survival tips" to things newcomers should know about the cultural and natural heritage of the state. "Go see the rock formations in Vedauwoo just a little east outside of Laramie." "Be sure you see more nature than only what's in Yellowstone." "Check out the history of mining ghost towns in South Pass City." When the last section of students came up to share their suggestions, the tone shifted dramatically yet again. A student told me that if I were to ever be in the town of Riverton, I should be wary of walking around at night because I could "get mugged by the Indians if they're drunk in the park." A slight sense of shock fell over me. What should I do? While I had moved to Wyoming full of trepidation that my commitment to teaching for critical pedagogy would meet staunch resistance from ideologically conservative students and teachers, I had hoped this would be something I could ease into, not confront on the first day of my teaching. How could I effectively respond to this publically shared thinking that perpetuated numerous problematic assumptions: that Native Americans are violent, often drunk, and that I should beware their presence? I knew that Riverton was situated aside the Wind River Indian Reservation and, having had driven throughout both Riverton and the reservation in the previous weeks, I knew from casual conversations in local bars there that tensions between White and Native communities have long been strained over a painful history of forced relocation, boarding schools, water rights, access to land, and internal conflicts between the peoples of the Eastern Shoshone and the Northern Arapahoe forced to resettle within the boundaries of the reservation. Suddenly everything I had previously learned about Wyoming through my engagement with popular culture crystalized into a diffracted lens for seeing the U.S. West in which I now resided: cowboys and Indians, shoot outs and knife fights, bar brawls and seedy saloons, lawlessness and violence.

I responded to the student in the most ambivalent of ways: "I am sad to hear that. I look forward to spending more time in Riverton and I hope I can learn more about the cultural politics of the different groups of people who reside there and the nearby reservation." In a cowardly move wishing to seek a confrontation interrogation of the student's remarks and space of thinking, I quickly moved on to the few remaining students. With a grand pedagogical flourish, I stood up and congratulated all of the students for enacting their first pedagogical act as social studies educators. They had just taught me about the history, geography, culture, and politics of Wyoming and we set about doing a task grouping and classifying the suggested responses to the purposes and practices of social studies education. I have not yet since had a student share a suggested piece of knowledge about Wyoming so charged with the painful residue of race, class, and violence that saturates the high plains of this place, but I have had in the ensuring semesters numerous conversations with teachers, students, and folks throughout Wyoming about what Wyoming was and is and what the notion of "the West" might have been, might be now, and what it might be in the future. In this chapter I consider ideas and themes that emerged from a focus group study I did with my students in 2016. I dwell inside the perspectives and perceptions my students express to critically read the curriculum of Wyoming's rurality, a curriculum the United States has used as part of its national fantasy of the Old West or the Wild West now displaced by an inherited violence and its fraught engagement with isolation, abandonment, and loss that characterize what many scholars of Western history and literature term as the "post-West" (Baym, 2006; Campbell, 2008, 2013; Comer, 2013; Kollin, 2007). In this chapter I consider Wyoming's contested space as part of a "post-Western" curriculum on rurality. The traces, tropes, and iconographies of Laramie, Wyoming appear paradoxically as absent present signifiers of violence and hatred against national fantasies of bravery, ruggedness, and resilience in the mythic West that is a more established curriculum of the U.S. West.

HISTORICIZING THE WEST

During my first month of living in Wyoming a state news story grabbed my attention online: "Wyoming Railroad Employee Hijacks Train." A 22-year-old train driver allegedly stole a train from the North Antelope Rochelle mine and recklessly drove the train before plowing it into another train (Jarmusz, 2014). I had joked that upon moving to Wyoming I was living in the Disneyland version of Frontierland, the themed area of its amusement park that contains attractions, landscaping, and piped-in instrumental music reminiscent of the Old West. Now, with this news story, I felt I truly was living in a version of Frontierland as one of its signature attractions is Big Thunder Mountain Railroad, a ride on a runaway mine train through a haunted gold-mining town. The mythology of the Old West, as with all mythological structures, begins in reality, mutates through fabulation, and resurfaces in real, lived experiences. The Old West in many ways is what we imagine when, as Comer (2011) describes, we call forth:

> cultural belonging and identity in a region defined as arid lands west of the 98th meridian … narratives linked to the demand of the modern state for a unifying national soul on ostensible display in the natural lands and mythologies of the West. (p. 159)

Indeed, Wyoming structures its tourism industry largely in part on mythologizing the Old West and the Wild West as it manifests in the popular imagination (Lehan, 2014). The Wyoming Territorial Prison State Historic site in Laramie was built as a federal prison for the Wyoming Territory in 1872 and served as the state's penitentiary until the early 20th century after Wyoming achieved statehood. Today the prison structure and grounds operate as a museum to arrest visitors' interest in Butch Cassidy and other celebrated bandits of the Wild West who were incarcerated in the prison in the late 1800s. In Cody, Wyoming, aficionados of the Old West can visit the Old Trail Town, an oddly assembled collection of real buildings erected throughout Wyoming in the 1800s now relocated to this site that plays up imagery and exhibits on the Wild West, including the grave of Liver-Eating Johnson, a 19th century mountain man immortalized in Robert Redford's portrayal of him as Jeremiah Johnson in the film of the same name. The story of the relocation of Johnson's grave begins as a project a high school U.S. history teacher orchestrated with his students. I can think of no better hands-on history lesson than a social studies teacher and his students actively leading for the exhumation and relocation of a dead person, literally bringing the past alive in a rather undead way. In almost every incorporated community in Wyoming there is a museum or cultural attraction that in some way attempts to enshrine, memorialize, and market historical (mis)representations of the Old West, sometimes through the vernacular of the Wild West associated with Hollywood Westerns and Italian "spaghetti" Westerns, and sometimes through a tacit distancing of the Wild West. One staple of the romantic imagination of the Wild West is in depictions of brothels, saloons, and other places of ill repute that position the Wild West as an illicit space of lawlessness, vice, crime, and morals run amok when countered against the sophisticated aesthetics of "the East" in 19th century Americana.

One example of such a depiction can be found in the officially sanctioned and promoted walking tour of downtown Laramie titled "Legends of Laramie." This tour keenly sizes up the aesthetic elements of the Old West in its partnership project with the Historical Living Project, described as "a video-based journalism initiative that provides residents and visitors with a historical narrative of the people and historic homes of Laramie, from its beginnings as a railroad town, to a thriving community that values its sustainable architecture and historic heritage (www. visitlaramie.org). One of the stops along the Legends of Laramie walking tour is the 2nd Street brothel area. Two of Laramie's independent bookstores take up space within the original brothel area on 2nd Street and provide signage to visitors to read about "the soiled doves of Laramie." A scan of the signs' QR codes leads visitors to multimedia narration of the many devastating hardships prostitutes in Laramie endured in the late 1800s and early 1900s. I have yet to come across in any piece of social studies curriculum or textbook material dealing with the historical significance and economic issues of prostitution and brothels in the Old West.

The Old West remains the most entrenched form of the West in U.S. social studies curriculum, a rather unsurprising conclusion my students at the University of Wyoming and I have found through both our analysis of United States history textbooks and through focus group interviews conducted with pre-service social studies educators in our college of education. Consider the curricular framing of the Old West in one popular U.S. history textbook, *An American Promise* (Roark, Johnson, Cohen, Hartmann, & Stage, 2014). In this textbook the Old West first appears hazily as a portion of sixteenth-century European colonies in North America. A map of New Spain shows lands commonly associated with the Old West as a part of New Spain, but neither the map nor the accompanying text do little to contextualize how the borders of New Spain imparted issues of conflict between indigenous peoples of these lands and the Spanish colonialists that left as the periphery of their New World conquests (p. 40). As of this chapter's writing public discourse in Wyoming is dominated by issues of insider/outside cultural contact as many communities resist Wyoming Governor Mead's request to consider the resettlement of refugees from Syria and elsewhere. Wyoming is the only state in the U.S. that has never participated in the UN/US State Department Refugee Admissions Program. As xenophobic calls build for erecting a wall between the U.S. and Mexico, I suspect few Wyomingites realize that the land of their state were, for many centuries, part of Mexico.

The Old West reappears in this textbook several chapters later in a section titled "The Westward Movement." Consolidating all of the myriad, disparate human migration in a westward direction under the conceptual rubric of "manifest destiny," the textbook authors argue that "as important as national pride and racial arrogance were to manifest destiny, economic gain made up its core" (Roark et al., 2014, p. 313). In the same section a photograph of a White pioneer family traversing the Oregon Trail prompts the typical textbook question on the Old West: "What were some of the difficulties faced by pioneers traveling west?" (p. 316). A photograph of a miner with a pick, pan, and shovel has as its caption: "this young man exhibits the spirit of individual effort that was the foundation of free-labor ideals" (p. 325). A few chapters later the textbook begins to bring the Old West to a close, curricularly, in a chapter titled "The Contested West, 1865–1900." The authors begin this closing of the West (literally and figuratively) by invoking the Turner Thesis, an idea associated with the writing of Frederick Jackson Turner who argued in his essay "The Significance of the Frontier in American History" that "the existence of an area of free land, its continuous recession, and the advance of settlement westward explained American development" (in Roark et al., 2014, p. 448). The authors signal that the mythic West, as materialized by Buffalo Bill Cody's traveling western show, dime store novels, cowboy songs, the Western genre in comics, television, and film, is contained within larger narratives of how "in the decades following the Civil War, the United States pursued empire in the American West" and that representations of the mythic West "obscured the complex reality of the West as a fiercely contested terrain" (p. 449).

Such historiographic moves that query what we think we know about the history of the American West are the hallmark of a critical vein that questions and interrogates assumptions of the Old West as it is commonly framed in national discourse. As Limerick (1987) demonstrates in her field defining book *The Legacy of Conquest: The Unbroken Past of the American West* identified for historians a growing concern with the assumptions of the Turner Thesis that had been taken for granted over much of the 20th century. What the work of Limerick and other post-West historians call for is the rethinking of the west and teaching the history of the west "as conquered terrain, that the west had always been a scene of economic exploitation not democratic opportunity, that the frontier on the one hand had never existed and on the other had never closed" (Baym, 2006, p. 815). This is a visioning of the U.S. West that is more diverse than cowboys and Indians as it includes the gendered concerns placed upon women and children, of homosocial relationships, of racial and ethnic encounters amongst Blacks, Latina/os, Asians, and Europeans. The curriculum made out of a national fantasy of the Old West was replaced with a curriculum made out of a national fantasy of new Wests made possible to imagine with the insights from cultural studies, critical historians, and multiculturalism's advocates in the 1980s, 1990s, and early 2000s.

If the Old West is mapped out through romantic imagery of white settlers taming nature and staking claims in unexplored lands, a mythic wilderness constructed out of transcendental notions of nature and beauty in which national stories of resilience and adaptability, the post-West is mapped out by how it rethinks and redraws these older borders forged by historians, artists, literary writers, and filmmakers. Thinking of this post-West requires an interpretive paradigm that examines stories of the American West as resisting the settler colonial discourse of Manifest Destiny, the Wild West, and its narratives and the romantic, mythic depictions of a community coming together despite numerous hardships. The ways in which my students expressed a curriculum of the post-West all involved contesting representations of Wyoming the American West as savage, backwards, and stifled by autonomous individualism and distrust of the commons and collective public assemblages (such as "national" or "global").

IDENTIFYING (WITH) THE WEST

This complicated existence of multiple "Wests" is what appears most resoundingly in the perspectives, outlooks, and understandings of the students I have worked with at the University of Wyoming in their social studies education program. In the spring of 2016 I conducted a series of four focus group interviews with this group of 25 students, 20 of whom were seniors preparing to graduate and five of whom were recently graduated students returning for a post-baccalaureate teacher certification program. Two of the students had spent most of their lives living in Colorado, one had lived in Arizona, one in South Dakota, and one in California. The other 20 students in the course had lived their lives entirely in Wyoming. As a whole they represented the spaces and places of the U.S. West. In the next section I examine what these students articulate in their conceptualization of both Wyoming and the U.S. West as curricular constructs to examine in their teaching of social studies subject matters. I was compelled to investigate what my students from the west knew about the west. The focus group studies I conducted were to help give shape to what increasingly struck me as an amorphous curriculum of many different wests, a curriculum I wanted to study in social studies classrooms throughout Wyoming. With a tape recorder and a series of open-ended questions my students and I talked, for hours, about Wyoming and the west and what we thought they were.

Initially conversations percolated over debating how we define the West. Was the west any land located westward of the Mississippi River? If so, that would include California, Oregon, and Washington, states that one student, Jeremy, said "were not part of the real west." When I asked why he claimed it was because those three states are part of "the coast" and all happened to be a locus for liberalism. To Jeremy "the real west" was Montana, Wyoming, Idaho, the two Dakotas, Nebraska, and Colorado, despite the growing "purple" political color of Colorado as its becomes seen as a more progressively liberal state through the decriminalization of marijuana and the booming population of its capital city, Denver. Indeed, as Jeremy and other students indicated, large populations are antithetical to the West. The Pacific coastal states are seen as teeming with crowded and densely populated cities.

Yet is is undeniable that to be a part of the U.S. West is to be a part of a land that is sparsely populated. Wyoming, as all of my students I interviewed knew quite well, was the least populated state in the United States and the second least densely populated state, second only to Alaska. Hovering around 600,000, the entire population of Wyoming is well under half of many large cities in the United States. One student, Jenny, described Wyoming in the way many others have described Wyoming to me: "Wyoming is just one big small town with really long roads." The oxymoronic structure of this phrase requires a bit of deconstruction to understand its full import. My students conceive of Wyoming as a singularity of "one," a homogenous state despite vast differences in its physical regions that vary from the Red Desert of the southwest, to the impenetrable national forests in the northwest, to the Wind River and Big Horn mountain ranges in the central and northern reaches of the state, to the sprawling sea of grasslands of the east and the windswept high plans of the southeast. Just as there is no one "true West," there is no one true Wyoming. There are multiple Wests and multiple Wyomings. The notion of a one true authentic Wyoming is in keeping with the pervasive notion that there is one true West, even if the hallmarks that are used to signify the authentic "realness" of the U.S. West are in conflict with the evolving economic, political, and sociocultural realities of how the west has evolved in recent decades (Handley & Lewis, 2004).

Despite this incommensurate association of a classically "real" U.S. West seen in Wyoming and the multiple changes that have shifted the rural landscapes in the west after globalization, neoliberalism, and other conditions of postmodernity, the belief still exists that Wyoming is merely one communal space in which everyone knows everyone else. How else could that reality be conceived with a population so small in comparison to every other state? When I take my university's jet to fly to the communities of Gillette or Casper to supervise student teachers or do work with local teachers, I am known and recognized by people despite that Laramie and the university are at least a six-hour drive away in a remote corner of the state. Even when I do not traverse the "really long roads" that Jenny invoked, I still feel intimately connected to rural communities across the state. And yet these places are marked by an immense emptiness. As soon as I leave the city limits of Laramie my cell phone loses its signal. Driving through the Shirley Basin to Casper, or through Elk Mountain to Rawlins, or past Muddy Gap north on U.S. 287 towards Lander, I am engulfed by emptiness. The emptiness of Wyoming, its "there is nothing there, there"-ness, is as much a physical and affective condition as it is ideological. Harding (2007) cautions us to be suspicious of what she terms the myth of emptiness, arguing that "empty cannot be taken at face value" because emptiness is an unstable category that shapes one's perception of a rural place, it can be attached to anything signifying rurality, "deserted, desolate, or out-of-the-way places" as well as "mountains, lakes, forest, or oceans" (p. 13). This allows almost anyone to render an empty space suitable for their ideological purposes, from preservationists to homesteaders, from ranchers to land developers, from oil barons to religious leaders in search of an empty space to start a new utopia.

As I learned from interviewing my students, this sense of emptiness is heavily scrutinized when considered as a characteristic in need of revision in our consideration of a post-West. Kristin, a non-traditional adult student who has returned to the university to pursue teacher certification in social studies, considers the national narratives about Wyoming to be grossly inaccurate and unfair:

> This isn't just empty nothingness, and we're not backwards rednecks who only like country music. We have the same concerns, desires, and perspectives that people in other parts of the country have. We just like our privacy probably a bit more than other states.

This acknowledgment of the cultural importance that privacy holds within Wyoming underscores the significance of privacy and individuality in Wyoming. As Loffreda (2000) writes in her account of teaching at the University of Wyoming during the year of Matthew Shepherd's murder there is an immense sense of loneliness that festers under the cultural tropes of privacy and individuality that uphold Wyoming as a state of quietude and solace, wild open spaces perfect for roughing it alone without nosy neighbors or city slickers. To take one illustration of this concept, many tourist souvenir postcards of Wyoming play on the idea of rush hour traffic in the state as one truck on a dirt road stuck behind a herd of cattle or antelope. This is a significant part of Wyoming's sense of rurality. There are numerous facts about Wyoming that exploit its rural character: there are only two sets of escalators in the entire state (each located in a separate bank in the city of

Casper); the tallest building in the state is White Hall, a modest dormitory of 200 feet at the University of Wyoming (which is the only four-year college in the state); the entire population of the state is about equal to the population alone of the city of Albuquerque, New Mexico; and 54% of all land in Wyoming is owned by either the federal or state government (Arthur, 2014). If, as according to Woods (2011), the modern etymology of the word "rural" once referred to "open space," the Wyoming may indeed be the most rural of all states in the U.S. (p. 17). It is this volatile mixture of hostile privacy, rugged independence, and vast open, lonely spaces that helped give shape to the sense of place in the minds of many Americans when the town of Laramie became synonymous with a place of hate in the wake of Matthew Shepard's murder in 1998.

SHIFTING THE WEST

I brought up Matthew Shepard during the focus group interview in which my student Kristin participated. Triggered by her association of extreme privacy with Wyoming, how, I ask, do residents of Wyoming and Laramie understand the position Matt (as he is intimately referred to by locals in Laramie) plays in larger national discourses of tolerance, acceptance, and hate? This and related questions occupy my thinking quite frequently. What does it mean for me, a white gay male educator who, as a closeted high school teenager, saw Matthew Shepard's murder unfold on nightly news reports half a country away in October of 1998? And what, if anything, did it mean for my own identity and my own life history to now live and teach in the community that—unfairly or not—is synonymous with homophobia and violence against queer persons? Emily was the first to respond. She claims she knew Matt when he was a student at the university. "You know, it's really hard," she says, with a tear welling in her eyes:

> I knew Matt and he would not have wanted to be seen as a martyr. He would not have wanted to be seen this way all these years later. He just wasn't that kind of guy. And people just don't know the whole story about Matt, about Laramie. Really about anything.

I have reflected often on Emily's assessment. One cannot live in Laramie and inquire about Matthew Shepard without immediately running into a surprisingly wide array of competing thoughts about "the whole story" as Emily alludes to the murder and the events surrounding Shepard's death. Emily, and many other people in Laramie whom I have asked about Matthew Shepard, people I would be quick to describe as liberally open minded and progressive in their stance as allies to queer people and queer causes, briskly deny Matthew Shepard's murder was a hate crime. They invoke either drugs (specifically meth) as the primary vice that threw these horrific events into motion, or they awkwardly express that Shepard was sexually and/or romantically involved with the men who were found guilty of murdering him. These statements always appear to me as rhetorical moves to absolve Laramie and Wyoming as unequivocal spaces of hatred and violence. I still do not know what to make of them.

I wonder, as with all things about Wyoming and the U.S. West, what the consequences could be of allegorizing Matthew Shepard as a cautionary tale we now use in education to narrativize and teach the history of securing civil rights for queer citizens in the U.S. In the play *The Laramie Project* (Kaufman, 2001) Wyoming is distilled into the voices and memories of residents of Laramie who were interviewed by members of the Tectonic Theater Project, interviews that would become the dramatic material for *The Laramie Project*. Wangh (2005) wonders if the play is "simply a lie," one that perhaps paints a "rosy picture" of Laramie complicating our national narratives of revenge and forgiveness (p. 5). I, too, wonder about this condition of the play. However, I agree with Wangh that one way to think about potential lessons of Matthew Shepard and of Laramie and Wyoming is to consider how such events and narratives help "steer human voyages from unpleasant beginnings toward happy endings, or at least toward endings that bring some resolution to the terrors of the middle passage" (Wangh, 2005, p. 5). Responding to Emily during the same interview, another student, Keith, suggests Matthew Shepard's murder, regardless of cause or intent, are crucial in rethinking Wyoming and the U.S. West as "innocent and undisturbed" to use his words. "Matt's death reminds us that the Wild West was founded on violence and getting tied to a buck and rail fence, left to die in the sun, is about as violent and Western as one could get" Keith adds. This is how Tigner (2002) reads the role of Laramie and Matthew Shepard's death in refiguring the rural Western narrative in the service of seeing the New West: "as much as Laramie represents innocence impossible in a metropolis, Laramie also represents mythological or historical violence—the violence of the Western" (p. 140).

If the desires, myths, and symbols of Matthew Shepard are far from settled and stable, what can we do to honor the complexity of his life? The same can also be asked for how we imagine the rural spaces of the U.S. West as settled and stable spaces. The conceptual paradigm of the New West unsettles our mythologized curriculum of the U.S. West, resisting a traditional curriculum of heritage and history, of community and national identity, and of progress and growth (Finnega, 2008; Jones & Wills, 2009). If Wyoming is truly one small town with really long roads, then what I have learned from both my students and my own introspections in living here is that there is a transformative demand for recognizing the limits of what we mean by rural, empty, and wild. Life in Laramie, and, I would argue, in Wyoming and our post-West region, requires a refusal to look away from and ignore the horrifying events of the past that are the countenance of the Old West. A reparative response can to this history can be found in ideas of a post-Western curriculum, other ideas, other voices, and other ways of thinking or being "Western" that not only marks this region's unsettled past through colonial settlement, but also through a radical uncertainty of what the U.S. West once was, might have been, or will be in the future. As I write this chapter the University of Wyoming is in the throes of an unprecedented fiscal crisis, triggered by the state legislature's decimation of public funding as a result of a cataclysmic bust in the energy industry. The "boom and bust" cycle that characterizes Wyoming and so much of the U.S. West could very well be lurching towards its final oscillation in the face of changing global attitudes towards mineral extraction and climate change. Wyoming is, then, truly inhabiting a post-Western moment.

REFERENCES

Arthur, B. (2014). *Top 50 Wyoming facts.* Retrieved from http://www.movoto.com/blog/opinions/wyoming-facts/

Baym, N. (2006). Old west, new west, postwest, real west. *American Literary History, 18*(4), 814–828.

Campbell, N. (2008). *The rhizomatic West: Representing the American West in a transnational, global, media age.* Lincoln, NE: University of Nebraska Press.

Campbell, N. (2013). *Post-Westerns: Cinema, region, west.* Lincoln, NE: University of Nebraska Press.

Comer, K. (2011). Exceptionalism, other wests, critical regionalism. *American Literary History, 23*(1), 159–173.

Comer, K. (2013). Introduction: Assessing the postwestern. *Western American Literature, 48*(1&2), 3–15.

Finnega, J. (2008). *Narrating the American West: new forms of historical memory.* Amherst, NY: Cambria Press.

Handley, W. R., & Lewis, N. (2004). *True west: Authenticity and the American West.* Lincoln, NE: University of Nebraska Press.

Harding, W. (2007). *The myth of emptiness and the new American literature of place.* Iowa City, IA: University of Iowa Press.

Jarmusz, T. S. (2014, October 12). Disgruntled employee steals train. *Gillette News Record.* Retrieved from http://www.gillettenewsrecord.com/

Jones, K. R., & Wills, J. (2009). *The American West: Competing visions.* Edinburgh: Edinburgh University Press.

Kaufman, M. (2001). *The Laramie project.* New York, NY: Dramatists Play Service.

Kollin, S. (Ed.) (2007). *Postwestern cultures: Literature, theory, space.* Lincoln, NE: University of Nebraska Press.

Lehan, R. (2014). *Quest west: American intellectual and cultural transformations.* Baton Rouge, LA: Louisiana State University Press.

Limerick, P. N. (1987). *The legacy of conquest: The unbroken past of the American West.* New York, NY: W. W. Norton.

Loffreda, B. (2000). *Losing Matt Shepard: Life and politics in the aftermath of anti-gay murder.* New York, NY: Columbia University Press.

Roark, J. L., Johnson, M. P., Cohen, P. C., Hartmann, S. M., & Stage, S. (Eds.) (2014). *The American promise: A concise history*. New York, NY: Bedford/St. Martin's Press.

Tigner, A. L. (2002). *The Laramie Project*: Western pastoral. *Modern Drama, 45*(1), 138–156.

Wangh, S. (2005). Revenge and forgiveness in Laramie, Wyoming. *Psychoanalytic Dialogues, 15*(1), 1–16.

Woods, M. (2011). *Rural*. New York, NY: Routledge.

PART FOUR

International
Rural Contexts

Reconstructing THE Deficit Discourse IN A Multi-Remote School IN far North Queensland

JON AUSTIN AND AMELIA JENKINS

One of the long-standing images and identity markers of the continent of Australia in the international imagination is of large open spaces ["the Bush"], housing remote and sparsely populated communities or settlements. The image of the remoteness of Australia has sustained national narratives of an enduring frontier-type lifestyle, embodied in the mythic construction of the Drover, for example. To a lesser degree, notions of remoteness also anchor myths and narratives regarding the indigenous population of this place, Australian Aboriginal and Torres Strait Islander peoples.

With a current population somewhere in the order of 24 million located within an area of 7.6 million square kilometres (approximately 3 million square miles), Australia is indeed a land of large space and relatively small population. In reality, it is a highly urbanized place, with somewhere around 90% of the population living in large metropolises and sizeable provincial cities and towns in very close proximity to the coast, such that around 85% of the country has a population density of no more than 1 person per square kilometre. Geographically, remote here is very remote, and those who live in these areas find themselves with the challenges of distance insofar as the provision of and access to public facilities, transport and other infrastructural amenities, and central social services such as health and education.

In addition to, and further complicating the geographic dimension of remoteness for some groups in a particular society, culture acts as another dimension of proximity and remoteness. As much as one can be physically or geographically remote from centers of population one might also be at distance from dominant or mainstream cultures. This is certainly the case with Australian Aboriginal and Torres Strait Island peoples, who, despite being at times geographically located close to the center are at great distance culturally, politically, economically, and spiritually from the dominant mores of the community. The impact of such cultural alienation in many ways parallels those of being physically remote; where the physically remote find difficulty in securing access to services readily available in the metropolis, the culturally remote find similar difficulties in being able to locate and access—that is, to deal directly with—the epistemologies, ideologies, hegemonic ways of knowing and being that those culturally close take as universal or commonsensical.

This chapter looks to explore the effect of being both physically and culturally remote in broadly cultural but more specifically educational terms. The chapter touches on the ways in which Indigenous Australian people have essentially been discursively positioned as uneducable through the operation of a deceitful discourse of deficit. We then move on to feature an example of alternative practices in the education of culturally remote students in a far North Queensland State [public] school. The physical remoteness of this particular school brings with it a number of advantages for affecting a critical indigenous education, one that seeks to secure understanding, respect, and acceptance of the ways of the Other. In this, we hope to excavate some of the facets of critical education work where the embrace of schooling as a means to securing a stronger democratic environment and civic engagement beyond that of being merely good consumers and compliant workers figures prominently in both individual and collective philosophies and imperatives.

THE CONTEXT OF AUSTRALIAN INDIGENOUS EDUCATION: STANDARDIZED TESTING, DEFICIT DISCOURSE AND THE "INEDUCABILITY" OF INDIGENOUS STUDENTS

In ways typical of many other colonizer countries, responsibility for the provision of education—essentially, schooling—for Australian Aboriginal and Torres Strait Islander peoples has been a multi-level governmental undertaking. Whilst under the Australian Constitution, responsibility for education resided with the six State governments, decades of constitutional evolution have seen the reality of much of this responsibility being taken over by the Commonwealth (Federal) government. This has occurred largely as a result of the complex development of conditional or "tied" budgetary grants made by the Commonwealth to the States.

The "official" image of Aboriginal and Torres Strait Islander students in Australian schools is one essentially of ineducability, there being perhaps no more indicative "compensatory" program title than *Closing the Gap* (COAG, 2012) to reflect this deficit view of the educational capacities of Australian indigenous students. The then Prime Minister's (Tony Abbott) opening statement in the

2015 Closing the Gap: Prime Minister's Report makes it very clear that the official narrative of learning is tethered to formal Western senses of what and where it means to be educated: *"It's hard to be literate and numerate without attending school"* (AustralianGovernment, 2015, p. 2). This report then starkly acknowledges a failure on the part of the myriad projects nestled together under the *"Closing the Gap"* funding banner to make any real progress towards the 2018 target of halving the gap between the reading, writing and numeracy achievements of non-indigenous and Indigenous students, (unusually) confessing that *"There has been no overall improvement in Indigenous reading and numeracy since 2008"* (AustralianGovernment, 2015, p. 4). The unwritten ending of this statement is probably along the lines of "despite governments spending large amounts of money over many decades on this". If the commitment of government—and by extension, the community as a whole—hasn't been wanting, then the problem must surely lie on the side of the recipients of this social concern and consequent financial largesse. There must be, goes the logical extension here, an inherent problem, a lack or deficit in the cognitive capacities of Aboriginal and Torres Strait Islander people. They simply aren't able to learn these things, or, at least, those things required by the formal school curriculum.

An interwoven discourse surrounding the casual factors of indigenous learning deficit is that of environment. One might see all of the facets of "environment" as falling within the general purview of the notion of cultural capital, particularly in the complex constellation of two of the three forms in which such capital manifests and exists; viz.

> in the embodied state, i.e., in the form of long-lasting dispositions of the mind and body;[and] in the objectified state, in the form of cultural goods (pictures, books, dictionaries, instruments, machines, etc.) (Bourdieu, 1986, p. 243)

In other words, in this discursive regime, the learning deficits of Aboriginal and Torres Strait Islander students are the product of a lack of the types of cultural knowledge, expertise and material possessions sufficient to connect with the ways of knowing and being expected, required and taught by the formal schooling process. As such, these students lack the cultural capital necessary to secure social and economic normalcy, legitimacy, acceptance, and in the logic of the dominant culture, success.

Intertwined, these two narratives of indigenous ineducability paint pictures of contemporary forms of the primitivism and sub-human status that has marked previous depictions of Aboriginal and Torres Strait Islander peoples. In one very thorough historical exploration of the representations of indigenous peoples in the Australian context, Heather Sharp (2010) analysed the representations of Aboriginal Australians in official syllabus and associated teaching materials (textbooks, school papers, children's storybooks, etc) used in Queensland schools over an approximately 100-year period. Whilst she was looking largely at the history curriculum, Sharp's summation of the place of Indigenous Australians in the official school narrative of nationhood is important here:

> Indigenous Australians are not excluded from the narrative, although their inclusion is constructed based on a passive and subjugated identity (p. 410)

In her study, Sharp identified persistent themes in official school materials that are highly relevant to the point being made here. She identified what she called discourses of Indigenous Australians as being "savages/primitives" (p 309), "monocultural" (p. 358), "on the fringe of history" (p. 352), and presenting as "problem-laden" (p. 357). The crucial point is that over an extended time period, generations of children have absorbed ("learned") certain things about Aboriginal and Torres Strait Islander peoples; teachers have presented ("taught") such problematically one-dimensional and culturally-pernicious ideas about Indigenous Australians; and these peoples have come to see themselves represented in these ways repeatedly and consistently in the various forms of official knowledge (Apple, 1993).

This last effect is a major tool in the armoury of colonisation and both leads to and reinforces the intergenerational alienation of Aboriginal and Torres Strait Islander peoples from their cultures and ways of life. The power and impact of a process of learning to see oneself as seen by dominant forces in a society has been the focus of attention and concern for well over a century, from du Bois' notion of double consciousness *(this sense of always looking at one's self through the eyes of others, of measuring one's soul by the tape of a world that looks on in amused contempt and pity.* (1903, p. 9) through Franz Fanon's exhortation to the colonised to pursue what he called resistance to cultural amputation (1967, p. 140) *(resisting the colonizing knowledge system that constantly pathologizes and criminalizes blackness and misrepresents it as an agent of malevolent powers there to cause harm to the white world* (Adjei, 2010, p. 87) to Albert Memmi's analysis of *the colonialist hoax* (1967, p. 91).

In the Australian context, Martin Nakata (2007), writing from a Torres Strait Islander perspective, comprehensively charts the development of Western knowledge about and representations of Torres Strait Island peoples and cultures that flowed from the activities of various agents of colonisation—religious, scientific (especially anthropological) and educational—that for all intents and purposes has come to assume the non-partisan status of "knowledge":

> My task was not simply to know my position but to know first how I was positioned in and by Western disciplines and knowledge practices. My task then was to know how such a knowledge system created a position for Islanders through which we have all come to view Islanders and their problems. (p. 11)

A further significant piece of work relevant to the arguments of this chapter is that of Australian sociologist, Raewyn Connell in her book *Southern Theory* (Connell, 2007). Connell's purpose in this particular book was to explore the ways in which academic disciplinary knowledge—particularly that of sociology—developed from a Western center, mirroring the physical exploitation of the colonized worlds [mining, plant and animal trafficking, etc.] through the ways in which it effectively "mined" non-Western knowledge resources and proclaimed the output as its own. In the pursuit of such an appropriation of intellectual resources of the colonized world, Connell argues, the power and significance of such intelligence resident within the Periphery (the colonised) had to be largely rendered invisible or at the very least, derided as primitive or superficial. One can see this strategy in place with regard to Australian Indigenous knowledge systems and ways of knowing, and arguably this process continues apace through the application of Western-based processes of assessment, evaluation, and categorization of Indigenous peoples as holding both an inferior "traditional" or cultural knowledge and a seeming inability to "succeed" within the Western canon.

To flesh out further the situation regarding Aboriginal and Torres Strait Islander students, and to use the current dominant language of assessment—statistics—we can draw out a number of inevitable conclusions regarding the constructed reality of learning of Indigenous Australian students. The primary source of such statistical—and thereby accepted commonsensically as apolitical and objective; that is, "accurate"—knowledge is the annual National Assessment Program—Literacy and Numeracy (NAPLAN). NAPLAN operates under the auspices of the Australian Curriculum, Assessment and Reporting Authority (ACARA). The annual NAPLAN tests have been visited upon students, teachers and schools since 2008, and are claimed to test achievement in *the sorts of skills that are essential for every child to progress through school and life, such as reading, writing, spelling and numeracy* (ACARA, 2013).

What do current statistics tell us about the competencies—a.k.a. learning achievements—of Aboriginal and Torres Strait Islander students? Drawing from the most current set of figures available at the time of writing, the 2015 NAPLAN Report (ACARA, 2015), Indigenous Australian students "lag behind" their non-indigenous counterparts across all of the several areas of testing. The areas tested in years three, five, seven and nine of formal schooling annually are Reading, Persuasive Writing, Spelling, Grammar and Punctuation and Numeracy. In the area of Reading, for example, the official image of Aboriginal and Torres Strait Islander students in year nine of formal schooling tells us that currently:

- 71.7% nationally meet expected standards in reading compared with nonindigenous students, 93.6% of whom meet these standards;
- this disparity is consistent across the four school years of NAPLAN testing [years three, five, seven, and nine];
- the percentage of Australian Indigenous students meeting minimum expectations in reading decreases markedly across the four geographical

regions—metropolitan, provincial, remote, and very remote. 87.2% of Indigenous students in metropolitan areas meet minimum reading standards as opposed to 54.7% in very remote areas; and that

- less than 55% of Australian indigenous students in very remote areas meet minimum national reading standards compared to 96.5% of nonindigenous students in the same geographic regions.

So, from within this particular paradigm it would seem—in fact, the statistics prove—that Aboriginal and Torres Strait Islander students are significantly challenged in the basic tents of reading, and the more removed from urban areas students are, the more significant the challenge. As such, these statistics present as major markers of an educational crisis, with all of the attendant impacts on and consequences for life chances. The fact that there has been no improvement in these "objective" measures of educational achievement over many years, despite the dedication of billions of dollars, points to an underlying assumption of an Australian Indigenous incapacity to think or reason numerically. But is this the total picture, and how should educators respond to such statistics?

A commencing point would be for educators (in the first instance) to come to acknowledge that these two groups of students typically identified as being "behind" in most areas of the formal school curriculum—viz. Australian Aboriginal and Torres Strait Islander students—inhabit and straddle multiple and complex cultural and educational lifeworlds (Guy, 2015), the successful navigation of which requires adeptness at what might be seen to be a version of the originally linguistic concept of code switching:

> In general terms, codeswitching can be used to refer to situations in which bilingual people alternate between languages, either between or within utterances. (Greer, 2007, p. 28)

The importance of the concept of lifeworlds to considerations of matters such as the concrete contexts of learning of Aboriginal and Torres Strait Islander students cannot be overstated. Jill Guy, in her 2015 doctoral thesis that set out to explore the complexity of education and schooling of young Australian Aboriginal males, provides a useful summary of this phenomenon:

> A lifeworld is a "communicative locale for affirming individual agency and forming cultural identity" (Ludert, 2010, p. 3). Husserl explained the lifeworld as the world of human activity and everyday sociability, taken-for-granted and always there as a background to other dimensions of life (Husserl, 1970). According to Nakata (2002) Aboriginal and Torres Strait Islanders' lifeworlds are situated in a cultural interface, a complex intersection of Indigenous and Western epistemological domains. It is the place where we live and learn, the place that conditions our lives, the place that shapes our futures and more to the point the place where we are active agents in our own lives, where we make decisions. (p. 285)

In this intensely personal research project grounded in the very concrete experiences of her participants, Guy documented the significant tensions experienced by these young Australian Aboriginal people as they tried to move effectively between and within Aboriginal and Western educational contexts. Clearly, there is not space within the confines of this chapter to delve more deeply into the specifics of Guy's research, but the crucial point for this current chapter might well be summed up by quoting from her concluding section:

> The participants within this project highlighted some of the challenges that are experienced with biculturality within Australia. There are many people, not only Aboriginal and Torres Strait Islander peoples, who inhabit complex educational lifeworlds that are comprised of more than the white, middle class cultural capital that is promoted within the formal schooling arena. It appears as if many of these people will continue to experience the educative tensions that arise when these worlds clash, unless action is taken to change societal views. The cultural interface, the site where the Indigenous and Western epistemological domains meet (Nakata, 2002) has the potential to create a vibrant, strong and empathetic Australia. (Guy, 2015, p. 172)

On a systemic basis, Australian Aboriginal and Torres Strait Islander students will likely continue to be positioned as "behind", as being "deficient". This is one of the strategies of subjugation attendant upon the colonization process, working in tandem with an ongoing process of epistemicide, *the murder of knowledge* (Santos, 2016, p. 92) whereby

> Dominant epistemologies have resulted in a massive waste of social experience and, particularly, in the massive destruction of ways of knowing that did not ft [sic] the dominant epistemological canon. (Santos, 2016, p. 238)

This is what Andrade (1990 [1928]), a Brazilian poet, early last century called anthropopaphy: *the* American's [coloniser's] *capacity to devour all that was alien to him and to incorporate all so as to create a complex identity, a new, constantly changing identity (Santos, 2016, p. 52)*

Until schools come to acknowledge, incorporate and value the power of the biculturality of their Indigenous students and communities, Aboriginal and Torres Strait Islander people will continue to be judged against less-than-honest criteria of educational attainment and found wanting.

Schools, however, that do operate from a strengths and needs based model, honouring the biculturality of Indigenous students, incorporating Aboriginal and Torres Strait Islander perspectives and building bridges within communities, have been able to assist Indigenous students achieve remarkable academic attainments, ultimately working to expose and white-ant the discourse of deficit blemishing and restricting such Indigenous students in Australia.

CASE STUDY: ROSSVILLE STATE SCHOOL

Rossville State School is a small school located approximately 40 km south of Cooktown, tucked away in the coastal rainforest ranges adjacent to Cedar Bay National Park on the remote Cape York Peninsula. The local area boasts spectacular natural beauty set amongst the world's oldest living rainforests along the legendary Bloomfield Track that until recently was exclusively accessible by 4-wheel drive.

The school is on the traditional lands of the Kuku Nyungul. In the past, families were relocated, voluntarily and involuntarily, to missions such as Bloomfield River which lies 46 km south. Recently, there has been a move to return to live on country, with many families choosing to return to their ancestral grounds and join a growing community on Traditional Kuku Nyungul Freehold Land located on Shipton's Flat road or in local housing provided by the local Gungarde Aboriginal Corporation.

The school population is very diverse across a number of demographic categories. The majority of families who reside in the Rossville catchment area are chronically and often generationally unemployed. Socio-economic demographics of the school vary but average out to the sixteenth percentile Australia wide. There is a lot of variation, however, with some students coming from families with very limited formal education and generational poverty while other students come from families where both parents have post graduate qualifications and work in highly regarded professional roles. The school has a much higher proportion of its students identifying as Aboriginal and/or Torres Strait Islander people (27% of students enrolled in 2014) than the Australian average of 5.3% and the Queensland average of 7.6%.

In many ways, despite its remote location, Rossville State School is faced with the type of challenges typical of schools looking to equitably support students and families who have been traditionally disadvantaged while holding high expectations to extend all students. In meeting these challenges, Rossville State School has found itself positioned within the "cultural interface", that point at which Indigenous and Western epistemological domains meet (Nakata, 2002) realising "the potential to create a vibrant, strong and empathetic Australia" (Guy, 2015, p. 172) and articulated in the school's vision to empower and equip confident, connected and creative citizens. Moreover, significant improvements in student outcomes became evident quickly, in some instances immediately, demonstrating that meaningful change should not necessarily take a generation to achieve.

THE CHALLENGE

2014 presented the school with a number of challenges and opportunities with an entire turnover of administrative staff and most of the teaching staff. The immediate priority, therefore, was collaboratively creating a shared vision for the school and developing consistent school wide practices.

Official school performance data indicated that at the time student engagement was of particular concern as overall attendance for 2013 was 89.5%. The end of 2013 also saw an increasing amount of disciplinary absences and behaviour incidents, predominantly within the Indigenous student cohort.

Initial observations and data collection further revealed the diversity and complexity of the student population with 14% of students at least 2 years behind academically in formal (Western) literacy and/or numeracy. In addition, 23% of students required literacy support and 12.5% needed numeracy support. Altogether, 43% of students required literacy or numeracy intervention or extension. At the same time, analysis from a strengths based mindset revealed opportunities to extend students in areas where they excelled. Ignoring these opportunities and simply prioritising remedial interventions for funding and resources would have been the typical response of a deficit or Closing the Gap mentality. However, Rossville staff and community determined that a more culturally-appropriate and student-centred response to formal pressures to improve formal measures of educational attainment/achievement were both necessary and respectful of all students and their home cultures.

During term one, the entire teaching team came together to analyse school and student data, evaluate evidence based strategies and pedagogies and to consolidate the curriculum. Community outreach meetings were held and outside agency support solicited. Individual staff and school goals were set and plans put in place to achieve these targets. The result was an enhanced Whole School Approach: Confident, Connected and Creative Citizens.

A year later, attendance, behaviour and academic data showed significant improvements across the school. Analysis of 2015 NAPLAN data show that the intentional, targeted strategies enacted made obvious and sizeable impacts for all students. For the first time ever, 100% of students achieved above the national minimum standard in literacy and numeracy. Student attendance rates came within half a percent of the state average and school disciplinary absences were the lowest on record. There has also been a dramatic increase in parent participation as caregivers are continually being connected to their child's learning.

TARGETED AND HOLISTIC INTERVENTION AND EXTENSION

To guarantee success for every child, Rossville's Pedagogical Framework relies on a continuum of multi-layered or multi-tiered support and extension services to meet the cultural, academic, physical and social/emotional needs of each child.

Mind

At Tier 1, the emphasis is on quality teaching and ongoing monitoring of learning. The Whole School Pedagogy, Curriculum, Assessment & Reporting Plan sets out how triangulated data is to be collected and used to plan and enact the Australian Curriculum to integrate curriculum where appropriate and backward map assessment and learning episodes to formal (mandated) ACARA Achievement Standards.

Students identified as requiring extension or additional support benefit from intentional strategies aimed at those students' particular needs. These Tier 2 interventions are focussed, increasing in intensity of instruction and frequency of monitoring.

Students who have not responded to Tier 1 or Tier 2 levels of intervention benefit from Tier 3 support that is highly personalised and individualised. Other professional expertise is engaged to determine students' needs and to assist in setting goals and action plans.

A core value that underpins Rossville's response to intervention strategies is that educational achievement, very broadly defined, is a human right. Everyone has the right to succeed and feel proud of and to be recognised for their accomplishments. Every student should be given strategic opportunities to excel in their areas of strength. It is vitally important that teachers recognise each student's strength and intentionally create learning episodes within which students can identify and revel in their respective gifts.

For example, it is a school wide expectation that a student on tier 3 support with an individual curriculum plan be given the opportunity as part of that plan to develop their particular interests and talents. A student who is more than 2 years behind in official literacy and numeracy benchmarks would still be given the chance to learn robotics, computer coding, digital design or other pursuits that are frequently reserved for the "gifted and talented". Moreover, these subjects are delivered with rigour and are not simply treated as a "reward time" when students complete their literacy and numeracy tasks. All skills and knowledges are valued to promote student self-efficacy and life-long learning.

Body

To promote physical fitness and health, Rossville's Learning and Wellbeing Framework was developed as part of the Tier 1 Systems and include school wide routines to encourage healthy living.

Conductive hearing loss is a medical condition commonly suffered by children throughout Cape York, and is more prominent in Indigenous children. It usually involves a reduction in sound level or the ability to hear faint sounds. This has particular implications for young children's oral language and literacy. Children find it difficult to develop phonological or phonemic awareness which makes learning to read more challenging.

Because the condition isn't painful, it can be difficult for children to identify whether they are suffering from an episode of hearing loss so the school partners with outside agencies to regularly screen students and provide advice to teachers regarding universal and targeted supports to ensure every student can access quality teaching of the curriculum.

Students are encouraged to find a physical activity or sport that they enjoy and can excel at with an emphasis put on setting goals to extend one's personal best. Cooperative skills are promoted through team sports and participation in district regional sporting competitions and camps gives students the chance to extend their athletic skills and talents. Year 6 students with sporting interests and abilities are also often encouraged to apply for sporting scholarships to high schools. Over the past 2 years, a number of graduating students have secured scholarships or positions in elite sporting programs.

Spirit

Student engagement is paramount to success in school and later in life. Attendance and disciplinary incident data provided feedback that made student engagement a priority focus in 2014. Behaviour incidents started to increase in frequency and intensity and it became clear that the whole school behaviour system in place wasn't meeting the needs of all of our students.

Referrals were made to outside government and community agencies to assist with wraparound family support. An experienced social worker and psychologists were engaged to assist with developing new strategies to support high needs students suffering from trauma, grief and loss, features that are common and persistent for colonised peoples worldwide.

Cultural engagement was also identified as a priority. A Cultural Connections intervention was designed with local elders and an Indigenous teacher aide. As part of this strategy, Rossville hosted its inaugural National Aboriginal Day of Celebration in partnership with local Aboriginal community members.

Throughout these consultations, it became evident to the leadership and teaching team at Rossville State School that a significant shift was needed in theory and practice used to "manage behaviour", to use official nomenclature. In fact, the very notion of managing behaviour was deemed contrary to the moral purpose of the school as it did not seek to challenge, extend and support students to become self-regulated members of society able to make sensible decisions.

A deliberate whole school move from enforcing compliance to maintaining connection saw the teaching team explore a variety of research, theory and evidence in search of a better way. A professional learning community was set up around analysing a variety of disciplines including neuroscience and positive psychology.

As a result, BOOST!, a home grown positive education program, was designed specifically to equip the students at Rossville with socio-emotional skills to practice resilience, mindfulness, empathy and collaboration.

Additionally, the language and practice around redirecting and responding to "misbehaviour" has changed significantly as the focus has shifted from rewarding and punishing to promote compliant behaviour to challenging each child to set goals and seek out support when faced with a challenge moment. Students are equipped and encouraged to self-regulate and seek out support to help them make positive decisions. Better self-regulation, risk taking and decision making is carefully scaffolded for each individual child. Improvements are evident and often celebrated before new goals and higher expectations set and supported.

HIGHLY EFFECTIVE TEACHING AND LEARNING

To plan for intentional differentiation to meet the specific learning needs of students, professional development was delivered to teachers to enable them to share the results of formal diagnostic testing with their students in order to set learning goals to mutually "project manage" the students' pathway to continued and enhanced achievement based on the Australian Curriculum Achievement Standards.

School Resources were primarily directed towards accelerating the learning of the 43% of students identified (or marked) by the national testing regimen as requiring intervention and extension. All students who were 12 months or more behind these reading or numeracy benchmarks were complex case managed with individual learning plans developed. In addition, a comprehensive before school intervention program was developed to target very specific skills to accelerate these students so that they could access the curriculum and begin to achieve at or beyond their year level.

Base-line data informed individual learning plans for every prep (kindergarten) student. A highly differentiated prep program was implemented and reading achievement was monitored fortnightly to inform targeted planning. Oral language and phonological awareness intervention was delivered to specific students and reading extension delivered to others.

Students requiring extension and acceleration were identified along with long term strategies to promote profound and lasting improvement articulated in a Whole School Data & Advancement Plan to make it explicit when and how students would be supported and extended.

EXPLICIT TEACHING AND EXPERIENTIAL LEARNING: A CLASH OF PEDAGOGIES

Research indicates that direct instruction, teacher clarity, feedback and consistent classroom practices produce enhanced educational outcomes for students (Hattie, 2009). These practices are all features of a highly prescribed pedagogical practice identified as Explicit Teaching. The goal of Explicit Teaching is for students to acquire new skills by directing student attention toward specific learning in a highly structured environment. It is teaching that is focused on producing specific learning outcomes.

Content Strands are broken down into small parts and taught individually. This involves explanation, demonstration and practise. Students are provided with guidance and structured frameworks. Topics are taught in a (really, *one*) logical order and directed by the teacher (Archer & Hughes, 2011).

Another important characteristic of explicit teaching involves the teacher modelling skills and behaviours and modelling thinking. This involves the teacher thinking aloud when working through problems and demonstrating processes for students. Of course given the dominant whiteness of the teaching profession in Australia [as in many parts of the world] this "modelling of thinking" proceeds from a Western epistemological and ontological base. The attention of students is important and listening and observations are key to imitation and, consequently, "success".

The goal of experiential learning, however, is to help students personally construct meaning of important ideas and processes. Explicit Teaching sets the groundwork for teaching all new skills and concepts but experiential learning develops deep understanding, promotes problem solving and enhances creativity. It allows for, and in many ways is strengthened by, multiple ways of knowing. It creates a space for multilogicality (Austin, 2011; Kincheloe & Steinberg, 2008)

By the beginning of 2014, Rossville's existing pedagogical framework relied exclusively on explicit teaching as its signature pedagogy. In developing a more balanced and enhanced pedagogical plan, the teaching team sought out to define examples of best practice to encourage experiential learning where effective and appropriate. A key priority in 2014 was reading. In 2012 and 2013, the school worked hard to develop consistent practices for the explicit teaching of reading including structured guided reading scripts and daily consolidations. While data showed that reading scores were improving for the lowest performing students, it was evident that strategies needed to be enacted to extend high achieving students. Philosophy was introduced across the school as a component of the literacy program to promote discussion, analysis and reflection.

Play based learning is an important element of the early years program (at the very least) and all children should be involved in guided play to develop social skills, problem solving and creativity. The arts lend themselves to exploration and play based pedagogies. Over the past few years, the curriculum focus at the school was the introduction of the Australian Curriculum in English, Mathematics and Science. Additional pressure to achieve school and system wide set benchmarks in literacy and numeracy measured by the NAPLAN tests have further provoked a narrowing of the enacted curriculum. As a result, the arts had been relegated to the margins of the classroom.

The development of an enhanced curriculum framework provided the staff, students and community to reflect on the role of the arts in school, reprioritise its inclusion in the curriculum and consider best practice pedagogies. Resources were budgeted towards engaging a music teacher one day a week. All students in the school worked in small groups so that they could receive individual coaching with a focus on expression, composition and team work.

Further school-based research revealed that student voice and choice would engage more students and promote deep learning through specialised projects. From term 4, 2014, weekly Art and Innovation electives were introduced to provide students with an opportunity to go into detail in an arts specialty each term.

So far, clowning, fashion design, robotics, cooking, drama, dance, digital design, stop-go animation, painting, drawing, computer coding, typography and collage have been offered. Projects have culminated in end of term performances and permanent school signage and displays. Last year the fashion design students designed their own labels, catalogues and lines of jewellery that they displayed and sold at a local music festival.

Coaching

Educating students to have high, challenging, appropriate expectations is among the most powerful influences in enhancing student achievement (Hattie, 2009). The goal of coaching is to support the learner's ability to transfer their learning autonomously and effectively to new situations.

Rossville's enhanced pedagogical framework emphasised coaching as a powerful pedagogy. A suite of tools was developed to enable teachers to effectively conference with students to analyse their own reading, writing and maths data to identify areas for future development. Together, student and teacher set specific goals to project manage the way to achievement. Goals are shared with parents and homework is differentiated for each child so that they work towards their goal.

To embed coaching across the school, teachers participated in peer observations and reflection to enhance proficiency in executing all elements of the pedagogical framework. Then, they set a goal with the Principal and activate strategies to project manage the way forward. The Professional Learning Plan is then differentiated for each staff member so that everyone has access to professional development tailored towards their goals.

CONFIDENT, CONNECTED AND CREATIVE CITIZENS

By the end of 2015, Rossville State School could demonstrate that student engagement and achievement had dramatically shifted and that students were indeed beginning to realise their vision to empower and engage as confident, connected and creative citizens.

Confident

Students grow academic confidence when they acquire the skills they need to succeed. Targeted intervention had gone to making significant improvements in students who were already profoundly behind their State-mandated year level benchmarks. By the end of 2015, reported academic achievement had improved significantly. Report card data from semester 1, 2014 indicated that 23.1% of students were failing against the Australian Curriculum achievement standards. By the end of 2015, that number had been reduced by more than half to 9.3%. Students achieving 2 or more years below year level benchmarks dramatically reduced from 4.7% to 0.7%.

Achievement on the NAPLAN tests also showed remarkable improvements, particularly in the areas of reading and numeracy. All students achieved above the national minimum standard in all areas of the tests in 2015. 50% of year 3 students achieve in the upper 2 bands (top levels of achievement) in both reading and numeracy. Year 5 students improved on average at 150% of the national average.

By opening up the curriculum beyond official literacy and numeracy basics and exposing students to more variety as well as promoting artistic and, most importantly, cultural knowledge and participation, students actually demonstrated greater improvement in literacy and numeracy. Moreover, a more equitable delivery of the Australian curriculum was achieved to give students a world class 21st century education in one of the most remote locations in the state.

Connected

Initiatives such as Cultural Connections and National Aboriginal and Islander Day Organising Committee (NAIDOC) implemented resulted in a dramatic decrease in behaviour incidents and continuous improvement in attendance rates. Attendance rates in particular improved steadily with the school coming within half a percent of the state average attendance for the first time since attendance data have been recorded and analysed system wide. Of particular note, unexplained absences have fallen to zero as solid relationships built on trust have been established with every family in the school. This is particularly the case with Aboriginal and Torres Strait Islander students.

Creative

There has been an explosion of creativity at Rossville State School. Students are continuously working creatively in their arts electives evidenced by student showcases of the latest examples of their visual and performing arts weekly at parade (assembly) or shown off in the community. Much of the evidence of this aspect of the school program can be seen in the physical environs, with Indigenous motifs and stylistic touches prominently on display.

CONCLUSION

From the brief notes above regarding recent significant pedagogical and curricular development at Rossville State School, a number of potent strategies and tactics utilized in effecting a more culturally respectful and life world enhancing approach to the formal schooling aspect of the education of Aboriginal and Torres Strait Islander peoples specifically, but for all students more generally, might be identified. In summary, the remoteness of the school, frequently seen as perhaps carrying more problems than advantages, has in this case allowed the school and its community to develop a quite individual approach to the educational operations of the school. Being "off the beaten track" geographically as well as culturally, the school has been able to conceptualize and put into practice and approach to education that, whilst acknowledging the administrative necessity to work within the NAPLAN framework and to use reporting language attendant upon this [statistics, mean, behind, average, etc.] is also able to "fly under the radar" sufficiently to enable pedagogical innovation to gestate and develop relatively unhindered by external administrative visits, etc.

The physical remoteness has also tended to support something of a more enclosed epistemological and pedagogical hybridization, with "traditional" and colonizer cultures being intertwined as much as possible in the formal school curriculum. For Indigenous students at the school, the everyday visibility, acceptance, and celebration of their home cultures, including teaching of aspects of these cultures to all students [Indigenous and non-Indigenous] through language programs, the creative/arts emphasis, performance work, and aspects of science and history, marks one fairly significant step towards a reconciliation of a bifurcated life world—Home culture and Western culture. Such a recognition of the utter complexity of being "multi-cultural" is a major contribution towards cultural, emotional, and physical well-being for individuals and communities. There is no doubt that the elders of the local Indigenous communities connected to the school see their children developing competencies in formal Western schooling competencies as essential. But they are equally as determined to ensure that "home" cultural learning also is accorded value, time, and attention in the school curriculum. It is in this area that, in many ways, pedagogical developments of Rossville State School seem to be, at least in the short term, working to narrow the space between remoteness from dominant culture and the immediacy of Home cultures. From this perspective, *Closing the Gap* assumes a far more palatable and transformational meaning. The educators working in this school appeared to be assuming positions close to what Kincheloe and Steinberg (2008, p. 139) described as critical multi-logical educators: *critical multilogical teachers begin to look at lessons from the perspectives of individuals from different race, class, gender, and sexual orientations ... they are dedicated to the search for new perspectives.*

To sum up, instances such as Rossville State School and its community provide encouraging signs of the ongoing incubation of possibilities for and the evolution of critical pedagogies and education in remote regions, where an essential concern is to ensure the place of the local [culturally and geographically] in the face of continuing engulfment by the systemic.

REFERENCES

ACARA. (2013). *NAPLAN: National Assessment Program—Literacy And Numeracy.* Retrieved from http://www.nap.edu.au/naplan/naplan.html

ACARA. (2015). *National Assessment Program Literacy and Numeracy: Achievement in Reading, Persuasive Writing, Language Conventions and Numeracy National Report for 2015.* Sydney: Australian Curriculum, Assessment and Reporting Authority Retrieved from http://www.nap.edu.au/verve/_resources/2015_NAPLAN_national_report.pdf

Adjei, P. (2010). Resistance to Amputation: Discomforting truth about colonial education in Ghana. In G. J. S. Dei & M. Simmons (Eds.), *Fanan & Education: Thinking through pedagogical possibilities* (pp. 78–104). New York, NY: Peter Lang.

Andrade, O. d. (1990 [1928]). *A Utopia Antropofagica.* Sao Paulo: Globo.

Apple, M. W. (1993). *Official knowledge: democratic education in a conservative age.* New York, NY: Routledge.

Archer, A. L., & Hughes, C. A. (2011). Exploring the foundations of explicit instruction. In K. R. Harris & S. Graham (Eds.), *Explicit instruction: Effective and efficient teaching* (pp. 1–21). New York: The Guilford Press.

Austin, J. (2011). Decentering the WWW (White Western Ways): enacting a pedagogy of multilogicality. In R. Brock, C. S. Malott, & L. E. Villaverde (Eds.), *Teaching Joe Kincheloe* (pp. 167–184). New York, NY: Peter Lang.

AustralianGovernment. (2015). *Closing the Gap—The Prime Minister's Report 2015*. Commonwealth of Australia Retrieved from http://www.dpmc.gov.au/pmc-indigenous-affairs/publication/closing-gap-prime-ministers-report-2015

Bourdieu, P. (1986). The Forms of Capital. In J. G. Richardson (Ed.), *Handbook of theory and research for the sociology of education* (pp. 241–258). New York, NY: Greenwood Press.

COAG. (2012). *Closing the Gap in Indigenous Disadvantage*. Retrieved from https://www.coag.gov.au/closing_the_gap_in_indigenous_disadvantage

Connell, R. (2007). *Southern Theory: The global dynamics of knowledge in social science*. Crows Nest NSW: Allen & Unwin.

Du Bois, W. E. B. (1903). *The Souls of Black Folks: Essays and sketches*. Chicago: A. C. McClurg.

Fanon, F. (1967). *Black Skin, White Masks*. New York, NY: Grove Weidenfeld.

Greer, T. (2007). *Accomplishing identity in bilingual interaction: codeswitching practices among a group of multiethnic Japanese teenagers*. (Ed D), University of Southern Queensland. Retrieved from http://eprints.usq.edu.au/3592/

Guy, J. (2015). *Round pegs in square holes: an ethnographic study of the educational lifeworlds of Aboriginal Australian students*. (Ph D), University of Southern Queensland, Toowoomba.

Hattie, J (2009). *Visible Learning: A synthesis of over 800 meta-analyses in education*. Routledge: Oxford, England.

Kincheloe, J., & Steinberg, S. (2008). Indigenous Knowledges in Education: Complexities, dangers, and profound benefits. In N. K. Denzin, Y. S. Lincoln, & L. T. Smith (Eds.), *Handbook of critical and indigenous methodologies* (pp. 135–156). Los Angeles, CA: Sage.

Memmi, A. (1967). *The colonizer and the colonized* (expanded edition/ed.). Boston, MA: Beacon Press.

Nakata, M. (2002). Indigenous knowledge and the cultural interface: Underlying issues at the intersection of knowledge and information systems. *IFLA Journal, 28*(5/6), 281–291.

Nakata, M. (2007). *Disciplining the savages, savaging the disciplines*. Canberra: Aboriginal Studies Press.

Santos, B. d. S. (2016). *Epistemologies of the South: Justice against epistemicide*. New York, NY: Routledge.

Sharp, H. (2010). *Constructing history: selective representations of Indigenous Australians and British heritages in Queensland history curriculum*. (PhD unpublished), University of Southern Queensland.

CHAPTER TWENTY

Teaching IN THE Country

A Critical Analysis of the Experiences of Rural Teachers in the United States and Jamaica

ELEANOR J. BLAIR

Teaching in a rural community brings about challenges in many ways. Many of my students live in poverty. Their parents are not involved in participating in school events or having visitors in their homes. Most of my students have never left the county. The biggest thing that ever happens for them is a trip to Wal-Mart. Therefore, in implementing technology in my classroom, I am able to take them on global "trips" to see and learn more about life outside of our rural area. It's truly rewarding!

—RURAL TEACHER, UNITED STATES (2016, INTERVIEW)

Being a teacher in (rural) Jamaica is an awesome task. The classroom sizes are large, integration of students with special education issues without assistance from government agencies is the norm. Parents and students are disrespectful. However, some parents and students place trust in teachers and work with you to help students achieve required skills.

—RURAL TEACHER, JAMAICA (2015, INTERVIEW)

INTRODUCTION

Rural education and the experiences of rural teachers are important dimensions of the educational history of both the United States and Jamaica; both countries regularly acknowledge the contrasts between urban and rural education, but most research focuses on demographics and statistics related to levels of achievement, per pupil expenditures and school completion rates. Few studies look at the experiences of rural teachers and even fewer focus on the cross-cultural similarities among teachers working in rural schools. A review of articles and journals revealed a database "heavy" on rural education essays from the first half of the twentieth century, but very little work done in the past fifty years; "well over one hundred years ago, school reformers in the United States began to talk about what came to be known as the 'rural school problem'" (Kannapel and DeYoung, 1999; Tyack, 1972; cited in Schafft & Jackson, 2010, p. 1). And so, the "rural school problem" was popular fodder for scholarly essays at a time when significant numbers of students lived in rural communities. Time passed and as population centers were established in large urban and suburban communities, rural education became associated with a quaint aspect of "earlier times," and not surprisingly, rural schools were further isolated as an educational relic represented by pictures of the "little red schoolhouse" where both teaching and learning methods were defined as "not progressive" and more likely, backward and representative of how it "used to be." Research agendas focused on rural schools emphasized a lack of efficiency and progressivism in an age of modernity. Elwood Cubberley (1914, 1922) referred to rural schools as standing still and lacking the forward motion of urban schools that were exploding with growth reflecting the changing demographics and goals of twentieth century education. Challenges to these notions are hard to find. In the book, *Rural education for the twenty-first century: Identity, place, and community in a globalizing world*, edited by Kai A. Schafft and Jackson (2010), an absence of contemporary research that considers the relationship of identity, place and community in rural communities is noted. While urban education if frequently mediated by ideological shifts that challenge the goals and purposes of schooling as a product of identity, place and community, twenty-first century rural education has not proven worthy of the same kinds of challenges to the status quo that would have produced critical scrutiny and an in-depth analysis of the unique qualities that define the rural experience. As such, explorations of the lives of rural teachers, are equally hard to find; rural schools are different, but questions about the people who teach in these schools and discussions of their experiences are ignored. Most discussions of the profession focus on generic descriptions of teachers' work that ignore the qualities of rural schools that make teachers' lives and experiences different from their urban counterparts. Even the training of teachers for rural schools disregards the qualities of rural education that demand a critical ideology that challenges the unequal distribution of resources and paucity of teachers qualified to teach higher level classes in science and math. Fred Yeo (2001) found that,

> the specialized knowledge taught in most of teacher education is geared toward the urban and devaluing of the rural. This is often the case even in colleges of education located in predominantly rural areas. All too often, teacher education sustains understandings of perceived inadequacies of rural schools by failing to note either the difference in community-oriented cultural values or the problematic of impoverished resources resulting from discriminatory state funding allocations which give rise to differential educational measurements. (p. 518)

Twenty-first century schools have historically focused upon measures of success that are objective, efficient and promote consolidation of resources; bigger may not be better, but small is equated with higher costs and unwieldy bureaucratic structures that would be more appropriate for the management of small industrial complexes, not small schools in isolated, sparsely populated communities.

First, however, I have to consider how rural education became a part of my life. I am a "city girl;" I grew up in Memphis, Tennessee, I knew nothing about rural life or living in the country during the first half of my life. The streets were my playground and working-class neighborhoods of small houses built on top of each other were the norm. I never hung out in the woods and the wildest animals I knew anything about were the domestic pets in my home; dogs and cats. Our schools were behemoth concrete jungles built in the late 1940s to serve the needs of burgeoning populations of children. We had trees, but no gardens. I didn't know what a trailer looked like; poor people lived in projects. And parks were the only places where you went to find nature. My grandparents did occasionally take me to a lake in rural Arkansas to fish, but I didn't know how to swim; all of the pools in Memphis were closed because of the threat that desegregation might ultimately mean that Blacks and Whites would swim in the same water. All I knew about rural life was related to stereotypes that I encountered in popular media representations on television; *The Beverly Hillbillies, Green Acres* and *Petticoat* Junction were my guides to rural life. I was left to assume that people who live in the country, talk and act "funny" and that while they may be smart, it wasn't "book smart," it was "street smart;" they knew how to survive on the land and in the woods. So, life took an interesting turn and twenty-three years ago I moved to a small town in western North Carolina. I took a job at a university in a rural Appalachian community in the mountains which included in my responsibilities the opportunity to regularly teach in various communities across the island of Jamaica. Previously, I had only worked in urban communities and now I was training teachers to work in rural schools. Initially, I thought that the differences were negligible, teaching is teaching, but I was very wrong. As I visited rural schools and encountered the myriad accents and the poorly resourced classrooms, I knew that I needed to be preparing teachers to adapt. Students challenged the urban educational literature that I used, and while there were similarities between poor city kids and poor country kids, there were also profound differences. Overnight, I was reminded that we must always be teachers AND learners; I had a lot to learn about teaching in the country, and thus, began a journey that has lasted twenty-three years.

My work as a teacher educator was enriched by my work in the rural communities of western North Carolina, but also by the time I have spent visiting and working in Jamaica. My work in Jamaica each year can be brief, 2–3 weeks per course, but in some years I have spent the equivalent of 3–4 months on the island teaching multiple courses in different locales. Working with teachers in both North Carolina and Jamaica transformed the ways that I thought about teaching and learning. The rural communities in both countries are quite different, and yet, there are unexpected similarities. Teachers in both North Carolina and Jamaica experience the impact of negative stereotypes, lack of resources, isolation and exclusion, in addition to challenges associated with recruiting and retaining highly qualified teachers who view rural schools as undesirable. This chapter will critically examine issues associated with rural education generally, but more specifically discuss the experiences of teachers in the rural communities of North Carolina and Jamaica.

A PLACE CALLED RURAL

While much of my work in the social foundations of education had focused on the issues that affect teachers working in urban environments, I quickly discovered that there was a richness and complexity to rural life that intersected with the urban experience, but yet, was completely different; a different place. Theobald and Nachtigal (1995) suggest that "the work of the rural school is no longer to emulate the urban or suburban school, but to attend to its own place" (p. 132). My introduction to rural life was not an easy transition; I was forced to re-evaluate all of the stereotypes I had about life in rural communities. I quickly came to realize that the issues I was confronting in the rural communities I visited everyday were complicated due to the fact that not only did geography define the rural experience, but more importantly, there was a significant role played in how local culture, history, values and beliefs intersected with the public school experience.

My earlier training in qualitative research methods focused on emic and etic perspectives, and in this environment, I became keenly aware of the chasm between insider and outsider views of life in the country. In the rural communities where I have worked, there was an acknowledgement of the difficulties attached to rural life, but simultaneously, there was an honoring of the family/community traditions, history, values and beliefs that have defined their lives. Most parents had attended, and played sports, in the same schools their children now attended. There was a continuity to this experience, and despite challenges to the adequacy of the schools, parents often don't want anything to change. From a distance, from the outside, I am also able to see how the negative stereotypes as well as the isolation and exclusion that were associated with notions of rurality had impacted education and the lives of teachers in rural schools in unique ways. Rural sociologists, Schwarzeller and Brown (1962) claim that in Appalachia, "the school is the primary or only cultural bridge between regional subcultures and the national culture" (cited in DeYoung, 1995, p. 174). As such, the school assumes an even more important role in the lives of rural communities, a role with added dimensions not evident in urban schools and one with unexplored purposes and goals. A critical analysis of the role a "cultural bridge" plays for teachers in rural schools is worthy of consideration.

Definitions of rural are confusing at best. Researcher Mike Arnold with the Mid-Continent Regional Educational Laboratory observed the following:

> We do need a better definition of "rural" and the different kinds of "rural." There is "poor rural" and "wealthy rural." There's "rural" with no minorities, and "rural" with high minorities. There's "rural" with high limited English proficiency. ... [and] big rural communities versus small rural communities. In some parts of the country a community of 20,000 might be considered rural while, in most of the Great Plains, that would be a major community" (The National Center for Education Statistics, 2013, n.p.).

In the same report, it was documented that in the school year 2010–2011, over half of all operating regular school districts and about one-third of all public schools were in rural areas, while about one-quarter of all public school students were enrolled in rural schools (The National Center for Education Statistics, 2013, n.p.). On January 5, 2016, *The Atlantic*, ran an essay by Rachel Martin entitled, "Salvaging Education in Rural America." Rachel Martin (2016) described the following situation in rural America:

> When teachers, theorists, and pundits analyze America's educational system, they usually focus on urban centers, but rural school systems make up more than half of the nation's operating school districts, according to the National Center for Education Statistics. Like many of their urban peers, children there fight to overcome scant funding, generational poverty, rampant malnutrition, and limited job prospects. (n.p.)

When discussing rural education with teachers in both Jamaica and the United States, two ideas regularly emerge: the notion of challenges and the idea that there are both good and bad things associated with rural education; comparisons with urban counterparts are frequently noted. A 1994 report by the U.S. Department of Education is still valid over twenty years later, rural schools and rural school districts are different from than urban schools in many important ways:

- Rural school and rural school districts usually enroll small number of pupils (i.e., fewer than 1,000 pupils per school district).
- Rural school districts commonly are experiencing significant enrollment decline.
- Rural residents report incomes significantly less than their urban and suburban peers.
- Rural school districts usually employ school buildings that house smaller numbers of pupils.
- Rural school districts typically are sparsely populated.

- Due primarily to small numbers of pupils generally located large geographic areas, per-pupil transportation costs for total schools inordinately high.
- Due to the absence of significant trading centers, rural school districts often are nearly exclusively dependent on real property taxations for their local revenue. (Stern, 1994, p. 48)

Not surprisingly, teachers in both the United States and Jamaica, discuss the challenges associated with being rural; exclusion and isolation as well as a lack of resources both in the school and the community are frequently mentioned. And yet, at the same time, teachers talk about the rewards of providing important services as a role model, mentor and teacher to students and communities where they are needed. This sense of "doing good," however, is mediated by the difficulties associated with working in schools where the work can be hard and the resources limited. However, recent statistics do demonstrate that that the "bad" associated with rural education is often balanced by many qualities that reinforce a sense of difference that is at times neutral and at other times, quite good:

- In rural areas, 71% of public school students were White, 10% were Black, 13% were Hispanic, 2% were Asian/Pacific Islander, 2% were American Indian/Alaska Native, and 2% were of two or more races.
- However, a larger percentage of rural children lived in poverty than suburban children (19 vs. 15%). There were regional differences in the percentages of rural children living in poverty in 2010. The percentage of rural children living in poverty was highest in the South, at 22%, followed by the West (20%), Midwest (15%), and Northeast (12%).
- On average, public school students in rural areas perform better on the National Assessment of Educational Progress (NAEP) than their peers in cities and towns but generally not as well as their peers in suburban areas.
- Students in rural districts experienced higher graduation rates than their peers in districts in cities and towns. Nationally, during the 2008–2009 school year (the latest year for which these data are available), the averaged freshman graduation rate (AFGR) for the 47 states that reported data (California, Nevada, and Vermont did not) and the District of Columbia was 77% (see the National Center for Educational Statistics (NCES) Rural Education in America website). The rate was higher in rural areas (80%) than across the 47 reporting states and the District of Columbia. The rate was also higher in rural areas than in cities (68%) and towns (79%) but was lower than the rate in suburban areas (81%). (National Center on Education Statistics, 2013, n.p.)

Stern (1994) also noted that "another problem concerns stereotypical images of rural life that inhibit understanding the wide diversity that exists not only across regions of the country but even within states" (p. 48).

As noted earlier, stereotypical images of rural life in popular culture representations are often the only knowledge that "outsiders" have of what it means to be rural. Recently, I looked at popular culture images of life in the southern United States, a large geographic area frequently referred to as rural despite many large urban areas. These popular culture characterizations, included images from shows like *The Beverly Hillbillies, Green Acres* and *Petticoat Junction*, as well as more contemporary images from *Honey Boo Boo, Duck Dynasty*, and *Moonshiners*. While many may view the images in these programs as benign and harmless, they regularly presented rural communities as places where language, values and beliefs are contrary to a more strictly regulated norm, and most importantly, a place where intelligence can be defined as a special kind of knowledge and truth that emerges from life experiences, not education. "Outsiders" frequently refer to individuals who live in rural communities as hicks, white trash, yokels and hillbillies; terms that are most often used generically without any understanding of how rural residents might define or understand the use of this language. In this previous work, I observed the following about "hickality" television:

> Television programming in the 21st century provides an entirely different twist on Southern life as a focus of entertainment. Tired of fictional accounts of life in the South, these reality shows are being characterized as "hickality" television programming (Bass, 2013). And yet, unsurprisingly, the themes are similar to those from Hooterville: It's ok to be ignorant, and often obnoxious, but there is a native intelligence among those from the rural South that endows them with an air of superiority despite their marginalized and often disenfranchised status in the rest of the world. From *Honey Boo Boo* to *Moonshiners* to *Duck Dynasty*, although the themes of these shows are different and their stories distinctive, the message is still the same: The South is a place where academic knowledge is viewed with disdain, and it is really cool if one is smart about the workings of the real world, and proficient in turning this "special knowledge" into profit. (Bass, 2013, n.p.; cited in Blair, 2014, pp. 138–139)

Interestingly, images of rural life in contemporary popular culture television programs continue to proliferate with new renderings of familiar themes.

> In dozens of shows—ranging from *Hillbilly Handfishing* and *Swamp People* to *Bayou Billionaires, Rocket City Rednecks* and *American Hoggers*—sons (and daughters) of the South make moonshine, chase wild hogs, stuff dead pets, carve duck calls, wrestle alligators, catch catfish with their bare hands, mess around in swamps and generally hoot and holler. While these shows often play it for laughs by highlighting the antics of their rural stars, TV executives say the shows also appeal to viewers who want to see regular folks on television. (Catlin, 2012, n.p.)

Catlin's (2012) definitions of "regular folks" is open to debate; however, he provides assurances from Marjorie Kaplan, president and general manager of Animal Planet, home to the popular *Hillbilly Handfishing*:

These shows are not painting people in a derogatory way, because they're affectionate. I think some people see themselves in the show, but for others it's reflective of an iconic way of life. The shows are popular because of the desire to connect back to something that's a little more raw and a little bit more real. … and hillbillies are the epitome of that—no artifice, living in the moment, the real deal" (n.p.).

I am not sure when rural life became synonymous with hillbillies and hicks or when assumptions were made that ruralites live in the moment, but somehow I don't find these images affectionate portrayals of rural life. These popular culture images are a part of a rural identity. While some may find them liberating, others might find them limiting. When discussing the experiences of teachers in rural communities, stereotypical images that define education and schooling in ways that limit rather expand global connections, reality often becomes destiny. Too much critique breeds contempt from those who find these images "affectionate," however, the images are disturbing. The formation of a rural identity involves constructions that affirm values and beliefs and reify a history, politics and culture that perpetuate a way of life that is not often subject to the scrutiny it deserves.

TEACHING IN THE COUNTRY: THE UNITED STATES

Teaching is not what I expected. When I grew up in rural West Virginia and went to school. I remember what teachers did and I remember the role that they played. There was pride in teaching. High School teachers were looked at as leaders in the community and people that you looked up to. Those days are gone. People feel and I didn't realize this until I was teaching, it's kind of degrading to say, "I'm a high school teacher." You have to say it under your breath. I used to think people had a lot of respect for high school teachers, but I feel that they don't anymore. It's just a guy who wants to teach school is just the attitude I get now. That's kind of an embarrassment to me because I do enjoy it.

—High School Teacher, United States (Interview)

Teachers in both urban and rural communities suffer from the various problems that afflict the profession; lack of status, low pay, limited autonomy. Alexandra Ossola (2014) found that rural schools face very different problems from urban schools,

In the 2010–2011 school year, rural students made up about a quarter of all students enrolled in public schools in the United States. These rural districts tend to be less wealthy than urban or suburban ones, so facilities and infrastructure are limited. Transportation costs are higher because students live farther away. Fewer students are enrolled in each school, which means that, when administrators apply for federal grants to pay for technology and special education classes, they don't have enough clout to make a difference. While the educators don't necessarily strive to send every kid to college, they are working hard to give students a sufficient understanding of STEM topics as a baseline for future work and education. (Ossola, 2014, n.p.)

Complicating these issues are the difficulties associated with recruitment, retention and staffing. Finding teachers willing to locate to rural, isolated communities is difficult; principals will often resort to creative ways to find teachers licensed and willing to work in rural schools The public recognizes the important role played by teachers in American education; however, there is a lack of support for widespread reform that would impact teachers in both urban and rural communities. While the privatization of schools and school choice have impacted the structure and delivery of education in urban communities in myriad ways that are not all good, rural schools have been impervious to change. Small school size and limited resources seem to have led to schools that seem "frozen in time." Recent research on teaching in rural schools reveals the following facts:

> As of 2008, the National Center for Education Statistics reported an estimated 7,757 rural school districts across the country, with about 11.3 million students enrolled in primary or secondary rural schools. The NCES offers a table of the percentages of public primary and secondary schools with teaching vacancies in different subjects. The table shows high percentages of job vacancies in rural schools in subjects ranging from special education to vocational education. Furthermore, after the No Child Left Behind Act of 2001, schools were met with new requirements and standards to increase the quality of education. The act required states to, among other educational reforms, guarantee that every teacher is qualified in their subject area. All core classes (science, history, math, English, etc.) are required to be taught by qualified teachers. Qualifications entail the necessary degrees and certifications for teachers mandated by the Department of Education, and for rural schools, this demand proves difficult. The act set deadlines for schools to institute a plan that ensures their teachers are "highly qualified." The jobs are there: rural schools need teachers, and if you're looking to make a tangible difference and have a lasting impact on students' lives, you should consider teaching at a rural school. It's true, the average salary of teachers in rural schools is less than in other areas, with base salaries ranging from $44,000 for teachers with a bachelor's degree, to $51,600 with a doctorate. But then again, the cost of living in these areas is also lower. Teaching in a rural area may also pose other difficulties for teachers. Rural schools face challenges in attracting and retaining teachers and administrators, limited financial resources and issues with long-distance transportation. (Teach Make a Difference, n.d., n.p.)

In contrast to their urban counterparts, however, the news for rural teachers is not all bad. A March, 2015, report entitled, *The Supply and Demand for Rural Teachers*, Daniel Player found that,

> rural teachers report participating in slightly fewer professional development opportunities, although this is not clear whether it is because such opportunities are not available or not of interest. However, rural teachers report more control over the teaching that occurs in their classrooms and somewhat greater influence in school policy than urban teachers. Overall, rural teachers appear to be among the most satisfied with their jobs, but report lower satisfaction with their salaries. (p. 23)

Teaching in the country is different, and as noted earlier, the best descriptions of the experience discuss challenges occurring within a context of both strengths and weaknesses. Important to this discussion, however, is a consideration of how to best understand this experience from a critical perspective. For American teachers, the issues of teaching in the country are wrapped up in the complex mythology and stereotypes that shape conceptions of a rural identity. Yes, poverty, isolation and exclusion contribute to this identity, but it is important for teachers to challenge themselves and their students to consider the impact of these factors on their ability to gain access to the same kinds of educational experiences of teachers and learners in more urban, adequately resourced, main-stream environments. Access and choice become key pieces of this critical analysis of schools. Paulo Freire (1993) argued that "projecting an absolute ignorance onto others, a characteristic of the ideology of oppression, negates education and knowledge as processes of inquiry" (p. 72). Encouraging a critical consciousness of rural education would initiate an in-depth examination of both the social and political contradiction inherent in rural versus urban schools.

TEACHING IN THE COUNTRY: JAMAICA

I would want others to know that despite the lack of resources, bad working conditions, being underpaid and neglected by the government we are still making a difference and doing the best with what we have because we love our jobs.

—RURAL TEACHER, JAMAICA (2015, INTERVIEW)

While the official motto of Jamaica is, "Out of Many People, One People," this motto while reflecting admirable goals needed to maintain peace and stability among a diverse population, it obscures the vast differences in ethnicity that exist in Jamaica. Jamaicans include people of African, European, Arabic (Lebanese descendants known as "Syrians"), Chinese, and East Indian descent. Equally important is the other motto frequently associated with Jamaicans, "No problem, Mon." Phrases like this and "No pressure, no problem" reflect the carefree, happy-go-lucky spirit of the Jamaican people, but once again ignores the dire circumstances that define the lives of many people living in poverty, both rural and urban communities. "It is significant that for most Jamaicans there is a distinction between 'town' and 'country'. Country people are thought to be good and town people are thought to be bad" (Folk, 2001, n.p.). Stephanie Folk (2001) described Jamaican rural life in the following,

The housing in rural areas is not much better than that found in the slum towns of the city. The advantage to living in the country is that you are living close to nature and housing conditions do not really make a difference. Many of the houses found in rural Jamaica are known as "wattle and daub" dwellings. They are houses built with sticks, covered with wattle,

> plastered with clay and a little cement, and then whitened with lime. Thatch palms typically cover the roof. Only one fourth of these houses has electricity or running water. (n.p.)

Similar to the United States, in Jamaica, teachers in rural schools face problems that are complex, multi-dimensional and not easily solved; poverty is only one of the more obvious issues afflicting educational opportunities. Recent findings from the National Education Inspectorate (NEI) (2015) indicated that

> schools located in the urban areas of Jamaica are far ahead of their rural counterparts in key areas which were used to assess schools. These areas included leadership and management, teaching and support for students' learning, students' progress in English and mathematics, students' personal and social development, use of human and material resources, curriculum and enhancement programmes and safety, security, health and wellbeing. (n.p.)

In many rural schools, teachers teach in multi-grade classrooms where one teacher serves the needs of students at several different grade levels,

> multi-grade schools exist in many countries and play an important role in providing access to education for children in isolated and underdeveloped rural areas. ... The typically low student population at some of these rural schools contributes to their multi-grade status, as the Ministry of Education, more often than not, discourages the employment of new teachers, since teachers are engaged based on the size of the student population at a school. ("Three classes, one classroom, one teacher," 2011, n.p.)

However, in Jamaica, the multi grade classrooms are frequently over-crowded and combine students with varying degrees of learning and behavioral challenges with average students. This results in teachers who are frustrated and quickly burn-out; one Jamaican principal noted that,

> our problem is resources, the resources are limited, because we do not get anything extra from the ministry. (We get) the same as other schools, because you know that schools are paid per student in terms of grants. ... additional resources such as computers and special educators would help his school to enrich its offerings to the students. ... it takes special teachers to operate in multi-grade schools. It is at that level that the child is either made or broken. If the teacher does not understand how to operate in a multigrade setting, you are going to find that the teacher becomes frustrated and the students then become frustrated. ("Three Classes, One Classroom, One Teacher," 2011, n.p.)

Teaching in the country in Jamaica is further complicated by the high rates of absenteeism, illiteracy and lack of resources that are frequently documented (Cook & Ezenne, 2010; Illiteracy Rising in Rural Schools, 2010, n.p.). Marianne McIntosh Robinson associated with the TEACH Caribbean programme observed that

> Maths and English are foundation competencies which students need to move forward; however, many children continue to face serious challenges with the subjects. And our students, particularly in our rural institutions, do not always get the same attention as those in urban schools with similar challenges. ("Rhodes Scholars Focus on Rural Schools," 2015, n.p.)

And finally, just as teachers in rural communities in America struggle with issues related to non-standard dialects and accents, similar problems exist in Jamaica.

> Although, Standard Jamaican English (SJE) is the official language of Jamaica, many school children tend to speak Jamaican Creole, which is often the language of the home, playground, and churches. Jamaican Creole is derived from the languages of the colonizers and the colonized and is considered low in language status and prestige. Standard Jamaican English is closely associated with the upper- and middle-classes and has more prestige and status. This language structure is aligned with Standard British English and is often acquired through education. (Evans, 2001; cited in Williams and Staulters, 2010, pp. 98–99)

Additionally, while many rural schools struggle with recruitment and retention of teachers to fill their classrooms, the training of these rural teachers is often limited and inadequate. Williams and Staulters (2010) noted that just like the United States, Caribbean countries struggle to locate, train and retain talented teachers, and consequently, the relationship between teacher training and educational achievement becomes one of central importance (p. 99). Of additional concern to these researchers are the questions that arise from confronting the inadequacies associated with a majority of educators trained at the initial level of teacher preparation who lack the skills to meet the demands of educating the disenfranchised members of their communities. Williams and Staulters (2010) ask us to consider concerns regarding "what instructional strategies do teachers employ in raising the literacy rate of their Creole-speaking population?" (p. 99). Finally,

The findings of the NEI baseline report echoes research conducted by founder and director of the Institute for Educational Administration and Leadership-Jamaica (IEAL-J) and Reader in Education at Brunel University in the United Kingdom, Professor Paul Miller. Miller, in a research paper published in 2014, argued that schools located outside of the immediate reach of the central officers of the Ministry of Education, what he calls the centre, are generally under-resourced and do not have sufficient support for principals. ("Rural Schools Underperforming—NEI Report," 2015, n.p.)

These kinds of problems in country schools are frequently acknowledged in Jamaican newspapers with calls for school reform and improvement, and yet, change is slow to come and country schools due to small size and remote location are seldom a high priority.

CONCLUSION: RURAL TEACHERS, RURAL LEADERS

In summary, the problems that afflict rural teachers in BOTH Jamaica and the United States fall into the following six areas:

1. Teacher recruitment
2. Teacher retention
3. Teacher licensure in STEM subjects
4. Lack of access to technology
5. Negative stereotypes attached to language and culture
6. Lack of resources

Related to these problems are the issues of salary, status and autonomy that afflict the profession generally. However, these problems are also the foundation for problems unique to rural schools; student related problems of absenteeism, multi grade classrooms, and low rates of literacy and college attendance. There are no simple answers for complex problems; each of the aforementioned issues requires a thorough understanding of the problem before we seek to generate solutions. Obviously, resource allocation is not adequate, but the underlying reasons for the inequitable distribution of resources require critical analysis and an ideological shift that makes social justice a priority. The choices available to rural teachers and their students are limited by place and identity; their attempts to prepare for a global marketplace are restricted by the local marketplace. School reform in both Jamaica and the United States focuses on testing and accountability while attempts to scrutinize what actually happens in schools and classrooms are thwarted by adults more concerned with political agendas and bottom line economics than the efforts of teachers who devote their lives to doing the impossible: preparing students to function in a world very different from the one we currently live in.

My teacher education students in both Jamaica and western North Carolina are equally brilliant; I have spent twenty-three years learning about the culture, values and beliefs that inform and shape their lives. I have learned about their dreams and about their willingness to envision a future that is tenuous, at best, considering their limited resources. I have also learned about the courage required to "push" past the confines of racism, poverty and stereotypes that attempt to define one's intelligence by language and culture. I appreciate the closeness and inter-connectedness of their communities; the sense of community and strong identity. Stephanie Folk's description of rural schools is not an exception; I have visited too many schools in Jamaica with overcrowded classrooms and no running water; I have also come to appreciate the sense of exclusion and isolation that permeate the rural experience; and yet, simultaneously melds a community together in a mutual sense of strength and identity. While rural North Carolina schools may not face the same kinds of physical plant issues, the schools are often run-down and neglected. In far too many poor rural schools, I enter the school property and immediately feel as though I have arrived at a place that is simply forgotten; these schools are not a part of anyone's conversation about meaningful school reform. I still remember vividly a school that I visited in Westmoreland, Jamaica, where upon driving up to the school with colleagues, I heard the children yelling, "white people, white people" and running into the building to hide. I was never given a satisfactory explanation for the reaction of these students, but I was struck by the fact that these children were so isolated and their experiences in the world so limited that a vision of white people arriving at the school was accompanied by panic and fear. Who did they think we were? What were we going to do to them? I will never know the answers to these questions, but I know that these children were not being prepared to move beyond their colonial history and take their places in a global society where the intersection of poverty, racism and politics in the public educational arena must be critically analyzed; it is imperative that teachers find connections with an advocacy ideology that informs and leads this movement while simultaneously transforming the lives and work of rural teachers. The words of McLaren and Giroux (1990) still ring true today,

> Central to the conception of a critical pedagogy for rural schooling is the relationship between authority and the responsibility of leadership. We believe that teachers must wield authority in the interests of creating conditions for students and others to eventually exercise it with an equal sense of its importance as the basis for critical agency and dialogic learning. In this sense teachers must constantly reflect on the use of their own authority as part of a pedagogy of place. This means understanding the epistemological limits of their position so that they can be open to other arguments. It means understanding the limits of the forms of ethical address they use to construct particular narratives that frame relationships between self and others. It also means understanding how their own location within institutional structures positions them in the service of power. At the same time, teachers need to subvert power's most oppressive features. Hence, the notion of teachers as critical and public intellectuals is not a call to a limited notion of critical rationality, it is an epistemological, ethical, and experiential form of address that lends itself to creating social relations steeped in a sense of justice, compassion, radical empathy, and civic courage. (p. 163)

In earlier work, I argued that it was a sense of differentness that defined the rural southern experience. And indeed, a consideration of popular culture images of the South reinforced the notion that life in southern communities is rural and that it is defined by a language, culture and set of values that are different, even if those qualities are portrayed as both negative and positive; sometimes enviable and at other times despised. However noble the work of rural teachers may be, it is not easy work; teachers who persevere despite the frustrations find limited rewards and frequently negotiated outcomes; they are the heroes in this struggle for equity and opportunity for our most vulnerable students. The negative images of rural communities and their inhabitants do ultimately impact rural education and the lives of teachers in rural communities; the link between our laughter at parodies of rural life and the allocation of resources for rural schools is, unfortunately, too clear. Teachers are transformative leaders and change agents in their communities and rural schools are the keys to change; changing the content and context of teachers' work is the first step towards understanding the progress of change. McLaren and Giroux (1990) noted that with regard to rural schools and teachers, the following needs to occur:

> A critical pedagogy for rural schooling needs to be understood and practiced in a way that redefines how teachers view their role as cultural agents. Cultures occur to the extent that students and teachers live them. Consequently, it is as important to pay attention to the contradictions and disharmonies within cultures as it is to their appearances of uniformity and consensus. The cultural field of the school should not be viewed as a monadic site of harmony and control but rather as a site of disjuncture, rupture, and contradiction-a point which we tried to underscore in the story about our local high school. We want to argue that school culture is better understood as the loci of multivalent voices and powers as well as competing interests. Rural teachers need to disturb the popular assurance of received orthodoxies about the cultural fields that inform the classrooms where they teach. They must resist embracing monocultural views of democratic society that privilege the ideology of the dominant white culture. (p. 164)

The culture of rural communities and schools are defined by the values and beliefs that reflect the unique characteristics of the geography that shapes their different-ness. However, in and of itself, this differentness is not bad or less or negative in any way; rural diversity offers us a chance to critically examine the many ways that our perceptions of intelligence and ability are tempered by narrow conceptions of education and schooling. The challenge for teachers working in rural schools and communities is the preservation of rural values and identity while also embracing the types of reforms that will give students access to the knowledge and skills needed to navigate a rapidly expanding world where the exclusion and isolation of rural schools is unacceptable and demands for inclusion take priority in the public discourse regarding the future of 21st century schools; all schools, all students involved in meaningful and sustainable change.

In conclusion, DeYoung and Lawrence (1995) asked important questions in their essay entitled, *On Hoosiers, Yankees, and Mountaineers*,

> Throughout rural America for almost a century and in urban America for more than 30 years, we have been exhorted to achieve magical world-class standards in the compe-tition for global markets, as if succeeding in such an arena is an end in itself or can ever be completely accomplished. Meanwhile, some important questions have gotten lost. Is formal schooling only a matter of more and better instruction? Is the real purpose of the school to supply workers and consumers for a national economy, regardless of other human and social costs? Whom does the school serve, and whom might it serve if building com-munities rather than careers were to become the aim of education reform? And what price do we pay by educating students to flee the communities that nurtured them? We believe that these are worthy questions to ponder and to act upon. (p. 112)

These questions are appropriate for both Jamaican and American teachers. Ultimately, the answers will require rural teaching to be synonymous with rural leadership; leadership that is grounded in critical analysis and builds leadership capacity in the school and community. Central to these efforts will be a recognition of the close relationship between rural education and an understanding of rural as a place. Rural teachers acting as leaders in rural schools and communities must lead efforts to articulate a collective challenge to the benign neglect, isolation and exclusion that threaten the viability and integrity of rural education. The problems and issues that impede the progress of rural education were not born in rural communities, but rather they originated in public spaces where decisions are being made regarding both the training of teachers, the allocation of resources, and the goals and purposes of education in the absence of any serious regard for the differences between urban, suburban and rural schools. Rural schools suffer from invisibility; they are ignored because the public agenda focuses attention and resources on urban/suburban schools that have more visibility and capture the public imagination regarding "doable" school reform that produces quick, easily documented results for the largest number of students. In many instances, the impact of the neglect of rural schools has been so devastating that efforts to turn around these schools will require a long-term commitment to communities that have been excluded from having a voice in school reform efforts. These efforts accompanied by a renewed focus on the needs of rural teachers working in rural schools have the potential to change the landscape of rural education. In both Jamaica and the United States, sustainable school reform efforts require the skilled involvement of an educational leadership that includes both teachers and administrators. Rural issues and topics associated with educational administration and leadership must incorporate views that reflect local, national and/or international perspectives and contexts. This chapter attempts to accomplish these goals through the intersection of research, data and the documentation of the personal experiences and perspectives of rural teachers in two countries. This kind of knowledge should be integral to the work of educational leaders and policymakers in both countries. Rural communities represent a significant portion of the educational landscape, and as such, understanding the current realities of rural education is prerequisite to shaping future possibilities and potentialities.

REFERENCES

Bass, J. (2013, January 7). *Honey Boo Boo*, and the rise of "hick" culture on reality TV. *Policymic*. Retrieved from http://www.policymic.com/articles/22180/honey-boo-boo-and-the-rise-of-hick-culture-on-reality-tv/336076?vm=r

Blair, E. J. (2014). *Here Comes Honey Boo Boo, Moonshiners, and Duck Dynasty*: The intersection of popular culture and a Southern place. In W. M. Reynolds (Ed.), *Critical studies of southern place* (pp. 132–146). New York, NY: Peter Lang Publishers.

Catlin, R. (2012, June 7). Reality TVs Explosion of Southern Stereotypes. *The Washington Post.* Retrieved from https://www.washingtonpost.com/entertainment/tv/reality-tvs-explosion-of-southern-stereotypes/2012/06/06/gJQA3bXbLV_story.html

Cook, L. D., & Ezenne, A. (2010). Factors influencing students' absenteeism in primary schools in Jamaica: Perspectives of Community Members. *Caribbean Curriculum, 17,* 33–57.

Cubberley, E. (1914). *Rural life and education: A study of the rural school problem as a part of the rural life problem* (pp. 105–106). Boston, MA: Houghton Mifflin.

Cubberley, E. (1922). *A brief history of education; A history of the practice and progress and organization of education.* Boston, MA: Houghton Mifflin Company.

DeYoung, A. J. (1995, June). Constructing and staffing the cultural bridge: The school as change agent in rural Appalachia. *Anthropology & Education Quarterly, 26* (2), 168–192.

DeYoung, A. J., & Lawrence, B. K. (1995, October). On Hoosiers, Yankees, and Mountaineers, *The Phi Delta Kappan, 77* (2), 104–112.

Evans, H. (2001). *Inside Jamaican Schools.* Kingston, Jamaica: University of West Indies Press.

Folk, S. (2001). *Rural paradise or concrete jungle.* Retrieved from https://debate.uvm.edu/dreadlibrary/folk02.htm

Freire, P. (1993). *Pedagogy of the oppressed.* New York, NY: Continuum.

Illiteracy Rising in Rural Schools. (2010, March 24). *The Gleaner.* Retrieved from http://jamaica-gleaner.com/gleaner/20100324/lead/lead92.html

Kannapel, P. J., & DeYoung, A. J. (1999). The rural school problem in 1999: A review and critique of the literature. *Journal of Research in Rural Education, 15,* 67–79.

Martin, R. (2016, January 5). Salvaging education in Rural America. *The Atlantic.* Retrieved from http://www.theatlantic.com/education/archive/2016/01/americas-rural-schools/422586/

McLaren, P. L., & Giroux, H. A. (1990, Summer). Critical pedagogy and rural education: A challenge from Poland. *Peabody Journal of Education, 67* (4), A Look at Rural Education in the United States, 154–165.

The National Center on Education Statistics. (2013, May). *The status of rural education.* Retrieved from http://nces.ed.gov/programs/coe/indicator_tla.asp

Ossola, A. (2014). The challenge of teaching science in Rural America. *The Atlantic.* Retrieved from http://www.theatlantic.com/education/archive/2014/11/the-challenge-of-being-a-rural-science-teacher/382309/

Player, D. (2015, March). *The supply and demand for rural teachers.* Retrieved from http://www.roci-idaho.org/wp-content/uploads/2015/03/ROCI_2015_RuralTeachers_FINAL.pdf

Rhodes Scholars Focus on Rural Schools (2015, July 12). *The Jamaica Gleaner.* Retrieved from http://jamaica-gleaner.com/article/news/20150712/rhodes-scholars-focus-rural-schools

Rural Schools Underperforming—NEI Report. (2015, September 21). *The Jamaica Gleaner.* Retrieved from http://jamaica-gleaner.com/article/news/20150921/rural-schools-underperforming-nei-report

Schafft, K. A., & Jackson, A. Y. (2010). *Rural education for the twenty-first century: Identity, place, and community in a globalizing world.* University Park, PA: Penn State University Press.

Schwarzeller, H., & Brown, J. (1962). Education as a cultural bridge between eastern Kentucky and the great society. *Rural Sociology, 27,* 357–373.

Sherwood, T. (2001, March). *Where has all the 'rural' gone: Rural education research and current federal reform.* Retrieved from *http://www.ruraledu.org/user_uploads/file/Where_Has_All_the_Rural.pdf*

Stern, J. D. (1994). *The condition of education in rural schools* (Ed.). Washington, DC: U.S. Department of Education.

Teach Make a Difference. (n.d.). Retrieved from http://teach.com/where/types-of-schools/other-types-of-schools/rural-schools

Theobald, P., & Nachtigal, P. (1995, October). Culture, community, and the promise of rural education. *The Phi Delta Kappan, 77* (2), 132–135.

Three Classes, One Classroom, One Teacher. (2011, September 18). *The Jamaica Observer*. Retrieved from www.jamaicaobserver.com/news/Three-classes--one-classroom--one-teacher_9710663

Tyack, D. (1972). The "one best system": A historical analysis. In H. Walberg & A. Kopan (Eds.), *Rethinking Urban education* (pp. 231–246). San Francisco, CA: Jossey-Bass.

Warrican, S. J., Down, L., & Spencer-Ernandez, J. (2008). Exemplary teaching in the Caribbean: Experiences from early literacy classrooms. *Journal of Eastern Caribbean Studies, 33*, 1–30.

Williams, S. A. S., & Staulters, M. L. (2010). Literacy instruction in rural elementary schools in Jamaica: Response to professional development. *The Journal of Negro Education, 79* (2), 97–111.

Yeo, F. (2001). Thoughts on rural education: Reconstructing the invisible and the myths of country schooling. In S. Steinberg (Ed.), *Multi/Intercultural conversations: A reader* (pp. 511–526). New York, NY: Peter Lang Publishing.

CHAPTER TWENTY-ONE

Learning FROM THE Margins

A Case of Critical Community Pedagogy in Rural Thailand

MARK VICARS

INTRODUCTION

This chapter narrates teaching and learning interactions with culturally prescribed discourses of practice to situate English language learning and teaching in rural Thai school communities as a critical encounter. It draws upon data taken from two projects that sought to provide a pedagogic reframing of English language teaching in rural schools in Thailand. In both projects teacher educators and pre-service education students worked alongside Thai English language teachers in rural Thai schools recording in journals reflexive narratives that documented pedagogic practices and curriculum development. The chapter references the introduction of a Thai Core Curriculum and how the repositioning of English language pedagogy in rural Thai schools generated opportunities for a collaborative and reflexive re/thinking of teaching practice.

Situating the notion of encounter as a pedagogical process, this chapter draws on the development and delivery of a teaching and learning English project in rural primary schools in Thailand by Australian teacher educators in 2013 and pre-service education students in 2014. The rationale for the pre-service teaching placements, in which seventeen pre-service teachers undertook a practicum in rural primary schools located on the outer margins of Bangkok for three weeks, was drawn from an Australian Government funded project that partnered with a Thai University in 2012.

This partnership had sought to Strengthen the teaching of English language and literacy in Thai Schools and had been designed with the following objectives:

1. To provide Thai English language teachers with up-to-date knowledge of research in teaching and learning practices in EFL classrooms;
2. To develop Thai English language with teacher's knowledge of praxis enquiry in order for them to start to investigate their classroom practice and reflect on ways to: motivate students, to introduce new EFL methods, to increase learner to learner interaction, to design syllabus and effectively teach large mixed ability EFL classes;
3. To provide in-service training on English speaking and listening and writing skills;
4. To supplement localised EFL teaching methods by demonstrating how different models of language pedagogy can be used to scaffold communicative competence in English.

The team on the intial project had consisited of five Australian academics with experience in critical qualitative iquiry and English Language learning and six Thai academics who had expressed an interest in being part of the project, all of whom had expressed an interest in critical qualitative approaches to researching English language teaching and learning. Preceding the project, the Thai government had instigated the Basic Education Core Curriculum in 2008 that had the objective of refocusing the public education system towards the development of communicative curriculum. The introduction of standardized frameworks for the assessment of teaching and learning and the underlying rationale of many the revisions in the 2008 Core Curriculum was to refocus schools towards pedagogical change.

The "quality" metric, it was explained to us by our Thai academic partners, was being applied throughout the Thai public school sector specifically in the teaching and learning of English language, the focus of development on an inquiry based student-centered pedagogy, had the intention to transform existing teaching and learning practices and further ensure the development of new knowledge and skills required of Thai citizens in an increasingly globalized world. In the new curriculum, English language had been identified as being a compulsory foreign language subject starting from level 1 in primary education (6 years of age) and the teaching of English was increasingly being structured toward students improving their English language communication skills and developing understanding of the culture of native speakers.

The presence of of English as a lingua Franca in Thailand, was already shaping social and economic capital, with access to and competence in English a mitigating factor in employability and access to the tourist dollar. Spivak's (1990) notion of "worlding of the West as world" a process through which the interests of the West are naturalised and performatively inculcated as a process of cultural and linguistic production in developing countries supports Suksirpakonchai's (2015) observation of how the presence of English language in Thailand in rural areas had resulted in the impossibility for Thais to avoid having to adjust their attitudes towards the use of English as a necessity in their daily communication. Sa Nguan Ying (2004) had noted the proliferation of English Programs in Thai schools in which only English is used as a medium of instruction and the epistemic threat to local languages and cultural diversity had been noted by Suwilai (2016) by education policy that had shifted focus towards standardizing language instruction and language of instruction.

It goes without saying that for many children in rural Thai communities English might well be the third or fourth language to be learned and the requirement of learning and using English, it could be argued, might well further be a disconnect for children in rural communities already disadvantaged by poverty and/or other emblematic indicators. This disparity between language policy and language practice was central to how an understanding of how we were to work alongside our Thai colleagues in English language classrooms. A key question was: How would we be able to include and represent, in Thai classrooms, the diversity of cultural and linguistic positions in the teaching of English? As we grasped the positioning of English in rural communities and how it was becoming a vital skill for developing economic capital in areas of the country that experienced high levels of poverty, we also provided with explanations of how the official mandated language policy and schooling curriculum in Thailand was struggling with the Teaching of English as a foreign language. A starting point for finding ways to work with teachers was to develop texts and draw upon textual practices that represented local indigenous linguistic and cultural diversity.

Recognizing how for many of students in the school access to English language teaching may well be something that is only possible within the institutional walls of the classroom further alerted us to the linguistic gap that existed between the everyday life in rural community and the situated language learning in the classroom. As the introduction of the Core Curriculum in to Thai Public schools had stressed the development of communicative competence, a rethinking and a replacement of what could at best be characterized as a didactic and grammar translation orientated pedagogy was also in need of development, but one that recognized the importance of situating English connected to local context and usage. A further divergence between rural and urban schools was in terms of access to native speakers and language resources. As English language learners themselves, the Thai teachers expressed how they were already struggling to upgrade their own language skills and ability. A component of the education reform outlined in the 2008 Core Curriculum was teacher development with Thai teachers being offered continuous training every two years to develop professionally and learn new teaching methodologies. Identifying the opportunity to provide in-service to the Thai teachers, we started to develop workshops with the aim to create self-sustaining professional teaching and learning networks that would focus on the sharing and disseminating of best practices in EAL pedagogy.

ENCOUNTERS NOT INTERVENTIONS

Documenting my encounters with teachers and schools in my journal throughout the project, I was reminded of the visceral differences that are created by periphery/centre dialectic in Thailand. The chasm between rich and poor, urban and rural I had never found a comfortable space and living everyday amongst visible inequality had framed my prior knowledge of the country and its schooling system. This knowledge had been acquired from living and working in Bangkok for six years. In the late 90s, I had taught at a prestigious international school, one of the first to be granted a license to accept Thai students and the only school at that time permitted to do so in Bangkok. Prior to the change in policy only Thai students with a foreign passport could access international schooling. The relatively few number of established international schools were imposing a quota on the number of local Thai children they would accept, however, with the relaxation of and renegotiation of this policy the volume of schools offering English language as medium of instruction quickly proliferated. In Thailand, the increase in recent years, of an affluent middle class has spawned a growing number of fee paying private international schools delivering English language instruction; an international curriculum and native speaker teachers. Accessible at a price, the schooling system for the urban Thai elite was regarded as a pathway to participation in an increased globalized economy and Wiriyachitra (2016, p. 2) has noted how:

As of last year, there were 56 international schools around the country. There were three foreign colleges and universities in Thailand. In private Thai universities, there were 77 undergraduate, 30 graduate and five Ph.D curricula using English as the language of instruction. In governmental higher education institutions, there were 143 undergraduate, 205 graduate and 77 doctoral international programs in English which have been established either independently by Thai institutes or have links with overseas institutes. It is expected that most new programs to be opened in universities in the future will be international programs.

The economic changes sweeping the country in the late 90s and early 2000 policy led to the rise of the "Thai Tiger" amongst ASEAN nations and birthed an unprecedented demand for English language education. The high demand for private tutoring meant that I was oversubscribed for private English lessons and I tutored students in the evening and at weekends from what locally is termed as the "high society" families. These were Thais whose economic wealth provided an economic privilege well beyond the means of the average Thai and certainly beyond the means of rural Thais. My private life in contrast was spent "hanging out" with my Thai friends of my partner all of whom had grown-up in Esarn, an area geographically located in the central eastern region and known for high levels of poverty. These disparate worlds could never have been conjoined, each domain making the conditions in which the lives of each group irreconcilable.

Experiencing the gap between the "have" and "have not" had driven the conceptualization of the project. The ways in which classrooms in rural communities all too easily became spaces of marginalization that systemically inscribe and re/produce economic and social binaries was/is in large part to how English language had become an issue of access. The lack of access in rural areas language schools, native teachers and resources revealed the disparity between educational provision, income and geographical location. Building professional knowledge in the teaching and learning of English was therefore an organizing principal and a driver to the reframing of our pedagogic encounters in the schools in which we were to work.

Picture, if you will a classroom in which 30–40 students sit side by side on small wooden benches and desks facing front to a blackboard half hanging off the wall. There are no brightly covered displays covering the peeling plaster, no air conditioner whirring away in the corner of the room to mitigate against the incessant heats that enters through the windows cracked ajar to catch the upwind. The occasional breeze that does make it through half ajar window is accompanied by the sounds of labourers working in the rice paddies; Soi dogs can be heard barking as they chase passing motor cycle taxis and the aroma of freshly steamed noodles lingers in the air. The teacher stood at the front of her/his class glances at the heads bowed over the rows of desk monitoring the precise copying of grammar based sentences in to notebooks, oversees learning that graphically demonstrates the numerous hours spent learning English. The neatness of this learning belies the messiness involved in language learning and teaching. The wrestling with strange sounds demanded by the reconfiguration of tongue against teeth and lips shaped by the play of making words mean is strangely silent; the taking ownership of a language in the free play and practise of words breathed in to life is an absent presence within the classroom walls. The impeccable handwriting that fuels the learning amasses, pages in carefully kept notebooks: no ripped covers or torn pages in this class. Lines are copied and populated with well rehearsed functional phrases translated from English to Thai and Thai to English.

BEING CRITICAL

Underpinning our work in schools were the principles of critical and transformative pedagogy. Critical in the ways we sought to contest and problematizes understandings of the practice of the teaching and learning of English in rural Thai classrooms and transformative for instigating a generative motion for reflection, agency and action. Luke (2004, p. 26) has noted:

To be critical is to call up for scrutiny, whether through embodied action or discourse practice, the rules of exchange within a social field. To do so requires an analytic move to self-position oneself as Other even in a market or field that might not necessarily construe or structurally position one as Other ... This doubling and positioning of the self from dominant text and discourse can be cognate, analytic, expository, and hypothetical, and it can, indeed, be already lived, narrated, embodied, and experienced.

Turning to the journal recount of an initial visit to one of my schools: a rural school located two hours by road from Metropolitan Bangkok that served a dominantly fishing and farming community illustrated to me how the knowledge that derives from self as Other can become a tricky encounter. The aim of the visit was to work with the Thai English language teacher to support existing school curriculum and generate a contextual student-centred approach to communicative English language learning and teaching.

The timing of my visit to the school coincided when annual school reports were being written for submission to the Thai Ministry of Education. The principal was immersed in the collating of the school' submission and had arranged for me to be "looked after" by her staff. I waited in the staff room for four hours eventually visiting a classroom to observe a lesson. The teacher, who I had assumed was the English teacher did not speak English and the students were amusing themselves as best they could, gingerly fingering the standard BANA produced English text books with topics such as "Christmas Celebrations in Britain" and "A day shopping at a local London market". Looking around the room I was somewhat taken aback as the blackboard peppered with holes was precariously hanging off the wall, attached only by a couple of screws. The students were talking amongst themselves, looking out of the window and the teacher informed me he was the Physical Education teacher as the English teacher was assisting the School Principal in the collation of the submission of the annual report.

Returning to the school on the second day, I requested a meeting with the Principal to discuss my observations of the first day and sought assistance from my Thai academic partner to translate. I listened as the Principal explained that her role was to manage the school and the teaching was left to the expertise of her staff. I was also informed that the school population were "good students" but not academically orientated and would, in the future join their family professions: farmers and fishermen. Walking around the school and observing classroom after classroom I was left wondering as to what the best and possible course of action I could take. On the long drive back to Bangkok, I started to question what had occurred reappraising expectations and evaluating my communication protocols all of which led me to stumble upon a significant moment of unlearning.

Moore-Gilbert (1997) refers to unlearning as the "imperative to reconsider positions that once seemed self-evident and normal" (p. 98) and the more I "unlearnt" about English language education teaching in the schools in which we were working the efficacy of my knowing presence to deliver effective pedagogical practices became increasingly in doubt.

As the project came to its close it was apparent that English language-learning in some of the schools was neither meaningful or was connected to what Gee (2008) has identified as being the "other stuff" of language, namely: "social relations, cultural models, power and politics, perspectives on experience, values and attitudes, as well as things and places in the world" (p. 1). It was with this knowledge in mind that when the opportunity to return to work in Thai rural schools was presented, with 17 pre-service teacher education students, we knew we had to focus on the local context to start to build-up communities of language practice in schools.

LEARNING AND UNLEARNING

As the pre-service education students prepared for their teaching practicum in rural Thai schools, they initially planned and resourced English Language lessons based on a local curriculum to be taught across year levels Years 2–6 (7–11 years). They had been told that the Thai teachers were under increased pressure to produce curriculum that engaged with new methods and theories of language teaching. They were briefed on how English language had become an increasingly dominant cultural and linguistic presence in Thailand and how the challenge for the Thai teachers was to unlearn pedagogies with "The tension between domesticating and transformative pedagogies best captured in Freire's (1972, p. 58) description of what he terms the 'banking model of education" (Austin & Hickey, 2007, p. 22).

Working with the pre-service teachers prior to departure to Thailand, we sought to encourage them to "see teaching as something more than the reproduction of existing social relations ... that a socially transformative education requires authentic knowledge of and connection with the experiences, histories and hopes of those who inhabit the margins" (Austin & Hickey, 2007, p. 22). Identifying initiating questions such as, "How is English language learning shaped in Thai contexts?" "How does Thai culture impact on teaching and learning?" and "how will the experience of working in Thai schools change thinking collective about teaching and learning practices", the pre—service education students were asked to critically and reflexively account for their learning through four praxis inquiry journal entries that would comprise of:

Entry 1:   a contextual overview of Thailand—due on the day of departure aimed at a developing understanding of the Thai context including history and culture.

Entries 2–3:   accounts of the cultural and social experiences of that day that will reflect key questions that arise and that they are connected to teaching and learning in the placement school.

Entry 4:   a summary, evaluation, critique of the understandings you now have or those that are developing for you as a result of this experience.

Palmer (1998) maintains that good teaching includes understanding "the self that teaches" (p. 4) and the following excerpts from one if the students journal illustrates the development of a praxis in which "a socially transformative education draws both student and teacher into a consideration of their own positioning within the social dynamic": (Austin & Hickey, 2007, p. 23).

As I was planning my lesson last my night, I was bereft. I knew I wanted to teach a language point that was relevant and contextualised to the students' daily lives and the curriculum goals of the placement school, but I had little idea of how to achieve this. I did what I normally do in this situation: look to see what everyone else is doing. To this end, I started putting together a power point presentation including pictures of my life in Australia. I tried to scaffold these pictures with target language so that there was a learning objective with each image, but somehow it felt educationally flaccid and self-aggrandising. The questions that I was wrestling with, and have continued to struggle with on this trip, are how to articulate a simple language objective for a lesson? Moreover, once identified how do I plan, and conduct, a lesson to logically and sequentially build towards this objective? How much of my personality should I put into my language teaching?

To this end, the Communicative Language Teaching (CLT) theory that I have been introduced to as part of this trip is a revolutionary paradigm when applied to this question of learning objectives. It marries with my personal philosophy of teaching, namely that it should be contextualised and speak to the daily lives of students. I have continued to struggle identifying and reaching language objectives with classes over the last fortnight and as a neophyte teacher in charge of lesson planning and delivery for a class, it often feels as if I'm drowning in an ocean of my own uncertainty. With a narrow theoretical and pedagogical toolkit from which to build lessons, often it's the path of least risk that gets chosen and the focus becomes how best to entertain the students rather than how to best educate them. The instinctive movement towards a power point presentation was one such example.

But in CLT pedagogical framework it is not enough to teach words or grammar structures; each lesson must be scaffolded to build new and strengthen existing vocabulary, and dovetail this vocabulary into a communicative structure to assist students in communicating authentic information about themselves and the world they inhabit. As opposed to grammatical or rote teaching, CLT should focus on fluency over accuracy and "reflect natural … (and) require meaningful use of language" (Richards, 2006, p. 14). Richards (2006) proposed that the methodology to achieve this in a CLT classroom should be to teach in three distinct phases, mechanical, meaningful, and communicative practice.

Mechanical practice includes chorus work and drilling, and still has a place in the CLT classroom as it gives students the chance to become familiar with the target language without necessarily understanding what it means (Richards, 2006) … I have had success this week in reaching the meaningful practice phase, as students have taken the "I like/I don't like" structure and applied it to verb vocabulary that was taught at the beginning of the lesson. This felt like a breakthrough as I planned and facilitated effective controlled language activities that equipped students with a vocabulary, and now I had introduced a language focus, "I like" or "I don't like", that students could apply authentically to those verbs.

The next step for my teaching is the crux of CLT; Richards' communicative practice that Xia (2014) describes as "arousing" within students "the desire to communicate something" (p. 564). This stage involves a move beyond communicating a single language structure to using a range in a purposeful, free and student-directed manner, and demands that I as teacher "transform … from "teller" to "facilitator" (Nonkukhetkong, 2006). These activities should reflect real-life interactions that relate authentically to the students' lives. Students should concentrate on fluency rather than accuracy, and the teacher should not interrupt or provide any critique of the activity until it is concluded (Xia, 2014).

Like most of the Thai teachers, I am currently "more confident teaching language content than teaching communicative activities" (Nonkukhetkong, 2006, p. 5). However, I believe we have made solid progress in CLT practice and now have a much stronger grasp of the pedagogy and the methodology to implement it CLT. As previously mentioned, the final frontier still beckons: to facilitate authentic communication activities in future classes. Using a clear framework of mechanical, meaningful and communicative practice, to continue to hone my teaching and help students experience the thrill of communicating freely in English.

Furthermore, on this trip I have identified how do I transfer any positive regard that students may have for me into a genuine excitement for the subject matter being taught.

During the three weeks of studying and teaching in Thailand, I have no doubt that my self-awareness developed considerably, both as a student and as a teacher. Living in a foreign place with an unfamiliar cohort of students and lecturers takes away many of the familiar points of reference that we usually use to help identify ourselves. the cultural divide between us and our Thai buddies, mentor teachers and students could be described as a yawning chasm. I would argue that the way we learnt to frame, reflect and then bridge this cultural divide was the most valuable opportunity AS.

I certainly came to this teaching period with expectations and some of these expectations were supported during my Thai experience, such as the hierarchical nature of school bureaucracies, and the chaos of the teaching remit of a mother tongue English speaker in a lower socio-economic school. However other expectations, such as the automatic respect and good behaviour of students, were actually challenged significantly during this experience.

This ability to connect with and adapt to culturally alien situations is referred to as "cultural competence" AND becoming more aware of our own cultural proclivities; that is, understanding that we as individuals "function as the vehicles through which culture is expressed" (Weigl, 2009, p. 346), helps us to interact more adeptly in every context and situation in which we find ourselves, not just in the foreign one.

I would argue that one of my most profound learnings this trip was intrinsic to cultural competency. I quickly realised that the speaking activities and pair work that have served me well in teaching older students would only result in exponential stress levels for the teacher. My natural reaction to this frustration was to blame the students.

But as Dervin and Hahl (2014) "the intercultural never takes place in a power vacuum" (p. 2). I assumed, as the tall, bearded (and therefore manly), white male that I would be accorded a respect that had nothing to do with my competence as a teacher and everything to do with my status. In some ways I probably did get this respect, but the laws of physiology and concentration meant that if my teaching wasn't skilful in its pedagogy and methodology and tailored for the age group, I had no chance of success.

Finally, while observing and reflecting on some of my fellow pre-service teachers and the way they related to the Thai people we encountered in shops, restaurants, taxis and in the streets I realised something else. Being away from the familiarities of home can be stressful at the best of times, let alone in a bustling and chaotic Asian megalopolis, but dealing with the unfamiliar and foreign will be something that each of us will encounter regularly in the classrooms we manage upon graduation. To this end, it's important to understand what Cheng (2012) meant when she said that intercultural communication and competence is "an art" (p. 176). By understanding our own cultural originations more fully, we can develop our empathy for others and develop "the artistic and humanistic traits of respect, mutual understanding and empathy" (Cheng, 2012, p. 176) that are so vital to model as teachers.

This was a remarkable and deeply transformative trip. As I mentioned in my application letter, I had learned many things through my previous experiences teaching in China, but I did not have the mentoring to develop the pedagogical and methodological understanding that I craved. The opportunity to deeply immerse myself in teaching and cultural theory, practice, and reflection here in Thailand was invaluable.

While only mentioned briefly in this praxis inquiry, the cultural self-study model described by Weigl (2009) has fascinated me and I would like to learn more about this. Like most people from individualist cultures, before reading his journal article I would have told you that I am unique and have the ability to shape my own destiny through enterprise and innovation (Weigl, 2009). Now I am interested to discover my own cultural roots and more fully flesh out the picture of who I am; to dig deeper into the identity

that I bring to my teaching practice. As Weigl (2009) says, "those who feel culture oper-
ating in themselves are more likely to feel how culture operates powerfully in others."
(p. 348).

FRAMING AND REFRAMING

Becoming subject to the particularities of time, place and personal involvement, the students reflexive understandings of having an experience of teaching and learning in rural schools in Thailand produced narratives that involved a "complex layering [of understandings] formed and informed through discursive practices and social interactions" (Sikes, 2006, p. 21). Schön's The Reflective Practitioner (1983) articulates how knowing is in action and asserts that practitioners do not rely so much on espoused theory but develop their own theory-in-use and how understanding of practice is learned and developed as a result of day to day work. Calling this kind of rethinking process reflection-in action and reflection-on-action; reflection-in-action generates contextualising knowledge and in knowing-in-practice our journals formed the basis for everyday conversations about teaching and learning. They became a platform through which to consider what Andreotti (2007, p. 78) has called a: framework for an educational approach that could enable learners to value and learn from difference and to reconstruct their worldviews and identities based on an "ethical relation to the other".

Reflection has significantly been recognised as an important critical process and instrument for teachers to develop a consciousness not only of their practice but of how it feels to teach. To make that tacit knowledge visible and known to other people within the contexts in which it is located (Beauchamp & Thomas, 2009) structured how the student teachers worked in classrooms alongside the Thai teachers and there emerged a range of conversations that focused on the messiness of making pedagogy. The Thai teachers' anxieties had to do with the implementation of the new curriculum, the introduction of standardization, new models of assessment and how to teach using a CLT model framed many of the learning and relearning encounters. The pre-service education students on having to navigate the complexity of language and culture in the spaces of a Thai classroom. Each of these aspects involved thinking through the ways in which the British, Australian and North American language communities and cultures had become a hegemonic presence in English language classroom. As the students learned from the Thai teachers about how they taught English, the Thai teachers, in turn, observed and participated in lessons that introduced in to the pedagogical space: games, role-play and popular culture resources. Together, the pre-service students and Thai teachers 'as "subjects-in-discourse" [started to turn the critical lens on [them]selves to where everything about [their] professional lives [were held] to the light: [their] teaching, choice of pedagogic materials, discipline's orientations, valued genres, socialization practices". (Morgan & Ramanathan, 2005, p. 154).

Central to this re-accounting of pedagogy was learning about the ways of the classroom as a socially constructed practice and an encouraging of critical reflection on individual articulations of teaching and learning. Antonek, McCormick, and Donato (1997) claim it is impossible not to link with the concept of reflection with the self that teaches because an individual cannot talk about self without reflection as a method to develop teaching practices. The journals and conversations started to incorporate what the pre-service education students and Thai teachers considered as socially and culturally relevant imaginings of themselves as teachers (Korthagen, 2001), and Conway (2001) has noted how in educational contexts attention is seldom paid to teachers' formation of prospective practice.

Drawn out of the reflections on lesson there emerged more space for reflection of teacher development that better connected teachers to anticipating teaching actions in the future and possible models of practice for teaching and learning using a communicative approach in the Thai classrooms started to emerge. More tellingly the Thai teachers started to situate the 2008 Core Curriculum to pedagogic interrogation and as the practicum experience came a close the Thai teachers and the partner university organized a seminar in which the Thai teachers and Head Teachers of the school evaluated the program and the learning that it had generated. A common sentiment that was expressed was the benefit that had been brought to the schools in modelling a communicative approach to the teaching of English. Anxieties, fuelled by the imperative of: (i) Evidence-based approaches to the teaching of reading; ii) the introduction of new models of standardized assessments and the (iii) the requirements of on-going professional learning had lead the Thai teachers to feeling an increasingly pressure of being evaluated by a content knowledge = pedagogically competent model of practice. The complexities of the classrooms and of the schools in which we worked could never be fully grasped in a three week practicum. However, working alongside and in developing a partnership with the Thai teachers we sought to share and reflect upon pedagogy and develop shared understandings of practice around the teaching and learning of English. Baker and MacIntyre's (2003) observe that students in English as a foreign language settings usually only gain input from the target language in a classroom. The ostensible lack of opportunities for students to practice their English in rural communities could be regarded as a limitation but with the dissemination of English language TV and social media these limitations are diminishing. However, developing a perceived competence, fostering a willingness and confidence to communicate, and invest in increasing the frequency of authentic communication contexts can be a crucial aspect in becoming a speaker of English and is an aspect where language teaching in schools can be a decisive factor. Hines and

Barraclough (1995) argue that positive language experiences communicating in English can contribute to anxiety reduction, perceived competence improvement and reinforce motivation to participate in the target language and on our return to Australia the next phase of the project sought to connect Thai and Australian schools via social media to continue shared conversation and provide models of English language pedagogy.

SO, WHERE TO NOW?

Hatch (1978) argues: "language learning evolves out of learning how to carry on conversation" (p. 404) as does, I suggest, learning how to teach. At the time of writing this chapter, preparations are underway to return to the Thai schools and communities for a third practicum placement. The development of, and commitment to the work in the schools is orientated around a challenging of the idea that language teaching should transmit native speakers' perfect models of expressions We seeks to encourage the role of non-native teachers to explore and extend their learners' existing language competence because they have the "ability to see the target language through the learners' eyes" (Meddings & Thornbury, 2009, p. 84), and as such our work situated within "a rich tradition of alternative, progressive, critical and humanist educational theory" (Meddings & Thornbury, 2009, p. 7). Our support for developing emergent systems, modelling of communicative language teaching and task-based learning underpins our approach to critical community pedagogy and the practicum project remains a collaborative encounter in progress.

REFERENCES

Andreotti, V. (2007). An ethical engagement with the other: Spivak's ideas on education. *Critical Literacy: Theories and Practices, 1*(1), 69–79.

Antonek, J., McCormick, E., & Donato, R. (1997). The student teacher portfolio as autobiography: Developing a professional identity. *The Modern Language Journal, 81*(1), 15–27.

Austin, J., & Hickey, A. (2007). Pedagogies of self: Conscientising the personal to the social, *International Journal of Pedagogies and Learning, 3*(1), 21–29.

Baker, S. C., & MacIntyre, P. D. (2003). The role of gender and immersion in communication and second language orientations. In Z. Dörnyei (Ed.), *Attitudes, orientations, and motivations in language learning: Advances in theory, research, and applications. Oxford:* Blackwell Publishing.

Beauchamp, C., & Thomas, L. (2009). Understanding teacher identity: An overview of issues in the literature and implication for teacher education. *Cambridge Journal of Education, 39*(2), 175–189.

Conway, P. F. (2001). Anticipatory reflection while learning to teach: From a temporally truncated to a temporally distributed model of reflection in teacher education. *Teaching and Teacher Education, 17*(1), 89–106.

Cheng, C. (2012). The influence of college EFL teachers' understandings of intercultural competence on their self-reported pedagogical practices in Taiwan. *English Teaching: Practice and Critique, 11*(1), 164–182.

Dervin, F., & Hahl, K. (2014). Developing a portfolio of intercultural competences in teacher education: The case of a Finnish international programme. *Scandinavian Journal of Educational Research, 59*(1), 95–109.

Freire, P. (1972). *Pedagogy of the oppressed.* London: Sheed and Ward.

Gee, J. P. (2008). *Social Linguistics and Literacies: Ideologies in Discourses,* London: Falmer.

Hatch, E. (1978). Discourse analysis and second language acquisition. In E. Hatch (Ed.), *Second language acquisition* (pp. 401–435). Rowley, MA: Newbury House.

Hines, S. C., & Barraclough, R. A. (1995). Communicating in a foreign language: Its effects on perceived motivation, knowledge, and communication ability. *Communication Research Report, 12*, 241–247.

Korthagen, F. A. J. (2001). *Linking practice and theory: The pedagogy of realistic teacher education.* Mahwah, NJ: Lawrence Erlbaum Associates.

Luke, A. (2004). Two takes on the critical. In B. Norton & K. Toohey (Eds.), *Critical pedagogies and language learning* (pp. 21–29). Cambridge: Cambridge University Press.

Meddings, L., & Thornbury, S. (2009). *Teaching unplugged.* Peaslake: Delta Publishing.

Moore-Gilbert, B. (1997). *Postcolonial theory: contexts, practices, politics.* London: Verso.

Morgan, B., & Ramanathan, V. (2005). Critical literacies and langauge education: Global and local perspectives. *Annual Review of Applied Lingustics, 25*, 151–169.

Nonkukhetkong, K. (2006, January 19–21). Learner-centredness in teaching English as a foreign language. *Paper Presented at 26 Thai TESOL International Conference,* Chiang Mai, Thailand.

Palmer, P. J. (1998). *The courage to teach.* San Francisco, CA: Jossey-Bass.

Richards, J. (2006). *Communicative language teaching today.* New York, NY: Cambridge University Press.

Sa Nguan Ying. (2004). *English Program (EP).* Retrieved June 2, 2014 from http://www.epsyschool.org/

Schön, D. (1983). *The reflective practitioner.* New York, NY: Basic Books.

Sikes, P. (2006). Travel broadens the mind or making the strange familiar? A story of a visiting academic. *Qualitative Inquiry, 12*, 523–540.

Spitzberg, B., & Chagnon, G. (2011). Conceptualizing intercultural competence. In Deardorff, D. (Ed.), *The Sage handbook of intercultural competence* Thousand Oaks, Califormia. SAGE (pp. 2–52).

Spivak, G. (1990). *The post-colonial critic: interviews, strategies, dialogues.* New York, NY and London: Routledge.

SuksirpakonChai, W. (2015). English as lingua franca and its status in Thailand: Implications for teaching English pronunciation. *Journal of Asian Critical Education, 3*(1), 1–9.

Suwilai, P. M. (2016). Model for the preservation of language diversity: Thailand experience, Unpublished Paper, Mahidol University.

Weigl, R. (2009). Intercultural competence through cultural self-study: A strategy for adult learners. *International Journal of Intercultural Relations, 39*, 346–360.

Wiriyachitra, A. 2016). A. *English teaching and learning in Thailand in this decade.* Retrieved June 1, 2016 from http://citeseerx.ist.psu.edu/viewdoc/download?doi=10.1.1.475.4155&rep=rep1&type=pdf

Xia, Y. (2014). Language theories and language teaching—from traditional grammar to functionalism. *Journal of Language Teaching and Research, 5*(3), 559–565.

Contributors

Faith Agostinone-Wilson is Professor of Education at Aurora University. She is the author of Dialectical Research Methods in the Classical Marxist Tradition, Marxism and Education beyond Identity: Sexuality and Schooling and co-editor for The Handbook for Undergraduate Research Advisors, along with being published in several journals and edited books. A member of the Rouge Forum educational collective, Faith lives in Waukegan, Illinois and her research interests include education policy, copyleft movement, sexuality, and counter-hegemonic research methodologies. Outside of academic life, Faith knits, sews historical clothing, and works on restoring her Victorian home.

Jon Austin is currently an Associate Professor in the School of Linguistics, Adult and Specialist Education at the University of Southern Queensland, Toowoomba, Australia. Coming from an early childhood education background, he has worked in university-based teacher education for 30 years. He has a long history of critical teaching and research, particularly in the areas of race, Whiteness, identity, and anti-racist education, and in Indigenous research methodologies. His current work explores Indigenous public pedagogical use of social media formats for cultural connection and revitalization, and for social and political activism.

Jennifer A. Beech is Professor of English at the University of Tennessee at Chattanooga, where she teaches undergraduate and graduate courses in style, research methods, composition pedagogy, and race and class-based rhetorics.

At the national level, she co-chairs the Working-Class Culture and Pedagogy Standing Group for the Conference on College Composition and Communication.

Frank Bird III has been in education directly or indirectly for over forty five years, currently teaching high school and college. My educational background includes psychology, seminary and extensive graduate studies in curriculum and instruction. My interest in Foxfire goes back to the purchase of the book Foxfire II in 1972. I was reintroduced through graduate school and have been teaching about the Foxfire Approach and researching the past fifteen years. I live in Between, Georgia, with my wife Pat. My spare time is devoted to continued teaching, grandbabies, reading, writing, and gardening.

Eleanor J. Blair received her Ph.D. from the University of Tennessee, Knoxville. She is an Associate Professor at Western Carolina University where she teaches foundations of education courses in curriculum, teacher leadership and history/philosophy of education at WCU and in Jamaica through the WCU-Jamaica program. She is a frequent presenter at regional, national and international conferences and has authored chapters and essays in numerous books and journals. Additionally, she is the editor of four readers: Thinking about Schools: A Foundations of Education Reader (2011), Teacher Leadership: The "new" Foundation of Education (2011, 2016) and The Social Foundations Reader: Critical Essays on Teaching, Learning and Leading in the 21st Century (co-edited with Yolanda Medina) (2016). She is also the author of Foundations of Education: Teachers, Teaching and Teacher Leadership in Diverse 21st Century Schools (forthcoming in 2017). Her work utilizes qualitative methodologies and critical pedagogical frameworks to explore teaching, learning and leading in contemporary schools. References to her research on teacher moonlighting and the significance of place in the preparation of teacher leaders in rural communities occur in both popular and professional publications.

Andy Blunden is an independent scholar of social theory who lives in Australia. He is Managing editor of the journal, Mind, Culture, and Activity. Andy has published 4 books: An Interdisciplinary Theory of Activity (2010); Concepts. A Critical Approach (2012); Collaborative Projects. An Interdisciplinary Study (2014); and Origin of Collective Decision Making (2016). His email address is ablunden@mira.net

Erin Bowers is an illustrator and muralist living in St. Augustine, Florida. She draws material from plant life, counter culture, thoughts of other realms and traditional sentimentality.

Michael Boyer is a public school teacher at a Spanish- English dual immersion elementary school in Corvallis, Oregon where he currently lives with his wife and four children. Over the past twenty years, he has taught general education, ESOL, and history courses at the elementary, middle, and high school levels. In addition, he has taught foundations of education courses at Boise State University where he recently earned his doctorate. His research and writing focus on developing critical literacies with migrant children and their families to confront and dismantle systemic inequities.

Rebekah Cordova is a teacher educator at the University of Florida where she supports teachers across Florida to advance their action research work in pursuit of social-justice aims. With a focus on rural and Southern communities, Dr. Cordova's scholarship focuses on the perception of educative experiences, in and outside of schools. Her work contributes to a better understanding of emotional learning theory, public pedagogy, self-directed constructs of learning, and explorations of mis-education. Cordova's most comprehensive research has focused on educative healing as response to educative trauma. She currently resides in San Mateo, Florida.

Kristi Dickey is a doctoral student at Oklahoma State University and works for the Institute of Teacher and Learning Excellence at OSU. She is from Oklahoma.

Bevin Etheridge recently received her Ed.D in Curriculum and Instruction from Boise State University. Her dissertation focused on the school experiences of early school leavers, their reasons for leaving, and how they felt about the purpose of secondary school in their lives. She is currently an adjunct professor at Galen University in Belize - teaching action research, alternative assessment and research writing in the primary education program. Her research interests include student voice and experience, action and participatory action research, and transforming educational environments to be more generative and responsive to students.

Derek R. Ford is an educational theorist, teacher, and organizer. He is assistant professor of education studies at DePauw University. Informed by marxism, post-structuralism, queer theory, and critical geography, his research emerges from the knot of pedagogy, subjectivity, and revolutionary movements. Derek has written and edited six books, including Communist Study: Education for the Commons (Lexington, 2016). He is chair of the education department at The Hampton Institute and an organizer with the Answer Coalition. He can be reached at derekford@depauw.edu.

Matthew Guy earned his Ph.D. in Comparative Literature from Louisiana State University, and teaches literary theory and criticism as a professor of English at the University of Tennessee at Chattanooga. He has published and presented on a range of topics, from pop culture, phenomenology, and ethics, to the works of Emmanuel Levinas and Julia Kristeva.

Mark Helmsing teaches in the College of Education at the University of Wyoming. His work integrates theories and methods from the fields of curriculum studies, critical regional studies, and American studies to examine how conceptions of national heritage, belonging, and identity in different regions of the United States are pedagogically constructed and taught in schools, classrooms, museums, historic sites, national parks, and popular culture. His research has been published in numerous books and journals including Theory & Research in Social Education; the Journal of Social Studies Research; the Journal of Adolescent & Adult Literacy; and Race, Ethnicity, & Education

Randy Hewitt is Associate Professor in the School of Teaching, Learning, and Leadership at the University of Central Florida. Hewitt's current research focuses on the critical sense of the American pragmatist, social reconstructionist traditions, and on the art of democratic pedagogy. He is the author of Dewey and Power: Renewing the Democratic Faith and co-editor with his old friend Joe Kincheloe of Regenerating the Philosophy of Education: What Happened to Soul? And despite all of the above, he still is as working class as the day he was born.

Amelia Jenkins originally from Canada, has been teaching in Queensland (Australia) schools for several years. She was principal of Rossville State School (in the Daintree forest area of Far North Queensland) for three years and during her time there, she worked to incorporate local Australian Indigenous language and other cultural knowledges into the formal school curriculum. As a result, the school received two Regional Showcase Awards for Excellence in Education for Inclusive Education and for Primary Schooling. She is currently continuing this work in her position as Principal of Flying Fish Point State School south of Cairns.

Jennifer Job is an Assistant Professor of Curriculum Studies at Oklahoma State University. Her research focuses on the political contexts of education, media literacy, and how political trauma is taught in schools. She is a section editor for The Journal of Curriculum Theorizing. Her work has been seen in The Handbook of Educational Research, National Teacher Education Journal, The High School Journal, and Critical Literacy.

Kelsey Dayle John (Dineǧ) is a member of the Navajo Nation and a Ph.D. student in the Cultural Foundations of Education Program at Syracuse University. She has a C.A.S. in Women's and Gender Studies and is currently a National Science Foundation Graduate Research Fellow. Her work is on Indigenous and Decolonizing Methodologies. Specifically, she centers relationships in methodological interventions as a way to build research frameworks for Native researchers, students, and communities.

Susan Kirk is a doctoral student at Oklahoma State University. She teaches at Connors State College and has lived in Oklahoma for 42 years.

Robert Lake is an Associate Professor of Social Foundations of Education at Georgia Southern University. He teaches undergraduate and graduate courses in diversity and multicultural education from both a local and global perspective. Robert is the author of (2012) Vygotsky on Education for Peter Lang and (2013) A Curriculum of Imagination in an Era of Standardization: An Imaginative Dialogue with Maxine Greene and Paulo Freire: Information Age. His email address is boblake@georgiasouthern.edu

Justin McCrackin is a doctoral student at Oklahoma State University. He teaches history at Jenks High School and has lived in Oklahoma for 36 years.

Gina Morris is a doctoral student at Oklahoma State University and works for the Institute of Teaching and Learning Excellence at OSU. She has lived in Oklahoma her entire life.

Priya Parmar PhD is an Associate Professor of Secondary Education at Brooklyn College-CUNY. Her scholarly publications center around critical literacies, youth and Hip Hop culture, and other contemporary issues in the field of Cultural Studies in which economic, political, and social justice issues are addressed. A few of her published scholarly works include From Education to Incarceration: Dismantling the School to Prison Pipeline (co-edited with Anthony Nocella and David Stovall, 2014 and 2nd edition forthcoming 2017), Critical Literacy in English Literature: Primer (co-authored with Hindi Krinsky, 2013), and Knowledge Reigns Supreme: The Critical Pedagogy of Hip Hop Artist KRS-ONE (2009).

Daniel R. Paulson has been an educator 43 years. He earned a D. Ed. from the University of Florida in curriculum and instruction. His experiences range across elementary, middle and high schools in Minnesota, Florida and Wisconsin. He has taught in a rural elementary school on the edge of the everglades and in a small intercity charter school focused on experiential learning where he accompanied students on expeditions around the country and twice to Ghana, Africa. He has taught in large suburban schools and in small rural schools in Minnesota and Wisconsin where half of the male staff ran to the fire hall when there was a fire. He has been an Assistant Professor at UW-Stout and a M. Ed Learning Community Facilitator for St. Mary's

University, Winona, Minnesota and UW-River Falls. He currently resides in Menomonie Wisconsin where he frustrates absent teachers by never following their lesson plans but has fun creating a dialog with their students.

Todd Alan Price is Director of Policy Studies and Chair of Educational Foundations and Inquiry in the National College of Education, National Louis University. With a University of Wisconsin-Madison Ph.D. in Curriculum and Instruction—Educational Communications Technology specialization—his current scholarly work centers around the curricular implications of contemporary educational policy and educational reform on teacher education specifically and on K-12 public education more broadly.

William M. Reynolds teaches at Georgia Southern University. He has authored, co-edited and co-authored several books most recently Critical Studies of Southern Place: A Reader (2014). Practicing Critical Pedagogy: The Influences of Joe L. Kincheloe (2016) and Expanding Curriculum Theory: Dis/positions and Lines of Flight (2016). He is editor of a series with Intellect Books entitled, Critical Cultural Studies: Toward Transformative Curriculum and Pedagogy, co-editor of a series with Lexington Books entitled, Youth Culture and Pedagogy in the 21st Century and editor of Critical Media Literacies and Youth with Sense Publishing. His current research interests are the politics of youth culture, critical pedagogy, critical media literacy, foundations of education and curriculum studies.

Derrick M. Tennial is founder/CEO of Let's REThink That, a literary services agency. A published author and national presenter, his research interests include culturally responsive teacher education, education for social justice and equity, oral history, black orality, HIV/AIDS education, and identity, sexuality, and spirituality. He has authored six books and contributed to magazines, blogs, and several books as well. A proud son, brother, uncle, and godfather, he resides in Atlanta, Georgia.

Paul L. Thomas Professor of Education (Furman University, Greenville SC), taught high school English in rural South Carolina before moving to teacher education. NCTE named Thomas the 2013 George Orwell Award winner. His teaching and scholarship focus on literacy and the impact of poverty and race on education, as well as confronting the political dynamics influencing public education in the U.S. Follow his work @plthomasEdD and the becoming radical (http://radicalscholarship.wordpress.com/).

Mark Vicars is a Senior Lecturer in the College of Education at Victoria University, Melbourne. His main research interests are literacy education, practitioner inquiry, and narrative methodologies. An overarching concern of his work is the connectivities between literacy and identity practices in everyday life with a particular focus of interest being intercultural literacy. In 2010, he was awarded the Australian Learning and Teaching Council Citation for pedagogical approaches that motivate, inspire and support socially disadvantaged and culturally diverse students to overcome barriers to learning and to experience and attain success.

Reta Ugena Whitlock is Professor of Curriculum & Instruction and Chair of the Department of Educational Leadership at Kennesaw State University. She is the author of This Corner of Canaan: Curriculum Studies of Place and the Reconstruction of the South (Peter Lang, 2007) and editor of Queer South Rising: Voices of a Contested Place (Information Age Press, 2013). She is co-editor of the book series from Palgrave Macmillan, Queer Studies in Education. In addition to her continued writing on co-constructions of self and place, her latest work explores how theology, particularly queer theology, informs curriculum and how we make meaning of it.

Studies in Criticality

General Editor
Shirley R. Steinberg

Counterpoints publishes the most compelling and imaginative books being written in education today. Grounded on the theoretical advances in criticalism, feminism, and postmodernism in the last two decades of the twentieth century, Counterpoints engages the meaning of these innovations in various forms of educational expression. Committed to the proposition that theoretical literature should be accessible to a variety of audiences, the series insists that its authors avoid esoteric and jargonistic languages that transform educational scholarship into an elite discourse for the initiated. Scholarly work matters only to the degree it affects consciousness and practice at multiple sites. Counterpoints' editorial policy is based on these principles and the ability of scholars to break new ground, to open new conversations, to go where educators have never gone before.

For additional information about this series or for the submission of manuscripts, please contact:

Shirley R. Steinberg
c/o Peter Lang Publishing, Inc.
29 Broadway, 18th floor
New York, New York 10006

To order other books in this series, please contact our Customer Service Department:

(800) 770-LANG (within the U.S.)
(212) 647-7706 (outside the U.S.)
(212) 647-7707 FAX

Or browse online by series:
www.peterlang.com